T0213080

Lecture Notes in Computer Science   10106

Commenced Publication in 1973
Founding and Former Series Editors:
Gerhard Goos, Juris Hartmanis, and Jan van Leeuwen

More information about this series at http://www.springer.com/series/7407

Jose Acacio de Barros · Bob Coecke
Emmanuel Pothos (Eds.)

Quantum Interaction

10th International Conference, QI 2016
San Francisco, CA, USA, July 20–22, 2016
Revised Selected Papers

 Springer

Editors
Jose Acacio de Barros
San Francisco State University
San Francisco, CA
USA

Emmanuel Pothos
City University of London
London
UK

Bob Coecke
University of Oxford
Oxford
UK

ISSN 0302-9743   ISSN 1611-3349   (electronic)
Lecture Notes in Computer Science
ISBN 978-3-319-52288-3   ISBN 978-3-319-52289-0   (eBook)
DOI 10.1007/978-3-319-52289-0

Library of Congress Control Number: 2016963661

LNCS Sublibrary: SL1 – Theoretical Computer Science and General Issues

Printed on acid-free paper

This Springer imprint is published by Springer Nature
The registered company is Springer International Publishing AG
The registered company address is: Gewerbestrasse 11, 6330 Cham, Switzerland

Preface

QI 2016, the 10th International Conference on Quantum Interactions, was part of a series of international conferences on applications of the quantum formalism outside of physics. This now traditional conference started in 2007 as part of the Association for the Advancement of Artificial Intelligence, AAAI, Spring Symposia, and has taken place annually ever since, mostly in Europe. The tenth conference was held on the Downtown Campus of San Francisco State University (SFSU), in San Francisco, California, during July 20–22, 2016. It was hosted by the School of Humanities and Liberal Studies, an interdisciplinary unit within the College of Liberal and Creative Arts at SFSU.

The title of the conference, "Quantum Interactions," was concocted by Peter Bruza and William Lawless, who co-organized, together with C.J. van Rijsbergen and Don Sofge, the 2007 symposium at the AAAI at Stanford University. In their original proposal to the AAAI symposium, they were referring to social interactions. Social interactions, so was their argument, were prone to context-dependent effects the same as quantum observables. Therefore, it was reasonable to assume that the conceptual structure of quantum mechanics could shed light on them. Currently, quantum interactions refers more broadly to the use of the quantum mathematical, conceptual, or probabilistic structures outside of physics, often in social and computer sciences. Social sciences, in particular psychology, have many examples where observable quantities are contextual, and as such do not fit well within a classic probability theory. Since quantum mechanics was a theory developed to deal with quantum contextuality, as happens, for example, in the case of the double-slit experiment, researchers started asking whether the extended probabilistic apparatus developed could be used to describe contextual systems outside of physics. As such, we should not think of quantum interactions as the use of quantum mechanics outside of physics, but instead as the use of the *mathematics* of quantum mechanics to non-quantum systems.

In this year's conference we had many distinguished speakers, and we are happy to have contributions to this volume from Professors Bas van Fraassen and Ehtibar Dzhafarov. Professor van Fraassen's paper takes the idea of the quantum formalism as a way to describe contextual systems, and then tries to create a formal theory of epistemology based on it. Professor Dzhafarov, in collaboration with Janne Kujala, developed in detail his theory of contextuality based on classic probability theory and random variables. These papers were grouped in the fundamentals session, along with a paper by Hou Yau. Hou Yau presented a modified theory of the Klein–Gordon equation where time is itself a dynamical variable, with the hopes that such an approach might have some applications outside of physics.

Papers for the conference were naturally grouped into applications of quantum formalism to psychology (quantum cognition), language and applications, and quantum-like measurements outside physics. In the quantum cognition group, Irina Basieva and Andrei Khrennikov discussed the two- and three-slit experiments as metaphors to the modeling of cognitive processes, especially the difficulties associated with pushing this metaphor to experiments in psychology. J. Acacio de Barros, Carlos Montemayor, and Leonardo De Assis used the results of quantum cognition, in particular of contextuality in quantum cognition, to argue that some empirical theories of consciousness are inadequate and need revision. J. Acacio de Barros, Leonardo de Assis, and Petr Bob used data from experiments in stress research to argue that stress may show order effects in a way that is consistent with the collapse model used by Busemeyer in psychology. Diederik Aerts, Lyneth Beltran, Massimiliano Sassoli de Bianchi, Sandro Sozzo, and Tomas Veloz provided a modified hidden-variable model of quantum mechanics that could describe order effects in a way consistent with experimental findings. Finally, Peter beim Graben and Reinhard Blutner discussed the use of the quantum formalism in music theory.

For language and applications, the paper by David Windridge and Raja Nagarajan discussed bootstrap aggregation in quantum machine learning. Yaared Al-Mehairi, Bob Coecke, and Martha Lewis created a model of categorical compositional cognition by fitting the integrated connectionist/symbolic architecture within categorical compositional semantics. Trevor Cohen, Dominic Widdows, Jason A. Vander Heiden, Namita T. Gupta, and Steven H. Kleinstein extended their previous vector model based on a quantum description to represent protein sequences with graded vectors. Aditya Joshi, Johan Halseth, and Pentti Kanerva used random indexing to identify the language of text samples.

In the quantum-like measurement session, Jacob Denolf attempted to broaden the theory of measurement with operators in a Hilbert space to account for ordinal measurements common in social sciences. François Dubois and Zeno Toffano extended the measurements from a Boolean logic to a fuzzy logic. Kevin Dunne tries to connect two different approaches to quantum theory: topos and monoidal.

This year we also had a very successful special session on "Contextuality and the Foundations of Probability." Contextuality, in line with the meaning put forth in Dzhafarov and Kujala's contribution to this volume, is an essential feature of the quantum formalism used in the applications outside of physics. In this session, the papers by Victor Cervantes and Ehtibar Dzhafarov and by Ru Zhang and Ehtibar Dzhafarov presented a series of experiments to test the existence of contextuality in psychology. Contextuality in database theory was also discussed by Peter Bruza and Samson Abramsky. Finally, some papers addressed modified theories of probability to model contextual phenomena, as, for example, Federico Holik et al.'s contribution on non-monotonic subadditive probabilities, and Mark Burgin's symmetric inflated (signed) probabilities, which may take values outside of the [0, 1] interval of standard probability theory.

From the 39 papers submitted to the conference, 21 were accepted, and are included in this volume. These 21 papers are based on the conference presentations, and incorporate feedback received not only by the peer-review process, but also during the talks. With the exception of the invited presentations and associated papers of Professors Bas van Fraassen and Pawel Kurzinsky, which were reviewed by the editors after the conference, each paper was single-blind peer-reviewed prior to the conference by at least two reviewers, and the conference presentations were based on the revised papers. We thank the Program Committee members for their timely and dedicated work on reviewing the papers, a particularly daunting task, given the interdisciplinarity of the QI 2016 contributions.

This year we received many submissions of papers whose main authors were students or junior researchers. Owing to their high quality, the conference organizers created for the first time at the QI conference a best paper award by a student or young researcher. This year's recipients were Ru Zhang for Best Post-Doctoral/Young Researchers Paper Award, and Aditya Joshi for Best Undergraduate/Graduate Paper Award. We wish to congratulate both recipients, as well as the many other finalists, for submitting excellent papers to the conference.

We would like to thank the Downtown Campus staff of San Francisco State University, in particular Kasey Wood and Dania Russel, for their hospitality and help, which ensured the success of the conference. Alfred Hofmann and Anna Kramer at Springer provided support for the speedy publication of the proceedings in the Springer series *Lecture Notes in Computer Science*. We also thank the local Organizing Committee, Leonardo Paulo Guimarães De Assis (Stanford University) and Margarida Duque de Castela (SFSU), without whom the conference would not have worked smoothly. Finally, we thank the support of the School of Humanities and Liberal Studies, through its director, Professor Cristina Ruotolo, and of the College of Liberal and Creative Arts, San Francisco State University.

November 2016

J. Acacio de Barros
Emmanuel Pothos
Bob Coecke

Organization

General Chair

José Acacio de Barros   San Francisco State University, USA

Program Chairs

Emmanuel Photos   City University London, UK
Bob Coecke   Oxford University, UK

Steering Committee

Peter Bruza   Queensland University of Technology, Australia
Trevor Cohen   University of Texas at Houston, USA
Bob Coecke   Oxford University, UK
Ariane   Paris School of Economics, France
   Lambert-Mogiliansky
Dominic Widdows   Grab Technologies Inc., USA

Program Committee

Irina Basieva   Linneaus University, Sweden
Peter Beim Graben   Humboldt-Universität zu Berlin, Germany
Reinhard Blutner   University of Amsterdam, The Netherlands
Peter Bruza   Queensland University of Technology, Australia
Stephen Clark   University of Cambridge, UK
Trevor Cohen   University of Texas, Houston, USA
Vedran Dunjko   Institute for Quantum Optics and Quantum
     Information, Austria
Ehtibar Dzhafarov   Purdue University, USA
Chris Heunen   University of Edinburgh, UK
Andrei Khrennikov   Linnaeus University, Sweden
Kirsty Kitto   Queensland University of Technology, Australia
Bill Lawless   Paine College, USA
Martha Lewis   University of Oxford, UK
Massimo Melluci   University of Padua, Italy
Jian-Yin Nie   University of Montreal, Canada
Gary Oas   Stanford University, USA
Paavo Pylkkanen   University of Helsinki, Finland, and University
     of Skovde, Sweden
Mehrnoosh Sadrzadeh   Queen Mary University of London, UK

Sonja Smets   University of Amsterdam, The Netherlands
Sandro Sozzo   University of Leicester, UK
Dominic Widdows   Grab Technologies Inc., USA

Organizing Committee

Margarida Duque de Castela   San Francisco State University, USA
Leonardo P.G. De Assis   Stanford University, USA

Contents

Fundamentals

Interpretations of QM with Applications for Formal Epistemology   3
  Bas C. van Fraassen

Contextuality-by-Default 2.0: Systems with Binary Random Variables.   16
  Ehtibar N. Dzhafarov and Janne V. Kujala

Probabilistic Nature of a Field with Time as a Dynamical Variable   33
  Hou Y. Yau

Quantum Cognition

Testing Boundaries of Applicability of Quantum Probabilistic Formalism
to Modeling of Cognition: Metaphors of Two and Three Slit Experiments . . .   49
  Irina Basieva and Andrei Khrennikov

Contextuality in the Integrated Information Theory   57
  J. Acacio de Barros, Carlos Montemayor, and Leonardo P.G. De Assis

Is Stress Quantum-Like?   71
  J. Acacio de Barros, Leonardo Guimarães De Assis, and Petr Bob

Quantum Cognition Beyond Hilbert Space: Fundamentals and Applications   81
  Diederik Aerts, Lyneth Beltran, Massimiliano Sassoli de Bianchi,
  Sandro Sozzo, and Tomas Veloz

Toward a Gauge Theory of Musical Forces   99
  Peter beim Graben and Reinhard Blutner

Language and Applications

Quantum Bootstrap Aggregation   115
  David Windridge and Rajagopal Nagarajan

Categorical Compositional Cognition.   122
  Yaared Al-Mehairi, Bob Coecke, and Martha Lewis

Graded Vector Representations of Immunoglobulins Produced in Response
to West Nile Virus   135
  Trevor Cohen, Dominic Widdows, Jason A. Vander Heiden,
  Namita T. Gupta, and Steven H. Kleinstein

Contextuality and Foundations of Probability

Testing Contextuality in Cyclic Psychophysical Systems of High Ranks   151
  Ru Zhang and Ehtibar N. Dzhafarov

Probabilistic Programs: Contextuality and Relational Database Theory.   163
  P.D. Bruza and S. Abramsky

On Peculiar Relations Between Measurement Incompatibility
and Contextuality   175
  Dagomir Kaszlikowski and Paweł Kurzyński

Exploration of Contextuality in a Psychophysical Double-Detection
Experiment.   182
  Víctor H. Cervantes and Ehtibar N. Dzhafarov

On the Interpretation of Probabilities in Generalized Probabilistic Models . . .   194
  Federico Holik, Sebastian Fortin, Gustavo Bosyk, and Angelo Plastino

An Introduction to Symmetric Inflated Probabilities.   206
  Mark Burgin

Quantum-Like Measurements

A First Attempt at Ordinal Projective Measurement.   227
  Jacob Denolf

Eigenlogic: A Quantum View for Multiple-Valued and Fuzzy Systems   239
  François Dubois and Zeno Toffano

A New Perspective on Observables in the Category of Relations:
A Spectral Presheaf for Relations   252
  Kevin Dunne

Language Geometry Using Random Indexing.   265
  Aditya Joshi, Johan T. Halseth, and Pentti Kanerva

Author Index   275

Fundamentals

Interpretations of QM with Applications for Formal Epistemology

Bas C. van Fraassen[(✉)]

Department of Philosophy, San Francisco State University,
San Francisco, CA 94132, USA
fraassen@princeton.edu

Abstract. Associated with the Copenhagen school, the External Observation View of quantum mechanics depicted a quantum state as evolving deterministically, but with interruptions when 'collapsed' by measurement interactions. I will point to an analogy with the doxastic state studied in epistemology, and show that this analogy suggests an application of the quantum mechanical formalism that leads to a proof of one solution of a central problem in formal epistemology. I will end with some critical remarks.

1 The External Observation View Versus the Closed Universe View

Until the 1950s their were two main views of how we are to understand QM, separated by the Iron Curtain. One view, dominant among scientists in the West, traced its origin to Bohr and the Copenhagen scientists. John Wheeler described it: "The 'external observation' formulation of quantum mechanics ...associates a state function with the system under study—as for example a particle—but not with the *ultimate* observing equipment. The system under study can be enlarged to include the original object as a subsystem and also a piece of observing equipment [....]. However, the *ultimate* observing equipment still lies outside the system that is treated by a wave equation." [1].

As Wheeler points out, within this view it would not make sense to think of the Universe as a whole as a quantum system. Yet quantum mechanics represents that as a deterministic evolution of a wave function subject to Schroedinger's equation.

This view was characterized as positivist and idealist in the Soviet Union, where Academician D.I. Blokhintsev was intent on developing a view of QM *as mechanics*, properly speaking, in line with dialectical materialism [2, 3]. On that view a quantum state is not essentially what the scientist *attributes* on the basis of measurements, but a mechanical state in the same way that states were in classical physics.

Remarkably, beginning in the 1950s, the latter view seemed to become wholeheartedly adopted among philosophers in the West. The popular term there was not "materialist" but "realist". This began, arguably, with Wheeler's commentary of Hugh Everett's dissertation [1, 4]. Wheeler, a cosmologist, welcomed this development since it allowed for the conceptual possibility of representing the cosmos as a quantum system. But in this 'turn to objectivity' Everett's interpretation, or the subsequent Many-Worlds interpretations that drew on his work, was not alone: interpretations

© Springer International Publishing AG 2017
J.A. de Barros et al. (Eds.): QI 2016, LNCS 10106, pp. 3–15, 2017.
DOI: 10.1007/978-3-319-52289-0_1

developed in the 70s and 80s generally regarded the state and the values of observables as physical, measurement-independent characteristics of physical systems.

2   Information-Theory Approach from 1950s to the Present

Since then the focus on information led to new interpretations that we can think of as continuing, whether explicitly or surreptitiously, the Copenhagen external observer view, without any implication of a role for consciousness. Examples include e.g. Carlo Rovelli, Christopher Fuchs, and Jeffrey Bub.

Conceptual changes usually have their harbingers and predecessors. In the 1950s the Dutch physicist H.J. Groenewold advocated that we should regard quantum states as just summaries of *information* obtained through measurement [5–7]. He proposed a formulation of the theory centering on the effect of a series of measurements, represented by a series of observables (the ones being measured) interspersed with evolution operators (governing evolution between measurements). The sole real problem to be addressed is then: *given the outcomes of preceding measurements, what are the probabilities for outcomes of later measurements in the series?*

Imagine that each measurement apparatus in the series records its outcome. After the entire series has been concluded, a physicist O inspects those recorded results, and assigns states to the system measured for the times of those outcomes using von Neumann's Projection Postulate recipe (which everyone agrees is fine for such narrowly focused predictive tasks). To begin, O assumes some initial state. (When there is no prior substantive information, that will be the entirely uninformative mixture represented by the identity operator on the space.) Suppose now that successive measurements are made on the same system at times t_1, t_2, t_3, ... of various observables O_1, O_2, O_3, ... yielding eigenvalues of those observables λ_1, λ_2, λ_3, ... This process can be represented theoretically as the evolution of a state, interrupted at those times by projections into the relevant eigenspaces, and between those times governed by the Schroedinger equation – more precisely by a group of unitary operators, the 'evolution operators, indexed by the time intervals between those times. However that would be a representation 'after the fact' when the outcomes are known. Before they are known the state is represented as a mixture corresponding to the possible outcomes, with 'weights' reflecting the probabilities of those outcomes. What can be read off this representation, *and can be empirically tested*, are the *transition probabilities*: the probability that if the sequence of outcomes so far is λ_1, λ_2, ..., λ_n, the next outcome at time t_{n+1} will be λ_{n+1}.

The contentious part is Groenewold's insistence that no other significance is to be accorded to the assignment of states. The states are nothing more than compendia of information assumed, known, or gathered through measurements, and thus determined entirely by a specific history, the 'observer's' history.

> The conditionality or relativity of the quantum states is just as much a matter of choice of reference as e.g. the relativity in special relativity theory with respect to the choice of inertial systems [5].

Later interpretations which apply information theory, such as Carlo Rovelli's *Relational Quantum Mechanics* echo this analogy to what is meant by states relative to an observer in relativity theory, and emphasizes that similarly any system can serve in the role of 'anchoring' relative states of information:

> The quantum system represents something real and independent of us; the quantum state represents a collection of subjective degrees of belief about something to do with that system [8].

> A quantum theory is best understood as a theory about the possibilities and impossibilities of information transfer, as opposed to a theory about the mechanics of nonclassical waves or particles [9].

"Information" is here understood as Groenewold specified, in the technical sense of information theory, as measured classically by the Shannon entropy or by the von Neumann entropy for quantum states.

3   The Analogy: Information States Evolving with Interruptions

The External Observation View and the later information theory oriented interpretations view the quantum state as subject to a deterministic evolution constantly interrupted by measurements, with the measurement outcome characterizing an abrupt change in the state. This provides the basis for an analogy that can be explored for suggestions to solve problems in formal epistemology.

Independently of the differences between sorts of interpretations, what has to be interpreted includes:

- representation of pure states by vectors, of mixed states by statistical operators, and of physical quantities by self-adjoint linear operators,
- representation of measurement as physical interactions that establish correlations between measured system and measurement apparatus
- representation of the evolution in time of an isolated system as governed by the Schroedinger equation (more abstractly, by a one-parameter group of unitary operators).

On the information theory approach the measurement operations are affecting changes in the *information state* of the 'observer', the 'measurer', however conceived. And crucially, the information state is mathematically representable in the way that quantum states were represented all along.

The information state may be called "subjective" to the extent that, and in the sense that, it is relative to the observer, but the changes in information are induced (in some way) by the input from physical measurement operations. Within this approach, the classical theory of information understood in terms of subjective probability, the changes of state as subjective probability updating.

A state of information, in which the information consists in a combination of probabilities and certainties, is precisely how in epistemology one regards a subject's *epistemic* (or etymologically more accurately, *doxastic*) state. The analogy is therefore to the External Observation View, where the steady evolution of the state is depicted as interrupted by measurement, with its unforeseen outcome used to adjust that state. In the epistemic case, the steady evolution of one's subjective probabilities is depicted as interrupted by the 'deliverances of experience', with their unforeseen content evoking an adjustment of that doxastic state. So we can begin to set up a possibly illuminating analogy for conceptual exploitation:

- **target:** state of opinion over time
  - represented as an evolving probability function, interrupted by external input
- **base:** quantum state over time
  - deterministic process between interruptions (data input)
  - states are elements of a vector space,
  - the deterministic process is transformation by a dynamic group (unitary operators).

4   Representing Opinion: Possibilities, Probabilities, and Quantities

We begin with a space of possibilities. There will be many; for example, for a large set of real numbers N there will be many possibilities that include that the mass of the moon in kg is N. In some of these, my average daily wage in dollars is K, in some it is K + 1, and so forth. For each N, the proposition that the mass of the moon is N kg singles out a region of possibilities in which that is so. We call these regions *cells* of the *partition* we have thus imposed on this possibility space.

The single requirement on our probability assignment is that the probabilities of the cells of any given partition are never less than 0, and together sum to one. The mass of the moon and average daily wage define relevant partitions in a natural way, namely in terms of the values that a quantity may have. Such a quantity is called, in statistics jargon, a *random variable*. It is (represented by) a function that assigns to each point in the possibility space a real number as its value. But usually, perhaps always, the quantity will have the same value in a variety of possible circumstances. So by listing its values, we are specifying a corresponding partition: for example, the one in which the Nth cell is the region of those possibilities in which my average daily wage is K.

While I will be talking about results that may actually be significant, non-trivial, only for cases involving infinity, this discussion will be limited to quantities and probabilities assigned to cells of a finite partition.

Probability assignments are just a special case of random variables: their values are non-negative and sum to 1. But that is the only difference from the general case.

Keeping things simple suppose that the partition is finite, say it has N cells, and let's think of them as ordered sequentially for convenience. Then each random variable, and so automatically also each probability assignment, is in effect being represented by a vector, with N components. For example <1/6, 2/6, 3/6> represents probability assignment to a three-cell partition, which might have been defined by a quantity which takes values 1, 2, and 3 in the first, second and third cell respectively.

The *expectation value*, for that quantity, in this state of opinion, is defined to be

$$(1/6) \cdot 1 + (2/6) \cdot 2 + (3/6) \cdot 3 = 14/6$$

which is 14/6. It is generally most useful to think about expectation values rather than specific probabilities. When $\mathbf{p}$ is a probability function and $\mathbf{x}$ is a random variable, let us designate the expectation value for that case as $EX(\mathbf{p}, \mathbf{x})$.

Thinking about the random variables as vectors brings us now into familiar territory. The inner product (also called dot product, scalar product) of two vectors is defined to be:

$$<x_1, \ldots, x_N > \cdot <y_1, \ldots, y_N > = x_1 y_1 + \ldots + x_N y_N$$

Using the boldface notation $\mathbf{x}$ for $<x_1, \ldots, x_N>$, and so forth, we put this succinctly:

$$\mathbf{x} \cdot \mathbf{y} = \Sigma \, x_k y_k$$

So the expectation value is the inner product of the two vectors that represent the probability (the state of opinion) and the quantity. From this it follows at once, e.g. that expectation is linear.

5 Representing Opinion Change

Considering the input that may require a change of opinion, we typically think of something concrete, like a witness report or the outcome of a measurement. But whatever that is, it functions as input only if the person in question takes it to place a *constraint on his or her future (posterior) opinion.*

What can these constraints be? The simplest example is the case where a measurement outcome is accepted as definitive, and a certain proposition is then taken to be definitely true, and assigned probability 1. But there a number of different constraints on one's posterior opinion that may be accepted in response to 'experience' (which can include reports from trusted sources, not just observer perceptions). So these may include:

> ! change your probability for rain to 1 !
> ! change your probability for rain to 0.7 !
> ! let your probabilities for rain and for snow be equal !
> ! change your odds for rain vs. snow to 7: 3 !
> ! change your conditional probability of rain given snow to 2/3 !
> ! change your expectation value for precipitation in inches to 3 !

How is the agent to satisfy such a constraint? For the first and second example we have theorems to answer this question. For the remainder, answers remain controversial, and we will see how an analogy to quantum mechanics might help.

The simplest constraint on the posterior opinion is that it should assign probability 1 to a particular proposition (region in the possibility space) E (then called the *evidence*). Bayes' famous idea was that the only other relevant consideration is the prior, which is to be modified, and that the posterior is *function* of just the prior and the proposition E.

That there must be a function, with only certain specific factors admitted as relevant, is the very stuff of symmetry arguments. When that idea is assumed for the case of opinion change, there is a beautiful symmetry argument [10] that demonstrates that there is only one probability function that fits, the very one that Bayes displayed.

Simple Conditionalization. Given prior probability function p, and the constraint on posterior probability function p* that it must assign 1 to E, and that p* is a function of only p and E,

p* must be:

$$\mathbf{p}^* = \mathbf{p}(\ |E),$$

which is defined by

$$\mathbf{p}(\ |E) : \mathbf{p}(A|E) = \mathbf{p}(A \cap E) / \mathbf{p}(E), \text{for A in the domain of p}$$

(and thus undefined if $\mathbf{p}(E) = 0$).

If we represent p as a vector $<p_1, ..., p_N>$ with reference to a partition with cells $A_1, ..., A_N$ then E must be the union of some of those cells. The recipe in question then has two steps: (1) If A_j is a cell disjoint from E, change p_j to 0; for j = 1, ..., N. (2) Multiply the resulting components by a number so that their sum is 1. Only the first step is really important, for the odds between the components is what matters. That the numbers should add up to 1 is just a convention.

Richard Jeffrey created the new subject of *probability kinematics* [11] and introduced a new rule, *Jeffrey Conditionalization*, that generalized Simple Conditionalization, for the constraint

! change your probability for E to r !

To see how Jeffrey's prescription works, consider first the choice of conditionalizing on E or alternatively on the negation $\sim$E. That is a choice between two possible posteriors, produced by Simple Conditionalization. Instead of choosing between them, you assign them relative 'weights', namely r and (1 − r). Thus you arrive at the *mixture* (convex combination)

$$\mathbf{p}^* = r\mathbf{p}(...|E) + (1 - r)\mathbf{p}(...|\sim E)$$

Again there is a beautiful symmetry argument that shows there is just one way to do that, namely, the one prescribed by Jeffrey [10].

For each such *Jeffrey shift*, as I will call the operation, there is of course a corresponding effect on the expectation values. In fact we form the posterior expectation value function by inserting the multipliers $[q_i/p(A_i)]$, which depend solely on the prior and the constraints that the shift is meant to satisfy.

This change in the coefficients in the sum that constitutes the expectation value is a simple operation, and in fact, it is the effect of a linear operator on the vectors that represent random variables such as quantity $\mathbf{x}$ [12].

6   Representing Opinion Change: Generalizing Probability Kinematics

What about all the other forms of constraint? The solution of the general problem consists in defining a function Φ, which takes the given constraint as input, and which will turn an arbitrary given prior p into an appropriate posterior $p' = \Phi p$ (provided Φ is applicable). Unless we have further desiderata for Φ, the problem does not make sense.

Before exploring or exploiting quantum mechanical analogies, I want to mention the best known candidate that has been proposed for the role of Φ.

6.1   The Best Known Candidate, Jaynes' MAXENT: a. k. a. Minimize Relative Information

An often introduced intuition is that the change in the information state should be conservative, that is, that by some measure, the posterior should be 'as close to' the prior as possible. The best known candidate for that measure is *relative information*. Minimizing the relative information is equivalent to maximizing the relative entropy, as first proposed by the physicist E.T. Jaynes [13].

How much the posterior $\mathbf{p^*}$ differs from the prior $\mathbf{p}$ can be described in various ways. One good way in or present context would seem to be to list the ratios p_i^*/p_i, $i = 1, \ldots, n$. In order to satisfy various desiderata for what a relative information function should look like, these ratios are found enmeshed in a somewhat complicated function:

$$INF(\mathbf{p^*}, \mathbf{p}) = \Sigma p_i^* \ln \left(p_i^*/p_i\right)$$

So the recipe variously titled INFOMIN or MAXENT says that the posterior should be chosen in such a way that the given constraints are satisfied while minimizing this relative information (Note: the function is not well-defined when either the posterior or prior has a 0 component).

Notice that INF is the *posterior expectation value* of a quantity, whose value on the ith cell of the partition is $\ln(p_i^*/p_i)$ So what it represents is the *information in the posterior relative to the prior, as evaluated posteriorly*. The logarithmic function is introduced to have a formula with nice mathematical properties; the genuinely crucial part is the set of ratios (p_i^*/p_i). These are what 'conceptualize' the 'distance' between prior and posterior, as answer to 'how close the one is to the other'.

The arguments supporting Jaynes' proposal spell out desiderata of various sorts, both conceptual and mathematical. There are disagreements about their force; moreover, Jaynes' proposal has been roundly rejected in a number of articles in which it was discussed [14, 15].

Without purporting to settle those disputes here, I want to explore our analogy to quantum mechanics for the possibility of a symmetry theorem for this proposal.

7 Steps Toward a Symmetry Theorem

The set of probability vectors is a convex region in the vector space, but not a subspace. To apply familiar results concerning vector spaces, it is therefore more convenient to switch attention to odds rather than probabilities.

Since we know that $p(A_1) + \ldots + p(A_n) = 1$, we would also have specified **p** completely if we were just given certain ratios, such as $p_1/p_2, p_1/p_3, \ldots, p_1/p_n$.

To give an example, suppose the probabilities that the television or radio, or neither, is on (when at most one can play at any given time) initially (at $t = 0$) equal 0.5, 0.3, 0.2. That information is conveyed equally well by saying that the odds are 5 : 3 : 2. So this probability function can be represented by the *probability vector* <0.5, 0.3, 0.2> or by the *odds vector* <5, 3, 2> , or the odds vector <10, 6, 4> . While it would be unusual to see it at a horse race, negative numbers would do as well: these odds are equally represented by <−5, −3, −2> for the ratios are the same. The odds vectors comprise the entire vector space except for the null vector.

A odds vector is a scalar multiple of a probability vector. And we call odds vectors **x** and **y** *equivalent* iff there is a positive real number k such that $\mathbf{x} = k\mathbf{y}$ (i.e. $x_i = k y_i$ for $i = 1, \ldots, n$).

We must also give proper regard to partial comparisons, such as that the odds of $E_1 : E_2$ according to $\mathbf{p}_1$ are 17 times the odds of $E_1 : E_2$ according to $\mathbf{p}_2$. Indeed, if those probability functions are the prior and posterior opinion, that is just the sort of item that would go into a description of how much the posterior differs from the prior.

Definition. The *quotient* $(\mathbf{x}/\mathbf{y})$ is the vector $<x_1/y_1, \ldots, x_n/y_n>$.

This does not qualify as well-defined measure of the 'distance' between the vectors, but will serve us as an intuitive guide (Just as we noted with respect to the MAXENT formalism, there is a problem about division by zero; the quotient is undefined then).

When I present the conditions leading to the main theorem I will show how they are related to the idea that the 'distance' reflected in the quotient between prior and posterior is to be kept as small as possible.

The *symmetries* of the set of odds vectors are the transformations that leave that structure intact.. They are isomorphisms, and for a finite real vector space they are thus the one-to one linear transformations. These are the transformations representable by a diagonal matrix and are therefore the following transformations:

Transformation U of the set of odds vectors is a *uniform transformation* if and only if there are constants $u_1, \ldots, u_N$, not all of them 0, such that for all vectors **x**.

$$U\mathbf{x} = <u_1 x_1, \ldots, u_n x_n >$$

In quantum mechanics, during the time between disturbances from outside (such as measurements) the state of a system evolves in accordance with Schroedingers's equation. Put in a more abstract fashion: this evolution, the 'motion', is governed by a one-parameter group of unitary operators. The parameter in question is time, and the unitary operators are precisely the symmetries of the space of possible states:

the state ψ at t evolves to become the state $U_z\psi$ at time $t + z$.

On the analogy that I proposed, what happens 'between' prior and posterior is something that looks very much like what we see in QM, at least in an abstract sort of way.

Now we have just seen what the relevant symmetries are, namely the uniform transformations. In geometry or physical kinematics, we denote as "rigid motion" any continuous transformation which remains isometric, i.e., preserves distances. Let us here define the analogous notion of a uniform motion. Take the prior $\mathbf{x}$ as the state of opinion at time $t = 0$, and write $\mathbf{x} = \mathbf{x}(0)$. We may imagine this state developing in time as the vector $\mathbf{x}(t)$, and require that $\mathbf{x}(t + d)$ results from $\mathbf{x}(t)$ by a uniform transformation U_d.

These operators $\{U_d\}$ include U_0 which is the identity, and form a semi-group with $U_{d+e} = U_d U_e$, because $U_d U_e \, (\mathbf{x}(t)) = \mathbf{x}(t + d + e) = U_{d+e} \, \mathbf{x}(t)$. Note also that these operators commute, by similar argument.

Let us denote as a *uniform motion* any such one-parameter semigroup of uniform transformations.

For readability of the superscripts, I will describe a quantity $\mathbf{k}$ as having values denoted interchangeably as either "k_i" or "$k(i)$".

Theorem. If $\{U_z: z \geq 0\}$ is a uniform motion then there are numbers $k_1, \ldots, k_n$ such that $U_z\mathbf{x} = <e^{\,k(i)z}x_1, \ldots, e^{\,k(n)z}x_n>$.

This equation has many familiar models, such as Lambert's Law of light absorption, radio-active decay, and continuously compounded interest in economics.

Proof. To prove this theorem, recall the preceding one and let

$$U_z(\mathbf{x}) \; = \; <u_1(z)x_1, \ldots, u_n(z)x_n).$$

Because $U_{z+w} = U_z U_w$, we also have for each index i:

$$u_i(z+w) \; = \; u_i(z)u_i(w)$$

Switching now to the natural logarithm, it follows that the function $ln(u_i)$ is additive (on the same domain, the non-negative real numbers). By a theorem of analysis it then follows that

$$ln(u_i)(z) \; = \; k_i + z, \text{for some real number } k_i$$

Hence, switching back from the logarithm and using our notation, $u_i(z) = e^b \cdot e^{\,k(i)z}$ for some number b. For the case $z = 0$, U_0 is the identity, so $e^b = 1$. This ends the proof.

8 A Symmetry Theorem for Jaynes' MAXENT

What is it like, for a prior opinion, in response to a new constraint, to change into a posterior opinion by a uniform motion?

As I mentioned, a uniform motion has familiar instances in the scientific literature, and also in economics, where it is used to represent continuously compounded interest. That is such a down to earth example, that it will help our imagination:

a capital V invested at interest rate k, continually compounded, grows to $e^{kt}V$ over time t.

In a typical situation a capital can consist of parts for which the investor has different aims; for example it might be prudent keep several savings accounts in different banks. That would be a constraint on the desired growth, in addition perhaps to the main aim of achieving a certain capital, apportioned selectively, by the age of retirement. At this point the investor faces an *optimality problem*. We can imagine that accounts with higher interest require longer term commitments (penalties for withdrawal before certain lengths of time) hence offer less liquidity. If liquidity is important to the investor, he will ask how his main aim can be achieved while maximizing expected liquidity, which in this case means minimizing expected interest rates.

At this point the example may not look like a great candidate for modeling rational change of opinion, but let me state it first. Then I will offer the proper motivation and go on to show that if we do take it as our guide, we will have a truly gratifying result.

Optimality Postulate. The transformation of prior odds $<x_1, ..., x_n>$ to posterior odds $<y_1, ..., y_n>$ subject to the constraint $F(y_1, ..., y_n) = m$ is by a uniform motion $\{U_z: z \geq 0\}$, such that there are constants k_i with $u_i(z) = e^{k(i)z}$, for $i = 1, ..., n$, for which the posterior expectation value of the quantity $\mathbf{k}$ is minimal (equivalently, such that $\Sigma\{y_ik_i: i = 1, ..., n\}$ is minimal).

As motivation, we can take a look at the quotient between a prior and a thus produced posterior. The quotient $U\mathbf{x}/\mathbf{x} = <(e^{k(i1)z}x_1)/x_1, ..., (e^{k(n)z}x_n)/x_n> = <(e^{k(i1)z}), ..., (e^{k(n)z})>$. Thus minimizing the expectation value (whether prior or posterior) of the quotient terms is equivalent to minimizing that quantity $\mathbf{k}$.

Theorem. For the simultaneous constraints $\Sigma\{y_i : I = 1, ..., n\} = 1$ and $\Sigma\{y_iq_i: i = 1, ..., n\} = r$ (the posterior expectation value of quantity $\mathbf{q}$), there exists a constant w such that the transformation of prior odds $<x_1, ..., x_n>$ to posterior odds $<y_1, ..., y_n>$ is by a uniform motion $\{U_z: z \geq 0\}$, with $u_i(z) = e^{wq(i)z}$, for $i = 1, ..., n$.

The importance of this theorem is that it gives exactly the same answer, to the question of how we are to update to a new expectation value for a given quantity, as Jaynes' MAXENT. I'll comment more on this below, but first let's look at the proof of the theorem.

Proof. We have here a dual constraint: $\Sigma\{y_i : I = 1, ..., n\} = 1$ and $\Sigma\{y_iq_i: i = 1, ..., n\} = r$. The Optimality Postulate says that these constraints will be satisfied by a transformation of prior $\mathbf{x}$ into posterior $\mathbf{y}$, by a uniform motion of a certain form:

$$<y_1, ..., y_n> = U_t <x_1, ..., x_n> = <e^{k(1)t}x_1, ..., e^{k(n)t}x_n>$$

for a certain time period t (however long it takes for the mind to change opinion in this way). For convenience we can choose the units of time such that this period has duration 1, that is, t = 1. So

$$<y_1, \ldots, y_n> \; = \; U_1 <x_1, \ldots, x_n> \; = \; < e^{k(1)}x_1, \ldots, e^{k(n)}x_n >$$

such that the expectation value of quantity **k** is minimized. What can we deduce about what **k** is like?

This sort of problem can be solved with the Lagrange multiplier method. To use this method we introduce special variables, say w and u, and assert that the minimum is found where all the partial derivatives (with respect to w, u, y_1, …, y_n) of the following function are zero:

$$y_i k_i + w(r - y_i q_i) + u(1 - \Sigma y_i).$$

That point is thus characterized by:

$$r - \Sigma y_i q_i = 0$$
$$1 - \Sigma y_i = 0$$
$$k_1 - w q_1 - u = 0$$
$$\vdots$$
$$k_n - w q_n - u = 0$$

First then, we see how **k** is a function of **q** and the two unknowns w and u:

$$k_i = w q_i + u$$

which means that

$$y_i = x_i e^{wq(i+u)} = x_i e^{wq(i)} \cdot e^u$$

Given the second constraint (in effect that the posterior is a probability vector) it is clear that the multiplication by e^u serves to normalize the vector, that is, that $e^u = 1/\Sigma x_i e^{wq(i)}$. So now the only unknown remaining is w.

Hence the posterior **y** is a function just of the prior **x** and that number w. However, the first constraint can then be brought into play: the expectation value of **q** equals r – this will determine a unique value for w, when we are told what **q** is. And we are done.

9 Applying the Theorem, an Example

To show how the value of w appears in an application, let us consider as example the simple constraint:

> ! set the odds even for A_1 versus A_2!

where we envisage a partition A_1, A_2, A_3.

Suppose the initial odds vector is, $<x_1, x_2, x_3> = <1/6, 1/3, 1/2>$.

The calculation, applying the above theorem, goes as follows. The way to state the constraint in terms of expectation value is this:

the posterior expectation of q equals 0,
where q is the quantity that has:
value 1 on A_1,
value -1 on A_2,
and value 0 on A_3.

That will clearly be so iff the posterior odds on A_I, A_2 are the same.

The prior expectation of q equals -1/6; we let the odds grow over unit time by "interest rates" proportional to q's proper values:

There is a constant w such that the posterior odds vector (ignoring normalization) is

$$<y_1, y_2, y_3>, \text{ with } y_i = x_i e^{wq(i)}, \text{ in other words,}$$
$$<y_1, y_2, y_3> = <(1/6)e^{w.1}, (1/3)v^{w.-1}, (1/2)e^{w.0}>$$
$$= <(1/6)e^{w}, (1/3)e^{-w}, (1/2)>$$

At the same time, the posterior expectation value of q equals 0, hence

$$1.y_1 + -1. y_2 + 0.y_3 = 0$$
$$\text{so } (e^{w}/6) = (1/3e^{w})$$
$$\text{hence } e^{w} = \sqrt{2}$$

which means that the posterior odds are $<(\sqrt{2})/6, \sqrt{2})/6, 1/2>$ approximately equal to the probability vector $<0.24, 0.24, 0.52>$.

That is, as the (essentially same) calculations make clear, the same answer as that obtained by Jaynes' MAXENT method. Notice that the third probability has grown a little. although the constraint was just on the first two. That is reminiscent of the Judy Benjamin example, and should of course raise the same eyebrows.

10 Conclusion

What can we figure out, about rational change of subjective probability, the transformation of prior into posterior opinion, through analogies with quantum mechanics? In the approach I presented
the most general pictures of the relevant 'motions' coincide:

- In quantum mechanics, the way in which a state changes over time is depicted as a frequently interrupted deterministic evolution. The interruptions are the measurements, interferences 'from outside', easy to think of as coming from the free decisions of experimentalists. The normal evolution between those interruptions are governed by Schroedinger's equation.
- In rational management of opinion, the way in which a state changes over time is also depicted as a frequently interrupted deterministic evolution. The interruptions are the acceptances of new constraints on one's opinion, prompted in response to experience – easy to think of as the exercise of free decisions by the agent. The normal evolution that leads from prior to posterior, in a way that satisfies the

accepted constraints, is by a process that has the same abstract form as Schroedinger's equation.

But now I want to enter a demurral, on my own behalf. In the three symmetry arguments noted or presented above, the main assumption was in each case that the posterior opinion would be literally a *function* of the prior and the constraint that was accepted in response to the 'input' or 'experience'. That is in effect an assumption of determinism, of a single unique 'way to go', which is in the case of rational management of opinion the idea that rationality requires rule-following, with no leeway for free choice.

In my view, a liberal probabilism, that assumption is not warranted and epistemology ought to have a greater respect for freedom of choice, within the bounds of reason [10, 15].

References

1. Wheeler, J.: Assessment of everett's 'Relative State' formulation of quantum theory. Rev. Mod. Phys. **29**, 463–465 (1957)
2. Blokhintsev, D.I.: My way in the science. In: Barbashov, B.M., Sissakian, A.N. (eds.) Self-review of Works. JINR Publishing, Dubna (2007)
3. Cross, A.: The crisis in physics: dialectical materialism and quantum theory. Soc. Stud. Sci. **21**, 735–759 (1991)
4. Everett, H.: 'Relative state' formulation of quantum mechanics. Rev. Mod. Phys. **29**, 454–462 (1957)
5. Groenewold, H.J.: Information in quantum measurement. Koninklijke Nederlandse Akademie van Wetenschappen **B55**, 21–27 (1952)
6. Groenewold, H.J.: Objective and subjective aspects of statistics in quantum description. In: Körner, S. (ed.) Observation and Interpretation in the Philosophy of Physics Proceedings of the Ninth Symposium of the Colston Research Society, pp. 197–203 (1957)
7. Groenewold, H.J.: Quantal Observation in Statistical Interpretation. In: Bastin, T. (ed.) Quantum Theory and Beyond: Essays and Discussions Arising from a Colloquium, pp. 43–54. Cambridge University Press, Cambridge (1971)
8. Fuchs, C.A.: Quantum mechanics as quantum information (And only a little more). quant-ph/0205039
9. Bub, J.: Why the quantum? Stud. Hist. Phil. Mod. Phys **35**, 241–266 (2004)
10. van Fraassen, B.C.: Laws and Symmetry. Oxford University Press, Oxford (1989)
11. Jeffrey, R.C.: Probable knowledge. In: Lakatos, I. (ed.) The Problem of Inductive Logic. Elsevier, Amsterdam (1968)
12. van Fraassen, B.C.: The geometry of opinion: Jeffrey shifts and linear operators. Philo. Sci. **59**, 163–175 (1992)
13. Jaynes, E.T.: Information theory and statistical mechanics. Phys. Rev. **106**, 620–630 (1956)
14. van Fraassen, B.C.: A problem for relative information minimizers in probability kinematics. Br. J. Philos. Sci. **32**, 375–379 (1981)
15. van Fraassen, B.C., Halpern, J.Y.: Updating probability: tracking statistics as criterion. Br. J. Philos. Sci. February 2016. doi:10.1093/bjps/axv027

Contextuality-by-Default 2.0: Systems with Binary Random Variables

Ehtibar N. Dzhafarov[1(✉)] and Janne V. Kujala[2]

[1] Purdue University, West Lafayette, USA
ehtibar@purdue.edu
[2] University of Jyväskylä, Jyväskylä, Finland
jvk@iki.fi

Abstract. The paper outlines a new development in the Contextuality-by-Default theory as applied to finite systems of binary random variables. The logic and principles of the original theory remain unchanged, but the definition of contextuality of a system of random variables is now based on multimaximal rather than maximal couplings of the variables that measure the same property in different contexts: a system is considered noncontextual if these multimaximal couplings are compatible with the distributions of the random variables sharing contexts. A multimaximal coupling is one that is a maximal coupling of any subset (equivalently, of any pair) of the random variables being coupled. Arguments are presented for why this modified theory is a superior generalization of the traditional understanding of contextuality in quantum mechanics. The modified theory coincides with the previous version in the important case of cyclic systems, which include the systems whose contextuality was most intensively studied in quantum physics and behavioral sciences.

Keywords: Contextuality · Connection · Consistent connectedness · Cyclic system · Inconsistent connectedness · Maximal coupling · Multimaximal coupling

1 Introduction: From Maximality to Multimaximality

The Contextuality-by-Default (CbD) theory [7–12,14,16,23–25] was proposed as a generalization of the traditional contextuality analysis in quantum physics [2,3,5,18,19,21,26,32]. The latter has been largely confined to *consistently connected* systems of random variables, those adhering to the *"no-disturbance"* principle [27,31]: the distributions of measurement outcomes remain unchanged under different measurement conditions (*contexts*). CbD allows for *inconsistently connected* systems, those in which context may influence the distribution of measurement outcomes for one and the same property [11,14–17,23,25]. In accordance with the CbD interpretation of the traditional contextuality analysis, this generalization is achieved by replacing the *identity couplings* used in dealing with consistently connected systems by *maximal couplings*.

© Springer International Publishing AG 2017
J.A. de Barros et al. (Eds.): QI 2016, LNCS 10106, pp. 16–32, 2017.
DOI: 10.1007/978-3-319-52289-0_2

Recall that, given a set of random variables $X, Y, \ldots, Z$, a coupling of this set is any set of jointly distributed random variables, $(X', Y', \ldots, Z')$, with

$$X \sim X', \ Y \sim Y', \ \ldots, \ Z \sim Z',$$

where $\sim$ stands for "has the same distribution as." The coupling $(X', Y', \ldots, Z')$ is maximal if (using Pr as a symbol for probability) the value of

$$p_{eq} = \Pr \left[X' = Y' = \ldots = Z' \right]$$

is maximal possible among all possible couplings of $X, Y, \ldots, Z$. The identity coupling is a special case of a maximal coupling, when $p_{eq} = 1$. The latter is possible if and only if all random variables $X, Y, \ldots, Z$ (hence also $X', Y', \ldots, Z'$) are identically distributed:

$$X \sim Y \sim \ldots \sim Z.$$

The notion of a maximal coupling, however, is not the only possible generalization of the identity couplings. And it has recently become apparent that it is not the best possible generalization either. The maximal-couplings-based definition of (non)contextual systems adopted in CbD does not have a certain intuitively plausible property that is enjoyed by the identity-couplings-based definition of consistently connected (non)contextual systems. This property is that *any subsystem of a consistently connected noncontextual system is noncontextual.* A subsystem is obtained by dropping from a system some of the random variables. An inconsistently connected noncontextual system in the previously published version of CbD ("CbD 1.0") does not generally have this property: by dropping some of its components one may be able to make it contextual.

In the new version, "CbD 2.0," preservation of noncontextuality for subsystems is achieved by replacing the notion of a maximal coupling in the definition of (non)contextual systems by the notion of a *multimaximal coupling.* This term designates a coupling every subcoupling whereof is a maximal coupling for the corresponding subset of the random variables being coupled (see Definition 1 below).

The remainder of the paper is a systematic presentation of this idea and of how it works in the analysis of contextuality. CbD 1.0 and CbD 2.0 coincide when dealing with consistently connected systems (as they must, because they both generalize this special case). They also coincide when dealing with the important class of cyclic systems [16,24,25] (see Sect. 4). None of the principles upon which CbD is based changes in version 2.0 (Sect. 2). The recently proposed logic of constructing a universal measure of contextuality [12] also transfers to version 2.0 without changes (Sect. 5).

2   Contextuality-by-Default Theory: Basics

We briefly recapitulate here the main aspects of the Contextuality-by-Default theory. We recommend, however, that the reader look through some of the recent accounts of CbD 1.0, e.g., Refs. [11,14], or (especially) Ref. [12].

Each random variable in CbD is double-indexed, R_q^c, where q is referred to as the *content* of the random variables, that which R_q^c measures or responds to, and c is referred to as its *context*, the conditions under which R_q^c measures or responds to q.

Remark 1. Following Ref. [12] we will write "conteXt" and "conteNt" to prevent their confusion in reading. The conteXt and conteNt of a random variable uniquely identify it within a given system of random variables.

Two random variables R_q^c and $R_{q'}^{c'}$ are jointly distributed if and only if they share a conteXt: $c = c'$. Otherwise they are *stochastically unrelated*. All random variables sharing a conteXt form a jointly distributed *bunch* of random variables. All random variables sharing a conteNt form a *connection*, the elements of which are pairwise stochastically unrelated. It is necessary that all random variables in a connection have the same set of possible values (more generally, the same set and sigma-algebra).

The present paper is primarily about systems in which all random variables are binary. It is immaterial for contextuality analysis how these values are named, insofar as they are identically named and identically interpreted within each connection. For instance, if $R_q^c = 1$ means "spin-up along axis z in particle 1" and $R_q^c = 2$ means "spin-down along axis z in particle 1," then all random variables $R_q^{c'}$ ($c' \neq c$) should have the same possible values, 1 and 2, with the same meanings. Note that for another conteNt q', the values of $R_{q'}^c$ need not be denoted in the same way even if they have analogous interpretations: e.g., we may have $R_{q'}^c = 3 =$ "spin-up along axis z in particle 2" and $R_{q'}^c = 4 =$ "spin-down along axis z in particle 2".

The matrix below provides an example of a *conteXt-conteNt system* (c-c system) of random variables:

R_1^1	R_2^1	$\cdot$	R_4^1	c_1
R_1^2	$\cdot$	R_3^2	$\cdot$	c_2
R_1^3	R_2^3	R_3^3	R_4^3	c_3
q_1	q_2	q_3	q_4	$\boxed{\mathcal{R}_{ex}}$

Each row here is a bunch of jointly distributed random variables, each column is a connection ("between bunches"). Note that not every conteNt should be measured in a given conteXt.

The system $\mathcal{R}_{ex}$ can be conveniently used to illustrate the logic of contextuality analysis. We first consider the connections separately, and for each of them find all couplings that satisfy a certain property C. Let's call them C-*couplings*. Then we determine if these C-couplings are *compatible* with a coupling of the bunches of the c-c system (equivalently put, with a coupling of the entire c-c system).

The compatibility in question means the following. A coupling of (the bunches of) the c-c system is a set of jointly distributed random variables

S_1^1	S_2^1		S_4^1	c_1
S_1^2	$\cdot$	S_3^2	$\cdot$	c_2
S_1^3	S_2^3	S_3^3	S_4^3	c_3
q_1	q_2	q_3	q_4	$\boxed{S_{ex}}$

such that

$$\left(S_1^1, S_2^1, S_4^1\right) \sim \left(R_1^1, R_2^1, R_4^1\right),$$

$$\left(S_1^2, S_3^2\right) \sim \left(R_1^2, R_3^2\right),$$

$$\left(S_1^3, S_2^3, S_3^3, S_4^3\right) \sim \left(R_1^3, R_2^3, R_3^3, R_4^3\right).$$

Since the elements of S_{ex} are jointly distributed, the marginal distributions of the columns corresponding to the connections of $\mathcal{R}_{ex}$ are well-defined:

$\left(S_1^1, S_1^2, , S_1^3\right)$ is a coupling of connection R_1^1, R_1^2, R_1^3,

$\left(S_2^1, S_2^3\right)$ is a coupling of connection R_2^1, R_2^3,

$\left(S_3^2, S_3^3\right)$ is a coupling of connection R_3^2, R_3^3,

$\left(S_4^1, S_4^3\right)$ is a coupling of connection R_4^1, R_4^3.

In CbD we pose the following question: is there a coupling S_{ex} such that the subcouplings corresponding to the connections are C-couplings? If the answer is affirmative, then we say that the bunches of $\mathcal{R}_{ex}$ are compatible with at least some of the combinations of the C-couplings for its connections — and the c-c system is considered *partially* C-*noncontextual*. Otherwise, if no such a coupling S_{ex} exists, we say that the bunches of $\mathcal{R}_{ex}$ are incompatible with any of the C-couplings for its connections — and the c-c system is considered *completely* C-*contextual*. The intuition is that in a completely C-contextual c-c system the conteXts "interfere" with one's ability to couple the measurements of each conteNt in a specified (by C) way — while the connections can be coupled in this way if they are considered separately, ignoring the conteXts.

The adjectives "partially" and "completely" do not belong to the original theory. They are added here because one can also consider a stronger (more restrictive) notion of noncontextual c-c systems and, correspondingly, a weaker (less restrictive) notion of contextual c-c systems. We say that a c-c system is *completely* C-*noncontextual* if the bunches of $\mathcal{R}_{ex}$ are compatible with any combinations of the C-couplings for its connections; and it is *partially* C-*contextual* if the bunches of $\mathcal{R}_{ex}$ are incompatible with at least some of these combinations. The intuition is that in a completely C-noncontextual c-c system the conteXts "do not interfere" in any way with C-couplings of the measurements of any given conteNt (as if the connections were taken separately, ignoring conteXts).

In CbD 1.0 the C-couplings are maximal couplings, as defined in the opening paragraph of the paper. In CbD 2.0 C-couplings are multimaximal couplings, as defined below. We will see that if all random variables in a system are binary and C is multimaximality, then every connection has a unique C-coupling (Theorem 1-Corollary 1). In this case the notions of partial and complete (non)contextuality coincide, allowing us to drop these adjectives when speaking of (non)contextual c-c systems.

Remark 2. It is important to accept that noncontextuality of a c-c system (even if complete) does not mean that the conteXts are irrelevant and can be ignored. On the contrary, they are relevant "by defaults because, e.g., R_2^1 and R_2^3 in the second connection of $\mathcal{R}_{ex}$ are distinct and stochastically unrelated random variables. Moreover, the distributions of R_2^1 and R_2^3 may very well be different (i.e., the c-c system may be inconsistently connected), and this does not necessarily mean that the system is contextual (even if only partially) in the sense of our definitions. The measurements of the conteNt q_2 in conteXt c_3 can be "directly" influenced by the jointly-made measurements of q_3 (in which case we can speak of "signaling" or "disturbance"), while in context c_1 this influence is absent [1, 22]. It is also possible that the experimental set-up in context c_3 is different from that in context c_1, in which case we can speak of conteXt-dependent biases [28, 29]. All of this may account for the different distributions of R_2^1 and R_2^3, and none of this by itself makes the system contextual. See Refs. [11, 12, 17] for argumentation against confusing signaling and contextual biases with contextuality. (Of course, if one so wishes, they can be called forms of contextuality, but in a different sense from how contextulaity is understood in quantum physics and in CbD.)

3   Multimaximal Couplings for Binary Variables

Definition 1. Let $R_q^1, \ldots, R_q^k$ ($k > 1$) be a connection of a system. A coupling $\left(T_q^1, \ldots, T_q^k\right)$ of $R_q^1, \ldots, R_q^k$ is a *multimaximal coupling* if, for any $m > 1$ and any subset $\left(T_q^{i_1}, \ldots, T_q^{i_m}\right)$ of $\left(T_q^1, \ldots, T_q^k\right)$, the value of

$$\Pr\left[T_q^{i_1} = \ldots = T_q^{i_m}\right]$$

is largest possible among all couplings of $R_q^{i_1}, \ldots, R_q^{i_m}$.

The multimaximality plays the role of the constraint C in the definition of C-couplings given in the previous section. One finds multimaximal couplings for each of the connections and then investigates their compatibility with the c-c system's bunches.

It is known that a maximal coupling exists for any connection [33]. This is not true for multimaximal couplings in general: such a coupling need not exist if the number of possible values for the random variables in a connection exceeds 2.

Example 1. Consider a connection consisting of random variables R_q^1, R_q^2, R_q^3 each having values $1, 2, 3$ with the following probabilities

	1	2	3
R_q^1	0	1/2	1/2
R_q^2	1/2	0	1/2
R_q^3	1/2	1/2	0

If a multimaximal coupling (T_q^1, T_q^2, T_q^3) exists, we should have (see Ref. [33], or Theorem 3.3 in Ref. [12])

$$\Pr[T_q^1 = T_q^2 = 1] = 0 \quad \Pr[T_q^1 = T_q^2 = 2] = 0 \quad \Pr[T_q^1 = T_q^2 = 3] = 0.5$$

$$\Pr[T_q^2 = T_q^3 = 1] = 0.5 \quad \Pr[T_q^2 = T_q^3 = 2] = 0 \quad \Pr[T_q^2 = T_q^3 = 3] = 0$$

$$\Pr[T_q^1 = T_q^3 = 1] = 0 \quad \Pr[T_q^1 = T_q^3 = 2] = 0.5 \quad \Pr[T_q^1 = T_q^3 = 3] = 0$$

from which we have in particular

$$\Pr[T_q^1 = T_q^2 = 3] = \Pr[T_q^1 = T_q^3 = 2] = \Pr[T_q^2 = T_q^3 = 1] = 0.5.$$

But these three events are pairwise mutually exclusive, so the sum of their probabilities cannot exceed 1.   □

It can also be shown that, in the case of random variables with more than two possible values, a multimaximal coupling, if it exists, is not generally unique.

Example 2. Consider a connection consisting of random variables R_q^1, R_q^2, R_q^3 each having one of six values (denoted $1, 1', 2, 2', 3, 3'$) with the following probabilities

	1	1'	2	2'	3	3'
R_q^1	0	0	0	1/2	0	1/2
R_q^2	0	1/2	0	0	1/2	0
R_q^3	1/2	0	1/2	0	0	0

Then the distinct couplings whose distributions are shown below,

$$\left(\dot{T}_q^1, \dot{T}_q^2, \dot{T}_q^3\right) = (2', 1', 1) \; (3', 3, 2) \text{ otherwise}$$

prob. mass	1/2	1/2	0

and $\left(\ddot{T}_q^1, \ddot{T}_q^2, \ddot{T}_q^3\right) = (2', 3, 2) \; (3', 1', 1) \text{ otherwise}$,

prob. mass	1/2	1/2	0

are both multimaximal couplings. □

However, the situation is different if the random variables in a connection are all binary: multimaximal couplings in this case always exist and are unique. In the theorem to follow we denote the values of all variables R_q^i by $1, 2$, and we will write values of $\left(T_q^1, \ldots, T_q^k\right)$ as strings of 1's and 2's, without commas.

Theorem 1. *Let* $R_q^1, \ldots, R_q^k$ *be a connection with binary random variables arranged so that the values of* $p_i = \Pr\left[R_q^i = 1\right]$ *are sorted* $p_1 \leq \ldots \leq p_k$. *Then* $\left(T_q^1, \ldots, T_q^k\right)$ *is a multimaximal coupling of* $R_q^1, \ldots, R_q^k$ *if and only if all values of* $\left(T_q^1, \ldots, T_q^k\right)$ *are assigned zero probability mass, except for*

$$
\begin{bmatrix}
\text{value of } \left(T_q^1, \ldots, T_q^k\right) & | & \text{probability mass} \\
11\ldots1 & | & p_1 \\
21\ldots1 & | & p_2 - p_1 \\
22\ldots1 & | & p_3 - p_2 \\
\vdots & | & \vdots \\
\overset{l}{\overbrace{2\ldots2}}\underbrace{1\ldots1}_{k-l} & | & p_{l+1} - p_l \\
\vdots & | & \vdots \\
22\ldots2 & | & 1 - p_k
\end{bmatrix}.
\tag{†}
$$

Proof. Note that the distribution of $\left(T_q^1, \ldots, T_q^k\right)$ in the theorem's statement is well-defined, and that $\left(T_q^1, \ldots, T_q^k\right)$ is indeed a coupling of $R_q^1, \ldots, R_q^k$: for any $1 \leq l \leq k$,

$$\Pr\left[T_q^l = 1\right] = \sum_{m=0}^{l-1} \Pr\left[\overset{m}{\overbrace{2\ldots2}}\underbrace{1\ldots1}_{k-m}\right] = \sum_{m=0}^{l-1} (p_{m+1} - p_m) = p_l = \Pr\left[R_q^l = 1\right].$$

Sufficiency. The "if" part is checked directly: for any $1 \leq i_1 < \ldots < i_m \leq k$,

$$\Pr\left[T_q^{i_1} = \ldots = T^{i_m} = 1\right] = \sum_{m=0}^{i_1-1} \Pr\left[\overset{m}{\overbrace{2\ldots2}}\underbrace{1\ldots1}_{k-m}\right]$$

$$= \sum_{m=0}^{i_1-1} (p_{m+1} - p_m) = p_{i_1} = \Pr\left[T_q^{i_1} = 1\right],$$

which is the maximal possible value for the leftmost probability. Analogously,

$$\Pr\left[T_q^{i_1} = \ldots = T^{i_m} = 2\right] = \sum_{m=i_m}^{k} \Pr\left[\overbrace{2\ldots2}^{m}\underbrace{1\ldots1}_{k-m}\right]$$

$$= \sum_{m=i_m}^{k} (p_{m+1} - p_m) = 1 - p_{i_m} = \Pr\left[T_q^{i_m} = 2\right],$$

which is also the maximal possible probability. This establishes that $\left(T_q^{i_1}, \ldots, T^{i_m}\right)$ is a maximal coupling for $\left(R_q^{i_1}, \ldots, R^{i_m}\right)$.

  Necessity. The "only if" part of the statement is proved by (i) observing that $\Pr\left[22\ldots2\right] = 1 - p_k$, and (ii) proving that if l is the ordinal position of the first 1 in the value of $\left(T_q^1, \ldots, T_q^k\right)$, then

$$\Pr\left[\overbrace{2\ldots2}^{l-1}\underbrace{1\ldots1}_{k-l+1}\right] = p_l - p_{l-1},$$

and for all other strings with the first 1 in the lth position the probabilities are zero. We prove (ii) by induction on l. For $l = 1$, we have

$$p_1 = \Pr\left[11\ldots1\right].$$

Since

$$p_1 = \Pr\left[T_q^1 = 1\right] = \Pr\left[11\ldots1\right] + \sum \Pr\left[1\underbrace{\ldots}_{\text{not all 1's}}\right],$$

all the summands under the summation operator must be zero. Let the statement be proved up to and including $l < k$. We have

$$p_{l+1} = \Pr\left[T_q^{l+1} = \ldots = T_q^k = 1\right] = \Pr\left[\overbrace{2\ldots2}^{l}\underbrace{1\ldots1}_{k-l}\right] + \sum \Pr\left[\overbrace{\ldots}^{\text{not all 2's}}\underbrace{1\ldots1}_{k-l}\right].$$

By the induction hypothesis, all summands under the summation operator are zero, except for

$$\begin{bmatrix} \text{value of } \left(T_q^1, \ldots, T_q^k\right) & | & \text{probability mass} \\ 11\ldots1 & | & p_1 \\ 21\ldots1 & | & p_2 - p_1 \\ 22\ldots1 & | & p_3 - p_2 \\ \vdots & | & \vdots \\ \overbrace{2\ldots2}^{l-1}\underbrace{1\ldots1}_{k-l+1} & | & p_l - p_{l-1} \end{bmatrix}$$

These values sum to p_l. Hence

$$\Pr \left[\overbrace{2 \ldots 2}^{l} \underbrace{1 \ldots 1}_{k-l} \right] = p_{l+1} - p_l.$$

We also have

$$p_{l+1} = \Pr\left[T_q^{l+1} = 1\right] = \Pr \left[\overbrace{2 \ldots 2}^{l} \underbrace{1 \ldots 1}_{k-l} \right] + \sum \Pr \left[\overbrace{\ldots}^{\text{not all 2's}} \underbrace{1 \ldots 1}_{k-l} \right]$$

$$+ \sum \Pr \left[\overbrace{\ldots 1}^{l+1} \underbrace{\ldots}_{\text{not all 1's}} \right]$$

$$= (p_{l+1} - p_l) + p_l + \sum \Pr \left[\overbrace{\ldots 1}^{l+1} \underbrace{\ldots}_{\text{not all 1's}} \right]$$

whence the summands under the last summation operator must all be zero. $\square$

Corollary 1. *A multimaximal coupling $\left(T_q^1, \ldots, T_q^k\right)$ exists and is unique for any connection $R_q^1, \ldots, R_q^k$ with binary random variables.*

The significance of this result is that insofar as we confine our analysis to c-c systems of binary random variables, every bunch (a row in a c-c matrix) has a known distribution and every connection (a column in the c-c matrix) has a uniquely imposed on it distribution. The only question is whether the distributions along the rows and along the columns of a c-c matrix are mutually compatible, i.e., can be viewed as marginals of an overall coupling of the entire c-c system.

We can now formulate the CbD 2.0 definition of (non)contextuality in systems with binary random variables.

Definition 2. A coupling of a c-c system is called *multimaximally connected* if every subcoupling of this coupling corresponding to a connection of the system is a multimaximal coupling of this connection.

Definition 3. A c-c system of binary random variables is *noncontextual* if it has a multimaximally connected coupling. Otherwise it is *contextual*.

Remark 3. As explained in the next section, any (non)contextual system of binary random variables is completely (non)contextual. Because of this it is unnecessary to use the qualification "completely" in the definition above. Note that this definition applies only to systems of binary random variables. The extension of this definition to arbitrary random variables is not unique, and we leave this topic outside the scope of this paper (but will discuss it briefly in Sect. 6).

4   Properties of Contextuality

Contextuality analysis of the systems of binary random variables is simplified by the following theorem, proved in Ref. [13].

Theorem 2. *Let* $R_q^1, \ldots, R_q^k$ *be a connection with binary random variables arranged so that the values of* $p_i = \Pr\left[R_q^i = 1\right]$ *are sorted* $p_1 \leq \ldots \leq p_k$. *Then* $\left(T_q^1, \ldots, T_q^k\right)$ *is a multimaximal coupling of* $R_q^1, \ldots, R_q^k$ *if and only if* $\left(T_q^i, T_q^{i+1}\right)$ *is a maximal coupling of* $\left\{R_q^i, R_q^{i+1}\right\}$ *for* $i = 1, \ldots, k-1$.

In other words, in the case of binary random variables, multimaximality can be defined in terms of certain pairs of random variables rather than all possible subsets thereof, as it was done in Definition 1. As shown in Sect. 6 below, a pairwise formulation can also be used in the general case, for arbitrary random variables.

. The main motivation for switching from the maximal couplings of CbD 1.0 to multimaximal couplings is to be able to prove the following theorem.

Theorem 3. *In a noncontextual c-c system of binary random variables every subsystem (obtained from the system by removing from it some of the random variables) is noncontextual.*

Proof. Let S be a multimaximally connected coupling of a system $\mathcal{R}$. Let $\mathcal{R}'$ be a system obtained by deleting a random variable R_q^c from $\mathcal{R}$; and let S' be the set of random variables obtained by deleting from S the corresponding random variable S_q^c. Then S' is a multimaximally connected coupling of $\mathcal{R}'$. Indeed, S' is jointly distributed, its subcouplings corresponding to the system's bunches have the same distributions as these bunches (including the bunch for conteXt c), and its subcouplings corresponding to the system's connections are multimaximal couplings (including the connection for context q, by the definition of a multimaximal coupling). $\qquad\square$

There are other desirable properties of the revised definition of contextuality.

First of all we should mention a property shared by CbD 1.0 and 2.0, one that should hold for any reasonable definition of contextuality. If a c-c system is consistently connected (i.e., $R_q^c \sim R_q^{c'}$ for all q, c, c' such that q is measured in both c and c'), then the system is (non)contextual if and only if it is (non)contextual in the traditional sense (as interpreted in CbD): the multimaximal couplings for connections consisting of identically distributed random variables are identity couplings.

Another property worth mentioning is that, using the terminology introduced at the end of Sect. 2, whether a c-c system of binary random variables is contextual or noncontextual, it is always completely contextual (respectively, completely noncontextual). This follows from the fact that multimaximal couplings for connections consisting of binary random variables are unique, whence if the combination of these unique couplings is (in)compatible with the system's bunches then it is *all* combinations of the couplings that are (in)compatible with the system's bunches.

A third property we find important follows from the fact that if a connection contains just two random variables, then their maximal coupling is their multi-maximal coupling. As a result, the theory of contextuality for cyclic c-c systems [16, 17, 20, 25] remains unchanged. Recall that a cyclic c-c system of binary random variables is one in which (1) any bunch consists of two random variables, and (2) any connection consists of two random variables (and, without loss of generality, the c-c system cannot be decomposed into two disjoint cyclic c-c systems). The conteXt-conteNt matrix below shows a cyclic system with 3 conteNts and 3 conteXts (their numbers in a cyclic system are always the same, and called the *rank* of the c-c system):

R_1^1	R_2^1	·	c_1
·	R_2^2	R_3^2	c_2
R_1^3	·	R_3^3	c_3
q_1	q_2	q_3	$\boxed{\mathcal{CYC}_3}$

A prominent example of a noncyclic c-c system each of whose connections consist of two binary random variables is one derived from the Cabello-Estebaranz-Alcaine proof [4] of the Kochen-Specker theorem in 4D space: the system there consists of 36 random variables arranged into 9 bunches (shown below by columns) containing 4 random variables each, and 18 connections (shown by rows) containing two random variables each:

	c_1	c_2	c_3	c_4	c_5	c_6	c_7	c_8	c_9
q_{0001}	★	★							
q_{0010}	★					★			
q_{1100}	★		★						
q_{1200}	★						★		
q_{0100}		★				★			
q_{1010}		★						★	
q_{1020}		★		★					
q_{1212}			★	★					
q_{1221}			★		★				
q_{0011}			★				★		
q_{1111}				★	★				
q_{0102}				★				★	
q_{1001}						★			★
q_{1002}					★	★			
q_{0120}					★				★
q_{1121}							★	★	
q_{1112}							★		★
q_{2111}								★	★

Here, the star symbol in the cell defined by conteXt c_i and conteNt q_j designates a binary random variable R_j^i (the quadruple index at q represents a ray in a 4D real Hilbert space, as labeled in Ref. [4]). The contextual analysis of such systems generalizes the 4D version of the Kochen-Specker theorem in the same way (although computationally more demanding) in which cyclic c-c systems of rank 3,4,5 generalize the treatment of, respectively, the Suppes-Zanotti-Leggett-Garg [19,32], EPR-Bohm-Bell [2,5,18], and Klyachko-Can-Binicoglu-Shumovsky systems [20]. More general proofs of the Kochen-Specker theorem (e.g., by Peres [30]) translate into systems with more than two binary random variables per connection. The multimaximal-couplings-based analysis here will yield different results from the maximal-couplings-based one.

5   A Measure of Contextuality

In accordance with the linear consistency theorem proved in Ref. [12], a c-c system of random variables always has a *quasi-coupling* that agrees with a given set of couplings imposed on its connections. Let us clarify this.

A *quasi-random variable* X is defined by assigning to its possible values real numbers (not necessarily nonnegative) that sum to 1. These numbers are called *quasi-probability masses*, or simply *quasi-probabilities*. For instance, a variable X with values 1 and 2 to which we assign quasi-probabilities $\mathsf{qPr}\,[X=1]=-5$, $\mathsf{qPr}\,[X=2]=6$ is a quasi-random variable. A quasi-random variable is a proper random variable if and only if the quasi-probabilities assigned to its values are nonnegative. If a quasi-random variable X is a vector, $(X_1,\ldots,X_n)$, it can be referred to as a vector of jointly distributed quasi-random variables, even if each X_i is a proper random variable. A vector of jointly distributed quasi-random variables may very well have marginals (subvectors) that are proper random vectors.

A *quasi-coupling* of a c-c system $\mathcal{R}$ is a vector S of jointly distributed quasi-random variables in a one-to-one correspondence with the elements of $\mathcal{R}$, such that every subcoupling of S that corresponds to a bunch of the system has a (proper) distribution that coincides with that of the bunch. Finally, the quasi-coupling S agrees with a set of multimaximal couplings of the system's connections if any subcoupling of S that corresponds to a connection has the same (proper) distribution as this connection's multimaximal coupling.

As an example, consider again our c-c system $\mathcal{R}_{ex}$:

R_1^1	R_2^1	$\cdot$	R_4^1	c_1
R_1^2	$\cdot$	R_3^2	$\cdot$	c_2
R_1^3	R_2^3	R_3^3	R_4^3	c_3
q_1	q_2	q_3	q_4	$\mathcal{R}_{ex}$

Let all random variables be binary. Then, as we know, each connection has a unique multimaximal coupling. Let us denote these couplings (going from the leftmost column to the rightmost one in the matrix)

$$\left(T_1^1, T_1^2, T_1^3\right), \left(T_2^1, T_2^3\right), \left(T_3^2, T_3^3\right), \left(T_4^1, T_4^3\right).$$

The theorem mentioned in the opening line of this section says that one can always find a quasi-coupling S for $\mathcal{R}_{ex}$,

S_1^1	S_2^1		S_4^1	c_1
S_1^2	$\cdot$	S_3^2	$\cdot$	c_2
S_1^3	S_2^3	S_3^3	S_4^3	c_3
q_1	q_2	q_3	q_4	$\boxed{S_{ex}}$

such that

$$\left(S_1^1, S_1^2, S_1^3\right) \sim \left(T_1^1, T_1^2, T_1^3\right),$$

$$\left(S_2^1, S_2^3\right) \sim \left(T_2^1, T_2^3\right),$$

$$\left(S_3^2, S_3^3\right) \sim \left(T_3^2, T_3^3\right),$$

$$\left(S_4^1, S_4^3\right) \sim \left(T_4^1, T_4^3\right).$$

Clearly, the system $\mathcal{R}_{ex}$ is noncontextual if and only if among all such quasi-couplings S_{ex} there is at least one proper coupling.

It is convenient for our purposes to look at this in the following way (introduced in Ref. [12] but derived from an idea proposed in Ref. [6]). For each quasi-coupling S_{ex} one can compute its *total variation*. The latter is defined as the sum of the absolute values of all quasi-probabilities assigned to the values of S_{ex} (i.e., to all 2^9 combinations of values of $S_1^1, S_2^1, \ldots, S_4^3$). If S_{ex} is a proper coupling, this total variation equals 1, otherwise it is greater than 1. Therefore, if the system $\mathcal{R}_{ex}$ is contextual, then the total variation of its quasi-couplings is always greater than 1. As shown in Ref. [12], one can always find a quasi-coupling S_{ex}^* of $\mathcal{R}_{ex}$ that has the smallest possible value of the total variation. This value (perhaps, less 1, if one wants zero rather than 1 to be the smallest value) can be taken to be a *measure of contextuality*.

Generalizing, we have the following statement.

Theorem 4. *Any c-c system of binary random variables has a quasi-coupling whose subcouplings corresponding to the system's connections are their multi-maximal couplings. Among all such quasi-couplings there is at least one with the smallest possible value of total variation (which value is then considered a measure of contextuality for the system).*

6   Conclusion: How to Generalize

For c-c systems with binary random variables multimaximal couplings are definitely a better way of generalizing identity couplings of the traditional contextuality analysis than maximal couplings. A system that is deemed noncontextual in terms of multimaximal couplings has noncontextual subsystems. The contextuality of a contextual system and noncontextuality of a noncontextual system are both complete if one uses multimaximal couplings to define them. And the theory specializes to the previous version (CbD 1.0) when applied to cyclic systems and to other systems whose connections consist of pairs of random variables.

The question to pose now is what one should do with non-binary random variables. The most straightforward way to construct a general theory is to simply drop the qualification "binary" in Definition 3. There are, however, some complications associated with this approach. Connections involving non-binary variables may not have multimaximal couplings (Sect. 3) One has to decide whether such systems are contextual, and how to measure the degree of contextuality in them if they are. Another complication, shared with the CbD 1.0, is that multimaximal couplings are not unique if the random variables are not all binary, because of which one no longer can ignore the difference between complete and partial forms of (non)contextuality. Conceptual and computational adjustments have to be made.

At the same time, some of the properties mentioned in Sect. 4 hold for arbitrary random variables, at least for categorical ones (those with finite number of values). Theorem 3 obviously holds for arbitrary random variables if noncontextuality is taken to be partial. The definition of the (non)contextuality of a system of random variables reduces to the traditional one when a system is consistently connected. Theorem 2 also generalizes to arbitrary random variables, although in a somewhat weaker form due to the loss of the linear ordering of the distributions within a connection.

Theorem 5. *Let $R_q^1, \ldots, R_q^k$ be a connection. Then $\left(T_q^1, \ldots, T_q^k\right)$ is a multimaximal coupling of $R_q^1, \ldots, R_q^k$ if and only if $\left(T_q^c, T_q^{c'}\right)$ is a maximal coupling of $\left\{R_q^c, R_q^{c'}\right\}$ for all $c < c'$ in $\{1, \ldots, k\}$.*

Proof. The "only if" part is true because pairs are subsets. To prove the "if" part, assume the contrary: there is a subset of the connection (without loss of generality, the connection itself, $R_q^1, \ldots, R_q^k$) such that its coupling $\left(T_q^1, \ldots, T_q^k\right)$ is not maximal while $\Pr\left[T_q^c = T_q^{c'}\right]$ is maximal possible for all c, c'. Then, by the theorem on maximal couplings (see Ref. [33] or Ref. [12], Theorem 3.3) there is a value v in the common set of values for all random variables T_q^c such that

$$\Pr\left[T_q^1 = T_q^2 = \ldots = T_q^k = v\right] < \min_{c \in \{1,\ldots,n\}} \left(\Pr\left[T_q^c = v\right]\right),$$

while, for any $c, c' \in \{1, \ldots, k\}$,

$$\Pr\left[T_q^c = T_q^{c'} = v\right] = \min\left(\Pr\left[T_q^c = v\right], \Pr\left[T_q^{c'} = v\right]\right).$$

Then, by replacing each T_q^c with

$$\widetilde{T}_q^c = \begin{cases} 1 \; if \quad T_q^c = v \\ 2 \; if \; otherwise \end{cases},$$

and considering $\left(\widetilde{T}_q^1, \ldots, \widetilde{T}_q^k\right)$ a coupling for some connection consisting of binary random variables, we come to a contradiction with Theorem 2.   □

There is a complication, however, that seems especially serious for simply dropping the qualification "binary" in Definition 3: this approach allows a noncontextual system of random variables to become contextual under *coarsegraining*. The latter means lumping together some of the values of the variables constituting some of the connections. Thus, if R_q^c has values $1, 2, 3, 4$, one could lump together 1 and 2 and obtain a random variables with three values (and do the same for all other random variables in the connection for conteNt q). It is natural to expect that a system should preserve its noncontextuality under such course-graining, but this is not the case generally.

Example 3. The system consisting of the single connection with six values $(1, 1', 2, 2', 3, 3')$ in Example 2 is noncontextual, because it does have multimaximal couplings. However, if one lumps together i and i' and denotes the lumped value i $(= 1, 2, 3)$, one obtains the system considered in Example 1, which is contextual because it does not have a multimaximal coupling.   □

A radical solution for all the problems mentioned is to deal with binary random variables only. This can be achieved by replacing each non-binary random variable R_q^c in a system with a bunch of jointly distributed dichotomizations thereof (that thereby becomes a sub-bunch of the bunch representing conteXt c). For instance, if R_q^c has values $1, 2, 3, 4$, then it could be represented by $2^{4-1} - 1 = 7$ jointly distributed binary random variables. The joint distribution is very simple: of the 2^7 values of this bunch all but 4 have zero probability masses. Of course, every other random variable with conteNt q should be dichotomized in the same way, replacing thereby the corresponding connection with 7 new connections. Coarse-graining in this approach becomes a special case of extracting from a system a subsystem. The price one pays for the conceptual simplicity thus achieved is a great increase of the numbers of random variables in each bunch (becoming infinite if the original system involves non-categorical random variables), although the cardinality of the supports of the bunches remains unchanged. It is to be seen if this dichotomization approach proves feasible.

Acknowledgments. This research has been supported by NSF grant SES-1155956 and AFOSR grant FA9550-14-1-0318. We are grateful to Victor H. Cervantes for his critical comments on the manuscript.

References

1. Bacciagaluppi, G.: Leggett-Garg inequalities, pilot waves and contextuality. Int. J. Quantum Found. **1**, 1–17 (2015)
2. Bell, J.: On the Einstein-Podolsky-Rosen paradox. Physics **1**, 195–200 (1964)
3. Bell, J.: On the problem of hidden variables in quantum mechanics. Rev. Mod. Phys. **38**, 447–453 (1966)
4. Cabello, A., Estebaranz, J.M., Alcaine, G.G.: Bell-Kochen-Specker theorem: a proof with 18 vectors. Phys. Lett. A **212**, 183 (1996)
5. Clauser, J.F., Horne, M.A., Shimony, A., Holt, R.A.: Proposed experiment to test local hidden-variable theories. Phys. Rev. Lett. **23**, 880–884 (1969)
6. Barros, J.A., Oas, G.: Negative probabilities and counter-factual reasoning in quantum cognition. Physica Scripta T **163**, 014008 (2014)
7. de Barros, J.A., Dzhafarov, E.N., Kujala, J.V., Oas, G.: Measuring observable quantum contextuality. In: Atmanspacher, H., Filk, T., Pothos, E. (eds.) QI 2015. LNCS, vol. 9535, pp. 36–47. Springer, Heidelberg (2016). doi:10.1007/978-3-319-28675-4_4
8. Dzhafarov, E.N., Kujala, J.V.: A qualified Kolmogorovian account of probabilistic contextuality. In: Atmanspacher, H., Haven, E., Kitto, K., Raine, D. (eds.) QI 2013. LNCS, vol. 8369, pp. 201–212. Springer, Heidelberg (2014). doi:10.1007/978-3-642-54943-4_18
9. Dzhafarov, E.N., Kujala, J.V.: Contextuality is about identity of random variables. Physica Scripta T **163**, 014009 (2014)
10. Dzhafarov, E.N., Kujala, J.V.: Contextuality-by-default. In: Advances in Cognitive Neurodynamics, vol. IV, pp. 405–410 (2015)
11. Dzhafarov, E.N., Kujala, J.V.: Conversations on contextuality. In: Contextuality from Quantum Physics to Psychology, pp. 1–22. World Scientific, New Jersey (2016)
12. Dzhafarov, E.N., Kujala, J.V.: The contextuality-by-default theory. J. Math. Psychol (to appear). arXiv:1511.03516
13. Dzhafarov, E.N., Kujala, J.V.: Probabilistic foundations of contextuality. Fortschritte der Physik - Progress of Physics (2016, to appear). arXiv:1604.08412
14. Dzhafarov, E.N., Kujala, J.V., Cervantes, V.H.: Contextuality-by-default: a brief overview of ideas, concepts, and terminology. In: Atmanspacher, H., Filk, T., Pothos, E. (eds.) QI 2015. LNCS, vol. 9535, pp. 12–23. Springer, Heidelberg (2016). doi:10.1007/978-3-319-28675-4_2
15. Dzhafarov, E.N., Zhang, R., Kujala, J.V.: Is there contextuality in behavioral and social systems? Philos. Trans. R. Soc. A **374**, 20150099 (2015)
16. Dzhafarov, E.N., Kujala, J.V., Larsson, J.-A.: Contextuality in three types of quantum-mechanical systems. Found. Phys. **7**, 762–782 (2015)
17. Dzhafarov, E.N., Kujala, J.V., Cervantes, V.H., Zhang, R., Jones, M.: On contextuality in behavioral data. Philos. Trans. R. Soc. A **374**, 20150234 (2016)
18. Fine, A.: Hidden variables, joint probability, and the Bell inequalities. Phys. Rev. Lett. **48**, 291–295 (1982)
19. Leggett, A.J., Garg, A.: Quantum mechanics versus macroscopic realism: Is the flux there when nobody looks? Phys. Rev. Lett. **54**, 857–860 (1985)
20. Klyachko, A.A., Can, M.A., Binicioglu, S., Shumovsky, A.S.: A simple test for hidden variables in spin-1 system. Phys. Rev. Lett. **101**, 020403 (2008)
21. Kochen, S., Specker, E.P.: The problem of hidden variables in quantum mechanics. J. Math. Mech. **17**, 59–87 (1967)

22. Kofler, J., Brukner, C.: Condition for macroscopic realism beyond the Leggett-Garg inequalities. Phys. Rev. A **87**, 052115 (2013)
23. Kujala, J.V., Dzhafarov, E.N.: Probabilistic contextuality in EPR/Bohm-type systems with signaling allowed. In: Contextuality from Quantum Physics to Psychology, pp. 287–308. World Scientific, New Jersey (2016)
24. Kujala, J.V., Dzhafarov, E.N.: Proof of a conjecture on contextuality in cyclic systems with binary variables. Found. Phys. **46**, 282–299 (2016)
25. Kujala, J.V., Dzhafarov, E.N., Larsson, J.-A.: Necessary and sufficient conditions for maximal contextuality in a broad class of quantum mechanical systems. Phys. Rev. Lett. **115**, 150401 (2015)
26. Kurzynski, P., Ramanathan, R., Kaszlikowski, D.: Entropic test of quantum contextuality. Phys. Rev. Lett. **109**, 020404 (2012)
27. Kurzynski, P., Cabello, A., Kaszlikowski, D.: Fundamental monogamy relation between contextuality and nonlocality. Phys. Rev. Lett. **112**, 100401 (2014)
28. Lapkiewicz, R., Li, P., Schaeff, C., Langford, N.K., Ramelow, S., Wiesniak, M., Zeilinger, A.: Experimental non-classicality of an indivisible quantum system. Nature **474**, 490 (2011)
29. Lapkiewicz, R., Li, P., Schaeff, C., Langford, N.K., Ramelow, S., Wiesniak,M., Zeilinger, A.: Comment on "two fundamental experimental tests of nonclassicality with qutrits" (2013). arXiv:1305.5529
30. Peres, A.: Quantum Theory: Concepts and Methods. Kluwer, Dordrecht (1995)
31. Ramanathan, R., Soeda, A., Kurzynski, P., Kaszlikowski, D.: Generalized monogamy of contextual inequalities from the no-disturbance principle. Phys. Rev. Lett. **109**, 050404 (2012)
32. Suppes, P., Zanotti, M.: When are probabilistic explanations possible? Synthese **48**, 191–199 (1981)
33. Thorisson, H.: Coupling, Stationarity, and Regeneration. Springer, New York (2000)

Probabilistic Nature of a Field with Time as a Dynamical Variable

Hou Y. Yau$^{(\boxtimes)}$

FDNL Research, 119 Poplar Avenue, San Bruno, CA 94066, USA
hyau@fdnresearch.us

Abstract. Taking time as a dynamical variable, we study a wave with 4-vector amplitude that has vibrations of matter in space and time. By analyzing its Hamiltonian density equation, we find that the system is quantized. It obeys the Klein-Gordon equation and thus also the Schrödinger equation. Only a probability can be assigned for the detection of a particle. This quantized field has physical structures that resemble a zero-spin quantum field. The possibility to apply our formalism outside quantum physics is briefly discussed.

Keywords: Quantum field · Klein Gordon equation · Schrödinger equation · Vibrations in space and time · Quantization · Probability density

1 Introduction

In the formulation of classical and quantum theories, time is principally treated as a parameter in the equation of motion. The theories postulate a time parameter with respect to which the dynamics unfold. Time and space are treated separately. On the other hand, space-time in general relativity is dynamical interacting with matter and radiation. There is no globally defined time in the theory. Space-time is weaved as unity. Thus, the treatment of time in quantum theory and general relativity is rather different. The problems created by these differences in approach are striking especially when one tries to reconcile the two basic theories from a single framework [1,2].

Apart from the relativistic dynamics that require time to be treated on the same footing as space, there are many cases where time is expected to be associated with an operator in quantum theory, e.g. dwell time of a particle in a region of space [3,4], tunneling time [5,6], or decay time of an unstable particle [7]. In these cases, time seems to play a dynamical role. Although it has been known since Pauli's era about the difficulties of assigning time as a selfadjoint operator [8,9], extensive efforts have been dedicated to resolve the dynamical nature of time in quantum theory [10–19]. In addition to these efforts, various classical and quantum models have also been proposed by T.D. Lee that suggest time can be considered as a fundamentally discrete dynamical variable [20,21].

As there are many suggested reasons why time shall play a more dynamical role, we ask a few fundamental questions: in classical theory, the amplitude, X,

© Springer International Publishing AG 2017
J.A. de Barros et al. (Eds.): QI 2016, LNCS 10106, pp. 33–45, 2017.
DOI: 10.1007/978-3-319-52289-0_3

of a wave with vibrations in space can be defined as the maximum displacement of matter in the wave from its equilibrium coordinate. Since matter can have vibrations in the x coordinates, can it also has vibrations in the time coordinate t? In fact, if space and time are to be treated on same footing, it is theoretically possible to define an amplitude T for vibration in time [22]. Although it is feasible to construct a wave that has vibrations in both space and time, can its properties have something to do with our real physical world?

Here, we investigate the quantum properties of a plane wave with a 4-vector amplitude $(T, \boldsymbol{X})$ that has vibrations in space and time. We define the amplitude in time of a plane wave as the maximum difference between the 'internal time' of matter within the wave and the 'external time' measured by a stationary inertial observer outside the wave; its meaning will be further elaborated in Sect. 2. By studying the Hamiltonian density equation of this planes wave in Sect. 3, we find that a harmonic oscillating system with vibration of matter in proper time can be the generator for the energy of mass. In Sect. 4, we show that an oscillator with vibration in proper time can only have one unique amplitude. This leads to our subsequent reasoning that a real scalar field describing the vibrations of matter in space and time shall be quantized; it has no classical description. Furthermore, this quantized real scalar field obeys the Klein-Gordon equation and has properties that resemble a zero-spin quantum field as will be shown in Sect. 5. Probabilistic nature of the system in the non-relativistic limit will be further demonstrated in Sect. 6. The possibility to apply our formalism outside quantum physics is briefly discussed in the last section reserved for conclusions and discussions.

2   Plane Wave with Vibrations in Space and Time

Consider the background coordinates $(t, \boldsymbol{x})$ for the flat space-time as observed in an inertial frame O. Time in this background is the 'external time' as measured by clocks that are not coupled to the system under investigation [23–25]. We will first study a plane wave with matter that has vibrations in space and time relative to this background coordinate system.

The amplitude for vibration in space, $\boldsymbol{X}$, of a classical plane wave is well defined; it is the maximum displacement of matter in the wave from its equilibrium coordinate such as in the case for a flexible string under tension. Similarly, let us define a plane wave's amplitude for vibration in time, T, as the maximum difference between the time of matter inside the wave, t_f, and the external time, t. Therefore, if matter inside the plane wave carries a clock measuring its internal time, an inertial observer outside will see the matter's clock vibrates with time, t_f, as related to his own clock measuring time, t. In other words, we have assumed the matter's internal clock is running at a varying rate relative to the inertial observer's clock. The 'internal time' t_f is an intrinsic property of matter[1]. The amplitude $(T, \boldsymbol{X})$ is a 4-vector such that $T^2 = T_0^2 + |\boldsymbol{X}|^2$, where T_0 is an amplitude with vibration in proper time.

The vibrations in space and time can be written as

$$t_f = t + T\sin(\boldsymbol{k} \cdot \boldsymbol{x} - \omega t) = t + \mathrm{Re}(\zeta_t^+), \tag{1}$$

$$\boldsymbol{x}_f = \boldsymbol{x} + \boldsymbol{X}\sin(\boldsymbol{k} \cdot \boldsymbol{x} - \omega t) = \boldsymbol{x} + \mathrm{Re}(\zeta_{\boldsymbol{x}}^+), \tag{2}$$

where

$$\zeta_t^+ = -iTe^{i(\boldsymbol{k} \cdot \boldsymbol{x} - \omega t)}, \tag{3}$$

$$\zeta_{\boldsymbol{x}}^+ = -i\boldsymbol{X}e^{i(\boldsymbol{k} \cdot \boldsymbol{x} - \omega t)}, \tag{4}$$

and

$$\omega^2 = \omega_0^2 + |\boldsymbol{k}|^2. \tag{5}$$

Thus, time of matter inside the plane wave has this temporal vibration when observed with respect to the external time. This internal time, t_f, is a function of the external time, t, and a dynamical variable for the system. The external time is used as reference for measuring the temporal vibrations inside the wave..

For a plane wave with proper time vibrations only, matter has no vibration in space. In this case, $\omega = \omega_0$, $|\boldsymbol{k}| = 0$, $T = T_0$, and $|\boldsymbol{X}| = 0$ with

$$\zeta_{0t}^+ = -iT_0e^{-i\omega_0 t}, \tag{6}$$

and

$$t_f = t - T_0\sin(\omega_0 t), \tag{7}$$

$$\boldsymbol{x}_f = \boldsymbol{x}. \tag{8}$$

The internal time passes at the rate $1 - \omega_0 T_0\cos(\omega_0 t)$ with respect to the external time and has an average value of 1. Matter in this plane wave is stationary in space and will still appear to travel along a time-like geodesic when averaged over many cycles. The nature of this internal time will be further elaborated in Sect. 4.

We can further define a plane wave,

$$\zeta^+ = \frac{T_0}{\omega_0}e^{i(\boldsymbol{k} \cdot \boldsymbol{x} - \omega t)}, \tag{9}$$

such that ζ_t^+ and $\zeta_{\boldsymbol{x}}^+$ in Eqs. (3) and (4) can be obtained from ζ^+ as:

$$\zeta_t^+ = \frac{\partial \zeta^+}{\partial t}, \tag{10}$$

$$\zeta_{\boldsymbol{x}}^+ = -\boldsymbol{\nabla}\zeta^+. \tag{11}$$

Therefore, the vibrations of matter in space and time for a plane wave can be described by ζ^+.

---

[1] Unlike the 'intrinsic time' [23,24] suggested as a dynamical variable of the studied system (e.g. position of a clock's dial or position of a classical free particle [26]) that can function to measure time, the 'internal time' defined here is an intrinsic property of matter that has vibration in time.

3   Hamiltonian Densities

Let us investigate the properties of a system in a cube with volume V that can have multiple particles with mass m vibrating in space and time. We will impose periodic boundary conditions at the box walls. Instead of carrying out our analysis in terms of the plane wave ζ^+ and its complex conjugate ζ^-, we make the following ansätz

$$\varphi^+ = \omega_0 \sqrt{\frac{m}{2V}} \zeta^+ = T_0 \sqrt{\frac{m}{2V}} e^{i(\boldsymbol{k}\cdot\boldsymbol{x}-\omega t)}, \tag{12}$$

$$\varphi^- = \omega_0 \sqrt{\frac{m}{2V}} \zeta^- = T_0^* \sqrt{\frac{m}{2V}} e^{-i(\boldsymbol{k}\cdot\boldsymbol{x}-\omega t)}, \tag{13}$$

where T_0 here is taken as a complex time amplitude and periodic boundary conditions are imposed on the wave vector $\boldsymbol{k}$.

The plane wave $\varphi^{\pm}$ satisfies the equation of motion:

$$\partial_u \partial^u \varphi^{\pm} + \omega_0^2 \varphi^{\pm} = 0. \tag{14}$$

Equation (14) is similar to the Klein-Gordon equation, except that we have yet to understand how $\varphi^{\pm}$ can be related to a quantized field. (Note that the formulations described so far can also apply to a classical field.) The Hamiltonian density corresponding to the equation of motion is,

$$H^{\pm} = (\partial_0 \varphi^{\pm})^* (\partial_0 \varphi^{\pm}) + (\boldsymbol{\nabla} \varphi^{\pm})^* \cdot (\boldsymbol{\nabla} \varphi^{\pm}) + \omega_0^2 \varphi^{\pm *} \varphi^{\pm}. \tag{15}$$

In our analysis, we will work in natural units whereby $c = \hbar = 1$.

Let us look at each term on the right hand side (RHS) of this Hamiltonian density equation. From Eqs. (12) and (13), the first term of Eq.(15)

$$H_1^{\pm} = (\partial_0 \varphi^{\pm})^* (\partial_0 \varphi^{\pm}) = \frac{m\omega_0^2}{2V} T^* T, \tag{16}$$

is a Hamiltonian density for vibrations of matter in time. Indeed, $m\omega_0^2/2$ is an usual term that appears in the Hamiltonian of a harmonic oscillator with mass m except the vibration is in time and not in space. (Note that we have not taken into account the order of multiplication between complex conjugates here but shall be considered when the field is quantized.) Similarly, the second term

$$H_2^{\pm} = (\boldsymbol{\nabla} \varphi^{\pm})^* \cdot (\boldsymbol{\nabla} \varphi^{\pm}) = \frac{m\omega_0^2}{2V} \boldsymbol{X}^* \cdot \boldsymbol{X}, \tag{17}$$

has the familiar form of a Hamiltonian density with harmonic oscillation in space.

The plane wave $\varphi^{\pm}$ is a function of T_0 as shown in Eqs. (12) and (13). The third term on RHS of Eq.(15) is a Hamiltonian density related to vibrations of matter in proper time,

$$H_3^{\pm} = \omega_0^2 \varphi^{\pm *} \varphi^{\pm} = \frac{m\omega_0^2}{2V} T_0^* T_0. \tag{18}$$

After combining the three terms from Eqs. (16), (17) and (18), the total Hamiltonian density is

$$H^{\pm} = \frac{m\omega_0^2}{V} T^* T. \tag{19}$$

The energy corresponding to the vibration of matter in proper time is of special importance in our study. To better understand its properties, we consider the simple plane waves

$$\varphi_0^+ = T_0 \sqrt{\frac{m}{2V}} e^{-i\omega_0 t}, \tag{20}$$

$$\varphi_0^- = T_0^* \sqrt{\frac{m}{2V}} e^{i\omega_0 t}. \tag{21}$$

Matter inside this plane wave $\varphi_0^{\pm}$ has vibrations in proper time only, i.e. $|\boldsymbol{k}| = 0$ and $\boldsymbol{x}_f = \boldsymbol{x}$. Substitute Eqs. (20) and (21) into Eq.(15), the Hamiltonian density is

$$H_0^{\pm} = \frac{m\omega_0^2 T_0^* T_0}{V}. \tag{22}$$

The energy contained inside volume V is $E = m\omega_0^2 T_0^* T_0$ of a simple harmonic oscillating system in proper time. As discussed in the previous section, the vibration in proper time is an intrinsic property of matter. Energy E shall therefore correspond to some energy related to matter. However, we have only consider matter with mass m in this simple harmonic oscillating system without involving any of the various charges or force fields. No other energy is present in this system except the energy of mass m. Here, we will consider this energy as the internal energy of mass.

4   Proper Time Oscillator

The energy E for the vibration of matter in proper time is necessary on shell if it is the internal energy of mass. For a single particle system, we have

$$E = m\omega_0^2 T_0^* T_0 = m, \tag{23}$$

or simply

$$\omega_0^2 T_0^* T_0 = 1. \tag{24}$$

In addition to the classical concepts of mass [27], we suggest here a possibility that a point mass m can have oscillation in proper time with amplitude $|\tilde{T}_0| = 1/\omega_0$. Only an oscillator with such amplitude is observable in this single particle system.

Let us first consider the point mass in the plane wave φ_0^+. A point mass m at rest in space with angular frequency ω_0 and amplitude $T_0 = 1/\omega_0$ will have vibration in proper time relative to the external time. The internal time $\tilde{t}_f^+$ of the point mass's internal clock observed in frame O is:

$$\tilde{t}_f^+(t) = t - \frac{\sin(\omega_0 t)}{\omega_0}. \tag{25}$$

We will assume the point mass observed is located at the origin of coordinate x_0,

$$\tilde{x}_f^+(t) = x_0. \tag{26}$$

The internal time of the oscillator is running at a different rate relative to an observer at spatial infinity. However, the temporal oscillator has no movement in the spatial direction. Unlike time dilation in relativity, the vibration of matter in time from Eq. (25) is not the result of relative movement or gravity. It is an additional degree of freedom introduced to restore the symmetry between space and time in a matter field.

From Eq. (25), the internal time rate relative to the external time for this oscillator is

$$\frac{\partial \tilde{t}_f^+}{\partial t} = 1 - \cos(\omega_0 t). \tag{27}$$

The average of this time rate is 1. Its value is bounded between 0 and 2 which is positive. Thus, the internal time of a point mass moves only in the forward direction. It cannot move back to its past. If we assume this point mass is a typical particle that has high vibration frequency, e.g. $\omega_0 = 7.6 \times 10^{20}\,\mathrm{s}^{-1}$ and $|\tilde{T}_0| = 1.32 \times 10^{-21}\,\mathrm{s}$ for an electron, the particle will appear to travel along a smooth time-like geodesic if the inertial observer's clock is not sensitive enough to detect the high frequency and small amplitude of the vibration. In fact, as the angular frequency increases and approaches infinity ($\omega_0 \to \infty$), the amplitude of oscillation becomes negligible ($T_0 \to 0$). Such particle will travel along a near time-like geodesic with no vibration observed. On the other hand, if the oscillation of a particle is slow enough, we can observe its properties under different time rate within a cycle. For example, an unstable particle will have different decay rate observed at different phase of the oscillation.

The internal clock of the particle with angular frequency $\omega_0 \to \infty$ is a clock suitable for the observer at spatial infinity. Its near time-like geodesic nature is sensitive enough to detect the varying internal time rate of another particle with lower frequency. However, this clock's mass is infinite ($m = \omega_0 \to \infty$). As pointed out by Salecker and Wigner [28], to obtain infinite accuracy in measuring a clock's time means infinite uncertainty in the clock's mass, and thus the clock's mass needs to reach infinity. Some of the studies regarding quantum clocks in the context of time-energy uncertainty relation can be found in references [25, 29–33].

Equations (25) and (26) can be Lorentz transformed to another frame of reference O' with background coordinates (t', x') where the the particle will have vibrations in time and space with amplitudes $\tilde{T} = \omega/\omega_0^2$ and $\tilde{X} = k/\omega_0^2$ respectively. (We have assumed frame O is traveling with velocity $v = k/\omega$ relative to frame O' and the particle begins at origin of the x' coordinates at $t' = 0$). The vibrations in time and space are

$$\tilde{t}_f^+(t') = t' - \frac{\omega}{\omega_0^2}\sin\left(\frac{\omega_0^2 t'}{\omega}\right), \tag{28}$$

$$\tilde{x}_f'^+(t') = vt' - \frac{k}{\omega_0^2}\sin\left(\frac{\omega_0^2 t'}{\omega}\right). \tag{29}$$

The internal time $\tilde{t}_f^{\,+}$ is measured with respect to the external time in frame O' and is not the internal proper time of the particle's internal clock. In frame O', the particle is traveling with a velocity. The internal proper time measured by the particle's clock is $\tilde{t}_f^+ = \sqrt{(\tilde{t}_f^{\,+})^2 - (\tilde{x}_f^{\,\prime+})^2} = t - \sin(\omega_0 t)/\omega_0$ as shown in Eq. (25).

Equation (29) is the trajectory of the particle observed in frame O'. The particle travels with a velocity

$$\tilde{v}_f^+ = \frac{\partial \tilde{x}_f^{\,\prime+}}{\partial t'} = v[1 - \cos(\frac{\omega_0^2 t'}{\omega})]. \tag{30}$$

Apart from this variation in velocity, the internal time rate also varies. From Eq. (28), the internal time rate relative to the clock of the inertial observer is

$$\frac{\partial \tilde{t}_f^{\,\prime+}}{\partial t'} = 1 - \cos(\frac{\omega_0^2 t'}{\omega}). \tag{31}$$

We can calculate the amplitudes of vibration for a particle. For example, we can estimate the amplitude of spatial vibration for an electron:

$$|v| = 0.99999 \Rightarrow |\tilde{X}| = 8.6 \times 10^{-9} \text{ cm}, \tag{32}$$

$$|v| = 0.001 \Rightarrow |\tilde{X}| = 3.9 \times 10^{-14} \text{ cm}. \tag{33}$$

In the second, non-relativistic example, the amplitude of the spatial vibration is approximately equal to the diameter of a nucleus which is tremendously larger than the Planck length. However, this vibration also has a very short time scale ($\approx 10^{-21}$ s for electron). A particle will therefore appear to travel along a smooth trajectory if the measurements are not sensitive enough to detect the small vibrations. On the other hand, the amplitude of the spatial oscillation becomes larger when its velocity increases as shown in Eqs. (32) and (33). If the oscillation is slow and the particle is traveling fast enough, we may observe the deviations of its position from the smooth trajectory at different phase of the oscillation.

Comparing Eqs. (20) and (21), the plane wave φ_0^+ with a particle traveling forward in time is mathematically equivalent to the plane wave φ_0^- with a particle traveling backward in time – time reversal symmetry, a property of an antiparticle [34]. The internal clock of this antiparticle shall read

$$\tilde{t}_f^-(t) = -t + \frac{\sin(\omega_0 t)}{\omega_0}. \tag{34}$$

Thus, the internal time rate relative to the external time for the oscillator with amplitude $\tilde{T}_0^* = 1/\omega_0$ is

$$\frac{\partial \tilde{t}_f^-}{\partial t} = -1 + \cos(\omega_0 t). \tag{35}$$

The average of this time rate is -1. Its value is bounded between 0 and -2 which is negative. Thus, the internal time of this antiparticle moves only in the backward direction.

5 Field Quantization

The amplitude of a classical harmonic oscillator with a point mass vibrating in space can take on different values. This is unlike the case for a simple harmonic oscillator with vibration in proper time. The condition that mass is on shell imposes a constraint allowing only an oscillator with proper time amplitude $|\tilde{T}_0| = 1/\omega_0$ to be observed. The classical harmonic oscillator has no such constraint.

As shown in Eq. (22), the amplitude T_0 of the plane wave $\varphi_0^\pm$ determines the amount of energy in a volume V. On the other hand, amplitude T_0 is constrained by condition (24) which limits the energy observable in the system to the energy of one particle. We can extend this concept to a many particle system that has n integer number of oscillators. A plane wave with proper time vibrations has energy for $n = H_0 V/m$ oscillators to be observed in a volume V. Condition (24) can be generalized as

$$\omega_0^2 T_0^* T_0 = n, \tag{36}$$

which is a Lorentz invariant. The number of particles observed in the system shall remain the same under Lorentz transformations. Taking the point mass as a particle (antiparticle) with de Broglie's mass/energy ($m = \omega_0$) in Eq.(22),

$$H_0^\pm = \frac{n\omega_0}{V}. \tag{37}$$

The energy in this plane wave $\varphi_0^\pm$ with vibrations in proper time is quantized with $n = 0, 1, 2, \ldots$ Only the energy corresponding to integer number of oscillators can be observed in this system.

Under a Lorentz transformation, $\varphi_0^\pm \to \varphi^\pm$. Instead, let us consider a plane wave $\varphi_n^\pm$ which is normalized in volume V when $n = 1$,

$$\varphi_n^\pm = \gamma^{-1/2} \varphi^\pm, \tag{38}$$

where $\gamma = (1 - |\boldsymbol{v}|^2)^{-1/2}$. Replace $\varphi^\pm$ with $\varphi_n^\pm$ in Eq. (15), the Hamiltonian density for plane wave $\varphi_n^\pm$ is

$$H_n^\pm = \gamma H_0^\pm = \frac{n\omega}{V}. \tag{39}$$

The energy in this plane wave $\varphi_n^\pm$ is quantized with n particles (antiparticles) of angular frequency ω in a volume V.

We can obtain a real scalar field by superposition of plane waves,

$$\varphi(x) = \sum_{\boldsymbol{k}} \varphi_{n\boldsymbol{k}}^+(x) + \varphi_{n\boldsymbol{k}}^-(x)$$
$$= \sum_{\boldsymbol{k}} (2V\omega)^{-1/2} (\omega_0 T_{0\boldsymbol{k}} e^{-ikx} + \omega_0 T_{0\boldsymbol{k}}^* e^{ikx}),$$

which satisfies the Klein-Gordon equation. This field is an infinite array of quantized oscillators. Its Hamiltonian density equation is,

$$H = 1/2[(\partial_0 \varphi)^2 + (\boldsymbol{\nabla}\varphi)^2 + \omega_0^2 \varphi^2], \tag{40}$$

corresponding to the infinite sum of normal mode oscillator excitation, each one of which is quantized. The energy observable in this real scalar field is necessarily quantized. Therefore, φ has no classical analogue. It is strictly a quantized field.

In quantum field theory, the transition to a quantum field can be done via canonical quantization. Similarly, we can quantize our system following the same procedures. However, we will not go over this in detail since most of the formulations can be found in quantum theory. Instead, only the key points will be highlighted here. For example, $\varphi(x)$ and its field conjugate $\pi(x) = \dot{\varphi}(x)$ shall be treated as operators on quantization, satisfying the equal-time canonical commutation relations. Other physical observables shall also be promoted to operators. Condition (36) can be extended to the quantized field with

$$ N_{\boldsymbol{k}} = \omega_0^2 T_{0\boldsymbol{k}}^{\dagger} \dot{T}_{0\boldsymbol{k}}, \tag{41} $$

as the particle number operator after taking into account the ordering between $T_{0\boldsymbol{k}}$ and $T_{0\boldsymbol{k}}^{\dagger}$. We can also define the annihilation operator $a_{\boldsymbol{k}}$ and creation operator $a_{\boldsymbol{k}}^{\dagger}$ as,

$$ a_{\boldsymbol{k}} = \omega_0 T_{0\boldsymbol{k}}, \tag{42} $$

and

$$ a_{\boldsymbol{k}}^{\dagger} = \omega_0 T_{0\boldsymbol{k}}^{\dagger}, \tag{43} $$

such that $N_{\boldsymbol{k}} = a_{\boldsymbol{k}}^{\dagger} a_{\boldsymbol{k}}$. Substitute $a_{\boldsymbol{k}}$ and $a_{\boldsymbol{k}}^{\dagger}$ into φ, and taking the normal ordering of operators, Eq. (40) becomes

$$ H = \frac{1}{V} \sum_{\boldsymbol{k}} \omega_{\boldsymbol{k}} a_{\boldsymbol{k}}^{\dagger} a_{\boldsymbol{k}}, \tag{44} $$

which reminds one of the Hamiltonian density for a bosonic field. The real scalar field with vibrations in space and time has physical structures that resemble a zero-spin bosonic field.

6   Probability Density

To study the case in the non-relativistic limit, we will define a function:

$$ \psi_{\boldsymbol{k}} = \frac{\omega_0 T_{0\boldsymbol{k}}}{\sqrt{V}} e^{i(\boldsymbol{k}\cdot\boldsymbol{x} - \omega_c t + \chi)} \approx \left[\frac{\omega_0^2}{\sqrt{V}} e^{i(\omega_0 t + \chi)} \right] \zeta_{\boldsymbol{k}}^{+}, \tag{45} $$

where

$$ \omega_c = \frac{\boldsymbol{k} \cdot \boldsymbol{k}}{2m} \approx \omega - \omega_0, \tag{46} $$

and $e^{i\chi}$ is an arbitrary phase factor. Periodic boundary conditions for a cube with volume V are imposed on the wave vector $\boldsymbol{k}$. Here, $T_{0\boldsymbol{k}}$ is considered as a function and not an operator. As we can see, $\psi_{\boldsymbol{k}}$ is a solution for the Schrödinger equation of a free particle, $-i\partial\psi_k/\partial t = (2m)^{-1}\nabla^2\psi_k$. The superposition principle holds such that

$$\psi = e^{i\chi}\sum_k \frac{\omega_0 T_{0k}}{\sqrt{V}}e^{i(\boldsymbol{k}\cdot\boldsymbol{x}-\omega_c t)}, \tag{47}$$

is also a solution for the linear and homogeneous Schrödinger equation.

From Eq. (36), the product of ψ_k and its complex conjugate ψ_k^*,

$$\psi_k^*\psi_k = \frac{\omega_0^2 T_{0k}^* T_{0k}}{V} = \frac{n_k}{V}, \tag{48}$$

is a particle number density. In a quantum wave, the location where a particle can be observed is indeterminate. Only a probability can be assigned. For a plane wave, the probability density has an uniform distribution which is also the particle number density from Eq. (48). The amplitude $\alpha_k = \omega_0 T_{0k}/\sqrt{V}$ in Eq. (45) is a probability amplitude. Function ψ has the basic properties of a wave function in quantum mechanics.

It is commonly believed that a matter wave can only have a probabilistic interpretation because the overall phase of a wave function is unobservable. As we have shown, the introduction of the arbitrary phase factor $e^{i\chi}$ in Eqs. (45) and (47) does not change the the probability density $\psi^*\psi$ or the result that ψ satisfies the Schrödinger equation. In fact, the theory developed with wave functions ψ shall be invariant under global phase transformation χ but the relative phase factors are physical. Thus, the overall phase of ψ is unobservable. Function ψ is not required to have the same phase as ζ that describes the physical vibrations in space and time.

7 Conclusions and Discussions

In this paper, we treat time as a dynamical variable. Instead of considering proper time as an operator, for example in references [30,33], we study the possibility that matter can have vibrations in both space and time. We show that if the energy of a proper time harmonic oscillator is taken as the energy of mass, this energy is necessary on shell meaning only one unique amplitude for the harmonic oscillator can be observed, $|\tilde{T}_0| = 1/\omega_0$. This is unlike a classical harmonic oscillator with vibration in space that can take on different values as its amplitude. (There is no condition analogous to mass on shell that restrict amplitude of vibration in space to an unique value.) The Hamiltonian of the system is quantized. The real scalar field φ does not have a classical description but rather shall be treated as a quantized field. In addition, this real scalar field satisfies the Klein Gordon equation and Schrödinger equation. It has properties that resemble those for a zero spin quantum field.

Our mathematical formalism for the field with vibrations in space and time may have possible application outside quantum physics. Recent researches (see references cited in [35]) have shown that the mathematical formalism of quantum mechanics can be adapted to models in quantum cognition. This has proved to be successful in accounting for many human behavioral phenomena. The theory uses a probabilistic formalism borrowed from quantum mechanics. However, the underlying processes that govern it can be classical.

Brains are macroscopic objects where classical fields naturally exist. On the other hand, an important part of cognition is the extraction of selected information from the huge amount of information flowing into the brain. An observer might choose to retain partial incomplete information not because it is impossible to obtain complete information. Instead, it is profitable for an observer to ignore a part of information to increase the speed of computations. It is, therefore, possible that an observer can develop the ability to operate with incomplete information in a quantum like way.

As we shall recall, the main difference between the quantum and classical ways of information processing is that the former can consistently ignore a part of information. It is this information loss in the mathematical formalism of quantum theory that can be applied to the partial selection of information in a cognitive system. However, there is no easy way to adapt quantum formalism in cognition to extend quantum probabilities beginning from a classical theory. As such, it is important to understand how a classical field can be turned into a quantum field description. Several classical models have been proposed for this application [36–38]. Although the quantum mathematical formalism is adapted, the theory developed is not the result that the brain is some type of quantum computer.

In our mathematical formalism of the field with vibrations in space and time, we begin without specifying whether the matter field is quantized or classical. In fact, if we examine the mathematics describing the temporal and spatial vibrations in Sect. 2, the formalism can equally apply to a classical field. This part of our formalism, therefore, can be adapted to describe the classical fields in the brain. Here, we will assume the information carries initially in the brain can be mathematically represented in terms of waves with vibrations in space and time. At this initial stage without information loss, the field φ from Eq. (12) can be hypothetically treated as a classical field.

Next, we will impose a constraint $|\tilde{T}_0| = 1/\omega_0$ adapt from Eq. (24) leading to quantization of the field. As shown in Sects. 5 and 6, φ is found to be quantized after we consider the constraint that mass is on shell. Similarly, we can adapt this mathematical formalism in a cognitive system signaling information loss. A part of the information in the original classical field is ignored leading to a quantum like description for the field φ after imposing the constraint. Although it is not clear at this point how information in the brain can be mathematically represented by the waves with vibrations in space and time, our mathematical formalism can relate the transition of an original classical field to a quantum one which is a necessary step in quantum cognition. In this regard, it may worth explore further whether the formalism adapted from the field with vibrations in space and time can benefit the study of a cognitive system.

References

1. Rovelli, C.: Quantum Gravity. Cambridge University Press, Cambridge (2004)
2. Anderson, E.: Problem of time in quantum gravity. Annalen der Physik **524**, 757 (2012)
3. Munoz, J., Ruschhaupt, A., Campo, A. (eds.): Time in Quantum Mechanics - Vol 2. Lecture Notes in Physics, vol. 789, p. 97. Springer, Heidelberg (2009)
4. Yearsley, J., Downs, D., Halliwell, J., Hashagen, A.: Quantum arrival and dwell times via idealized clocks. Phys. Rev. A **84**, 022109 (2011)
5. Ordonez, G., Hatano, N.: Existence and nonexistence of an intrinsic tunneling time. Phys. Rev. A **79**, 042102 (2009)
6. Kiukas, J., Ruschhaupt, A., Werner, R.: Tunneling times with covariant measurements. Found. Phys. **39**, 829 (2009)
7. Madrid, R.: Time as a dynamical variable in quantum decay. Phys. A **913**, 217 (2013)
8. Pauli, W.: General Principles of Quantum Mechanics. Springer, Heidelberg (1980)
9. Muga, J., Leavens, C.: Arrival time in quantum mechanics. Phys. Rep. **338**, 353 (2000)
10. Aharonov, Y., Bohm, D.: Time in the quantum theory and the uncertainty relation for time and energy. Phys. Rev. **122**, 1649 (1961)
11. Holevo, A.: Probabilistic and Statistical Aspects of Quantum Theory. North-Holland, Amsterdam (1982)
12. Aharonov, Y., Oppenheim, J., Popescu, S., Reznik, B., Unruh, W.: Measurement of time of arrival in quantum mechanics. Phys. Rev. A **57**, 4130 (1998)
13. Olkhovsky, V., Recami, E.: Time as a quantum observable. Int. J. Mod. Phys. A **22**, 5063 (2007)
14. Wang, Z., Xiong, C.: How to introduce time operator. Ann. Phys. (N.Y.) **322**, 2304 (2007)
15. Galapon, E.: Post Paulis theorem emerging perspective on time in quantum mechanics. In: Muga, G., Ruschhaupt, A., Campo, A. (eds.) Time in Quantum Mechanics - Vol. 2. Lecture Notes in Physics, vol. 789. Springer, Heidelberg (2009). doi:10.1007/978-3-642-03174-8_3. And references therein
16. Brunetti, R., Fredenhagen, K., Hoge, M.: Time in quantum physics: from an external parameter to an intrinsic observable. Found. Phys. **40**, 1368 (2010)
17. Hegerfeldt, G., Muga, J.: Symmetries and time operators. J. Phys. A Math. Theor. **43**, 505303 (2010)
18. Strauss, Y., Silman, J., Machnes, S., Horwitz, L.: Study of a self-adjoint operator indicating the direction of time within standard quantum mechanics. C. R. Math. **349**, 1117 (2011)
19. Arsenovic, D., Buric, N., Davidovic, D., Prvanovic, S.: Dynamical time versus system time in quantum mechanics. Chin. Phys. B **21**, 070302 (2012)
20. Lee, T.D.: Can time be a discrete dynamical variable? Phys. Lett. B **122**, 217 (1983)
21. Lee, T.D.: Difference equations and conservation laws. J. Stat. Phys. **46**, 843 (1987)
22. Yau, H.Y.: Emerged quantum field of a deterministic system with vibrations in space and time. Conf. Proc. **1508**, 514 (2012)
23. Busch, P.: On the energy-time uncertainty relation. Part I: dynamical time and time indeterminacy. Found. Phys. **20**, 1 (1990)
24. Busch, P.: On the energy-time uncertainty relation. Part II: pragmatic time versus energy indeterminacy. Found. Phys. **20**, 33 (1990)

25. Hilgevoord, J.: Time in quantum mechanics: a story of confusion. Stud. Hist. Phil. Mod. Phys. **36**, 29 (2005)
26. Butterfield, J.: On Time in Quantum Physics - The Blackwell Companion to the Philosophy of Time. Wiley-Blackwell, Oxford (2013)
27. Jammer, M.: Concepts of Mass in Contemporary Physics and Philosophy. Princeton University Press, Princeton (2009)
28. Salecker, H., Wigner, E.: Quantum limitations of the measurement of space-time distances. Phys. Rev. **109**, 571 (1958)
29. Karolyhazy, F.: Sixty-Two Years of Uncertainty. Plenum, New York (1990). Ed. by Miller, A.I
30. Kudaka, S., Matsumoto, S.: Uncertainty principle for proper time and mass. J. Math. Phys. **40**, 1237 (1999)
31. Aharonov, Y., Reznik, B.: Weighing a closed system and the time-energy uncertainty principle. Phys. Rev. Lett. **84**, 1368 (2000)
32. Briggs, J.: A derivation of the time-energy uncertainty relation. J. Phys. Conf. Ser. **99**, 012002 (2008)
33. Greenberger, D.: Conceptual problems related to time and mass in quantum theory. arXiv:1011.3709. [quant-ph]
34. Feynman, R.: The theory of positrons. Phys. Rev. **76**, 749 (1949)
35. de Barros, A., Oas, G.: Some examples of contextuality in physics: implications to quantum cognition. Contextuality Quantum Phys. Psychol. **6**, 153 (2015). Ed. by Dzhafarov, E., Jordan, S., Zhang, R., Cervantes, V
36. Khrennikov, A.: Quantum-like brain: interference of minds. Biosystems **84**, 225 (2006)
37. Khrennikov, A.: Quantum-like model of processing of information in the brain based on classical electromagnetic field. Biosystems **105**, 250 (2011)
38. de Barros, A.: Quantum-like model of behavioral response computation using neural oscillators. Biosystems **110**, 171 (2012)

Quantum Cognition

Testing Boundaries of Applicability of Quantum Probabilistic Formalism to Modeling of Cognition: Metaphors of Two and Three Slit Experiments

Irina Basieva[1,2] and Andrei Khrennikov[2(✉)]

[1] Department of Psychology, City University of London, London, UK
[2] International Center for Mathematical Modeling in Physics and Cognitive Sciences, Linnaeus University, Växjö-kalmar, Sweden
Andrei.Khrennikov@lnu.se

Abstract. Analogy between the two slit experiment in quantum mechanics (QM) and the disjunction effect in psychology led to fruitful applications of the mathematical formalism of quantum probability to cognitive psychology. These quantum-like studies demonstrated that quantum probability (QP) matches better with the experimental statistical data than classical probability (CP). Similar conclusion can be derived from comparing QP and CP models for a variety of other cognitive-psychological effects, e.g., the order effect. However, one may wonder whether QP covers completely cognitive-psychological phenomena or cognition exhibits even more exotic probabilistic features and we have to use probabilistic models with even higher degree of nonclassicality than quantum probability. It is surprising that already a cognitive analog of the triple slit experiment in QM can be used to check this problem.

Keywords: Two and three slit experiments · Sorkin equality · Probabilistic structure of cognition

1 Introduction

Recently *quantum probability* (QP) started to be actively applied to a variety of problems in cognition, psychology, economics, finances, molecular biology, genetics and epigenetics, see, e.g., the monographs [1–4]. Researchers explore the possibility to relax some Boolean constraints assigned by the *classical probability* (CP) model (Kolmogorov, 1933). One of such constraints is given by the formula of total probability (FTP). In quantum mechanics (QM) this formula is violated [5] as can be demonstrated by statistical data collected in the famous two slit experiment. Thus QP violates the FTP-constraint. Such features were explored in modeling of probabilistic aspects of cognition and psychological behavior; in particular, in modeling of the disjunction effect [6].

© Springer International Publishing AG 2017
J.A. de Barros et al. (Eds.): QI 2016, LNCS 10106, pp. 49–56, 2017.
DOI: 10.1007/978-3-319-52289-0_4

However, QP also has its special laws and they can be considered as constraints on its applicability. The natural question arises:

Do all cognitive-psychological phenomena satisfy all constraints posed by QP?

This question was studied by a few authors [1,7–9]. For a moment, we cannot say that the answer is known. It became clear that one has to be careful in exploring the QM outside of physics. Simple cognitive effects cannot be modeled by using the projection type measurements of the Lüders type; we have to proceed by using theory of quantum instruments; in particular to represent the observables by positive operator valued measures (POVMs) [7]. However, we still do not know whether the use of quantum instruments can solve all problems discussed, e.g., in [7]; see [10] for the last update.

It is interesting that nowadays the same problem started to attract a lot of interest in QM; a few groups of experimental physicists work hard to test the boundaries of applicability of QP. Surprisingly this can be done by exploring the "one-step generalization of the two slit experiment", namely, the triple slit experiment. As was discovered by R. Sorkin [11], QP (based on Born's rule for calculation of probabilities from the complex amplitudes) leads to some equality which can be checked experimentally. Its violation would demonstrate that probabilistic behavior of micro-systems is even more exotic than described by QP. Sorkin's equality has been under experimental study by one of world's leading groups in quantum foundations [12,13]. However, technicalities related to functioning of quantum detectors led to difficulties in successful testing Sorkin's equality; so this problem is still under experimental study.

We propose to use the same Sorkin's equality as a QP constraint on probabilistic data collected for cognitive/psychological phenomena. This note is of merely conceptual nature and the experiment proposed here has to be considered as just an illustration.[1]

In Sect. 2 of this note we present Sorkin's equality as the probabilistic constraint in CP and QP; in Sect. 3 we present a possible experimental test.

2   Derivation of Sorkin's Equality of the Third Order

2.1   Classical Probability

In classical measure-theoretic framework, for two disjoint events A_1 and A_2 and an event B we have

$$p(B \wedge (A_1 \vee A_2)) = p(B \wedge A_1) + p(B \wedge A_2), \tag{1}$$

---

[1] When the first version of this note was prepared [14]; the authors contacted E. Pothos (City University, London) with the proposal to perform this experiment. He informed us that his group has been already working on the triple slit experiment, but problems of the organizational character postponed its completion. Now the research group of E. Guerci (University of Cote d' Azur; Nice) also works on preparation of this experiment; unfortunately, it also confronts some problems (to finance completion of the experimental study). So, now we are in the state of exciting expectation of the outputs of these experiments. In principle, we cannot exclude that they would be opposite...

where the symbols $\wedge$ and $\vee$ are used for the set-theoretical representations of the logical operations of *conjunction and disjunction* - as the intersection and the union of sets representing events.

This is the basic feature of classical probability - its additivity. As was pointed out by Feynman, quantum probability is not additive [15]. Formally, this is correct. However, one has to be careful in defining the probability of conjunction of "quantum events", because they can be incompatible. It seems that the only way to define rigorously such probability is to use quantum conditional probability which is well defined. Thus we want to explore a quantum analog of the classical equality:

$$p(B \wedge A) = p(A)p(B|A). \qquad (2)$$

This equality is a consequence of Bayes' formula

$$p(B|A) = p(B \wedge A)/p(A). \qquad (3)$$

The latter is the definition of conditional probability in the Kolmogorov model. Thus in classical probability we start with well defined probability of conjunction of events, the joint probability, and then define conditional probability. In quantum probability we proceed another way around. We shall start with conditional probability and the define joint probability. Taking into account the fundamental role which is played by conditional probability in our further considerations, it is useful to rewrite equality (1), additivity law, in terms of conditional probabilities:

$$p(B|A_1 \vee A_2) = \frac{1}{p(A_1 \vee A_2)}[p(A_1)p(B|A_1) + p(A_2)p(B|A_2)]. \qquad (4)$$

This is one of the basic elements of classical statistical inference, *the formula of total probability*. In particular, if $p(A_1 \vee A_2) = 1$, we get the standard formula of total probability

$$p(B) = p(A_1)p(B|A_1) + p(A_2)p(B|A_2). \qquad (5)$$

Preparing to quantum considerations, let us introduce the *"interference term"*:

$$\begin{aligned} I_{12} &= p(A_1 \vee A_2)p(B|A_1 \vee A_2) - p(A_1)p(B|A_1) - p(A_2)p(B|A_2) \\ &= p(B \wedge (A_1 \vee A_2)) - p(B \wedge A_1) - p(B \wedge A_2). \end{aligned} \qquad (6)$$

In classical probability theory $I_{12} = 0$ (but in quantum theory $I_{12} \neq 0$, see Sect. 3, Eq. (16)).

Now consider three events $A_i, i = 1, 2, 3$. Let $p(A_1 \vee A_2 \vee A_3) = 1$. Here the additivity law gives us

$$p(B) = p(B \wedge (A_1 \vee A_2 \vee A_2)) = p(B \wedge A_1) + p(B \wedge A_2) + p(B \wedge A_3). \qquad (7)$$

And the formula of total probability has the form:

$$p(B) = p(A_1)p(B|A_1) + p(A_2)p(B|A_2) + p(A_3)p(B|A_3). \qquad (8)$$

We introduce the corresponding "interference coefficient":

$$I_{123} = p(B) - p(A_1)p(B|A_1) + p(A_2)p(B|A_2) + p(A_3)p(B|A_3)$$
$$= p(B) - p(B \wedge A_1) - p(B \wedge A_2) + p(B \wedge A_3). \qquad (9)$$

In classical probability theory $I_{123} = 0$.

Since $I_{12} = I_{13} = I_{23} = 0$, we can write this term as

$$I_{123} = p(B) - p(A_1)p(B|A_1) - p(A_2)p(B|A_2) - p(A_3)p(B|A_3) \qquad (10)$$

$$-I_{12} - I_{13} - I_{23}.$$

Thus

$$I_{123} = p(B) - p(A_1)p(B|A_1) - p(A_2)p(B|A_2) - p(A_3)p(B|A_3)$$
$$- p(A_1 \vee A_2)p(B|A_1 \vee A_2) + p(A_1)p(B|A_1) + p(A_2)p(B|A_2) + ... \quad (11)$$

Finally, we obtain the triple-interference coefficient in the following form:

$$I_{123} = p(B) - p(A_1 \vee A_2)p(B|A_1 \vee A_2) - p(A_1 \vee A_3)p(B|A_1 \vee A_3)$$
$$- p(A_2 \vee A_3)p(B|A_2 \vee A_3) + p(A_1)p(B|A_1) + p(A_2)p(B|A_2) + p(A_3)p(B|A_3). \quad (12)$$

By using the joint probability distribution and by shortening notation, $p_{ij} = p(B \wedge (A_i \vee A_j)), p_i = p(B \wedge A_i)$, we write this coefficient as

$$I_{123} = p_{123} - p_{12} - p_{13} - p_{23} + p_1 + p_2 + p_3. \qquad (13)$$

Of course, in classical probability the expression in the left-hand side also equals to zero. Surprisingly the coefficient defined by the left-hand side of (13) also equals to zero, in spite non-vanishing (in general) of I_{ij}. And this was an interesting discovery of R. Sorkin [11]. We shall prove this in Sect. 3 by proceeding in the rigorous framework of quantum conditional probabilities, see equality (17). (In principle, we can proceed with only conditional probabilities, i.e., without joint probabilities at all. However, Sorkin formulated his equalities in terms of joint probabilities and we wanted two have similar expressions.)

Now we can forget about quantum probabilities and just to check whether some statistical data satisfies Sorkin's equality

$$I_{123} = p_{123} - p_{12} - p_{13} - p_{23} + p_1 + p_2 + p_3 = 0 \qquad (14)$$

or not. If Sorkin's equality were violated, both classical and quantum models should be rejected; in the opposite case, we would get another (nontrivial) confirmation of validity of the quantum model.

In coming experiments, instead of one event B, we shall consider a few disjoint events B_j. We shall use this j as the upper index for wprobabilities, e.g., $p_i^{(j)}$.

3   Quantum Probability

We restrict our consideration by standard quantum observables given by Hermitian operators a and b. We consider the finite-dimensional case. Unfortunately, we have to assume that their eigenvalues can be degenerate, because as was found in [1] (see also [8,9] for detailed analysis), it is impossible to represent some cognitive entities by operators with nondegenerate spectra. Such operators have to generate double-stochastic matrices of transition probabilities. However, the real data from cognitive psychology do not satisfy to this constraint. One of the possible interpretations of violation of double-stochasticity is that the dimension of the complete state space is higher than just the number of possible results of observables, e.g., possible answers to questions. Therefore we have to represent observables by operators with degenerate spectra. Another possibility is to work not with Hermitian operators, but with generalized observables given by positive operator valued measures (POVMs), see [7]. However, in this paper we shall not explore the latter possibility.

For reader's convenience, we recall that a matrix $P = (p_{ij})$ with nonnegative elements is called doubly-stochastic, if it satisfies to the system of equations:

$$\sum_i p_{ij} = 1, \quad \sum_j p_{ij} = 1.$$

Let $a_i, i = 1, 2, 3$, and $b_j, j = 1, 2, ..., m$, be the eigenvalues of a and b. Denote the corresponding projectors by P_i^a and P_j^b respectively. We shall also introduce projector $P_{ik}^a, i \neq k$, on subspaces consisting of eigenvectors of a corresponding to eigenvalues a_i and a_k. Thus $P_{ik}^a = P_i^a + P_k^a$.

Let ρ be a quantum state. Then we have: $p(a = a_i) = \mathrm{Tr} P_i^a \rho P_i^a, p(a = a_k \vee a = a_m) = \mathrm{Tr} P_{km}^a \rho P_{km}^a$. By definition of conditional probability in quantum probability theory

$$p(b = b_j | a = a_i) = \frac{\mathrm{Tr} P_j^b P_i^a \rho P_i^a}{\mathrm{Tr} P_i^a \rho P_i^a}.$$

We consider also "ordered joint probability distribution"[2] $p_i \equiv p(a = a_i) p(b = b_j | a = a_i)$, the index j is fixed and we omit it.

For $k \neq m$, we consider the two-slit interference:

$$p(b = b_j | a = a_k \vee a = a_m) = \frac{\mathrm{Tr} P_j^b P_{km}^a \rho P_{km}^a}{\mathrm{Tr} P_{km}^a \rho P_{km}^a}$$

$$= \frac{1}{\mathrm{Tr} P_{km}^a \rho P_{km}^a} \left(\mathrm{Tr} P_k^a \rho P_k^a \frac{\mathrm{Tr} P_j^b P_k^a \rho P_k^a}{\mathrm{Tr} P_k^a \rho P_k^a} + \mathrm{Tr} P_m^a \rho P_m^a \frac{\mathrm{Tr} P_j^b P_m^a \rho P_m^a}{\mathrm{Tr} P_m^a \rho P_m^a} + +I_{km} \right).$$

---

[2] Incompatible observables represented by non-commutative Hermitian operators cannot be measured jointly. Therefore the straightforward definition of the joint probability distribution is inapplicable. However, it is possible to explore the definition generalizing representation of the classical joint probability distribution through conditional probability. However, the order structure of observations has to be taken into account, because in general $p(a = a_i) p(b = b_j | a = a_i)$ is not equal to $p(b = b_j) p(a = a_i | b = b_j)$.

where $I_{km} = \text{Tr}P_j^b P_k^a \rho P_m^a + \text{Tr}P_j^b P_m^a \rho P_k^a$. We consider also "ordered joint probability distribution" $p_{km} \equiv p(a = a_k \vee a = a_m)p(b = b_j | a = a_k \vee a = a_m)$. Thus

$$p_{km} = p_k + p_m + I_{km}. \tag{15}$$

This is the quantum modification of the additivity law; in fact, this is the quantum analog of FTP, since joint probabilities are defined via conditional probabilities. R. Feynman emphasized [15] non-additivity of quantum probability; by using the language of conditional quantum probabilities one of the authors of this paper reformulated this violation as disturbance of FTP [1,16,17]. Thus in quantum theory we have that in general

$$I_{km} = p_{km} - p_k - p_m \neq 0. \tag{16}$$

Now we consider the triple-slit interference. We shall use the equality $I = \sum_i P_i^a$. We have:

$$p_{123} \equiv p(b = b_j) = p(b = b_j | a = a_1 \vee a = a_2 \vee a = a_3) = \text{Tr}P_j^b \rho$$

$$= \sum_i \text{Tr}P_i^a \rho P_i^a \frac{\text{Tr}P_j^b P_i^a \rho P_i^a}{\text{Tr}P_i^a \rho P_i^a}$$

$$(\text{Tr}P_j^b P_1^a \rho P_2^a + \text{Tr}P_j^b P_2^a \rho P_1^a) + (\text{Tr}P_j^b P_1^a \rho P_3^a + \text{Tr}P_j^b P_3^a \rho P_1^a) + (\text{Tr}P_j^b P_2^a \rho P_3^a + \text{Tr}P_j^b P_3^a \rho P_2^a).$$

$$= p_1 + p_2 + p_3 + I_{12} + I_{13} + I_{23} =$$

$$= p_1 + p_2 + p_3 + (p_{12} - p_1 - p_2) + (p_{13} - p_1 - p_3) + (p_{23} - p_2 - p_3)$$

Hence, as well as in classical probability theory, see Sect. 2,

$$I_{123} = p_{123} - p_{12} - p_{13} - p_{23} + p_1 + p_2 + p_3 = 0. \tag{17}$$

4   Experimental Illustration

We present a toy model of the cognitive analog of the triple-slit experiment. There is a homogeneous group of people recruited for the experiment.[3] They are informed that during the experiment they will answer to a few questions related to their possible emigration to other countries; for this experiment, three fixed countries; for example, we can select Brazil, Canada, Australia, $a = a_i = 1, 2, 3$.

We tell them the story: "Suppose you plan to emigrate to one of these countries." Thus in mathematical terms it is supposed that

$$p(a_1 \vee a_2 \vee a_3) = 1 \tag{18}$$

---

[3] Its homogeneity is important, because it will be divide into a few subgroups which will be used to collect different blocks of statistical data. And it is important that we can assume that the members of all subgroups have "the same mental state".

Then this group is divided into three subgroups G, G' and G''. People from the first two groups will participate in experiments with conditional questioning and in the last group in unconditional experiment.

Those from G first are asked the a-question: *To which of these three countries would you like to emigrate?* Those with the answers $a = i$ form the new groups G_i. We find the probabilities $p(a = i) \approx \frac{n_{G_i}}{n_G}$, where n_Q denotes the number of elements in the set Q.

Then we have to ask those in groups G_i another question, say b, which has to be "complementary" to the a-question. Selection of b is the delicate issue. For example, let us proceed with the question b: *Are you ready to change your profession?* (in the case of emigration to this country)[4] This is the dichotomous observable $b = 0, 1$ corresponding to the answers 'no', 'yes'. (In principle, we can consider b having any finite number of values, but it is enough to find violation of Sorkin's equality for a dichotomous b-observable.) Those in G_i who answered $b = j$ form the group denoted by $G_{j|i}$. Now we can find conditional probabilities, $p(b = j | a = i) \approx \frac{n_{G_{j|i}}}{n_{G_i}}$ and the "ordered joint probabilities" $p_i^{(j)} = p(a = i)p(b = j | a = i) \approx \frac{n_{G_{j|i}}}{n_G}$.

People from the group G' are asked about pairs of countries: *Which pair of these three countries would you select to emigrate?* The answers are pairs (k, m). The groups corresponding to concrete pairs are denoted as G'_{km}. And we can find the probabilities $p(a = k \vee a = m) \approx \frac{n_{G'_{km}}}{n_{G'}}$. Then we ask those in each group the b-question; depending on the answer $b = j$, we form the groups $G'_{j|km}$ and find the conditional probabilities $p(b = j | a = k \vee a = m) \approx \frac{n_{G'_{j|km}}}{n_{G'_{km}}}$. They determine the joint probabilities $p_{km}^{(j)} = p(a = k \vee a = m)p(b = j | a = k \vee a = m) \approx \frac{n_{G'_{j|km}}}{n_{G'}}$.

Now those in G'' are asked just the b-question; depending to the answers we find the probabilities $p(b = j) = p_{123}^{(j)}$.

Finally, we put collected probabilities into Sorkin's equality, to check whether the interference term $I_{123}^{(j)} = 0$.

Of course, it is useful before to start this "triple-slit experiment", to check whether the questions are really complementary, i.e., one has to start with the corresponding two slit versions of this experiment to see whether $I_{km}^{(j)} \neq 0$. (But for this experiment a new group of people has to be used.)

Acknowledgments. One of the authors (AKH) would like to thank G. Weihs for numerous discussions on the possibility to violate Born's rule, in particular on the triple-slit experiment, and the possibility to see the lab and performance of this test during the visit to Innsbruck in May 2013 and hospitality during this visit.

This work was supported (A. Khrennikov) by the EU-project "Quantum Information Access and Retrieval Theory" (QUARTZ), Grant No. 721321. It was also supported (I. Basieva) by a Marie Sklodowska-Curie Individual Fellowship, grant agreement 696331.

---

[4] Another proposal: *Do you think that your application for emigration (to this country) will be successful?*

References

1. Khrennikov, A.: Ubiquitous Quantum Structure: From Psychology to Finances. Springer, Heidelberg (2010)
2. Busemeyer, J.R., Bruza, P.D.: Quantum Models of Cognition and Decision. Cambridge University Press, Cambridge (2012)
3. Haven, E., Khrennikov, A.: Quantum Social Science. Cambridge University Press, Cambridge (2013)
4. Asano, M., Khrennikov, A., Ohya, M., Tanaka, Y., Yamato, I.: Quantum Adaptivity in Biology: From Genetics to Cognition. Springer, Heidelberg (2015)
5. Khrennikov, A.: Interpretations of Probability. VSP Int. Sc. Publishers, Utrecht/Tokyo (1999)
6. Pothos, E.M., Busemeyer, J.R.: A quantum probability explanation for violation of rational decision theory. Proc. Royal. Soc. B **276**, 2171–2178 (2009)
7. Khrennikov, A., Basieva, I., Dzhafarov, E.N., Busemeyer, J.R.: Quantum models for psychological measurements: an unsolved problem. PLoS ONE. 9. Article ID: e110909 (2014)
8. Boyer-Kassem, T., Duchene, S., Guerci, E.: Quantum-like models cannot account for the conjunction fallacy. GREDEG Working Papers 2015–41, Groupe de REcherche en Droit, Economie, Gestion (GREDEG CNRS), University of Nice Sophia Antipolis (2015)
9. Boyer-Kassem, T., Duchene, S., Guerci, E.: Testing quantum-like models of judgment for question order effects. GREDEG Working Papers 2015–06, Groupe de REcherche en Droit, Economie, Gestion (GREDEG CNRS), University of Nice Sophia Antipolis (2015)
10. Basieva, I., Khrennikov, A.: On a possibility to combine the order effect with sequential reproducibility for quantum measurements. Found. Phys. **45**, 1379–1393 (2015)
11. Sorkin, R.D.: Quantum mechanics as quantum measure theory. Mod. Phys. Lett. A **9**, 31119 (1994)
12. Sinha, U., Couteau, C., Medendorp, Z., Sillner, I., Laflamme, R., Sorkin, R., Weihs, G.: Testing Born's rule in quantum mechanics with a triple slit experiment. In: Accardi, L., Adenier, G., Fuchs, C., Jaeger, G., Khrennikov, A., Larsson, J.-A., and Stenholm, S. (eds). Foundations of Probability and Physics-5, vol. 1101, pp. 200–207. American Institute of Physics, Ser. Conference Proceedings, Melville (2009)
13. Sinha, U., Couteau, C., Jenewein, T., Laflamme, R.D., Weihs, G.: Ruling out multi-order interference in quantum mechanics. Science **329**, 418–421 (2010)
14. Khrennikov, A., Basieva, I.: Testing boundaries of applicability of quantum probabilistic formalism to modeling of cognition. arXiv:1603.03079 [q-bio.NC]
15. Feynman, R., Hibbs, A.: Quantum Mechanics and Path Integrals. McGraw-Hill, New York (1965)
16. Khrennikov, A.: Linear representations of probabilistic transformations induced by context transitions. J. Phys. A Math. Gen. **34**, 9965–9981 (2001)
17. Khrennikov, A.: Contextual viewpoint to quantum stochastics. J. Math. Phys. **44**(6), 2471–2478 (2003)

Contextuality in the Integrated Information Theory

J. Acacio de Barros[1,3(✉)], Carlos Montemayor[2], and Leonardo P. G. De Assis[3]

[1] School of Humanities and Liberal Studies,
San Francisco State University, San Francisco, CA, USA
barros@sfsu.edu
[2] Department of Philosophy,
San Francisco State University, San Francisco, CA, USA
cmontema@sfsu.edu
[3] Suppes Brain Lab, Center for the Study of Language and Information,
Stanford University, Stanford, CA, USA
lpgassis@stanford.edu

Abstract. Integrated Information Theory (IIT) is one of the most influential theories of consciousness, mainly due to its claim of mathematically formalizing consciousness in a measurable way. However, the theory, as it is formulated, does not account for contextual observations that are crucial for understanding consciousness. Here we put forth three possible difficulties for its current version, which could be interpreted as a trilemma. Either consciousness is contextual or not. If contextual, either IIT needs revisions to its axioms to include contextuality, or it is inconsistent. If consciousness is not contextual, then IIT faces an empirical challenge. Therefore, we argue that IIT in its current version is inadequate.

Keywords: Consciousness · Contextuality · Integrated information theory

1 Introduction

The Integrated Information Theory (IIT), developed by Giulio Tononi in a series of influential papers, promises to deliver not only an account of consciousness but also a concrete way to measure it [20,25]. In this paper, we focus on the second aspect of IIT. We shall argue that there are potential problems that require clarification concerning a tension between IIT's mathematical model of consciousness and contemporary models of contextuality.

Contextuality is important to measure consciousness for several reasons. Here we mention three salient ones. As IIT makes clear, the integration of semantic content is fundamental for understanding consciousness. IIT is so explicit about this semantic integration that it provides a set of definitions regarding not only conceptual content, but also how conceptual content is integrated into maximally specific experiences. But conscious content is always determined at a context of informational background, which is cognitive and perceptual, with many

© Springer International Publishing AG 2017
J.A. de Barros et al. (Eds.): QI 2016, LNCS 10106, pp. 57–70, 2017.
DOI: 10.1007/978-3-319-52289-0_5

variables that need to be determined at any moment in time. This is one of the main reasons why contextuality is central in linguistics and pragmatics—content depends on context and background assumptions.

A second reason to assume contextuality as a constraint on theories (and more pressingly measurements) of consciousness concerns attention. Attention, like conversational content, depends on background conditions and relevance. It also depends on conceptual content and is guided by many neural processes associated with voluntary and involuntary attention [19]. Context, therefore, is not only environmentally driven, but also motivationally determined.

Finally, a very important reason to take contextuality seriously into account in a theory of consciousness is the very nature of measurements. Measurements are notoriously contextual, a fact made quite vivid not only by quantum mechanics, but also by psychology and linguistics, disciplines who occupy a central role in studies about consciousness [3, 6, 17]. Thus, the contextuality of measurements is central to one of the main goals of IIT: to provide a measure for consciousness.

Our main argument is that IIT is empirically problematic, based on formal considerations concerning contextuality. One possibility is that IIT is problematic because, in its current formulation, it is incompatible with our current understandings of how to accommodate mathematically content that is contextual due to limited access to all processes. This would mean that IIT is in principle plausible, but in practice impossible to test. Alternatively, it could be that IIT is incomplete and needs critical amendments. This would mean that the theory could be compatible with our current understanding of contextuality but that it is unclear how it could be compatible with it. In either case, we believe that IIT is empirically problematic as it stands now, and that clarification is needed.

A more troublesome possibility, for which we will not argue as decisively as the previous empirical one, is that, in its current version, IIT is in principle incompatible with mathematical approaches to contextuality. Given the centrality of contextuality in understanding consciousness, this would make IIT internally inconsistent. This would mean that IIT needs to be abandoned. We will not develop this criticism and will only focus on the empirical one, but we mention this problem because we believe this is also an issue that demands further clarity, namely, it needs to be demonstrated that if IIT turns out to be incomplete, that it is at least in principle compatible with contextual data.

Before proceeding, two crucial clarifications are needed. First, our criticism is based on considerations concerning a notion of contextuality susceptible to mathematical analysis. IIT explicitly demands a mathematical treatment of the Φ measure and, as we will explain, this demand entails a mathematical treatment of contextuality. Our criticism only targets this formal, but still crucial, aspect of IIT. Because of our focus, whatever metaphysical commitments IIT has, for instance regarding panpsychism (or dualistic and monistic interpretations), are beyond the scope of this paper. Second, the notion of contextuality we work with here is relevant to linguistics, but we are not appealing to all cases of context sensitivity in linguistics. Rather, we use only a restricted sense of contextuality that can be formalized in terms of violations to sums of probabilities. Thus, we do not address forms of context dependence in pragmatics and forms of implicature in general.

To put forth our argument, we organize this paper in the following way. First, in Sect. 2 we discuss the current understanding of the mathematical theory of contextuality. Then, in Sect. 3, we present discussions of contextuality in IIT, and put forth our main argument. We end with some comments and discussions in Sect. 4.

2 Contextuality

Contextuality is an important concept in many different fields, such as in linguistics, physics and psychology. For that reason, there are many different definitions of contextuality, but here we focus on a mathematically precise definition that is relevant to IIT, as it directly relates to theories of measurement. Intuitively, contextuality is the idea that a quantity (say, the truth value of a proposition) depends on the overall environment in which it is present. To formalize such idea, the concept of random variables is used.

First, let us start with probabilities. The most straightforward way to define probabilities is axiomatic [18]. Accordingly, a probability space $(\Omega, \mathcal{F}, p)$, where Ω is a set of possible elementary events (the sample space), $\mathcal{F}$ an algebra (of events) over Ω, and p a function $p : \mathcal{F} \to [0, 1]$, is a triple satisfying:

1. $p(\Omega) = 1$
2. $p(\bigcup_i A_i) = \sum_i A_i$, for $i \neq j$ and $A_i \cap A_j = \emptyset$.

In this definition, $p(A)$ is the probability of event A happening.

A random variable $\mathbf{R}$ is a (measurable) function $\mathbf{R} : \mathcal{F} \to E$, where E is a set of real numbers. The idea of a random variable is to model the stochastic properties of the outcomes of a given experiment, where $e \in E$ corresponds to possible values of such outcomes. For example, imagine a hypothetical experiment measuring participants heights, with the minimum measurable height being 110 cm and the maximum 210 cm, with a resolution of 1 cm, the set of possible outcomes of measurements is $E = \{110, 111, 112, \ldots, 209, 210\}$. If we randomly select participants, the outcomes of their height measurement will follow some distribution (perhaps two superposed and truncated Gaussians, corresponding to female and male participants). A random variable modeling the height-measuring experiment should have all the same stochastic characteristics of it, and the random sampling of elements of Ω corresponds, intuitively, to the random sampling of participants and their respective heights.

The range of values of a random variable can be set to match that of any type of measurement, but the simplest ones are yes-no questions (e.g., "is this person taller than 170 cm?"). For such cases, two-valued random variables may be used to correspond to answers to the question "does the object/system have property P?". For example, E may be chosen as being either -1 (for "no") or 1 (for "yes"). If the property P is measured, then we record 1, and if it does not, we record -1. Since this is modeled with the random variable $\mathbf{R} : F \to \{-1, 1\}$ on a probability space $(\Omega, \mathcal{F}, p)$, we can think about the two-valued random variables as truth-values for propositions about the system, and the algebra $\mathcal{F}$ as corresponding to logical statements about such propositions (e.g. for two distinct elements $A_1, A_2 \in \mathcal{F}$, $A_1 \cup A_2$ and $A_1 \cap A_2$ are also in $\mathcal{F}$, and correspond to the logical connectives "or" and "and," respectively). In other words, random variables (and their corresponding probabilistic measures) correspond to a natural (stochastic) extension of logical statements about the nature of experimental outcomes. The logical structure of the statements come from the underlying Boolean algebraic structure that is derived from the ordering provided by the probability function p over the algebra $\mathcal{F}$.

So, how does contextuality come about in the language of random variables? As mentioned above, a system is contextual if it varies from one context to another. But what do we mean by "vary," and what do we mean by "context?" Let us start with an example, which will be useful below. Imagine we have a set of N properties (or concepts), denoted by P_i, $i = 1, \ldots, N$. The simplest contextual example could be though of as coming from $N = 2$, as in what happens with order effects. For example, consider the following two questions reflecting participants beliefs, discussed by [26, 27]: $P_1 = $ "Do you generally think Bill Clinton is honest and trustworthy?"; $P_2 = $ "Do you generally think Al Gore is honest and trustworthy?" Since those are two separate questions, they must be asked sequentially. We have only two possible ways to ask those questions: first P_1 and then P_2 or first P_2 and then P_1. It so happens that when doing so, the probabilities for P_i change. For instance, in a 1997 Gallup pool [26, 27], respondents answered yes to P_1 at a rate of 50% when P_1 was first, and 57% when P_1 was asked after P_2. Similarly, P_2 got a rate of 68% when first, and 60% when after P_1. This clearly shows an order effect, but more importantly, in a certain sense Clinton was considered by respondents as more trustworthy in the *context* of his relation with Al Gore than not, whereas Gore lost some of his trustworthiness when associated to Clinton.

In terms of random variables, if we think of $\mathbf{P}_1$ and $\mathbf{P}_2$ as representing those questions, then we have changes in the expectations of those random variables according to their order (or context). This is a situation where we have direct influences of one variable (which may also establish context) onto another. For example, in our Clinton/Gore example, we can think of the question P_1 (or P_2) directly influencing the respondent's belief about the following question: Gore gives Clinton a honesty bump. We call this explicit contextuality[1].

A more subtle case occurs when the random variables are not inconsistently connected. To see this, let us examine $N = 3$, and also that the properties are "yes" or "no." This is described by ±1-valued random variables, $\mathbf{P}_1$, $\mathbf{P}_2$, and $\mathbf{P}_3$, whose expectations are all equal to zero, meaning that we have equally random chances to either get $+1$ or -1 as outcomes of measurements of those variables. This case is more interesting because, as constructed, we do not allow for the type of explicit contextuality discussed in the paragraph

---

[1] This term was introduced by Pawel Kurzynski. See his contribution to this conference.

above. Variables $\mathbf{P}_1$, $\mathbf{P}_2$, and $\mathbf{P}_3$ may be correlated: their pairwise joint expectations (e.g. $E\left(\mathbf{P}_1\mathbf{P}_2\right)$) can take values between -1 and 1, corresponding to anti-correlated and perfectly correlated (with 0 meaning that they have no correlation)[2]. Imagine furthermore that experimental conditions are such that we can never observe all three random variables together, but only in pairs. It is possible to imagine an experimental setup that the measured correlations, given the impossibility of simultaneous observations of all three variables, be, for example, $E\left(\mathbf{P}_1\mathbf{P}_2\right) = E\left(\mathbf{P}_1\mathbf{P}_3\right) = E\left(\mathbf{P}_3\mathbf{P}_2\right) = -1$ (for a concrete example, see [5]). It is easy to see that there is a problem with the -1 correlations. For example, if $\mathbf{P}_1 = 1$, the first correlation implies $\mathbf{P}_2 = -1$, and the third implies that $\mathbf{P}_3 = 1$, which in turn, from the second correlation, implies $\mathbf{P}_1 = -1$, a clear contradiction. What is leading to the contradiction is the assumption that the variable $\mathbf{P}_1$ in the context of the experiment measuring $(\mathbf{P}_1, \mathbf{P}_2)$ is the same as the $\mathbf{P}_1$ in the context $(\mathbf{P}_1, \mathbf{P}_2)$[3]. If we were to, for example, index the variables (as proposed by Dzhafarov and Kujala [9,10][4]) according to their context, such contradictions would not appear.[5]

The above example shows how contextuality might be manifest as the impossibility of assigning the same values to a quantity in a way that is independent of the context. However, as it is presented, it comes from a logical contradiction. So, the question remains as to how one can extend the criteria for stochastic systems. A way to see this comes from the work of Abramsky and Hardy, where they showed that violations of logical consistency such as the one above are necessary and sufficient conditions the non-existence of a joint probability distribution (jpd) [1]. In other words, even when we have probabilistic outcomes, the existence of a single probability space $(\Omega, \mathcal{F}, p)$ is a necessary and sufficient condition for no logical inconsistencies, and therefore no contextuality. As a consequence, for the example of three variables, it can be shown [24] that the variables are not contextual iff

$$-1 \leq E\left(\mathbf{P}_1\mathbf{P}_2\right) + E'\left(\mathbf{P}_1\mathbf{P}_3\right) + E\left(\mathbf{P}_2\mathbf{P}_3\right) \tag{1}$$
$$\leq 1 + 2\min\left\{E\left(\mathbf{P}_1\mathbf{P}_2\right), E\left(\mathbf{P}_1\mathbf{P}_3\right), E\left(\mathbf{P}_2\mathbf{P}_3\right)\right\}.$$

The logical violation is a more subtle example of contextuality than the first one examined, where the statistical properties of a quantity changed with context. To distinguish the two types of contextuality above, one that is manifest

---

[2] Because of our choice of ± 1-valued random variables with zero expectation, their joint expectations coincide with their correlations.

[3] This example is examined in detail in Specker's Parable of the Over-Zealous Seer [cite], but was also discussed much earlier on by Boole [cite].

[4] The indexing idea is also related to Stalnaker's two-dimensional semantics; see [23].

[5] In the works of Dzhafarov and Kujala, when we can assign contextuality because of direct influences between the measuring conditions of random variables, such variables are said to be inconsistently connected [8, 10–12, 14]. To those author's, a system is contextual only if all context effects are not explainable by direct influences. So, for them the $\mathbf{P}_1$, $\mathbf{P}_2$, and $\mathbf{P}_3$ perfectly anti-correlated example is contextual, whereas the Clinton/Gore one is not. However, we emphasize that this is a nomenclature issue.

in the changed expectations from one context to another, and the other that is a consequence of the impossibility of attaching a consistent underlying logical structure via a jpd, we refer to systems that exhibit the former as exhibiting *explicit contextuality* or being *explicitly contextual* (or, according to [13], *inconsistently connected systems*) and the latter as exhibiting *hidden contextuality* or being *implicitly contextual*.

The example above can be generalized to more than three random variables, as well as to random variables that take multiple values. To represent this in terms of random variables in a way that makes the context explicit, we can use a contextual index in the following way. We start with the assumption that each experiment and its corresponding variables correspond to a context. We think of the random variables as contextual when we cannot associated to a variable P_i in one context the same probability space as the P_i in another context (i.e., there is no single jpd that describe P_i in all contexts). For our three random variable example above, only pairs are observable, namely (P_1, P_2), (P_1, P_3), or (P_2, P_3), but never triples, e.g. (P_1, P_2, P_3). Let us call C_1 the experimental condition (or context) (P_1, P_2), C_2 condition (P_1, P_3), and C_3 condition (P_2, P_3). To represent this explicitly in our notation, we add an index for context. For example, $P_{1,1}$ is P_1 in context C_1, whereas $P_{1,2}$ is P_1 in context C_2, and so on.

With this notation in mind, inconsistently connected systems are those in which it is not true that $\mathbf{P}_{1,1} \sim \mathbf{P}_{1,2}$, where this notation means "the random variable $\mathbf{P}_{1,1}$ has the same distribution as $\mathbf{P}_{1,2}$." As an example, let us revisit the Cliton-Gore order-effect survey, where two questions are asked in sequence in two different orders, C_1 and C_2:

C_1: $P_{1,1} =$ "Is Bill Clinton trustworthy?"; $P_{2,1} =$ "Is Al Gore trustworthy?";
C_2: $P_{2,2} =$ "Is Al Gore trustworthy?"; $P_{1,2} =$ "Is Bill Clinton trustworthy?".

It may be somewhat surprising that the expected answer to $P_{1,1}$, denoted by $E(\mathbf{P}_{1,1})$ and given by

$$E(\mathbf{P}_{1,1}) = \sum_{\omega_i \in \Omega} p(\omega_i) \mathbf{P}_{1,1}(\omega_i)$$
$$= p(\mathbf{P}_{1,1} = 1) - p(\mathbf{P}_{1,1} = -1),$$

is more positive toward Bill Clinton than $P_{1,2}$, but that is what was shown empirically [22] (i.e., $E(\mathbf{P}_{1,1}) > E(\mathbf{P}_{1,2})$). However, we should point out that mathematically, because we are using contextual indexing, it is not problematic to have different expectations for each context, whereas in the example with no contextual indexing, we would have a seemingly direct contradiction ($\mathbf{P}_1 \sim \mathbf{P}_1$).

In the hidden contextuality case with three random variables, the indexed notation can also be extended. As before, imagine the extreme case where $E(\mathbf{P}_{1,1}\mathbf{P}_{2,1}) = E(\mathbf{P}_{1,2}\mathbf{P}_{3,2}) = E(\mathbf{P}_{2,3}\mathbf{P}_{3,3}) = -1$. If we do not assume that the observed property is independent of context, we run into no problems. However, if we set $\mathbf{P}_{i,j} = \mathbf{P}_{i,j'}$, we run into the same type of problems as before, and reach a contradiction.

At this point it is worthwhile to discuss some aspects of contextuality that are directly relevant to our argument. Contextuality only exists when we cannot observe all quantities of interest simultaneously: measuring all random variables at the same time implies the existence of a jpd by simply creating a data table that can be used to compute the jpd and the relative frequencies for each marginal distribution. However, it is often the case that the random variables cannot be all measured simultaneously. This lack of simultaneous measurement may have two different origins: (i) it may be impossible *in principle* to measure $\mathbf{P}_1, \mathbf{P}_2, \ldots, \mathbf{P}_N$ simultaneously, or (ii) it may be empirically difficult, perhaps even impossible in practice.

For (i), there can be situations, particularly when the system is contextual by direct influences, where the observation of $\mathbf{P}_1$ precedes temporally and affects directly $\mathbf{P}_2$; this seems to be the case for the example of the Gore/Clinton questionnaire discussed above. One cannot ask a question about Al Gore's trustworthiness simultaneously with a question about Clinton; they must be asked in order. The same is the case for contextual examples in quantum mechanics, where there is no jpd. In entangled quantum systems, there are no direct influences, but we cannot measure non-commuting observables simultaneously, and depending on the choice of observables, no jpd exists [15].

For (ii), the situation is slightly different. There may not be a principled reason for not observing all three random variables simultaneously, but experimental design or measurement constraints may create a *de facto* impossibility of observing them. This was, for instance, the case of the contextual firefly introduced by Foulis (see [5] for an explicit contextual model). Because experimental constraints or technical limitations prevent us from observing all variables at the same time, the correlations between them may be enhanced, such that by this process the observations cannot fit a jpd. In other words, the marginal expectations of correlations change from context to context, in a way similar to explicit contextuality. Furthermore, it might be possible that when we observe a system, we may be unaware of the random variables being contextual, which is something that we only verify empirically. For instance, there is nothing strange about observing correlations $E(\mathbf{P}_1\mathbf{P}_2) = E(\mathbf{P}_1\mathbf{P}_3) = E(\mathbf{P}_3\mathbf{P}_2) = -1$. It is not until we put all three together, in an attempt to obtain a jpd, that we realize their inconsistency. That no jpd exists in certain circumstances is nontrivial for the three-random-variable example, and it becomes even more difficult to establish for more variables (consistency is checked with the satisfaction of inequalities whose complexities increase rapidly with the number of involved variables).

Contextuality shows up in many situations, from quantum mechanics to social sciences (see [6,16,17] and references therein). In particular, well-known examples exist in cognitive sciences, where human decision making has been shown to not follow classical probability theory, being therefore either explicitly or implicitly contextual (though recent work suggests that in psychology all examples are explicitly contextual [7]). Furthermore, the connection between speech and thought is well know to be contextual, with many examples discussed in the literature. Thus, a discussion of contextuality as it refers to proposed theories of consciousness is not only relevant, but essential. In the next section, we will turn our attention to one such theory, the Integrated Information Theory (IIT) [20].

3 Contextuality in IIT

It is unclear whether the measurable human mind (thought here to be equivalent to the brain and its physical states) is contextual in principle. It is not unimaginable (in fact, many theories do so) that, for example, quantum processes are important in the brain. If this is the case, it is possible (though we believe improbable, mainly due to decoherence) that entanglement of relevant neuronal processes exist. Such entanglement may produce contextual random variables, and would preclude the existence of a jpd.

Though the previous argument could be made that the brain is contextual, at the microlevel, we want to focus on the difficulties mentioned in Sect. 2. First, why should we bother with contextuality, at least from an empirical point of view, when thinking about the brain. The main reason is that contextuality shows up in many situations in the social sciences (see [6] and references therein). In particular, well-known examples exist on cognitive sciences, where human decision making has been show to not follow classical probability theory, in the sense of being incompatible with a jpd, therefore being contextual. Furthermore, as mentioned above, the connection between speech and thought is contextual. In other words, behavioral outcomes are contextual, and ultimately what we observe is tied, in one way or another, with behavioral outcomes.

It is possible that such contextuality comes from factors unknown to or uncontrollable by the experimenter. For example, in a real-world situation, where most learning happens, the brain is bombarded with huge amounts of disparate stimuli, some of them perhaps even seemingly contradictory to each other (e.g., simultaneous exposure to stimuli that represent pain and pleasure). Such stimuli are not forgotten, insofar as learned unconscious decision processes are concerned, by moving to a new environment in the protected conditions of controlled experiments. If we now think in terms of brain mechanisms, the presentation of a stimulus may activate not only neurons associated with this stimulus, but also other context-relevant neurons that were activated in the learned real-world situations. Furthermore, because we should expect neural activation to be stronger to the original stimulus, the detection of such neural patterns would be very difficult (particularly because we would not know what we should be looking for). If we could, perhaps, be able to measure all neurons in the brain, we would not have any implicit contextuality showing up (at least not in the measured firing patterns), though we could have explicit contextuality; however, as we will see below, this is very difficult empirically.

To see this, let us examine the well-known case of the "guppy" effect [2,21] in concept combination. The guppy effect refers to the established fact that when participants are asked to name objects that belong to the concept "pet" and objects that belong to "fish," guppies appear with very low frequency. However, when asked to name objects that belong to "pet-fish," guppies are high up on the list. What makes this example interesting is not that concept combination changes the frequency of "guppies," but instead that it changes such frequencies in a way that is incompatible with classical probability theory (i.e., with a jpd) [2]. In other words, concept combination as an internal process in the brain is contextual.

Now, let us say we try to approach the problem mentioned above, of measuring all the neurons associated to some cognitive process. How would we know which of the neurons are relevant. For instance, we know that once a concept (say, "fish") is presented, there is a spreading activation of neurons that are related to other concepts (e.g., "flounder," "cod," "tuna," "sushi," "Easter," etc.). Such web of activated neurons is strongly present in one context, but is not in another (such as "guppy"). That means that one would have to know what to look for, at the level of neurons, even when what we are looking for is not currently active. In other words, to be able to construct a jpd, if it exists, one would have to measure everything (including external conditions that might seem irrelevant to the experimenters under the situation, such as temperature, barometric pressure, amount of saliva in subject's mouth, heart beat, etc.), since any such variables could present contextual cues that are necessary for the construction of a jpd. However, as one could imagine, this would not only pose a huge measurement problem, from a practical point of view, but would also have so many variables that would make it impossible to obtain any type of statistical information about the system of interest, as every experiment would be, in a certain way, unique in terms of control variables. Of course, even if we maximally specify all those variables, it is still possible that the system displays explicit contextuality, and no jpd exists.

To summarize, we have the following empirical difficulty brought about by contextuality. Since contextuality exists in practice (numerous experiments corroborate this), we do not have a joint probability distribution. The only way to overcome the problem of contextuality would be to observe everything, clearly a daunting task. But even in such cases, however, no jpd exists, as we would move from implicit to explicit contextuality. As we will see below, those issues are a direct challenge for the current version of Tononi's IIT.

We now turn to IIT. As discussed above, Tononi's IIT is one of the most important theories of consciousness currently proposed [20]. IIT is an attempt to characterize consciousness both quantitatively and qualitatively, giving it a precise mathematical formulation. Unlike the traditional approach used in neuroscience, IIT takes as its starting point the phenomenology of consciousness, and postulates the properties the physical mechanisms, such as neurons with their synapses, shall respect so that consciousness can take place. One of goals of IIT is to quantify in what extent one system has consciousness, that is, what mechanisms belonging to that system contribute to the emergence of consciousness, and how much they contribute to it. The second goal is to build a theoretical tools able to discriminate the different kinds of consciousness that the system can display. In other words, define a qualia-space.

According IIT, a system that is capable of generating consciousness must have a high capacity to discriminate a large number of different states, which are related to the amount of information that distinct subsystems may generate. However, IIT also affirms that the ability to differentiate different states is not enough for the emergence of consciousness: the system must also be able to integrate information. This postulate is motivated by the fact that, under non-pathological conditions, the phenomenological experience does not occur in a fragmented way, i.e., we do not experience the colors of objects separated from their shapes.

Using concepts from mathematical information theory, Tononi proposes a measure of consciousness, Φ. In IIT the integrated information Φ is an information measure of the repertoires generated by the whole system, compared to the repertoires generated by the subsystems. Φ is defined in such a way that one of its consequences is the possibility of existence of different levels of consciousness. The set of elements within a system endowed with this property to generate a local maximum of conceptual information integrated is called complex.

For Tononi, systems that are able to generate consciousness are made of sub-mechanisms, and those sub-mechanisms can be combined in different ways to create mechanisms. It is the particular configuration of sub-mechanisms, at a given moment, that Tononi calls "context."

Though Tononi clearly sees the relevance of contexts to consciousness, in his model he makes the following assumption for the outcomes of mechanisms (see the supplementary methods of [20]):

$$p\left(ABC^t|ABC^{t-1}\right) = p\left(A^t|A^{t-1}\right) p\left(B^t|B^{t-1}\right) p\left(C^t|C^{t-1}\right). \tag{2}$$

Tononi's justification for (2) is that there are "no instantaneous interactions between mechanisms and causes precede their effects." It also seems to be an practical essential assumption to allow for computations in his model.

First, we should point out that the appeal to instantaneous interactions is misleading. To rule out instantaneous interactions, one would have to assure that the observations corresponding to, say, A^t or B^t, were separated by an spacelike interval (see [3] for a detailed argument in a different context). For example, if A^t and B^t were measured for an amount of time δt and were processes situated at a distance d, then any (non-instantaneous) interaction whose propagation speed is lower than the speed of light could account for violations of (2) if $\delta t \geq cd$. Since typical distances within the brain are at the order of 10^{-1} m, this means that for processes taking longer than 3×10^9 s, we can always explain them with non-instantaneous signaling. But most cognitive processes are believed to take much longer than 10^8 s. So, for biological processes, it is quite reasonable to assume that (2) may be violated due to physically plausible interactions between mechanisms (see [4] for a simple neural oscillator model exhibiting contextuality). Furthermore, we should point out that (2), as shown by Suppes and Zanotti [24], implies the existence of a jpd. Therefore, the assumption behind (2) is not, as Tononi claims, that of no instantaneous interactions: it is, instead, an assumption about *no* contextuality!

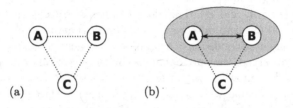

Fig. 1. (a) Contextual system of mechanisms, composed of six sub-mechanisms, A, B, and C. The sub-mechanisms are such that only pairs are simultaneously observable. (b) For example, when A is active, so is B, but not C. This is shown in the figure by the grayed area for the system.

To show how contextuality may appear in IIT, let us focus on the mechanisms shown in Fig. 1. This system behaves in a very simple way, and it is constructed merely to show how contextuality can emerge here. We start with three mechanisms, A, B, and C, each taking values ± 1, which we represent by the ± 1-valued random variables **A**, **B**, and **C**. Let us assume that those mechanisms are stochastic, but, more importantly, that we can only observe the following simultaneously: (A, B), (A, C), (B, C), and (A, B, C). If contextuality is present, it is possible to have pairwise correlations for the situations where (A, B), (A, C), (B, C) are observed such that (1) is violated. In other words, any measurements except (A, B, C), give strong negative correlations between **A**, **B**, and **C**. This mechanism is explicitly contextual, since the marginals from (A, B, C) cannot match the correlations from the pairwise observations, and it is also implicitly contextual, since the pairwise correlations lead to no jpd. Now, let us imagine that, in this case, the mechanism is such that at time t only one of the pairs (A, B), (A, C), (B, C) is observed, and at time $t-1$ the triple mechanism (A, B, C). It is clear, in this case, that Eq. (2) cannot hold, since there is no joint probability distribution.

One might argue that no mechanism is truly contextual, since we could, in principle, measure all quantities of interest simultaneously. This is not necessarily true for the following reasons. The first one is that in some cases it is not, *in principle,* possible to measure all quantities simultaneously. If, and we are not making this case here, there are underlying processes in the mechanism that are quantum, non-commuting observables cannot be simultaneously measurable, and contextuality may exist. This is what happens with entangled states in quantum mechanics, as in the famous Bell-EPR setup.

The second reason, which we consider more relevant, is simply empirical. It may be true that, for a certain system, it is possible *in principle* to measure all relevant variables simultaneously. However, for reasons of experimental limitations, it is close to impossible to measure them all. For example, imagine, that A, B, and C are neural oscillators that are measured with EEG. Because the activity strength of neural oscillators varies, and because EEGs are not spatially localized and are noisy, it is possible that under a certain stimulus, the only observable neural oscillators are a subset of the relevant oscillators involved in the mechanism (say, A, and B). This does not necessarily mean that the other oscillator C has no existing outcomes, but simply that it cannot be measured under the experimental conditions. As a result, because of contextuality, when correlations are observed, they are enhanced by the selection of a subset of oscillators, and no jpd compatible with the observations will exist, even though all quantities are in principle well defined simultaneously. This, of course, would provide an empirical difficulty to guarantee that the system is not contextual.

Finally, the third reason is that, for some contextual systems, the experiment of measuring the pairs (A, B), (A, C), (B, C) has different marginal expectations (for correlations) than what you would observe for the triple (A, B, C). In this case, one could have direct influences from context, as the marginal expectations change. We emphasize that such direct influences do not imply any non-local interactions, since, as argued above, their time scales are large compared to the distance scales. To summarize, we provided here a toy example showing how context-dependent mechanisms violate (2).

4   Conclusions

IIT is a remarkable theory that opens up the possibility of empirically measuring consciousness. As such, it has the potential to have a significant impact in the way we think about consciousness. This explains how IIT has become one of the main theories in consciousness study.

One of the main ideas in IIT is that consciousness comes from processes that integrate information. Therefore, to measure consciousness, one needs to be able to measure the integration of information, and, more basically, information itself. The question is how to measure information for contextual systems, in light of the trilemma we mentioned at the outset. We know, for instance, that Shannon's entropy is not adequate for some contextual systems, and in particular, we know that for the special type of contextuality constrained by the formalism of quantum mechanics, the more appropriate measure of information is given by von Neumann's entropy. However, a more general way of measuring information in more general contextual systems, such as those necessary for the description of consciousness, is yet to be developed.

Until such measures of information in contextual systems are developed, the use of IIT to measure consciousness needs to be clarified, in particular as to how it is to be applied to contextual systems, which candidate systems to consciousness are believe to be.

Acknowledgments. JAB and LPGA acknowledge support from the Patrick Suppes Gift Fund at Stanford University. Part of this work was developed at the Suppes Brain Lab in the Center for the Study of Language and Information, CSLI, and we thank CSLI and Professor John Perry for their hospitality.

References

1. Abramsky, S., Hardy, L.: Logical bell inequalities. Phys. Rev. A **85**(6), 062114 (2012)
2. Aerts, D., Broekaert, J., Gabora, L., Veloz, T.: The Guppy effect as interference. In: Busemeyer, J.R., Dubois, F., Lambert-Mogiliansky, A., Melucci, M. (eds.) Quantum Interaction. LNCS, vol. 7620, pp. 36–47. Springer, Heidelberg (2012)
3. de Barros, J.A., Suppes, P.: Quantum mechanics, interference, and the brain. J. Math. Psychol. **53**, 306–313 (2009)
4. Acacio de Barros, J.: Quantum-like model of behavioral response computation using neural oscillators. Biosystems **110**(3), 171–182 (2012)
5. de Barros, J.A., Kujala, J., Oas, G.: Negative probabilities and contextuality. arXiv:1511.02823 [physics, physics:quant-ph], November 2015
6. de Barros, J.A., Oas, G.: Some examples of contextuality in physics: implications to quantum cognition. In: Dzhafarov, E., Zhang, R., Jordan, S.M. (eds.) Contextuality from Quantum Physics to Psychology. World Scientific (2015)
7. Dzhafarov, E.N., Zhang, R., Kujala, J.: Is there contextuality in behavioural, social systems? Phil. Trans. R. Soc. A **374**(2058), 20150099 (2016)
8. Dzhafarov, E.N., Kujala, J.V.: Quantum entanglement and the issue of selective influences in psychology: an overview. In: Busemeyer, J.R., Dubois, F., Lambert-Mogiliansky, A., Melucci, M. (eds.) Quantum Interaction. LNCS, vol. 7620, pp. 184–195. Springer, Heidelberg (2012)
9. Dzhafarov, E.N., Kujala, J.V.: All-possible-couplings approach to measuring probabilistic context. PLoS One **8**(5), e61712 (2013)
10. Dzhafarov, E.N., Kujala, J.V.: Contextuality in generalized Klyachko-type, Bell-type, Leggett-Garg-type systems. arXiv:1411.2244 [physics, physics:quant-ph], November 2014
11. Dzhafarov, E.N., Kujala, J.V.: Context-content systems of random variables: the contextuality-by-default theory. arXiv:1511.03516 [quant-ph], November 2015
12. Dzhafarov, E.N., Kujala, J.V.: Conversations on contextuality. In: Dzhafarov, E., Sordan, S., Zhang, R., Cervantes, V. (eds.) Contextuality from Quantum Physics to Psychology, vol. 6. World Scientific Press, New Jersey (2015). arXiv: 1508.00862
13. Dzhafarov, E.N., Kujala, J.V., Larsson, J.Å.: Contextuality in three types of quantum-mechanical systems. Found. Phys. **45**(7), 762–782 (2015)
14. Dzhafarov, E.N., Kujala, J.N.: A qualified Kolmogorovian account of probabilistic contextuality. In: Atmanspacher, H., Haven, E., Kitto, K., Raine, D. (eds.) Quantum Interaction. LNCS, vol. 8369. Springer, Heidelberg (2014)
15. Fine, A.: Hidden variables, joint probability, and the bell inequalities. Phys. Rev. Lett. **48**(5), 291–295 (1982)
16. Haven, E., Khrennikov, A.: Quantum Social Science. Cambridge University Press, Cambridge (2013)
17. Khrennikov, A.: Ubiquitous Quantum Structure: from Psychology to Finance. Springer, Heidelberg (2010)
18. Kolmogorov, A.N.: Foundations of the Theory of Probability, 2nd edn. Chelsea Publishing Co., Oxford (1956)
19. Montemayor, C., Haladjian, H.H.: Consciousness, Attention, and Conscious Attention. MIT Press, Cambridge (2015)
20. Oizumi, M., Albantakis, L., Tononi, G.: From the phenomenology to the mechanisms of consciousness: integrated information theory 3.0. PLoS Comput. Biol. **10**(5), e1003588 (2014)

21. Osherson, D.N., Smith, E.E.: On the adequacy of prototype theory as a theory of concepts. Cognition **9**(1), 35–58 (1981)
22. Pothos, E.M., Busemeyer, J.R.: Can quantum probability provide a new direction for cognitive modeling? Behav. Brain Sci. **36**(03), 255–274 (2013)
23. Stalnaker, R.: Context and Content: Essays on Intentionality in Speech and Thought. Oxford University Press, Oxford (1999)
24. Suppes, P., Zanotti, M.: When are probabilistic explanations possible? Synthese **48**(2), 191–199 (1981)
25. Tononi, G., Koch, C.: Consciousness: here, there and everywhere? Philos. Trans. R. Soc. London B: Biol. Sci. **370**(1668), 20140167 (2015)
26. Wang, Z., Busemeyer, J.R.: A quantum question order model supported by empirical tests of an a priori and precise prediction. Topics Cogn. Sci. **5**(4), 689–710 (2013)
27. Wang, Z., Solloway, T., Shiffrin, R.M., Busemeyer, J.R.: Context effects produced by question orders reveal quantum nature of human judgments. Proc. Natl. Acad. Sci. **111**(26), 9431–9436 (2014)

Is Stress Quantum-Like?

J. Acacio de Barros[1(✉)], Leonardo Guimarães De Assis[2], and Petr Bob[3]

[1] School of Humanities and Liberal Studies,
San Francisco State University, San Francisco, CA, USA
barros@sfsu.edu
[2] Suppes Brain Lab, Center for the Study of Language and Information,
Stanford University, Stanford, CA, USA
lpgassis@stanford.edu
[3] Center for Neuropsychiatric Research of Traumatic Stress,
Department of Psychiatry and UHSL, Charles University, Prague, Czech Republic
petrbob@netscape.net

Abstract. In this paper we examine two well-controlled experiments where order effects were shown under stress. We show that for only one of those experiments the QQ equality of Wang and Busemeyer [21] seems to be fairly satisfied (under independence assumptions). Since the experiment satisfying QQ measures physiological variables, this may suggest that quantum order effect outside human judgment models.

1 Introduction

It is a well-known fact that the order in which two questions are asked affects the frequencies of their answers. Question order effects are observed by presenting two questions, Q_1 and Q_2, to two similar populations but in different orders. To one group, Q_1 precedes Q_2, whereas to the other group, Q_2 precedes Q_1. If there are changes in the frequencies for the answers to the questions between groups, then we see an order effect. This is known as the order effect, and it has been the subject of interest and study of social scientists for a while. Another well-know fact is that order effects also exist in physical measurements, in particular in quantum mechanics, where order effects exist *in principle*. They are associated to the existence of complementary variables whose observable operators in the Hilbert space do not commute, and therefore cannot have a simultaneous projector basis yielding repeatable experimental outcomes.

The main difficulty behind order effects is that they seem to violate standard probability theory, where the expectation of a random variable does not depend on which order we observe it. Therefore, it should not come as a surprise that among the first successful attempts to use quantum-like models in the social sciences were ones related to order effects. Furthermore, one may argue that all quantum-like effects in social sciences are actually order effects, mainly for two reasons. First, no experimental situation can preclude subliminal communication as a means of creating the superclassical (quantum-like) correlations, and therefore it is always possible to think of causal classical mechanisms that lead

J.A. de Barros et al. (Eds.): QI 2016, LNCS 10106, pp. 71–80, 2017.
DOI: 10.1007/978-3-319-52289-0_6

to such correlations. This means that the effects on the context-dependent probabilities could be seen as caused by this (perhaps difficult-to-observe) order. Second, it seems that all violations of contextual (Bell-type) inequalities may be explained by direct influences between the observables [11], which would be modeled in physics by order-effect like computations.

Be that as it may, quantum-like order-effect models make non-trivial predictions. For instance, in their seminal paper, Wang and Busemeyer [21] showed that for order effects described by the collapse of a state vector, the diagonal terms of the order effect matrix (see Sect. 2) would add to zero. This result is know as the Quantum Question (QQ) equality, and it not only holds for order effect models that use projections in a Hilbert space, but also for a vast set of data examined in [22].

In this paper we investigate order effects in stress. Stress can be thought of as, among other things, be caused by conflicting conditions. This is what is often seen in cognitive order effects, where the order of questions changes the assessment of the subsequent question. Here we investigate two experiments showing order effect under stress: one involving decision making under stress, and another measuring physiological effects. In both cases, the data suggests that the QQ equality is satisfied, thus supporting the idea that order effects are better described by quantum probabilities.

2   Quantum-Like Order Effects and the QQ Equality

In this Section, we will discuss how the Hilbert space quantum formalism leads to the order effect, in the same way that it is applied to the QQ model. For our purpose it suffices to examine a simple case. Imagine two propositions about the system of interest, P_A and P_B. Such propositions can be either true or false, depending on the state of the system. For example, P_A can be the question "Is the spin in direction $\mathbf{z}$ equal to $+1/2$?" To know whether this is the case, a spin measurement must be made, and the outcome would be either "yes, it is equal to $+1/2$," or "no, it is not equal to $+1/2$;" in this case the system of interest would be a particle with spin. P_B would then be a question that probes the same Hilbert space, e.g. "Is the spin in direction $\mathbf{e} \neq \mathbf{z}$ equal to $+1/2$?" Another example outside of physics, discussed in [22], is when P_A is the question "Is Bill Clinton honest and trustworthy?" and P_B is "Is Al Gore honest and trustworthy?" The system of interest here is a participant in an opinion pool, who may answer the question in the positive or negative.

To represent the stochastic outcomes of answers for the above cases, we use a standard quantum model for order effects (see [4,12,15]). We start with two yes-no questions, Q_A and Q_B, and associate to them projector operators $\hat{P}_A$ and $\hat{P}_B$ in a Hilbert space, $\mathcal{H}$. Because there is an order effect, originated from the impossibility of simultaneously measuring Q_A and Q_B, we assume that $\left[\hat{P}_A, \hat{P}_B\right] \neq 0$ (we remark that non-commuting operators are typical in quantum descriptions of cognitive systems). Prior to the first question, the participant's "cognitive state" may be represented by a quantum mixture ρ. However, after a question is asked, this state collapses into either $\hat{P}_i \rho \hat{P}_i$ or $\left(\hat{1} - \hat{P}_i\right) \rho \left(\hat{1} - \hat{P}_i\right)$, $i = A, B$, with the former expression corresponding to "yes" to question Q_i and the latter to "no." This new collapsed state is then measured again, by $\hat{P}_j, j \neq i$.

To understand where the order effect comes from, consider the example where the quantum state is not a proper mixture, but a pure state $\rho = |\psi\rangle\langle\psi|$ (where $|\psi\rangle$ is a vector in the Hilbert space and $\langle\psi|$ its associated dual vector) that is measured first by P_A and then by P_B. What is the probability that $P_A = 1$ and $P_B = 1$, when measured in that order? The probability that P_A is one is given by $p(P_A = 1|\rho) = \text{Tr}\left(\rho\hat{P}_A\right)$, and when such value is measure, the quantum state collapses to $\hat{P}_A \rho \hat{P}_A / \text{Tr}\left(\rho\hat{P}_A\right)$. Now, the probability of $P_B = 1$ for the state $\rho = |\psi\rangle\langle\psi|$ is $p\left(P_B = 1|\hat{P}_A|\psi\rangle\right) = \langle\psi|\hat{P}_A\hat{P}_B\hat{P}_A|\psi\rangle / \langle\psi|\hat{P}_A|\psi\rangle$. Therefore, the answer to our question is simply

$$p_{a:b} = \langle\psi|\hat{P}_A\hat{P}_B\hat{P}_A|\psi\rangle,$$

where we introduced the notation where $p_{a:b}$ corresponds to to the probability of $P_A = 1$ followed by $P_B = 1$, $p_{b:\bar{a}}$ to $P_B = 1$ followed by $P_A = 0$, and so on. From similar computations,

$$p_{b:a} = \langle\psi|\hat{P}_B\hat{P}_A\hat{P}_B|\psi\rangle,$$

$$p_{\bar{a}:\bar{b}} = \langle\psi|\left(1 - \hat{P}_A\right)\left(1 - \hat{P}_B\right)\left(1 - \hat{P}_A\right)|\psi\rangle,$$

and

$$p_{\bar{b}:\bar{a}} = \langle\psi|\left(1 - \hat{P}_B\right)\left(1 - \hat{P}_A\right)\left(1 - \hat{P}_B\right)|\psi\rangle.$$

Since $\hat{P}_A$ and $\hat{P}_B$ do not commute, it follows that $p_{a:b} \neq p_{b:a}$, which is what we understand as an order effect: the probability of answer P_A is different when asked before or after P_B.

From systems that present order effect (or any system, for that matter), we can define an effect size matrix

$$E = \begin{pmatrix} p_{a:b} - p_{b:a} & p_{\bar{a}:b} - p_{b:\bar{a}} \\ p_{a:\bar{b}} - p_{\bar{b}:a} & p_{\bar{a}:\bar{b}} - p_{\bar{b}:\bar{a}} \end{pmatrix}.$$

This matrix reflects how much the probabilities change given the order: if there are no order effects, then E is the zero matrix; if the elements of E are large, then there is a strong order effect, as the expectation s change considerably with orders. Notice that E has nothing to do with a quantum model, as it expresses the order effect in terms of measurable probabilities. However, from the above quantum model, it is straightforward to compute, from the algebra of projection operators (mainly their idempotent property), that the diagonal term sums to zero, i.e.,

$$q = (p_{a:b} - p_{b:a}) + (p_{\bar{a}:\bar{b}} - p_{\bar{b}:\bar{a}}) = 0.$$

This is called the QQ equality by [22], and it is exactly satisfied by quantum systems.

It is striking that most order effects in psychology seem to satisfy the QQ equality. In their paper [22], Wang et al. examined 72 datasets related to order effects to opinion-pool questions (the Clinton and Gore question above was part of a Gallup pool). With the exception of a few (pathological?) cases, the vast majority of the data satisfied the QQ equality. Perhaps more telling, Wang et al. [22] examined alternative models used to describe order effects, and none of them main alternatives in the literature fit the QQ equality. In the next section we will discuss order effects in the stress literature, and show not only that the QQ equality is satisfied in decision-making under stress, but also for physiological outcomes.

3 Order effects in Stress

Order effects are well established in stress research, thought with perhaps a different meaning from the ones discussed above. For instance, a physiological response seems to change with time in almost every cases of emotional responses, and repeating the same stimulus frequently decreases or increases a response, which just depends on the stimulus type. In the case of stimuli inducing adaptive behavior, most usually positive stimuli, repeating of the stimulus usually leads to a decreased response, which is called habituation (e.g. delicious food everyday) [3,20]. In cases of maladaptive responses most usually stressful stimuli, a frequent type of response is "sensitization" [10,14], i.e. a progressively increasing response to the same stimulus. Additionally, there is evidence that those types of responses work also for electric stimulation of the brain: upthreshold stimulus usually leads to epileptic discharges due to increasing responsibility to subthreshold stimuli related to "sensitization," and consequently very small sub-threshold electric stimulus at later times may cause epileptic discharges [16,18].

The order effects in the above paragraph present two challenges to testing the QQ model. First, it is not immediately clear how they actually correspond to the standard idea of order effect as modeled by a collapse of the wave function, since they do not seem to correspond to successive "measurements" (in the quantum sense) of two different operators. Second, as far as we know, and related to the first issue, they do not provide data sets that can be used to observe the QQ equality. For these reasons, we focus here on two well-controlled experiments with human subjects where order effects are shown: one where behavioral outcomes change with the order of stressors, and another where physiological outcomes did as well. In the subsection below, we describe the relevant experiments analyzed here. Then, in the following subsection, we analyze the QQ equality, showing that it is apparently satisfied also for those two experiments.

3.1 Order Effect Experiments

Well controlled experiments that provide enough information to allow for the computation of order effects in situations under stress are not widely available. At least as far as the authors can tell, the only (human) experiments that are set under the necessary criteria that allows us to estimate the QQ equality from the available published data are the experiments of Banis and Lorist [1] and Caceres and Burns [5]. We describe them briefly in the subsections that follow.

Behavioral Order Effect in Stress. In an interesting work, Banis and Lorist [1] studied the impact of acute noise stress on the feedback-related negativity (FRN), and whether the predictability of the stressor affected the results. FRN is an event-related potential (ERP) electroencephalogram component that is triggered by external feedback. Banis and Lorist used loud white noise, a stressor known to activate the hypothalamic-pituitary-adrenal axis and sympathetic nervous system that increases stress hormones, thus affecting the activity in brain areas responsible for feedback evaluation. Their goal was to test if acute noise stress had any influence on the cognitive control functioning of the anterior-cingular-cortex (ACC) through the analysis of the FRN feedback, and if the results depended on the predictability of the noise stressor. In their experiment, 32 healthy male undergraduates participated in an experiment where they performed a gamble task. Each trial started with a cross displayed at the center of a computer screen. After 500 ms, two white rectangles were displayed to the left and right side of the cross. Those rectangles remained on the screen until the subject selected one of them by pressing a button with their left or right index finger, corresponding to the equivalent location of the rectangle selected. The selected rectangle was then highlighted with a thick yellow border, for a random time interval between 800–1200 ms. After that, the highlighted rectangle was filled with one of two colors, cyan or magenta, corresponding to monetary gain or loss. Which color was associated with gain or loss varied across participants. Simultaneously to the appearance of cyan or magenta, the amount of gain or loss (±5 or ±25 cents of Euros) appeared inside the selected rectangle, informing the participant of how much money they won or lost during that trial. The values displayed inside the rectangles were selected randomly with equal probability for all of four possible values (though participants were not informed of this). This feedback was displayed for 1000 ms, and after that the next trial started. The experiment was conducted with five-minute trial blocks separated by 15 min of rest. Some trial blocks were performed first under a noise stressor, consisting of a discontinuous (75–95 dB) or continuous (85 dB) white noise, with intervals varying between 2 to 7 s, and then in silence; other blocks had the reverse order. Silence and noise condition trials were counterbalanced across subjects, with participants performing an equal number in each condition. At the beginning of the experiment, participants started with a balance of 5 euros, and were instructed to select whichever strategy they wished to maximize their gain: whatever balance they had at the end of the experiment was theirs to keep. At the end of each block, participants were informed about the amount of money they earned in the previous block. Though this experiment's main goal was to measure the effect of acute stress as a decreased in cognitive control by the ACC, it also showed that mean reaction time and mean stay percentages (i.e., how often a participant selected the same response as a strategy) depended on the condition order of the block (silence-noise vs. noise-silence conditions).

Physiological Order Effect in Stress. Many studies have shown a correlation between stress-induced physiological reactivity and indexes of pain sensitivity, but there was no proof whether such reactivity could affect consecutive levels of pain threshold, tolerance, and self-reported severity. To answer this question, Caceres and Burns [5] investigated if the indexes of pain sensitivity were influenced by physiological reactivity (namely, blood pressure and heart rate) induced by acute noise as a psychological stressor. To test that hypothesis, 52 individuals were randomly selected to perform one of two experimental protocols: mental arithmetic (MA) task followed by a cold pressor (CP) task or vice versa (we will refer to those two orders as MA/CP and CP/MA, respectively). Subjects were classified into low/high heart rate (HR) and low/high mean arterial pressure (MAP) based on reactivity to MA. The expectation was that stress-induced physiological changes would be able to modulate pain sensitivity. In such situation, the degree of sensitivity to pain could be predicted for the following task, since subjects with a high level of reactivity to the MA task would be more susceptible to exhibit characteristic pain threshold, tolerance, and self-reported pain severity. A second topic investigated was the hypothesis that there is a causal association between a presumed stress-pain mechanism evoked at the time of the initial task and pain sensitivity during a posterior task, or whether a common cause could explain both the presumed mechanism and subsequent pain. Their results showed that stress-induced MAP reactivity was related to pain threshold and tolerance only for subjects who received the MA task in the first phase of the experiment. In addition, their results showed that subjects in the MA/CP condition with high MAP increases during the first MA task exhibited a lower pain threshold and tolerance in a posterior CP task than low MAP reactors in the same condition. In the CP/MA case, the high and low MAP reactors the pain index had no significant differences. For high MAP reactors to the MA task in the MA/CP case had a lower pain threshold and tolerance if compared with high MAP reactors to the MA task in the CP/MA case. In other words, the mean arterial pressure under CP or MA presented an order effect.

3.2   QQ equality in Stress

In this subsection we examine the order effects observed in [1,5], in particular whether they satisfy the QQ model, in terms of obeying the QQ equality (how well the model fits the data is not interesting here, since the number of parameters for the quantum model is fairly large). Let us start with the data from [1], who report a strong and statistically significant order effect for the behavioral component of their experiment, where the mean stay percentage was observed. So, in terms of order effect, we have the following two random variables, S_N and S_S, corresponding to "Was the strategy, under noisy condition, to repeat the last response?" and "Was the strategy, under silence condition,

Table 1. Data, adapted from [1].

Silence-Noise	$S_N = 1$	$S_N = 0$		Noise-Silence	$S_N = 1$	$S_N = 0$
$S_S = 1$	.5289	.1323		$S_S = 1$	.3859	.2084
$S_S = 0$	.1388	.2000		$S_S = 0$	.2000	.2057

to repeat the last response?" Averaging over the mean stay percentages for large and small gains, given that trials were balanced, we obtain for the silent-noise order, $E(S_N) = 0.665$ and $E(S_S) = 0.665$, and for the noise-silence order $E(S_N) = 0.545$ and $E(S_S) = 0.558$. There is a clear order effect. To compute the order effect matrix E, we need to know the complete probability of events in both situations, namely, e.g., what is the probability that $S_N = 1$ in the first half and $S_S = 0$ in the second, what is the probability that $S_N = 1$ in the first half and $S_S = 1$ in the second, and so on. To do so, we obtained the original set of data from the authors, and computed the outcomes in Table 1.[1]

From this data, we can compute the order effect matrix,

$$E_{BL} = \begin{pmatrix} .1430 & -.0761 \\ -.0612 & -.0057 \end{pmatrix},$$

which gives a $q = 0.1373$, which does not corroborate the values predicted by quantum models.

More interesting than the previous result, however, is the experiment by Caceres and Burns, as it shows an order effect in physiological data, namely the mean arterial pressure (MAP). Once again, the data provided in [5] was the mean values of MAP (in $mmHg$) and their corresponding variance. We used this data to estimate, assuming a log-normal distribution for MAP [24], and comparing to the provided baseline, the probability for the following two questions, represented by the random variables P_M and P_C: "Was the mean arterial pressure above the baseline under the mental arithmetic task?" and "Was the mean arterial pressure above the baseline under the cold pressor task?" The estimated probabilities are given on Table 2. Once again, the order effect matrix can be computed from Table 2, yielding

$$E_{CB} = \begin{pmatrix} 0.0468 & 0.0011 \\ -0.0151 & -0.0327 \end{pmatrix},$$

which gives a $q = 0.014$, also close to quantum models.

---

[1] The assumption of statistical independence are possibly false. However, it is not possible to reconstruct the joint probability from the marginals without some additional assumptions.

Table 2. Order effect data for MA/CP and CP/MA conditions, adapted from [5].

MA/CP				CP/MA		
	$P_M = 1$	$P_M = 0$			$P_M = 1$	$P_M = 0$
$P_C = 1$	0.3403	0.1627		$P_C = 1$	0.2935	0.1616
$P_C = 0$	0.3362	0.1607		$P_C = 0$	0.3514	0.1935

4   Final Remarks

In this paper we examined two experiments in stress that observed order effects. For the Banis and Lorist experiment, we obtained the original data set and computed the joint probability distribution from it. For the other experiment examined, from the published data, we constructed (under simplifying conditions) data tables that allowed us to define an order effect matrix, from which the QQ equality could be computed. We saw that for the Banis and Lorist paper, the sum of the diagonals of the effect matrix was far from zero, thus not supporting the idea that the QQ equality holds, whereas for the simplifying assumptions used here the Caceres and Burn experiment satisfied the QQ equality. This shows that the QQ equality may be satisfied for some physiological experiments, though our results do not support it.

Our results relate to the broader literature in mental disorder that identifies disturbances in the synchronization connecting different regions of the brain [2,6]. For instance, quantum-like effects may appear in phase-synchronization models where incompatible stimuli are presented simultaneously [7–9]. Such quantum-like effects are similar to the order effects discussed, and recent studies on brain dynamics under stress conditions [13,17,19,23] suggest a decrease in synchronizing patterns compatible with those modeled in reference [8].

Our conclusions are limited, for many reasons. First, because of our limited access to experimental data limited to publicly available results in the literature, we could only obtain the order-effect matrix under very simplifying assumptions which are likely not true. Furthermore, without the actual data (except for [1]), we could not perform a χ^2 test to verify whether satisfying the QQ equality was done in a statistically significant way (that order effects were present were reported with statistical significance on the original papers). Second, the experimental protocols used in [1,5] were not conducive to accurately measure the order effect in a way defined by [21]. For example, the QQ equality was derived from quantum models where you have an ensemble of participants from a same population, and the first experiment does not fit this criteria. So, even with the raw data from experiments, we would expect to have problems constructing the data in Tables 1 and 2. Finally, we should point out that the data is not within subjects, so our conclusions for within subjects should be taken with a grain of salt.

As such, this paper should be seen only as an indication that quantum-like probabilistic order effects may possible not only for human judgments, but also that stress may affect such order effects. Furthermore, as we have seen, the quantum models seem to extend beyond human judgment, and fits with the description of order effects on the mean arterial pressure, a physiological variable. This is an exciting result, if actually found to be true once further experiments are carried out, where such effects could be measured in a more precise way, as they would raise the question as to why quantum probability would be a good descriptor of such types of processes.

Acknowledgments. We would like to thank Stella Banis for providing us with the original data set for their experiments. JAB and LPGA acknowledge support from the Patrick Suppes Gift Fund at Stanford University. Part of this work was done while JAB was a Visiting Professor at COPPE/UFRJ, and he also thanks Prof. Francisco Doria for his hospitality. Finally, we thank the anonymous referees for their helpful comments and suggestions.

References

1. Banis, S., Lorist, M.M.: Acute noise stress impairs feedback processing. Biol. Psychol. **91**(2), 163–171 (2012)
2. Basar, E., Schmiedt-Fehr, C., Mathes, B., Femir, B., Emek-Savas, D.D., Tulay, E., Tan, D., Duzgun, A., Guntekin, B., Ozerdem, A., Yener, G.: What does the broken brain say to the neuroscientist? Oscillations and connectivity in schizophrenia, Alzheimer's disease, and bipolar disorder. Int. J. Psychophysiol
3. Bouton, M.E.: Learning and Behavior: A Contemporary Synthesis, vol. 8. Sinauer Associates, Sunderland (2007)
4. Busemeyer, J.R., Bruza, P.D.: Quantum Models of Cognition and Decision. Cambridge University Press, Cambridge (2012)
5. Caceres, C., Burns, J.W.: Cardiovascular reactivity to psychological stress may enhance subsequent pain sensitivity. Pain **69**(3), 237–244 (1997)
6. de Assis, L.P.: Neural binding, consciousness, mental disorders: complexity as a common element. Activitas Nervosa Superior **57**(3–4), 110 (2016)
7. de Barros, J.A.: Joint probabilities and quantum cognition. In: AIP Conference Proceedings. vol. 1508, pp. 98–107. American Institute of Physics, Vaxjo, December 2012
8. Acacio de Barros, J.: Quantum-like model of behavioral response computation using neural oscillators. Biosystems **110**(3), 171–182 (2012)
9. de Barros, J.A.: Beyond the quantum formalism: consequences of a neural-oscillator model to quantum cognition. In: Liljenstrom, H. (ed.) Advances in Cognitive Neurodynamics (IV). Advances in Cognitive Neurodynamics (ICCN), pp. 401–404. Springer, Dordrecht (2015)
10. Domjan, M.: The Principles of Learning and Behavior. Nelson Education, Scarborough (2014)
11. Dzhafarov, E.N., Zhang, R., Kujala, J.: Is there contextuality in behavioural, social systems? Phil. Trans. R. Soc. A **374**(2058), 20150099 (2016)
12. Haven, E., Khrennikov, A.: Quantum Social Science. Cambridge University Press, Cambridge (2013)
13. Jacinto, L., Reis, J., Dias, N., Cerqueira, J.J., Correia, J.H., Sousa, N.: Stress affects theta activity in limbic networks and impairs novelty-induced exploration and familiarization. Frontiers Behav. Neurosci. **7**, 127 (2013)

14. Ji, R.-R., Kohno, T., Moore, K.A., Woolf, C.J.: Central sensitization and LTP: do pain and memory share similar mechanisms? Trends Neurosci. **26**(12), 696–705 (2003)
15. Khrennikov, A.: Ubiquitous Quantum Structure: From Psychology to Finance. Springer, Heidelberg (2010)
16. Morimoto, K., Fahnestock, M., Racine, R.J.: Kindling, status epilepticus models of epilepsy: rewiring the brain. Prog. Neurobiol. **73**(1), 1–60 (2004)
17. Oliveira, J.F., Dias, N.S., Correia, M., Gama-Pereira, F., Sardinha, V.M., Lima, A., Oliveira, A.F., Jacinto, L.R., Ferreira, D.S., Silva, A.M., Reis, J.S.: Chronic stress disrupts neural coherence between cortico-limbic structures. Front. Neural Circuits **7**, 10 (2013)
18. Post, R.M.: Transduction of psychosocial stress into the neurobiology of recurrent affective disorder. Am. J. Psychiatry **149**(8), 999–1010 (1992)
19. Sousa, N.: The dynamics of the stress neuromatrix. Mol. Psychiatry **21**(3), 302–312 (2016)
20. Thompson, R.F.: Habituation: a history. Neurobiol. Learn. Mem. **92**(2), 127–134 (2009)
21. Wang, Z., Busemeyer, J.R.: A quantum question order model supported by empirical tests of an a priori and precise prediction. Top. Cogn. Sci. **5**(4), 689–710 (2013)
22. Wang, Z., Solloway, T., Shiffrin, R.M., Busemeyer, J.R.: Context effects produced by question orders reveal quantum nature of human judgments. Proc. Natl. Acad. Sci. **111**(26), 9431–9436 (2014)
23. Yang, Q., Jiang, D., Sun, J., Tong, S.: Cortical synchrony change under mental stress due to time pressure. In: 2010 3rd International Conference on Biomedical Engineering and Informatics (BMEI), vol. 5, pp. 2004–2007, October 2010
24. Ziegler, D., Laux, G., Dannehl, K., Spüler, M., Mühlen, H., Mayer, P., Gries, F.A.: Assessment of cardiovascular autonomic function: age-related normal ranges and reproducibility of spectral analysis, vector analysis, and standard tests of heart rate variation and blood pressure responses. Diabet. Med. **9**(2), 166–175 (1992)

Quantum Cognition Beyond Hilbert Space: Fundamentals and Applications

Diederik Aerts[1], Lyneth Beltran[1], Massimiliano Sassoli de Bianchi[2], Sandro Sozzo[3(✉)], and Tomas Veloz[1]

[1] Center Leo Apostel (Clea), Brussels Free University (VUB), Pleinlaan 2, 1050 Brussel, Belgium
diraerts@vub.ac.be
[2] Laboratorio di Autoricerca di Base, 6914 Lugano, Switzerland
autoricerca@gmail.com
[3] School of Business and Institute IQSCS, University of Leicester, University Road, Leicester LE1 7RH, UK
ss831@le.ac.uk

Abstract. The 'quantum cognition' paradigm was recently challenged by its proven impossibility to simultaneously model 'question order effects' and 'response replicability'. In the present article we describe sequential dichotomic measurements within an operational and realistic framework for human cognition, and represent them in a quantum-like 'extended Bloch representation', where the Born rule of quantum probability does not necessarily hold. We then apply this mathematical framework to successfully model question order effects, response replicability and unpacking effects, thus opening the way toward 'quantum cognition beyond Hilbert space'.

Keywords: Cognitive modeling · Quantum structures · General tension-reduction model · Order effects · Response replicability · Unpacking effects

1 Introduction

'Quantum cognition' is the name given to the approaches that apply the mathematics of quantum theory in Hilbert space to model cognitive phenomena. Conjunctive and disjunctive fallacies, over- and under-extension effects in membership judgments, unpacking effects and expected utility paradoxes are some of the situations where quantum probabilistic approaches show significant advantages over the approaches in cognitive psychology that use classical probability theory (see, e.g., [1–12]). Notwithstanding this success, two well known experimental situations, 'question order effects' and 'response replicability', seriously challenge the acceptance of 'Hilbert space quantum cognition' as a universally valid paradigm in cognitive psychology [13–17], as we will emphasize in Sect. 2.

The difficulties of quantum approaches to model the statistics of responses of sequential questions where these cognitive effects occur led us to investigate

© Springer International Publishing AG 2017
J.A. de Barros et al. (Eds.): QI 2016, LNCS 10106, pp. 81–98, 2017.
DOI: 10.1007/978-3-319-52289-0_7

origins and range of applicability of the Born rule of quantum probability. To this end, we firstly developed an operational and realistic framework to describe cognitive entities, states and context-induced changes of states, individual and sequential measurements, measurement outcomes and their probabilities, etc. [18]. This general framework is applied in Sect. 3 to the operational and realistic description of a wide class of dichotomic measurements, including those exhibiting the above mentioned cognitive effects.

We also elaborated a 'general tension-reduction (GTR) model' [21,22] that extends some previous results obtained on the 'hidden measurements interpretation of quantum mechanics' [19]. This GTR-model, together with the associated 'extended Bloch representation (EBR)' [20], puts forward an explanation for the concrete effectiveness of the mathematical formalism of quantum theory in cognition. Indeed, the Born rule of quantum probability can be characterized in it as uniform fluctuations of the measurement context, and emerges as a 'universal average' over all possible forms of non-uniform fluctuations of the said context [20–22]. In this way, the GTR-model is also able to explain the difficulties of the Hilbert space formalism in the simultaneous modeling of question order effects and response replicability within a quantum-like framework where the Born rule does not generally hold [17].

Accordingly, in Sect. 4, we apply the GTR-model to represent dichotomic measurements that are performed individually and sequentially, together with the corresponding probabilities, and show that the GTR-model exhibits quantum-like aspects, although the Born rule of quantum probability is not generally valid in it. Hence, the GTR-model is generally non-Hilbertian. However, we also observe that the model is compatible with an operational and realistic framework for cognitive entities, and we also provide an intuitive illustration of how it can be interpreted in cognition.

In Sect. 5, we apply the model to the experimental data collected by Moore [24] and exhibiting question order effects. We then show, in Sect. 6, how question order effects and response replicability can be modeled together within the GTR-model, which is not the case in the Hilbert space quantum modeling [13,14]. Finally, in Sect. 7, we observe that another cognitive effect, the 'unpacking effect', also requires a non-Kolmogorovian probability framework, like the one provided by the GTR-model, when unpacking effects are interpreted in terms of the relationship between measurements and sub-measurements.

2   Challenges to Quantum Cognition in Hilbert Space

Quantum cognition in Hilbert space was recently challenged by 'question order effects' and 'response replicability' (the latter effect, however, is still waiting for a clear experimental confirmation). In the former, the response probabilities of two sequential questions, in an opinion poll, depend on the order in which the questions are asked, whereas in the latter the response to a given question should give the same outcome if repeated, regardless of whether another question is asked and answered in between [13]. More precisely, let us consider two dichotomic questions that are asked sequentially, in whatever order, on a sample of participants, such that probabilities of 'yes' and 'no' responses are collected as large number limits of statistical frequencies. The two questions thus correspond to two 'yes-no measurements' A and B. Their possible outcomes are 'yes' and 'no', which we denote by A_y, A_n, and B_y, B_n, respectively. Hence, performing first A then B produces the possible outcomes A_iB_j, while performing first B then A produces the possible outcomes B_jA_i, $i, j \in \{y, n\}$. A question order effect occurs when, in a given cognitive situation, the probability distribution of measurement outcomes depends on the order in which the two sequential measurements are performed, i.e. $p(A_iB_j) \neq p(B_jA_i)$.

Response replicability may instead appear in two forms, 'adjacent replicability' and 'separated replicability' [14]. Suppose that a measurement A (B) is performed twice sequentially in a given cognitive situation. Then, adjacent replicability requires that, if the outcome A_i (B_j) is obtained in the first measurement, then the same outcome A_i (B_j) should be obtained in the second measurement with certainty, i.e. with probability 1. Suppose now that the sequence of three measurements ABA (BAB) are performed in a given cognitive situation. Then, separated replicability requires that, if the outcome A_i (B_j) is obtained in the first measurement, then the same outcome A_i (B_j) should be obtained in the final measurement with certainty, i.e. with probability 1. We thus formalize response replicability by setting the conditional probability $p(A_i|A_i) = 1$ in a AA sequence, $p(B_j|B_j) = 1$ in a BB sequence, $p(A_i|A_iB_j) = 1$ in a ABA sequence, and $p(B_j|B_jA_i) = 1$ in a BAB sequence, $i, j \in \{y, n\}$.

Let us now come to the way in which the above class of psychological measurements are modeled in Hilbert space. The cognitive situation is represented by a unit vector $|\psi\rangle$ of a suitable Hilbert space, the measurements A and B are represented by the spectral measures $\{P_i^A\}$ and $\{P_j^B\}$, $i, j \in \{y, n\}$, and the Born rule is assumed to hold in both individual and sequential measurements, that is, $p_\psi(A_i) = \langle\psi|P_i^A|\psi\rangle$, $p_\psi(B_j) = \langle\psi|P_j^B|\psi\rangle$, $p_\psi(A_iB_j) = \langle\psi|P_i^A P_j^B P_i^A|\psi\rangle$, and $p_\psi(B_jA_i) = \langle\psi|P_j^B P_i^A P_j^B|\psi\rangle$, $i, j \in \{y, n\}$. Finally, this class of psychological measurements are assumed to be 'ideal first kind' measurements in a standard quantum sense, hence the state transformations induced by the measurements A and B are $|\psi\rangle \rightarrow \frac{P_i^A|\psi\rangle}{\|P_i^A|\psi\rangle\|}$ and $|\psi\rangle \rightarrow \frac{P_j^B|\psi\rangle}{\|P_j^B|\psi\rangle\|}$, respectively, for every $i, j \in \{y, n\}$, according to the Lüders postulate.

Recent studies confirm that, while the standard quantum formalism in Hilbert space is able to separately model question order effects and response replicability [3,7,9,12], the same formalism does not work in cognitive situations where both effects are simultaneously present [13,14,17]. Roughly speaking, while the latter effect requires the spectral measures representing measurements to commute, the former can only be reproduced by non-commuting spectral families – the possibility of solving this problem by using more general positive operator values measurements is still under investigation. One may then wonder whether cognitive experiments exist where question order effects and response replicability are effectively observed. In this respect, one typically accepts the latter effect as a natural requirement for a wide class of psychological measurements.

On the other hand, order effects in sequential measurements have been thoroughly studied since the seventies [23]. In particular, Moore reviewed a Gallup poll conducted in 1997, in which he reported interesting results of different experiments on question order effects [24].

Hilbert space models of question order effects predict that a so-called 'QQ equality' should be satisfied by the experimental data, for every initial state $|\psi\rangle$ [9]. The QQ equality is important, as it provides a 'parameter-free test of quantum models for question order effects', valid for projection operators of arbitrary dimension. Interestingly enough, this equality is approximately satisfied by some of the data collected by Moore, like those of the 'Clinton/Gore experiment', while it is significantly violated by others, like the 'Rose/Jackson experiment'. Furthermore, some authors [15,16], including ourselves [17], lately observed that a special version of the quantum model, the 'non-degenerate model', should satisfy further parameter-free conditions, which are instead generally violated by the data. As we will analyse more specifically in Sect. 5, we can thus already draw a major result from the preceding discussion: at the level of question order effects, not only when they are simultaneously present with response replicability, quantum modeling in Hilbert space is problematical, and a more general probabilistic framework becomes necessary.

3   An Operational and Realistic Framework for Cognitive Entities and Measurements

In this section, we apply an operational and realistic framework to describe cognitive situations of the type mentioned in Sect. 2 [18]. This framework rests on the operational and realistic foundations of quantum physics and quantum probability that were formalized by the SCoP formalism [25]. Here, the terms 'operational' and 'realistic' have a precise meaning. Our approach to cognition is 'operational', in the sense that the basic notions (states, measurements, outcomes and their probabilities, etc.) are defined in terms of the concrete operations that are performed in the laboratory of experimentation. Furthermore, our approach to cognition is 'realistic', in the sense that the state of the cognitive entity is interpreted as a 'state of affairs', hence it expresses a reality of the cognitive entity, albeit a reality not of a physical but of a conceptual nature.

In experimental psychology, we can introduce 'psychological laboratories', that is, spatio-temporal domains where cognitive experiments are performed. Let us focus ourselves on opinion polls, where a large number of human participants are asked questions in the form of structured questionnaires, and let the questions involve a 'cognitive entity' S (a concept, a combination of concepts, or a more complex conceptual situation). The experimental design, the questionnaire and the cognitive effect under study define a 'preparation' of the cognitive entity S, which is thus assumed to be in an 'initial state' p_S, and all participants interact with the cognitive entity in the state p_S. Suppose that the question, or 'yes-no measurement', A is asked to a participant as part of the opinion poll. The measurement has the possible outcomes A_y and A_n, depending on whether the response of the participant was 'yes' or 'no'. The interaction of the participant with the cognitive entity S, when the dichotomic measurement A is performed, thus leads to one of the two possible outcomes, and generally also gives rise to a change of the state of the entity from p_S to either p_{A_y} or p_{A_n}, depending on whether the response is 'yes' or 'no'. Hence, the participant acts as a measurement context for the cognitive entity in the state p_S. If the same measurement A is performed by making use of a large sample of participants, a statistics of responses is collected, which determines in the large number limit a 'transition probability' $\mu(p_{A_i}, e_A, p_S)$ that the initial state p_S of the cognitive entity S changes to the state p_{A_i}, $i \in \{y, n\}$, under the effect of the context e_A determined by the measurement A.

The above framework formalizes the situation of the 'Clinton/Gore experiment' mentioned in Sect. 2, where the participant is asked to answer 'yes' or 'no' to the question: "Is Gore honest and trustworthy?". If, for a given participant, the response is 'yes', the initial state $p_{Honesty}$ of the conceptual entity *Honesty and Trustworthiness* (which we will simply denote *Honesty*, for the sake of simplicity) changes to a new state p_{A_y}, which is the state the entity is in when the choice 'Gore is honest' is added to its original content. Let us now suppose that a second question B is asked to the participants as part of the opinion poll. This defines a measurement B, with possible outcomes B_y and B_n, on the cognitive entity in the state p_S. Also in this case, the response determines a change of the state of S from p_S to either p_{B_y} or p_{B_n}, depending on whether the response is 'yes' or 'no'. In the large number limit, we get a transition probability $\mu(p_{B_j}, e_B, p_S)$ that the initial state p_S of S changes to the state p_{B_j}, $j \in \{y, n\}$, under the effect of the context e_B determined by the measurement B.

The measurement B formalizes the situation where the participant is asked to answer 'yes' or 'no' to the question: "Is Clinton honest and trustworthy?". If, for a given participant, the response is 'yes', the initial state $p_{Honesty}$ of the conceptual entity *Honesty and Trustworthiness* changes to a new state p_{B_y}, which is the state the entity is in when the choice 'Clinton is honest' is added to its original content. Then, let us suppose that each participant is first asked question A and then question B. This defines a new measurement AB, with possible outcomes A_iB_j, $i, j \in \{y, n\}$, on the cognitive entity S in the state p_S. The probability $p_S(A_iB_j)$ of obtaining the outcome A_iB_j in the measurement AB, i.e. the outcome A_i when performing A, and then B_j when performing B, $i, j \in \{y, n\}$, on S in the state p_S, is given by the product $p_S(A_iB_j) = \mu(p_{A_i}, e_A, p_S)\mu(p_{B_j}, e_B, p_{A_i})$. Finally, let us suppose that each participant is first asked question B and then question A. This defines a new measurement BA, with possible outcomes B_jA_i, $i, j \in \{y, n\}$, on the cognitive entity S in the state p_S. The probability $p_S(B_jA_i)$ of obtaining the outcome B_jA_i in the measurement BA, i.e. the outcome B_j when performing B, and then A_i when performing A, $i, j \in \{y, n\}$, on S in the state p_S, is given by the product $p_S(B_jA_i) = \mu(p_{B_j}, e_B, p_S)\mu(p_{A_i}, e_A, p_{B_j})$.

To conclude this section, we stress that the state of a cognitive entity describes an element of a conceptual reality that is independent of the subjective beliefs of the persons questioning about that entity. Such subjective beliefs are rather incorporated in the measurement context, which describes the cognitive interaction between the entity and the persons deciding on it. As such, our operational and realistic approach to cognition departs from other approaches that apply the quantum formalism to model cognitive phenomena [3,7,8].

4   The GTR-model for Dichotomic Measurements

In this section, we present a geometric representation, in the 3-dimensional Euclidean space $\mathbb{R}^3$, of the operational and realistic entities we have introduced in Sect. 3, focusing on the representation of the sequential measurements AB and BA. Our results rest on [17], to which we refer for technical details and calculations. The model presented here is an application of the 'general tension-reduction (GTR) model, where quantum probabilities are recovered as 'universal averages' over all possible forms of non-uniform fluctuations [21,22]. When the state space is Hilbertian, as in quantum physics, the GTR-model reduces to the so-called 'extended Bloch representation' (EBR) of quantum theory [20].

Let us firstly consider individual measurements with two outcomes on a cognitive entity, and study how they are represented in the EBR representation. The cognitive entity S is represented by an abstract point particle that can move on the surface of a 3-dimensional unit sphere, called the 'Bloch sphere'. The initial state p_S of S is represented by a state of the point particle on the sphere corresponding to a given position $\mathbf{x}_\psi$ on the sphere. Dichotomic measurements on S are then represented by 1-dimensional breakable and elastic structures, anchored at two antipodal points, corresponding to the two possible outcome states. More precisely, the measurement A is represented by a breakable elastic band stretched between two points $\mathbf{a}_y$ and $\mathbf{a}_n = -\mathbf{a}_y$, $\|\mathbf{a}_y\| = \|\mathbf{a}_n\| = 1$, corresponding to the two outcomes A_y and A_n, respectively. Analogously, the measurement B is represented by a breakable elastic band stretched between two points $\mathbf{b}_y$ and $\mathbf{b}_n = -\mathbf{b}_y$, $\|\mathbf{b}_y\| = \|\mathbf{b}_n\| = 1$, corresponding to the two outcomes B_y and B_n, respectively. Accordingly, the outcome states p_{A_i} and p_{B_j} are represented by the positions $\mathbf{a}_i$ and $\mathbf{b}_j$, respectively, $i, j \in \{y, n\}$.

We assume that the points x of the two breakable elastics are parameterized in such a way that the end points coordinate $x = 1$ and $x = -1$ correspond to the outcome 'yes' and 'no', respectively, with $x = 0$ describing the center of the elastics, also coinciding with the center of the Bloch sphere. Each elastic represents a possible dichotomic measurement, and is described not only by its orientation within the sphere, but also by 'the way' it can break. More concretely, breakability of the elastic representing the measurement A is formalized by a probability distribution $\rho_A(x|\psi)$ such that $\int_{x_1}^{x_2} \rho_A(x|\psi)dx$ is the probability that the elastic breaks in the interval $[x_1, x_2]$, $-1 \le x_1 \le x_2 \le 1$, when the measurement A is performed and the point particle is in the initial position $\mathbf{x}_\psi$. The condition $\int_{-1}^{1} \rho_A(x|\psi)dx = 1$ guarantees that the elastic will break in one of its points, with certainty, i.e. that the measurement will produce an outcome.

Let us now describe the measurement A on the cognitive entity S in the state p_S as represented in the Bloch sphere. When the measurement A is performed

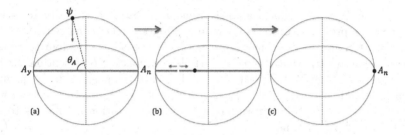

Fig. 1. The unfolding of the A-measurement, here producing outcome A_n.

and the point particle is in the initial position $\mathbf{x}_\psi$, a certain probability distribution $\rho_A(x|\psi)$ is actualized, which describes the way the A-elastic band will break, in accordance with the fluctuations that are present in the measurement context e_A. Then, the point particle "falls" from its original position $\mathbf{x}_\psi$, orthogonally onto the A-elastic band, and sticks to it. Next, the elastic breaks in some point, and its two broken fragments contract toward the corresponding anchor points, bringing with them the point particle (see Fig. 1). If x_A is the position of the point particle onto the elastic, i.e. $x_A = \mathbf{x}_\psi \cdot \mathbf{a}_y = \cos\theta_A$, and the elastic breaks in a point λ, with $x_A < \lambda$, then the particle attached to the elastic fragment $[-1, \lambda]$ is drawn toward the position $\mathbf{a}_y$. In this case, we say that the measurement A gives the outcome 'yes'. If instead $x_A > \lambda$, then the particle attached to the elastic fragment $[\lambda, 1]$ is drawn toward the position $\mathbf{a}_n$. In this case, we say that the measurement A gives the outcome 'no'. The transition probability $p_\psi(A_y)$ that the initial position $\mathbf{x}_\psi$ collapses to $\mathbf{a}_y$, and $p_\psi(A_n)$ that the initial position $\mathbf{x}_\psi$ collapses to $\mathbf{a}_n$, are given by:

$$p_\psi(A_y) = \int_{-1}^{\cos\theta_A} \rho_A(x|\psi)dx \qquad p_\psi(A_n) = \int_{\cos\theta_A}^{1} \rho_A(x|\psi)dx \qquad (1)$$

and represent the transition probabilities $\mu(p_{A_y}, e_A, p_S)$ and $\mu(p_{A_n}, e_A, p_S)$, respectively, which we have introduced in Sect. 3.

It is worth noticing that: (i) the probabilities in (1) formalize a lack of knowledge about the measurement process, i.e. the breaking point λ corresponds to a 'hidden measurement-interaction'; (ii) the Born rule of quantum probability is recovered when $\rho_A(x|\psi) = \frac{1}{2}$, i.e. when the probability distribution is globally uniform, in which case (1) becomes: $p_\psi(A_y) = \frac{1}{2}(1 + \cos\theta_A)$ and $p_\psi(A_n) = \frac{1}{2}(1 - \cos\theta_A)$. This result is not limited to dichotomic measurements, but has a general validity, i.e. it can be naturally generalized to degenerate and non-degenerate measurements having an arbitrary number of outcomes [20–22]. For the transition probabilities $p_\psi(B_y)$ and $p_\psi(B_n)$, associated with measurement B, one has the same formulae, simply replacing θ_A by θ_B and $\rho_A(x|\psi)$ by $\rho_B(x|\psi)$, with θ_B now defining the landing point $x_B = \mathbf{x}_\psi \cdot \mathbf{b}_y = \cos\theta_B$ of the point particle onto the B-elastic band, and $\rho_B(x|\psi)$ being the probability distribution associated with the latter (generally different from $\rho_A(x|\psi)$).

Let us then consider sequential measurements on a cognitive entity and study how they are represented in the GTR-model. Suppose that we firstly perform the measurement A and then the measurement B. We thus have the four transition probabilities $p_\psi(A_iB_j)$ that the point particle position $\mathbf{x}_\psi$, representing the initial state, first changes to the position $\mathbf{a}_i$ and then to the position $\mathbf{b}_j$ (sequential outcome A_i and then B_j), $i,j \in \{y,n\}$. If we set $\cos\theta = \mathbf{a}_y \cdot \mathbf{b}_y$, we can first write the conditional probabilities $p_{A_i}(B_j)$ that the position $\mathbf{a}_i$ changes to the position $\mathbf{b}_j$, $i,j \in \{y,n\}$, as

$$p_{A_y}(B_y) = \int_{-1}^{\cos\theta} \rho_B(x|A_y)dx \qquad p_{A_y}(B_n) = \int_{\cos\theta}^{1} \rho_B(x|A_y)dx$$

$$p_{A_n}(B_y) = \int_{-1}^{-\cos\theta} \rho_B(x|A_n)dx \qquad p_{A_n}(B_n) = \int_{-\cos\theta}^{1} \rho_B(x|A_n)dx \qquad (2)$$

where $\rho_B(x|A_y)$ (respectively $\rho_B(x|A_n)$) is the probability distribution actualized during the measurement B, knowing that the measurement A produced the transition from $\mathbf{x}_\psi$ to $\mathbf{a}_y$ (respectively to $\mathbf{a}_n$). Now, for every $i,j \in \{y,n\}$, we have $p_\psi(A_iB_j) = p_\psi(A_i)p_{A_i}(B_j)$ for the transition probabilities in the sequential measurement AB. More explicitly, using (2) and (1), we can write:

$$p_\psi(A_yB_y) = \int_{-1}^{\cos\theta} \rho_B(x|A_y)dx \int_{-1}^{\cos\theta_A} \rho_A(x|\psi)dx$$

$$p_\psi(A_yB_n) = \int_{\cos\theta}^{1} \rho_B(x|A_y)dx \int_{-1}^{\cos\theta_A} \rho_A(x|\psi)dx$$

$$p_\psi(A_nB_y) = \int_{-1}^{-\cos\theta} \rho_B(x|A_n)dx \int_{\cos\theta_A}^{1} \rho_A(x|\psi)dx$$

$$p_\psi(A_nB_n) = \int_{-\cos\theta}^{1} \rho_B(x|A_n)dx \int_{\cos\theta_A}^{1} \rho_A(x|\psi)dx \qquad (3)$$

and by exchanging the role of A and B in (3), we get similar expressions for the probabilities $p_\psi(B_yA_y)$, $p_\psi(B_yA_n)$, $p_\psi(B_nA_y)$ and $p_\psi(B_nA_n)$ of the sequential measurement BA. Clearly, these sequential probabilities coincide by construction with the probabilities $p_S(A_iB_j)$ and $p_S(B_jA_i)$, $i,j \in \{y,n\}$, given in Sect. 3.

Our general modeling of cognitive entities, states, dichotomic measurements and sequential measurement processes is thus completed. One realizes at once that it incorporates quantum aspects, as context induced changes of state, pure potentiality, unavoidable and uncontrollable uncertainty. In this sense, one can say that the model that we have presented is 'quantum-like'. However, it is more general than the standard Hilbert space representation, as the Born rule of quantum probability is only recovered in the specific case in which ρ_A and ρ_B are both globally uniform probability distributions (describing uniform elastic structures, having the same probability to break in all their points).

In order to find explicit solutions, to be used in specific applications, one needs to add some reasonable constraints to the measurements A and B, in particular for what concerns the probability densities ρ_A and ρ_B. Before doing so, let us observe that the elastic mechanism we have described also provides a possible representation of what we intuitively feel when confronted with decision contexts, and a neural/mental equilibrium is progressively built, resulting from the balancing of the different tensions between the initial state and the available mutually excluding answers. Indeed, an elastics stretched between two antipodal points in the Bloch sphere can be seen as an abstract representation of such equilibrium, which at some moment will be altered in a non-predictable way (when the elastic breaks), causing a sudden and irreversible process during which the initial conceptual state is drawn to one of the possible answers.

The compatibility of the GTR-model with our intuitive understanding of the human cognitive processes remains such also when psychological measurements with an arbitrary number N of outcomes are considered [20–22]. The elastics are then replaced by disintegrable hyper-membranes having the shape of $(N-1)$-dimensional simplexes. Similarly to the $N=2$ situation, the latter can still be viewed not only as mathematical objects naturally representing the measurements' probabilities, and their relations, but also as a way to 'give shape' to the different mental states of equilibrium, characterized by the existence of different competing 'tension lines' going from the on-membrane position of the point particle to the N vertices of the simplex, representing the different answers.

These 'tension-reduction processes' can also describe situations where the conflicts between the competing answers cannot be fully resolved, so that the system is brought into another state of equilibrium, between a reduced set of possibilities, which in the GTR-model correspond to lower-dimensional sub-simplexes [20–22]. These are situations describing sub-measurements of a given measurement, called degenerate measurements in quantum mechanics. As we see in Sect. 7, they may have some relevance in the description of unpacking effects.

Let us now provide an exact solution to the modeling of data about sequential measurements. For this, we will assume in the following that $\rho_A(x|\psi)$ does not depend on the initial state and that it is 'locally uniform', i.e. only characterized by two parameters $\epsilon_A \in [0,1]$ and $d_A \in [-1+\epsilon_A, 1-\epsilon_A]$, such that: $\rho_A(x) = 0$ if $x \in [-1, d_A - \epsilon_A] \cup (d_A + \epsilon_A, 1]$, and $\rho_A(x) = 1/2\epsilon_A$ if $x \in [d_A - \epsilon_A, d_A + \epsilon_A]$. To obtain compact expressions, we also assume that $\cos\theta_A \in [d_A - \epsilon_A, d_A + \epsilon_A]$. If we describe in a similar way a second dichotomic measurement B, then in addition to the three parameters ϵ_A, d_A and θ_A, characterizing A, we have three more parameters ϵ_B, d_B and θ_B, characterizing B, and a supplementary parameter θ, defined by $\cos\theta = \mathbf{a}_y \cdot \mathbf{b}_y$, characterizing the relative orientation of the two measurements within the Bloch sphere. In the following, we also assume that $\cos\theta \in [d_A - \epsilon_A, d_A + \epsilon_A]$ and $\cos\theta \in [d_B - \epsilon_B, d_B + \epsilon_B]$. Then, if we perform in sequence the measurement A followed by the measurement B (which we denote AB), the sequential measurement has the 4 outcomes A_iB_j, $i,j \in \{y,n\}$, and the associated probabilities are given by the products $p_\psi(A_iB_j) = p_\psi(A_i)p_{A_i}(B_j)$. Performing the integrals (1), one obtains:

$$p_\psi(A_yB_y) = \tfrac{1}{4}(1 + \tfrac{\cos\theta - d_B}{\epsilon_B})(1 + \tfrac{\cos\theta_A - d_A}{\epsilon_A})$$
$$p_\psi(A_yB_n) = \tfrac{1}{4}(1 - \tfrac{\cos\theta - d_B}{\epsilon_B})(1 + \tfrac{\cos\theta_A - d_A}{\epsilon_A})$$
$$p_\psi(A_nB_y) = \tfrac{1}{4}(1 - \tfrac{\cos\theta + d_B}{\epsilon_B})(1 - \tfrac{\cos\theta_A - d_A}{\epsilon_A})$$
$$p_\psi(A_nB_n) = \tfrac{1}{4}(1 + \tfrac{\cos\theta + d_B}{\epsilon_B})(1 - \tfrac{\cos\theta_A - d_A}{\epsilon_A}) \tag{4}$$

and by exchanging the role of A and B in (4), we get similar expressions for the probabilities $p_\psi(B_yA_y)$, $p_\psi(B_yA_n)$, $p_\psi(B_nA_y)$ and $p_\psi(B_nA_n)$ of the sequential measurement BA. These systems of equations are underdetermined, as the 8 outcome probabilities can determine all the parameters but one. Thus, we are free to choose one of the parameters, for instance ϵ_A, and by doing so all the others will be fixed. Since we must have $\epsilon_A(1 + \frac{d_A}{\epsilon_A}) \leq 1$, i.e. $\epsilon_A \leq 1/(1 + \frac{d_A}{\epsilon_A})$, this means that if $\frac{d_A}{\epsilon_A}$ is different from zero, it is not be possible to model the data by means of the standard quantum formalism (in a 2-dimensional Hilbert space), as the Born rule corresponds to the choice $d_A = 0$ and $\epsilon_A = 1$.

5   Modeling Moore's Data

We now use the system of Eq. (4), for the sequential measurement AB, and its reversed order version, for the sequential measurement BA, to 'exactly' model the data obtained in a Gallup poll conducted in 1997, as presented in a review of question order effects by Moore [24]. More precisely, we consider the probabilities given by [26] (see also [9]), where the participants who did not provided a 'yes' or 'no' answer have been excluded from the statistics. In one of the experiments, a thousand participants were subjected to a pair of questions, asked in a sequence. The first question, which we associate with measurement A, is Clinton's question, and the second question, which we associate with measurement B, is Gore's question, as we described them in Sect. 3. Half of the participants were submitted to the two questions in the order AB (first 'Clinton' then 'Gore') and the other half in the reversed order BA, and the collected response probabilities are: $p(A_y B_y) = 0.4899$, $p(A_y B_n) = 0.0447$, $p(A_n B_y) = 0.1767$, $p(A_n B_n) = 0.2887$, $p(B_y A_y) = 0.5625$, $p(B_y A_n) = 0.1991$, $p(B_n A_y) = 0.0255$, $p(B_n A_n) = 0.2129$.

These probabilities show a significant question order effect. Inserting them in (4), and in its reversed order version, one obtains, after some calculations, the following explicit values for the model's parameters (we refer to [17] for a detailed analysis): $\frac{d_A}{\epsilon_A} = 0.1545$, $\frac{\cos\theta_A}{\epsilon_A} = 0.2237$, $\frac{\cos\theta}{\epsilon_A} = 0.6316$, $\frac{d_B}{\epsilon_B} = -0.2961$, $\frac{\cos\theta_B}{\epsilon_B} = 0.2271$ and $\frac{\cos\theta}{\epsilon_B} = 0.5367$.

We see at once that the solution does not admit a representation by means of the Born rule, considering that $\frac{d_A}{\epsilon_A}, \frac{d_B}{\epsilon_B} \neq 0$. Furthermore, we see that we cannot have $\epsilon_A = \epsilon_B$ and $d_A = d_B$, i.e. the solution requires the two measurements to be characterized by different rules of probabilistic assignment ($\rho_A \neq \rho_B$). The structure of the probabilistic data is thus irreducibly non-Hilbertian. If we choose $\epsilon_A = 1/2$, we obtain for the other parameters (writing them in approximate form, to facilitate their reading): $\epsilon_A = 0.5$, $\epsilon_B \approx 0.59$, $d_A \approx 0.08$, $d_B \approx -0.17$, $\cos\theta \approx 0.32$, $\cos\theta_A \approx 0.11$, and $\cos\theta_B \approx 0.13$ – hence, $\theta \approx 72°$, $\theta_A \approx 84°$, and $\theta_B \approx 74°$.

In another experiment reported by Moore, always performed on a thousand participants, the opinion poll consisted in a pair of questions about the baseball players Pete Rose and Shoeless Joe Jackson. More precisely, question A was: "Do you think Rose should or should not be eligible for admission to the Hall of Fame?". Similarly, question B was: "Do you think Jackson should or should not be eligible for admission to the Hall of Fame?". The collected response probabilities are (also in this case we use the data given in [9,26]):

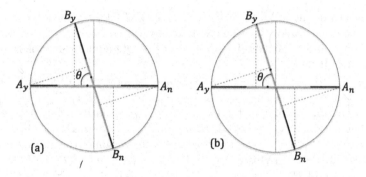

Fig. 2. The (a) Clinton/Gore and (b) Rose/Jackson probability distributions.

$p(A_yB_y) = 0.3379$, $p(A_yB_n) = 0.3241$, $p(A_nB_y) = 0.0178$, $p(A_nB_n) = 0.3202$, $p(B_yA_y) = 0.4156$, $p(B_yA_n) = 0.0671$, $p(B_nA_y) = 0.1234$, $p(B_nA_n) = 0.3939$, and the modeling now gives [17]: $\frac{d_A}{\epsilon_A} = -0.0995$, $\frac{\cos\theta_A}{\epsilon_A} = 0.2245$, $\frac{\cos\theta}{\epsilon_A} = 0.6224$, $\frac{d_B}{\epsilon_B} = 0.4369$, $\frac{\cos\theta_B}{\epsilon_B} = 0.4023$ and $\frac{\cos\theta}{\epsilon_B} = 0.4578$. Again, we can observe that these values are irreducibly non-Hilbertian. For $\epsilon_A = 1/2$, we obtain: $\epsilon_A = 0.5$, $\epsilon_B \approx 0.68$, $d_A \approx -0.05$, $d_B \approx 0.30$, $\cos\theta \approx 0.31$, $\cos\theta_A \approx 0.11$, $\cos\theta_B \approx 0.27$.

The two solutions are graphically represented in Fig. 2. The two black dots denote the values of $\cos\theta_A$ and $\cos\theta_B$, and the black regions are those where the probability distributions are zero (corresponding to the unbreakable elastic regions). What strikes the eye is that the Clinton/Gore and Rose/Jackson solutions are structurally very similar, despite the fact that only the former (almost) obey the 'QQ equality' [9,26]. This is because the latter is insufficient to fully characterize a Hilbertian structure and that both solutions are actually intrinsically non-Hilbertian [17].

It is worth mentioning that the QQ equality, i.e. the equality

$$p_\psi(A_yB_y) - p_\psi(B_yA_y) + p_\psi(A_nB_n) - p_\psi(B_nA_n) = 0 \tag{5}$$

simply follows by taking the average $\langle\psi|Q|\psi\rangle$ of the operatorial identity $Q = 0$, where $Q \equiv P_y^A P_y^B P_y^A - P_y^B P_y^A P_y^B + P_n^A P_n^B P_n^A - P_n^B P_n^A P_n^B = 0$ [17,18]. Now, it has been pointed out that the Clinton/Gore data are different from the Rose/Jackson, as for the latter, participants also received some sequential background information before answering the two questions, and this would explain why, contrary to the Clinton/Gore data, they violate the QQ equality. Indeed, if this supply of information is modeled by using two unitary operators U (for the information given before A) and V (for that given before B), we now have to write $p_\psi(A_iB_j) = \langle\psi|U^\dagger P_i^A V^\dagger P_j^B V P_i^A U|\psi\rangle$, and similarly for $p_\psi(B_jA_i)$. Thus, the relevant operator becomes:

$$\begin{aligned}
Q' &= U^\dagger P_y^A P_y^{\prime B} P_y^A U - V^\dagger P_y^B P_y^{\prime A} P_y^B V + U^\dagger P_n^A P_n^{\prime B} P_n^A U - V^\dagger P_n^B P_n^{\prime A} P_n^B V \\
&= [P_y^{\prime B} - U^\dagger P_y^{\prime B} U] + [V^\dagger P_y^{\prime A} V - P_y^{\prime A}] + [U^\dagger P_y^{\prime B} U P_y^{\prime A} - P_y^{\prime B} V^\dagger P_y^{\prime A} V] \\
&\quad + [P_y^{\prime A} U^\dagger P_y^{\prime B} U - V^\dagger P_y^{\prime A} V P_y^{\prime B}]
\end{aligned} \tag{6}$$

where we have defined $P'^A_i \equiv U^\dagger P^A_i U$, $P'^B_j \equiv V^\dagger P^B_j V$, $i,j \in \{y,n\}$. Since the average $\langle\psi|Q'|\psi\rangle$ can now in principle take any value within the interval $[-1,1]$ (unless $U = V = \mathbb{I}$), this could explain why the QQ equality is violated in the Rose/Jackson situation.

The above argument, however, is weakened by the observation that there are other quantum equalities that are strongly disobeyed both by the Clinton/Gore and Rose/Jackson data, like for instance, in the situation of non-degenerate measurements [17,18]: $q' \equiv p_\psi(A_y B_n)p_\psi(A_n B_n) - p_\psi(A_n B_y)p_\psi(A_y B_y) = 0$, which must be obeyed also when participants receive some background information. Indeed, we have in this case $p_\psi(A_i B_j) = |\langle A_i|U|\psi\rangle|^2|\langle B_j|V|A_i\rangle|^2$, where $P^A_i = |A_i\rangle\langle A_i|$ and $P^B_j = |B_j\rangle\langle B_j|$, $i,j \in \{y,n\}$, so that we can write:

$$q' = |\langle A_y|U|\psi\rangle|^2|\langle A_n|U|\psi\rangle|^2$$
$$\times \left[|\langle B_n|V|A_y\rangle|^2|\langle B_n|V|A_n\rangle|^2 - |\langle B_y|V|A_n\rangle|^2|\langle B_y|V|A_y\rangle|^2\right] \quad (7)$$

Using $|\langle B_y|V|A_n\rangle|^2 = 1 - |\langle B_n|V|A_n\rangle|^2$ and $|\langle B_y|V|A_y\rangle|^2 = 1 - |\langle B_n|V|A_y\rangle|^2$, it is easy to check that the terms in the above bracket cancel, so that $q' = 0$. Thus, we have a genuine quantum equality which must be satisfied also when some information is sequentially provided to the participants. However, it is strongly violated by the experimental data [17].

6   Response Replicability

As emphasized in [13], the standard quantum formalism is unable to jointly model question order effects and response replicability. The reason is simple to understand: response replicability, the situation where a question, if asked a second time, receives the same answer, even if other questions have been answered in between, requires commuting observables to be modeled. Indeed, since we have the operatorial identity $P^B_n P^A_y P^B_n - P^A_y P^B_n P^A_y = (P^B_y - P^A_y)[P^B_y, P^A_y]$, it follows that the difference $p_\psi(B_n A_y) - p_\psi(A_y B_n)$ can generally be non-zero only if $[P^B_y, P^A_y] \neq 0$, i.e. the spectral families associated with the A and B measurements do not commute. Thus, not only an exact description of question order effects requires to go beyond-quantum, but the combination of the latter with response replicability also creates a contradiction, which persists even when measurements are represented by positive-operator valued measures [13,14].

The reason why the above contradiction cannot be eliminated is that in quantum theory an observable automatically determines, via the Born rule, the outcome probabilities. This means that, once the initial state is given, and the possible outcomes are also given, there is only one way to choose them: that prescribed by the Born rule. This means that, if a specific participant were able to interact with a cognitive entity by employing different 'ways of choosing', at least one of them has to be non-Bornian. In our opinion, such a situation precisely occurs when considering the effect of response replicability. Indeed, in this case there are at least two possible ways of choosing an outcome from the memory of the previous interaction. In the standard formalism there is no place to describe such a memory effect, hence the impossibility to model it in a consistent way, beyond the so-called 'adjacent replicability' [14], which is built-in in all first-kind measurements. On the other hand, in the richer structure of the GTR-model, changes in the way outcomes are selected can be easily modeled as changes in the measurements' probability distributions [17]. In other words, the reason why 'separated replicability' can be taken into account in the GTR-model, jointly with possible question order effects, is that it allows not only to describe how the action of contexts can produce state transitions, but also how state transitions can determine a change of future contexts, via a change of the associated probability distributions.

To see how the above works, let us consider the sequence of three measurements ABA on a given cognitive entity (see also [17] for a more general discussion). Let ρ_A be the probability distribution describing the measurement A, and let us suppose that the outcome is A_y. We do not need to associate any change of the probability distribution ρ_A to this transition, as measurements are already first kind measurements in the GTR-model, as in quantum theory. Then, let us suppose that, when the measurement B is performed, with the entity now in the state associated with outcome A_y, the outcome B_y is obtained. Again, we do not need to associate any change of the probability distribution ρ_B to this second transition, but we now have to update the probability distribution describing the measurement A, to guarantee that, if we repeat the latter, the outcome A_y is certain in advance. In other words, we now associate a probability distribution transition $\rho_A \to \rho_A'$, to ensure response replicability. Similarly, when the measurement A is performed, giving A_y with probability 1, there will be a transition $\rho_B \to \rho_B'$, to ensure that a subsequent measurement B will give B_y with certainty, and from that point on subsequent A or B measurements can only deterministically reproduce the same outcomes, with no further changes of contexts. More precisely, the probability distributions ρ_A' and ρ_B' can be obtained by simple truncation and renormalization [17]:

$$\rho_A'(x) = \frac{\rho_A}{\int_{-1}^{\cos\theta} \rho_A dx}\chi_{[-1,\cos\theta)}(x) \qquad \rho_B'(x) = \frac{\rho_B}{\int_{-1}^{\cos\theta} \rho_B dx}\chi_{[-1,\cos\theta)}(x) \quad (8)$$

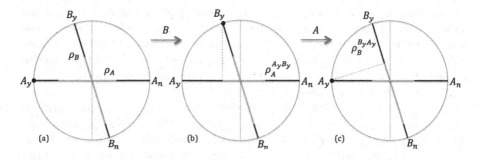

Fig. 3. The measurement sequence BA, in the GTR-model.

where $\chi_I(x)$ is the characteristic function of the interval I. Figure 3 illustrates this 'double transition process', where not only states but also probability distributions can change. Figure 3(a) represents the situation following the first measurement A, the outcome being A_y. Figure 3(b) describes the subsequent measurement B, the outcome being B_y, also producing the transition from ρ_A to ρ_A'. Figure 3(c) describes the second measurement A, giving again outcome A_y, with certainty, which is also accompanied by the transition from ρ_B to ρ_B'.

7   Unpacking Effects

In this final section, we analyze the so-called 'unpacking effects', usually modeled in the quantum formalism by assuming that the participants actually perform non-compatible sequential measurements, in a predetermined order [27]. Our thesis is that, if we consider these effects in relation to the notion of submeasurement, they point to an inadequacy of the quantum formalism in Hilbert space, as they describe situations that are incompatible with the quantum representation of degenerate measurements.

Two kinds of unpacking are usually considered, 'implicit' and 'explicit'. The implicit unpacking is when a question is addressed in two different ways, a 'packed way' and an 'unpacked way'. More precisely, if A and B are two dichotomic measurements with outcomes A_y and A_n, and B_y and B_n, respectively, we can define a measurement A', with outcomes A_y' and A_n', where A_n' is the same as A_n, and A_y' describes a possibility that is logically equivalent to A_y, expressed as an alternative over two mutually exclusive and exhaustive possibilities, defined by the outcomes of B. In other words, $A_y' = (A_y \wedge B_y) \oplus (A_y \wedge B_n)$, where the symbol $\oplus$ denotes the logical exclusive conjunction.

An example adapted from a list of experiments performed by Rottenstreich and Tversky [28] is the following. Measurement A is the question: "Is the winner of next US presidential election a non-Democrat?", with outcome A_y and A_n corresponding to the answers "Yes, is a non-Democrat," and "No, is a Democrat," respectively. Measurement B is the question: "If the winner of next US presidential election is a non-Democrat, will be an Independent?", with outcome B_y and B_n corresponding to the answers "Yes, an Independent," and "No, not an Independent," respectively. On the other hand, the implicitly unpacked measurement A' is defined by the question: "Is the winner of the next presidential election an Independent or Republican rather than a Democrat?", with outcome A_y' corresponding to the (unpacked) answer "Yes, is an Independent or a Republican rather than a Democrat" and outcome A_n' to the answer "No, is a Democrat," which is the same as A_n.

Following Sect. 3, we denote by p_S the initial state of the conceptual entity S, which in our case is: *The winner of next US presidential election*. Moreover, we denote by p_{A_i} and $p_{A_i'}$ the final states of S associated with the outcomes A_i and A_i', $i \in \{y, n\}$, respectively. Then, we can write the corresponding probabilities as $p_S(A_i) = \mu(p_{A_i}, e_A, p_S)$ and $p_S(A_i') = \mu(p_{A_i'}, e_{A'}, p_S)$, $i \in \{y, n\}$, where e_A and $e_{A'}$ are the contexts associated with A and A', respectively, causing the transitions from the initial state p_S to the observed outcome states p_{A_i} and $p_{A_i'}$, respectively. If $p_S(A_y')$ is found to be sensibly different from $p_S(A_y)$, one says that there is an unpacking effect, i.e. an effect where logically equivalent descriptions of a same possibility can produce different probabilities, thus violating the so-called principle of 'description invariance'. More precisely, one speaks of 'superadditivity' if $p_S(A_y) > p_S(A_y')$ and 'subadditivity' if $p_S(A_y) < p_S(A_y')$.

Let us also describe the situation corresponding to the 'explicit unpacking effect'. In this case the dichotomic measurement A' is further decomposed into a measurement having three distinct outcomes, transforming the implicit alternative into an explicit one. More precisely, this fully unpacked measurement, which we denote by A'', now has the three outcomes A_{yy}'', A_{yn}'' and A_n'', and the associated states $p_{A_{yy}''}$, $p_{A_{yn}''}$ and $p_{A_n''}$, respectively, where $A_n'' = A_n$, $A_{yy}'' = A_y \wedge B_y$ and $A_{yn}'' = A_y \wedge B_n$. Thus, participants can now choose among three distinct possibilities, with probabilities $p_S(A_i'') = \mu(p_{A_i''}, e_{A''}, p_S)$, $i \in \{yy, yn, n\}$. Again, one speaks of superadditivity if $p_S(A_y) > p_S(A_{yy}'') + p_S(A_{yn}'')$ and of subadditivity if $p_S(A_y) < p_S(A_{yy}'') + p_S(A_{yn}'')$.

Since superadditivity and subadditivity are in general both possible, the usual quantum analysis exploits the interference effects as a way to explain, by means of a single mechanism, both possibilities, as interference terms can take both positive and negative values [27]. The assumption behind this approach is that participants act in a sequential way, all with the same order for the sequence. Accordingly, one associates the non-commuting projection operators P_i^A and P_j^B to the outcomes A_i and B_j, respectively, $i, j \in \{y, n\}$, so that one can write, for every $i \in \{y, n\}$, $P_i^A = P_y^B P_i^A P_y^B + P_n^B P_i^A P_n^B + I_i$, for every $i \in \{y, n\}$, where $P_n^B = \mathbb{I} - P_y^B$ and $I_i = P_y^B P_i^A P_n^B + P_n^B P_i^A P_y^B$ is the interference contribution, responsible of the superadditivity or subadditivity effects.

The above analysis, however, has some weak points. Firstly, the above projection operators do not commute, hence the order of evaluation in the sequence becomes important, and one needs to assume that all participants always start by answering first the question B and only then the question A. However, since this sequentiality is not part of the experimental protocol, nothing guarantees that it will be carried out in practice, instead of considering A_{yy}'' and A_{yn}'' as outcomes of a single non-sequential measurement. Secondly, it is incompatible with the natural interpretation of the packed and explicitly unpacked outcomes as belonging to two measurements that are logically related, in the sense that A can be understood as the degenerate version of the non-degenerate measurement A'' or, to put it another way, as a sub-measurement of A''.

Considering the packed measurement A and the associated explicitly unpacked measurement A'', the question is: How should we use the quantum formalism to model these experimental situations? In both measurements we have a cognitive entity in the same initial state p_S. We also have outcomes that are the same for both measurements, A_n and A_n'', which therefore should be associated with the same state, describing the same intersubjective reality. Then, we have outcomes that are described in a packed way in one measurement and in an explicitly unpacked way in the other – in our example the outcome A_y that is decomposed into the two alternatives A_{yy}'' and A_{yn}''.

If quantum theory is taken as a unitary and coherent framework, one should then be able to use the notion of 'degenerate measurement' (the quantum notion of sub-measurement) to model these two logically related experimental situations. Considering the previous example of the entity *The winner of next US presidential election*, it is clear that a 'non-Democrat' president is either a 'Republican' or an 'Independent,' and that 'Republican' and 'Independent' presidents are always 'non-Democrat' presidents. This means that the 'Republican' or the 'Independent' specification is an additional specification for the 'non-Democrat' state, and this means that when comparing an experimental situation where this specification is made, to a situation where it is not made, the latter should be considered as a sub-measurement of the former, i.e. a 'degenerate measurement' in the quantum jargon. Indeed, when the outcome is just 'Non-Democrat', the experimenter has no information about the 'Independent' or 'Republican' element, this being not specified in the outcome state. Also, since 'Republican' and 'Independent' are excluding possibilities, within the quantum formalism one should certainly describe them by two orthogonal subspaces, or two orthogonal states. Considering all this, one would thus expect to get: $p_S(A_y) = p_S(A''_{yy}) + p_S(A''_{yn})$ and $p_S(A_n) = p_S(A''_n)$.

However, since explicit unpacking effects are observed (which are generally stronger than the implicit ones), equalities like the above can be expected to be significantly violated, meaning that sub-measurements in psychology would not allow themselves to be consistently represented in the Hilbert space quantum formalism. Again, this can be attributed to the fact that the latter only admits a single 'way of choosing' the available outcomes, the 'Born way', whereas it is more natural to assume that the selection process can generally depend on the overall cognitive situation that is presented to the participants. Indeed, participants' propensity of choosing a given outcome certainly depends on the nature of the alternatives that are presented to them, and this is a contextuality effect that the quantum formalism is unable to describe. Yet, it can be represented in the GTR-model and its EBR implementation, by assuming that the probability distribution ρ_A characterizing the degenerate measurement A is not the same as the probability distribution $\rho_{A''}$ describing the corresponding non-degenerate versions A'', associated with an explicitly unpacked situation.

Concerning the implicitly unpacked case, one would also expect, if the standard quantum formalism applied, that $p_S(A_n) = p_S(A'_n)$, implying that $p_S(A_y) = p_S(A'_y)$. However, since the packed and implicitly unpacked measurements are dichotomic measurements, sharing the same state $p_{A_n} = p_{A'_n}$, if follows that the two states corresponding to the outcomes A_y and $A'_y = (A_y \wedge B_y) \oplus (A_y \wedge B_n)$ should also be equal, implying the equality of the associated transition probabilities. Thus, also in this case a Hilbert space quantum formalism cannot be used to model the data. In fact, even the EBR is too specific in this case, as it also relies on the Hilbert space structure for the representation of states (in the EBR, if two non-degenerate two-outcome measurements share an eigenstate, they necessarily also share the other one, as to each point on the 3-dimensional Bloch sphere there is only one corresponding antipodal point).

This is a situation where the more general GTR-model is required, as it allows one to describe two dichotomic measurements by means of two probability distributions defined on line segments that share one of their vertex points (corresponding to the outcome A_n), but not the other.

To conclude, we observe that in [28] the protocol was such that respondents were partitioned in four groups, each group responding one of the four different 'yes/no' alternatives for *The winner of the next US presidential election*: 'Non-Democrat', 'Independent rather than Republican or Democrat', 'Republican rather than Independent or Democrat' and 'Independent or Republican rather than Democrat'. In other words, they were actually performing a single measurement with five distinct outcomes. The experimental situation we have discussed is different, although of course related, and to apply the data to our analysis one should repeat the experiment by splitting it into three measurements: (A) one with outcomes 'non-Democrat' and 'Democrat'; (A') another one with outcomes 'Independent or Republican rather than a Democrat' and 'Democrat'; (A'') and a last one with outcomes 'Independent', 'Republican' and 'Democrat'.

References

1. Aerts, D.: Quantum structure in cognition. J. Math. Psychol. **53**, 314–348 (2009)
2. Khrennikov, A.: Ubiquitos Quantum Structure: From Psychology to Finance. Springer, New York (2010)
3. Busemeyer, J.R., Bruza, P.D.: Quantum Models of Cognition and Decision. Cambridge University Press, Cambridge (2012)
4. Aerts, D., Broekaert, J., Gabora, L., Sozzo, S.: Quantum structure and human thought. Behav. Brain Sci. **36**, 274–276 (2013)
5. Aerts, D., Gabora, L., Sozzo, S.: Concepts and their dynamics: a quantum-theoretic modeling of human thought. Topics Cognitive Sci. **5**, 737–772 (2013)
6. Blutner, R.: Questions and answers in an orthoalgebraic approach. J. Logic Lang. Inf. **21**, 237–277 (2012)
7. Pothos, E.M., Busemeyer, J.R.: Can quantum probability provide a new direction for cognitive modeling? Behav. Brain Sci. **36**, 255–274 (2013)
8. Haven, E., Khrennikov, A.: Quantum Social Science. Cambridge University Press, Cambridge (2013)
9. Wang, Z., Solloway, T., Shiffrin, R.M., Busemeyer, J.R.: Context effects produced by question orders reveal quantum nature of human judgments. Proc. Natl. Acad. Sci. **111**, 9431–9436 (2014)
10. Aerts, D., Sozzo, S., Veloz, T.: New fundamental evidence of non-classical structure in the combination of natural concepts. Philosophical Trans. Royal Soc. A **374**, 20150095 (2015)
11. Aerts, D., Sozzo, S., Veloz, T.: Quantum structure of negation and conjunction in human thought. Front. Psychol. (2015). doi:10.3389/fpsyg.2015.01447
12. Bruza, P.D., Wang, Z., Busemeyer, J.R.: Quantum cognition: a new theoretical approach to psychology. Trends Cognitive Sci. **19**, 383–393 (2015)
13. Khrennikov, A., Basieva, I., Dzhafarov, E.N., Busemeyer, J.R.: Quantum models for psychological measurements: an unsolved problem. PLoS ONE **9**, e110909 (2014)

14. Khrennikov, A., Basieva, I.: On the possibility to combine the order effects with sequential reproducibility for quantum measurements. Found. Phys. **45**, 1379–1393 (2015)
15. Boyer-Kassem, T., Duchêne, S., Guerci, E.: Testing quantum-like models of judgment for question order effect. Math. Soc. Sci. **80**, 33–46 (2016)
16. Boyer-Kassem, T., Duchêne, S., Guerci, E.: Quantum-like models cannot account for the conjunction fallacy. Theory Decis. (2016). doi:10.1007/s11238-016-9549-9
17. Aerts, D., Sassoli de Bianchi, M.: Beyond-quantum modeling of question order effects, response replicability in psychological measurements (2015). arXiv:1508.03686 [cs.AI]
18. Aerts, D., Sassoli de Bianchi, M., Sozzo, S.: On the foundations of the Brussels operational-realistic approach to cognition. Front. Phys. **4**, 17 (2015). doi:10.3389/fphy.2016.00017
19. Aerts, D., Aerts, S., Coecke, B., D'Hooghe, B., Durt, T., Valckenborgh, F.: A model with varying fluctuations in the measurement context. In: Ferrero, M., van der Merwe, A. (eds.) New Developments on Fundamental Problems in Quantum Physics. Fundamental Theories of Physics, vol. 81, pp. 7–9. Springer, Dordrecht (1997)
20. Aerts, D., de Bianchi, M.S.: The extended bloch representation of quantum mechanics and the hidden-measurement solution to the measurement problem. Ann. Phys. **351**, 975–1025 (2014)
21. Aerts, D., de Bianchi, M.S.: The unreasonable success of quantum probability I. Quantum measurements as uniform fluctuations. J. Math. Psychol. **67**, 51–75 (2015)
22. Aerts, D., de Bianchi, M.S.: The unreasonable success of quantum probability II. Quantum measurements as universal measurements. J. Math. Psychol. **67**, 76–90 (2015)
23. Sudman, S., Bradburn, N.M.: Response Effects in Surveys. Aldine, Chicago (1974)
24. Moore, D.W.: Measuring new types of question-order effects: additive and subtractive. Public Opin. Q. **66**, 80–91 (2002)
25. Aerts, D.: Foundations of quantum physics: a general realistic and operational approach. Int. J. Theor. Phys. **38**, 289–358 (1999)
26. Wang, Z., Busemeyer, J.R.: A quantum question order model supported by empirical tests of an a priori and precise prediction. Top. Cogn. Sci. **5**, 689–710 (2013)
27. Franco, R.: Judged probability, unpacking effect and quantum formalism. In: Bruza, P.D., et al. (eds.) AAAI-Fall 2010. Quantum Informatics for Cognitive, Social, and Semantic Processes, pp. 56–61. Springer, Berlin (2010)
28. Rottenstreich, Y., Tversky, A.: Unpacking, repacking, and anchoring: advances in support theory. Psychol. Rev. **104**, 406–415 (1997)

Toward a Gauge Theory of Musical Forces

Peter beim Graben[1(✉)] and Reinhard Blutner[2]

[1] Bernstein Center for Computational Neuroscience Berlin,
Humboldt-Universität zu Berlin, Berlin, Germany
peter.beim.graben@hu-berlin.de
[2] Emeritus ILLC, Universiteit van Amsterdam,
1090 Amsterdam, GE, The Netherlands

Abstract. How well does a given pitch fit into a tonal scale or key, being either a major or minor key? This question addresses the well-known phenomenon of tonal attraction in music psychology. Metaphorically, tonal attraction is often described in terms of attracting and repelling forces that are exerted upon a probe tone of a scale. In modern physics, forces are related to gauge fields expressing fundamental symmetries of a theory. In this study we address the intriguing relationship between musical symmetries and gauge forces in the framework of quantum cognition.

1 Introduction

The application of physical metaphors is quite common in theories of tonal music. The basic assumption seems to be that our experience of musical motion is in terms of our experience of physical motion and their underlying forces. For example, Schönberg speaks of different forces when he explains the direction of musical forces in cadences where the tonic attracts the dominant [23, p. 58]. In a similar vein, Larson [14] proposed three musical forces generating melodic completions, which he calls *gravity*, *inertia*, and *magnetism*, respectively. These forces should be regarded as conceptual metaphors in the sense of Lakoff and Johnson [12]. They structure musical cognition in analogy with falling, inert and attracting physical bodies. Physical forces are represented in our naive (common sense) physics or folk physics.

In contrast to Larson, Mazzola [18] suggested a quite different analogy between music theory and modern (non-folk) physics. Modern foundational physics describes forces as being caused by the "exchange" of particular particles. Forces are basically connected with certain symmetries of the physical microworld. Mazzola was probably the first who saw the analogy between physics and music in connection with the existence of musical symmetries, especially for the domain of modulation. Although Mazzola did not directly apply quantum theory for his theoretical models, he made use of a simplified framework for handling the underlying symmetries.

Mazzola's insights are of highest importance for the present paper, because "exchange particles" in the standard model of elementary particle theory emerge from the quantization of gauge fields mediating symmetry transformations

© Springer International Publishing AG 2017
J.A. de Barros et al. (Eds.): QI 2016, LNCS 10106, pp. 99–111, 2017.
DOI: 10.1007/978-3-319-52289-0_8

between localized quantum states. Therefore, we investigate the central problem of tonal attraction in terms of quantum symmetries and gauge fields. The term "tonal attraction" refers to the idea that melodic or voice-leading pitches tend toward other pitches in greater or lesser degrees. The present conception sees a close relationship between the phenomenon of tonal attraction and the existence of tonal forces. After a short discussion of the music-psychological phenomenon of tonal attraction in the next section, Sect. 3 provides a quantum-cognitive model based on a qubit representation of tones along the lines developed in [3]. In Sect. 4 we outline a gauge theory of musical forces, presenting first the force-free case as a default model which essentially reproduces the findings of the qubit model. Second, it is demonstrated how the introduction of local phase factors can improve the descriptive power of the model. Gauge forces can be regarded as correction terms that apply to the force-free (default) case. Section 5, finally derives some general conclusions and gives an outlook on future works, e.g. the possible relationship of gauge theory and brain wave models [21] similar to existing proposals by de Barros and Suppes [1], Large [13], and most recently Friston and coworkers [25].

2   The Phenomenon of Tonal Attraction

In the last twenty years, there has been an enormous progress in the development of cognitive theories of tonal music. A central issue has been the question of tonal attraction. How well does a given pitch fit into a tonal scale or tonal key, let it be a major or minor key? In a celebrated study, Krumhansl and Kessler [11] asked listeners to rate how well each note of the chromatic octave fitted with a preceding context, which consisted of short musical sequences in major or minor keys. This finding plays an essential role in Lerdahl's and Jackendoff's generative theory of tonal music [16] and is one of the main pillars of the structural approach in music theory.

For illustration, Fig. 1(a) depicts the C major scale arranged around the circle of fifths comprising 12 semitones within one octave. The tonic, indicated with "0", defines the origin of the chroma circle [9]. Open bullets are members of the C major (diatonic) scale, while black bullets do not belong to the scale. One can see from Fig. 1(a) that the whole chromatic scale is divided into two connected subparts: the diatonic part (open bullets) and the remaining (nondiatonic) part. The empirical results of Krumhansl and Kessler [11] are replicated in Fig. 1(b) for the C major context. The probe tones are represented as real numbers $x = j\pi/6$ ($j = 0, \ldots 12$, with C(0) $\cong$ C'(12) one octave higher) at the x-axis corresponding to the radian angles at the chroma circle Fig. 1(a). The subjective ratings $y(x)$ are plotted at the y-axis. The results of this experiment clearly show a kind of hierarchy: the tonic pitch $j = 0$ which is mostly attracting received the highest rating, followed by the pitches completing the tonic triad (third $j = 1$ and fifth $j = 4$), followed by the remaining scale degrees, and finally the chromatic, nonscale tones.

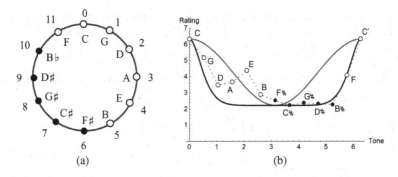

Fig. 1. Tonal attraction at the chroma circle. (a) The circle of fifths for C major scale as indicated by open bullets. (b) Rating data $y(x)$ of Krumhansl and Kessler [11] (dashed-bullets) and scaled quantum models of tonal attraction. Gray bold-solid: unmarked quantum model from Sect. 4.1 [Eq. (9)]. This model makes the same predictions as the qubit quantum model described in Sect. 3. Black bold-solid: marked quantum model from Sect. 4.2 [Eq. 11]. Obviously, the nondiatonic pitches (6–10 on the circle of fifth) are the pitches with the lowest attraction values as described by the traditional, hierarchic model.

3 Qubit Quantum Model of Tonal Attraction

One important model for the Krumhansl and Kessler [11] data was given by Lerdahl [15] and recently rephrased by Blutner [3] in terms of optimality theory [22]. In this framework, cognitive representations are described by several constraints that could either be satisfied of violated. The constraint violation profile of a construction accounts for its *markedness*. Unmarked constructions are generally easier to process in psychological experiments as is reflected by lower processing times and higher accuracies. On the other hand, marked constructions increase processing demands in terms of "mental energy" or "cognitive forces". Therefore it sounds reasonable to look for a similar relationship between tonal markedness in the sense of [3,15] and musical forces.

One of the fundamental ideas of quantum cognition is to apply the mathematics of the physical formalism to the domain of cognition. For example, we can use a series of qubit states to represent the 12 pitch classes used in tonal music. In addition, we can use the probability that one of these qubit state collapses into another one as a measure for the tonal attraction between the corresponding tones (see [3]).

For getting an explicit model of tonal states as states of a Hilbert space, the concept of symmetry is essential. Mathematically, symmetry is simply a set of transformations applied to given states such that the transformations preserve the properties of the states. In music, the most basic symmetry principle is the *principle of translation invariance*. It says that the musical quality of an episode is essentially unchanged if it is transposed into a different key. That means, the operations of the cyclic group $\mathbb{Z}_{12}$ are applied to the chroma circle from Fig. 1(a) [18]. Therefore, we can say that $\mathbb{Z}_{12}$ is the symmetry group of (Western) music.

More concretely, in the present case of tonal music, the underlying symmetry group could be represented by certain rotations of vectors in a two-dimensional vector space. For instance we can rotate the vector $\varphi_\rightarrow = \begin{pmatrix} 1 \\ 0 \end{pmatrix}$ in n steps to the original vector. In linear algebra, the elementary rotation steps can be described by the following rotation matrix γ:

$$\gamma = \begin{pmatrix} \cos \dfrac{2\pi}{n} & \sin \dfrac{2\pi}{n} \\ -\sin \dfrac{2\pi}{n} & \cos \dfrac{2\pi}{n} \end{pmatrix} \tag{1}$$

Performing a repeated application of the rotation matrix to our vector $\varphi_\rightarrow$ above, we can generate the 12 tones of the circle of fifth in the following way:

$$\psi_j = \gamma^j \begin{pmatrix} 1 \\ 0 \end{pmatrix} = \begin{pmatrix} \sin \dfrac{\pi j}{12} \\ \cos \dfrac{\pi j}{12} \end{pmatrix} \tag{2}$$

In the case of pure states, quantum theory defines structural probabilities. This means the probability that a state ψ collapses into another state depends exclusively on the geometric, structural properties of the considered states. How well does a given tone fit with the tonic pitch? What is the probability that it collapses into the (tonic) comparison state? The probability of a collapse of the state ψ_j into a state ψ_l can be calculated straightforwardly:

$$p_{\psi_l}(\psi_j) = \cos^2 \frac{\pi(j-l)}{12} = \frac{1}{2}\left[1 + \cos \frac{\pi(j-l)}{6}\right] \qquad \text{where } 0 \le j, l < 12 . \tag{3}$$

For a fixed element ψ_l the probabilities of the 12 tones indexed by $j (0 \le j < 12)$ sum up to one. Hence, formula (3) offers a probabilistic attraction profile relative to a given context tone ψ_l to which we refer to as a *kernel function*. If the context is not given as a single tone, but rather as a tonal region, a chord, or a series of chords, then we would consider the mixture of all the states conforming to all the involved single tonal elements. For simplicity, we could take all tones contributing to this mixture as being equivalent and give them the common weight $1/N$ (assuming N tonal elements are taken into account), thereby computing a density operator over different kernel functions [3]. This assumption is rather similar to Woolhouse's treatment of the problem of context effects in tonal attraction [26].

Figure 1(b) shows the attraction profile for the C major key as the kernel $p_{\psi_0}(\psi_j)$, obtained from the quantum model, and scales it to the Krumhansl and Kessler data [11] plotted in gray bold. Note that the quantum model is parameter-free. The correlation coefficient between the predicted profile and the Krumhansl-Kessler profile is $r = 0.7$ in the case of C major. That means that about 50 % of the variance is already explained by the default quantum kernel.

In order to permit the comparison with the symmetric model of Woolhouse [26], we fitted a kernel mixture, assuming symmetric phase parameters in the quantum model (i.e., the phases of the first seven tones of the circle of fifth are mirrored at the tritone point). The phase parameters were fitted as follows (starting from the tonic in the circle of fifth): $(0, \pi/2, \pi, 0, 0.9, 0, 0.99, 0, 0.9, 0, \pi, \pi/2, 0)$. In the present case of a symmetric kernel function, the correlation coefficient between the model fit and the Krumhansl-Kessler profile is $r = 0.82$ in the case of major keys. Moreover, an asymmetric distribution of phase angles improves the goodness of fit to $r = 0.95$ for major keys [3].

4   Gauge Theory of Tonal Attraction

In the following, we present an alternative treatment of tonal structures allowing the introduction of musical forces that is inspired by quantum gauge theory. In the last paragraph we have seen how the introduction of locally different phase factors could substantially improve the goodness of fit of the quantum model of tonal attraction. In modern physics, such phase functions lead naturally to the emergence of forces as frustrated connections of an underlying spatial structure.

In contrast to the qubit approach explained above, where a tone was represented by a state in the Hilbert space $\mathcal{H} = \mathbb{C}^2$ subjected to the cyclic group $\mathbb{Z}_{12}$ as symmetry, we strive here for a representation in terms of Schrödinger wave functions. A wave function is a state in a function Hilbert space $\mathcal{H} = L^2(\Omega)$ of complex-valued (square-integrable) functions $\psi : \Omega \to \mathbb{C}$ over a configuration space Ω. I.e., for a fixed "site" $x \in \Omega$, the value $\psi(x)$ belongs to a "local" Hilbert space $\mathcal{H}_x = \mathbb{C}$ attached to x. These local Hilbert spaces altogether form a "fiber bundle" over the configuration space Ω, which is the appropriate framework of gauge theory as required for the proper treatment of musical forces.

Our starting point is the chroma circle Fig. 1(a) representing tones as equivalence classes of pitches over one octave. This is essentially the continuum of the unit circle $S^1 = \mathbb{R} \pmod{2\pi}$ which contains the semitone cyclic group $\mathbb{Z}_{12}$ as a subgroup. A tone is then given through its radian angle $x = j\pi/6$ $(j = 0, \dots 12)$ as a spatial site of the unit circle. Therefore, the "tonal configuration space" of our quantum model will be taken as the chroma circle $\Omega = S^1$. A quantum state is then given as a wave function $\psi(x, t)$ that is dependent on tonal site $x \in S^1$ and time t solving the one-dimensional Schrödinger equation [24]

$$H\psi = \mathrm{i}\frac{\partial \psi}{\partial t} \tag{4}$$

with Hamilton operator H.[1] Finally, the complex value of a wave function $\psi(x, t)$ for fixed x, t will be regarded as a state in a local Hilbert space $\mathcal{H}_x = \mathbb{C}$ allowing for gauge transformations.

---

[1]   Note that we chose a natural unit system with particle's mass $m = 1/2$ and Planck's quantum of angular momentum $\hbar \equiv 1$ as necessary for quantum cognition applications.

4.1 Unmarked Behavior

In a first approximation for the unmarked behavior, we study the "movement" of a free particle with Hamiltonian

$$H = T = p^2$$

around the chroma circle. Here T denotes kinetic energy with $p = -i\partial/\partial x$ the momentum operator. Inserting the latter expressions into Eq. (4) yields

$$-\frac{\partial^2 \psi}{\partial x^2} = i\frac{\partial \psi}{\partial t} \tag{5}$$

which is solved by plane waves

$$\psi_k(x,t) = A_k e^{i(kx-\omega t)} \tag{6}$$

and their linear combinations, where A_k denote complex amplitudes. The wave number k and circular frequency ω depend on each other through the dispersion relation

$$\omega = k^2. \tag{7}$$

The final solution of the Schrödinger equation must obey the given initial and boundary conditions. As initial condition we may set $\psi(x_l, 0) = A$ for encoding the tonic of the context as a phase shift x_l with A as maximal attraction amplitude that is subjected to the normalization constraint

$$\int_\Omega |\psi(x,t)|^2 \, dx = 1.$$

Additionally we need Möbius-type periodic boundary conditions on the unit circle $\psi(x + 4\pi, t) = \psi(x, t)$ thus reflecting the double covering from Eq. (2). Therefore, the chroma circle exhibits the topology of a Möbius tape. Interestingly, Mazzola [18] has visionarily foreseen the putative relevance of these structures for mathematical music theory as well. Moreover, Möbius-type connectivities have been suggested as possible organizational principles of cortical structure and brain wave dynamics by Wright and coworkers [27,28]. The former yields the normalization $A = 1/(2\sqrt{\pi})$, while the latter gives a quantization constraint $e^{4\pi i k} = 1$, and hence $k \in \mathbb{Z}/2$. Choosing the two fundamental wave numbers $k = \pm 1/2$ yields $\omega = 1/4$ and $A_k = Ae^{-ikx_l}$. Finally, the superposition of fundamental solutions entails

$$\psi(x,t) = \frac{1}{\sqrt{\pi}} e^{-i\frac{t}{4}} \cos\frac{x - x_l}{2} \tag{8}$$

which is a standing wave along the unit circle with probability density

$$p(x) = |\psi(x,t)|^2 = \frac{1}{\pi} \cos^2\frac{x - x_l}{2}. \tag{9}$$

Inserting the semitones $x_j = j\pi/6$ around the circle of fifths for x, confirms the previous result obtained from the qubit quantum model [3] (Sect. 3).

$$p_j(x_l) = |\psi(x_j, t)|^2 = \frac{1}{\pi} \cos^2 \frac{\pi(j-l)}{12}. \tag{10}$$

This default distribution kernel characterizes *unmarked* music cognition and is plotted in gray bold after scaling in Fig. 1(b). The correlation with the Krumhansl-Kessler data [11] is $r = 0.7$ as reported above.

4.2   Marked Behavior

In order to understand marked behavior as well, we have to develop a theory of musical forces that complements the metaphoric notions of Larson [14] and Mazzola [18]. To that aim, we first realize that the distribution (10) simply reflects the similarity relations between tones along the chroma circle where C, G, and F are close neighbors and hence similar with respect to their attraction profiles, whereas C and the tritone F♯ are maximally distant and thus unrelated [Fig. 1(a)]. A suitable deformation of the distances along the chroma circle could lead to an improved description of the empirical data presented in Fig. 1(b). Therefore, we make the ansatz

$$\psi(x) = A \cos(\gamma(x)) \tag{11}$$

for the stationary wave function where $\gamma(x)$ is a spatial deformation function and A a normalization constant. For the sake of simplicity, we focus on the C major scale with $x_l = 0$ here. Differentiating (11) twice and eliminating trigonometric terms, we obtain the differential equation

$$-\psi''(x) + \frac{\gamma''(x)}{\gamma'(x)} \psi'(x) - \gamma'(x)^2 \psi(x) = 0 \tag{12}$$

which we compare with the stationary Schrödinger equation $H\psi(x) = E\psi(x)$ for the energy eigenvalue E. With

$$H = T + M + U$$

this comparison yields the following operators: The first term T is, as usual, the operator of kinetic energy

$$T = -\frac{\partial^2}{\partial x^2}.$$

The second term could be interpreted in the context of electromagnetism where the velocity-dependent contribution to the Hamilton operator is regarded as magnetic interaction energy

$$M = \frac{\gamma''(x)}{\gamma'(x)} \frac{\partial}{\partial x}$$

Finally, the last term, which is simply a scalar multiplication operator, receives its usual interpretation as potential energy

$$U = E - \gamma'(x)^2$$

which might be seen either as electrostatic or gravitational potential. Note that the constant

$$E = \gamma'(0)^2 \tag{13}$$

can be interpreted as the total energy of the tonal dynamics.

The marked Schrödinger equation obeys conservation of energy, as unveiled by multiplication with the adjoint solution ψ^* from the left. Introducing energy densities

$$t(x) = -\psi(x)^* \psi''(x) \tag{14}$$

$$m(x) = \psi(x)^* \frac{\gamma''(x)}{\gamma'(x)} \psi'(x) \tag{15}$$

$$u(x) = \psi(x)^* (E - \gamma'(x)^2) \psi(x) \tag{16}$$

yields

$$t(x) + m(x) + u(x) = E\psi(x)^* \psi(x) = Ep(x)$$

with $p(x) = |\psi(x)|^2$ the resulting probability distribution. Interestingly, this distribution describes the original Krumhansl-Kessler data [11] which therefore receive a straightforward interpretation as *total energy density* of tonal attraction.

From the general deformation ansatz Eq. (11) for the marked case we retain the unmarked wave function by the choice

$$\gamma_u(x) = \frac{x}{2}$$

rendering the force-free dynamics with $U(x) = E - \gamma_u'(x)^2 = E - 1/4$, i.e. $U = 0$ and $E = \omega = 1/4$. For the marked attraction profile we assume a symmetric polynomial of fourth order

$$\gamma_m(x) = a_0 + a_4(x - \pi)^4,$$

with boundary conditions $\gamma(0) = 0$, i.e. the tonic should not be deformed, and $\gamma(\pi) = \pi/2$, i.e. the tritone receives maximal deformation. This leads to the parameter-free model

$$\gamma_m(x) = \frac{\pi}{2} - \frac{(x - \pi)^4}{2\pi^3}. \tag{17}$$

Interestingly, the terms higher than linear order can be interpreted as spatially dependent phase shifts of the unmarked wave function which depends on the linear term only. From (17) we obtain the total energy (13) as $E = 4$ which is sixteen times larger than the energy required to the unmarked dynamics.

Inserting the deformation (17) into the wave function (11), yields the marked attraction kernel for the tonic context, plotted as the bold black curve

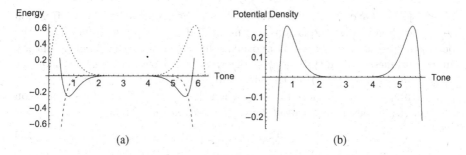

Fig. 2. Emergent energies of tonal attraction. (a) Energy densities: Solid: "inertia" $i(x)$, dashed: "gravity" $u(x)$, dotted: "magnetism" $m(x)$. (b) Density of potential energies $d(x)$ [Eq. (18)].

in Fig. 1(b). The correlation with the Krumhansl-Kessler data [11] is $r = 0.89$, i.e. our fit accounts now for 79% of the data's variance. Computing the mixture over the C major tonic triad context, improves the fit to $r = 0.97$, covering 95% of the data.

Finally, we compute the three energy densities (14–16) and also the density of potential energy alone

$$d(x) = m(x) + u(x). \tag{18}$$

The results are presented in Fig. 2.

Figure 2(a) shows the three densities "inertia" (solid), "gravity" (dashed), and "magnetism" (dotted). Both, "inertia" and "gravity" clearly indicate that the tonic at $x = 0 \pmod{2\pi}$ acts as a center of gravity, where the gravitation potential (16) approaches minus infinity while the kinetic energy (14) tends toward plus infinity. Therefore, the gravitational force which is the negative gradient of the potential is negative in the tonic's vicinity, i.e. the tonic is attracting, leading to high acceleration (14). The tonic is also attracting with respect to the "magnetic" force (15) which also has positive slope for small x-values. However, for tones in the interval $0.4 < x < 5.8$, corresponding to G – F, "magnetism" prevents tones from being attracted by the tonic. This makes the tritone F♯ a "magnetic trap" in this region.

Even more instructive is Fig. 2(b) depicting the summed potential energy density. Here again, the tonic appears as a center of force. Extrema of the potential $d(x)$ are equilibrium points which are either unstable for local maxima or stable for local minima. On the one hand, there are two unstable equilibria around $x = 0.8$ (D) and $x = 5.4$ (B♭). On the other hand, the only equilibrium at $x = \pi$ is stable, which is precisely the tritone. Because the total energy density is low in this region, tones are trapped by the tritone.

4.3   Gauge Invariance

Finally, we have to prove the local gauge invariance of our music quantum model. To that aim, we first realize that the probabilities $p(x)$ do not change under a shift of the wave functions's phases. Let ψ be an arbitrary wave function solving the Schrödinger equation (4) and $\varphi \in \mathbb{R}$ a real phase value. Then the operation $\psi \mapsto \tilde{\psi} = e^{i\varphi}\psi$ yields another solution of the Schrödinger equation simply obtained by multiplying Eq. (4) with $e^{i\varphi}$. However, this *global gauge transformation* does not affect the observable probabilities $\tilde{p} = |\tilde{\psi}|^2 = p$.

Yet, things get much more involved when the phase shift becomes a function of space,[2] $\varphi(x)$, describing a *local gauge transformation*. Writing

$$\tilde{\psi}(x) = e^{i\varphi(x)}\psi(x) \tag{19}$$

we have to take the spatial derivatives in (12)

$$\frac{\partial \tilde{\psi}}{\partial x} = i\frac{\partial \varphi}{\partial x}e^{i\varphi}\psi + e^{i\varphi}\frac{\partial \psi}{\partial x} = e^{i\varphi}\left(\frac{\partial}{\partial x} + i\frac{\partial \varphi}{\partial x}\right)\psi.$$

Repetition of the derivation yields the Laplacean

$$\frac{\partial^2 \tilde{\psi}}{\partial x^2} = \frac{\partial}{\partial x}\left[e^{i\varphi}\left(\frac{\partial}{\partial x} + i\frac{\partial \varphi}{\partial x}\right)\psi\right] = e^{i\varphi}\left(\frac{\partial}{\partial x} + i\frac{\partial \varphi}{\partial x}\right)^2\psi.$$

For the operator appearing in round brackets we introduce the notation

$$D_x = \frac{\partial}{\partial x} + i\frac{\partial \varphi}{\partial x} \tag{20}$$

which is called *covariant derivative*, thereby alluding to the curved space of general relativity which was the historically first formulated *local gauge theory*. The gradient of the phase function $\varphi(x)$ is called the *gauge field* in this connection.

The Schrödinger equation (12) is called *locally gauge invariant*, if the transformed wave function obeys a structurally equivalent equation with transformed coefficients

$$-\tilde{\psi}''(x) + \frac{\tilde{\gamma}''(x)}{\tilde{\gamma}'(x)}\tilde{\psi}'(x) - \tilde{\gamma}'(x)^2\tilde{\psi}(x) = 0. \tag{21}$$

Using covariant derivatives instead of the conventional ones (which emerge as limiting cases for $\varphi = $ constant) yields

$$-D_x^2\psi(x) + \frac{\tilde{\gamma}''(x)}{\tilde{\gamma}'(x)}D_x\psi(x) - \tilde{\gamma}'(x)^2\psi(x) = 0,$$

which gives after some rearrangements

$$-\psi''(x) + \left(\frac{\tilde{\gamma}''(x)}{\tilde{\gamma}'(x)} - 2i\varphi'(x)\right)\psi'(x) - \left[\tilde{\gamma}'(x)^2 - \varphi'(x)^2 + i\left(\varphi''(x) - \frac{\tilde{\gamma}''(x)}{\tilde{\gamma}'(x)}\varphi'(x)\right)\right]\psi(x) = 0.$$

This expression is invariant under the constraints

$$\frac{\tilde{\gamma}''(x)}{\tilde{\gamma}'(x)} - 2i\varphi'(x) = \frac{\gamma''(x)}{\gamma'(x)} \tag{22}$$

$$\tilde{\gamma}'(x)^2 - \varphi'(x)^2 = \gamma'(x)^2 \tag{23}$$

$$\varphi''(x) = \frac{\tilde{\gamma}''(x)}{\tilde{\gamma}'(x)}\varphi'(x), \tag{24}$$

---

[2] For the sake of simplicity, we neglect time-dependence of the gauge field in our exposition.

which restrict the freedom of choice for the local phase function $\varphi(x)$. Thus, our musical gauge theory has a broken symmetry that is not the full U(1) symmetry of quantum electrodynamics.

5 Discussion and Outlook

In this study we have discussed the phenomenon of tonal attraction in a quantum cognition framework. After reviewing a previous approach based on a qubit representation of the essential musical symmetry group [3], we formulated an alternative description in terms of wave functions. Solving the Schrödinger equation of a "free particle" over the circle of fifths as musical configuration space, we were able to reproduce the results of the unmarked qubit quantum model for the experimental findings of Krumhansl and Kessler [11]. In a second step we addressed the important issue of gauge symmetry of the Schrödinger equation and derived three expressions for musical forces which might be related to similar concepts discussed in the literature [14,23]. The introduction of gauge forces led to a spatial deformation of the circle of fifths that we approximated by a polynomial of fourth order, for which we could explicitly derive the musical forces of tonal attraction of the marked quantum model, in good agreement with the Krumhansl and Kessler data.

Sofar, our approach accounts for the effect of "static forces" which determine the center(s) of a series of tones or chords by means of stationary wave functions. Yet, there are also "dynamic forces" affecting melodic or harmonic progression and predictability, investigated, e.g. in [10]. The most interesting dynamical aspect of music theory is, notably, modulation, the dynamic transition from one scale or key into another one. Inspired by Schönberg's modulation theory [23], Mazzola [18] developed a sophisticated mathematical account based on musical symmetries and cadences. Its most important ingredient is, what he calls the "modulation quantum", a collection of chords mediating the dynamic transition from one key into another. It will be a challenging endeavor to further develop our gauge theory of musical forces into these fascinating directions.

In the recent literature of explaining tonal attraction, the spectral pitch class model [20] plays an essential role. In this model, the pitch perception of any musical sound is described by using spectral pitch class vectors. There are close similarities between this Helmholtzian model [8] and the present quantum approach which should be pursued in a later publication. At this point we only note that Schrödinger's idea of "quantization as eigenvalue problem" [24] was crucially influenced by Helmholtz' idea of oscillating strings.

Next, let us speculate about the putative relevance of our approach in the neurosciences. Partial differential equations are well-known in the discipline of neural field [5] and dynamic neural field theory [7,17] within computational neuroscience where they appear as brain wave equations [5,21]. In the latter, fields are regarded as functions over *abstract feature spaces* and we might consider the chroma circle in our approach as such a feature space. These neural fields are clearly real-valued functions in contrast to the generically complex wave functions solving the Schrödinger equation. However, according to Bohm [4], the Schrödinger equation for one complex field is equivalent to two coupled real fields describing the motion of a classical particle in a "quantum mechanical potential" and its respective field dynamics. In quantum theory this leads to disputably nonlocal representations. Yet in neural field theory, nonlocal interactions are ubiquitous due to long-range synaptic connectivity. Thus, our gauge theory of musical forces may find its neurophysiological counterparts in the organization of cortical areas [25, 28].

Finally, let us remark on the relationship between the process of musical perception and the musical composition process. A very naive understanding of the composition process is that it is nothing else than looking for the most probable continuation of a starting sequence of tones. Of course, this is simply to realize with the help of neural networks (e.g. [2]). A composer normally aims to generate emotions in the mind of the listener. Emotions are deeply connected with subjective expectancy [19]. However, it is crucially surprise that generates great musical effects. Hence, the process of composition cannot be described as a mechanism for finding the most probable continuation. If one insists to view the process of composing as an optimization algorithm, then one has to considering higher rules of optimization. These rules are directed to resolving conflicting aims in following particular emotional goals, optimally separating different voices and, at the same time, pursuing certain restrictions of a particular style.

References

1. de Barros, J.A., Suppes, P.: Quantum mechanics, interference, and the brain. J. Math. Psychol. **53**(5), 306–313 (2009)
2. Blutner, R.: Nonmonotonic inferences and neural networks. Synthese **142**(2), 143–174 (2004)
3. Blutner, R.: Modelling tonal attraction: tonal hierarchies, interval cycles, and quantum probabilities. Soft Comput., 1–19 (2015). doi:10.1007/s00500-015-1801-7
4. Bohm, D.: A suggested interpretation of the quantum theory in terms of "hidden" variables. I. Phys. Rev. **85**, 166–179 (1952)
5. Coombes, S., beim Graben, P.: Potthast: tutorial on neural field theory. In: Coombes et al. [6], pp. 1–43
6. Coombes, S., beim Graben, P., Potthast, R., Wright, J. (eds.): Neural Fields: Theory and Applications. Springer, Heidelberg (2014)
7. beim Graben, P., Potthast, R.: Universal neural field computation. In: Coombes et al. [6], pp. 299–318
8. von Helmholtz, H.: On the Sensations of Tones. Dover, New York (1877). Translated by Ellis, A.J
9. Krumhansl, C.L.: The psychological representation of musical pitch in a tonal context. Cogn. Psychol. **11**(3), 346–374 (1979)
10. Krumhansl, C.L.: Music psychology and music theory: problems and prospects. Music Theor. Spectr. **17**(1), 53–80 (1995)
11. Krumhansl, C.L., Kessler, E.J.: Tracing the dynamic changes in perceived tonal organization in a spatial representation of musical keys. Psychol. Rev. **89**(4), 334 (1982)

12. Lakoff, G., Johnson, M.: Metaphors We Live By. University of Chicago Press, Chicago (1980)
13. Large, E.W.: A dynamical systems approach to musical tonality. In: Huys, R., Jirsa, V.K. (eds.) Nonlinear Dynamics in Human Behavior. Studies in Computational Intelligence, pp. 193–211. Springer, Heidelberg (2011)
14. Larson, S.: Musical Forces: Motion, Metaphor, and Meaning in Music. Indiana University Press, Bloomington (2012)
15. Lerdahl, F.: Tonal pitch space. Music Perception **5**, 315–350 (1988)
16. Lerdahl, F., Jackendoff, R.: A Generative Theory of Tonal Music. MIT Press, Cambridge (1983)
17. Lins, J., Schöner, G.: A neural approach to cognition based on dynamic field theory. In: Coombes, S., beim Graben, P., Potthast, R., Wright, J. (eds.) Neural Fields: Theory and Applications, pp. 319–339. Springer, Heidelberg (2014)
18. Mazzola, G.: Geometrie der Töne. Birkhäuser, Basel (1990)
19. Meyer, L.B.: Emotions and Meaning in Music. Chicago University Press, Chicago (1956)
20. Milne, A.J., Laney, R., Sharp, D.B.: A spectral pitch class model of the probe tone data and scalic tonality. Music Percept. **32**(4), 364–393 (2015)
21. Nunez, P.L.: The brain wave equation: a model for the EEG. Mathematical Biosciences **21**(3–4), 279–297 (1974)
22. Prince, A., Smolensky, P.: Optimality: from neural networks to universal grammar. Science **275**, 1604–1610 (1997)
23. Schönberg, A.: Harmonielehre. Verlagsanstalt Paul Gerin, Wien (1911), translated by R. E. Carter as: Theory of Harmony. University of California Press, Berkeley (1978)
24. Schrödinger, E.: Quantisierung als Eigenwertproblem - Erste Mitteilung. Annalen der Physik **79**, 361–376 (1926)
25. Sengupta, B., Tozzi, A., Cooray, G.K., Douglas, P.K., Friston, K.J.: Towards a neuronal gauge theory. PLoS Biol. **14**(3), 1–12 (2016)
26. Woolhouse, M.: Modelling tonal attraction between adjacent musical elements. J. New Music Res. **38**(4), 357–379 (2009)
27. Wright, J.J.: Attractor dynamics and thermodynamic analogies in the cerebral cortex: synchronous oscillation, the background EEG, and the regulation of attention. Bull. Math. Biol. **73**, 436–457 (2011)
28. Wright, J.J., Alexander, D.M., Bourke, P.D.: Contribution of lateral interactions in V1 to organization of response properties. Vis. Res. **46**, 2703–2720 (2006)

Language and Applications

Quantum Bootstrap Aggregation

David Windridge[(✉)] and Rajagopal Nagarajan

Department of Computer Science, School of Science and Technology,
Middlesex University, London NW4 4BT, UK
{d.windridge,r.nagarajan}@mdx.ac.uk

Abstract. We set out a strategy for quantizing attribute bootstrap aggregation to enable variance-resilient quantum machine learning. To do so, we utilise the linear decomposability of decision boundary parameters in the Rebentrost *et al.* Support Vector Machine to guarantee that stochastic measurement of the output quantum state will give rise to an ensemble decision without destroying the superposition over projective feature subsets induced within the chosen SVM implementation. We achieve a linear performance advantage, $O(d)$, in addition to the existing $O(log(n))$ advantages of quantization as applied to Support Vector Machines. The approach extends to any form of quantum learning giving rise to linear decision boundaries.

1 Introduction

Quantum Machine Learning is a recent area of research initiated by the demonstration of a quantum Support Vector Machine (SVM) by Rebentrost, Mohseni & Lloyd [1] and the k-means algorithm by Aïmeur, Brassard & Gambs [2] (cf also [3–8]). The development of the quantum SVM can be regarded as particularly significant in that the classical SVM constitutes perhaps the exemplar instance of a *supervised binary classifier*, i.e. an entity capable of learning an optimal discriminative decision hyperplane from labeled vectors $\{(\boldsymbol{x}, y) \mid \boldsymbol{x} \in \tilde{X}, \ y \in \{-1, +1\}\}$ existing within a feature space.

Bootstrap Aggregation ('Bagging') is a well established method within stochastic machine learning for removing variance from classifiers via the production of bootstrap ensembles to refine the final decision accuracy. It shall be the argument of this paper that this decision ensemble can be equivalently represented via a quantum superposition, such that the final decision can be straightforwardly obtained via quantum measurement. Moreover, we shall demonstrate that this is necessarily more economic in both execution time and the total number of logic gates required in comparison to classical (and even parallelized quantum) SVM implementations.

2 Methodological Background

The Classical SVM. The standard SVM [9] seeks to maximize the margin (*i.e.*, the distance of the decision hyperplane to the nearest data point), subject to a constraint on the classification accuracy of the labelling induced by

J.A. de Barros et al. (Eds.): QI 2016, LNCS 10106, pp. 115–121, 2017.
DOI: 10.1007/978-3-319-52289-0_9

the hyperplane's delineation of a general decision boundary. In its primal form, the soft margin SVM optimization takes the form of a Lagrange optimization problem:

$$\arg\min_{(\boldsymbol{w},b)} \left\{ \frac{1}{2}\|\boldsymbol{w}\|^2 + C\sum_{i=1}^{M}\xi_i \right\} \quad \text{subject to:} \quad \forall_i\, y_i(\boldsymbol{w}\cdot\boldsymbol{x_i}-b) \geq 1-\xi_i,\ \xi_i \geq 0$$

where $(\boldsymbol{x_i}, y_i)$ $i = 1\ldots M$ are the training vectors/labels, $y_i \in \{-1, +1\}$, $\boldsymbol{w}$ is the weight orientation vector of the decision hyperplane, and b is its bias offset. (The margin is inversely proportional to $\|\boldsymbol{w}\|$). The ξ_i are slack variables that give rise to the soft margin with sensitivity controlled by hyper-parameter C.

In the dual form [9], the slack parameters disappear such that the problem is solved in terms of the Karush–Kuhn–Tucker (KKT) multipliers α_i:

$$\arg\max_{(\alpha_i)} \sum_{i=1}^{n}\alpha_i - \frac{1}{2}\sum_{i,j}\alpha_i\alpha_j y_i y_j(\boldsymbol{x}_i^T\boldsymbol{x}_j) \quad \text{subject to:} \sum \alpha_i y_i = 0 : \forall_i\, 0 \leq \alpha_i \leq C$$

The problem is one of quadratic programming. As the optimization proceeds, only a sparse set of the α_s's retain non-zero values. These denote the support vectors defining the decision hyperplane. This sparsity (i.e. the low parametric complexity of the decision boundary with respect to the training data) gives the SVM substantial resilience to over-fitting (and thus reduces classifier variance).

Notably, the term $(\boldsymbol{x}_i^T\boldsymbol{x}_j)$ in the above (equating to the training vector Gram matrix) may be freely replaced by any kernel function $K(\boldsymbol{x_i}, \boldsymbol{x_j})$ that satisfies Mercer's condition (i.e. positive semi-definiteness). This vastly extends the utility of the SVM by enabling the mapping of the input decision space into a large variety of alternative Hilbert spaces of potentially infinite dimensionality (thus guaranteeing linear separability). The decision boundary in the input space may thus undergo significant morphology variation while crucially retaining the low parametric support-vector characterization of the decision boundary within the Mercer embedding space (the space denoted $\phi(\boldsymbol{x})$ for which $K(\boldsymbol{x_i}, \boldsymbol{x_j}) \equiv \phi(\boldsymbol{x_i})^T(\phi(\boldsymbol{x_j}))$. Critically, at no stage are we required to compute $\phi(\boldsymbol{x_i})$). The KKT conditions guarantee the existence of ϕ, but the kernel itself may be calculated based on any similarity function that gives rise to a kernel matrix obeying Mercer's condition.

The Quantum SVM. The quantum SVM implementation proposed by Rebentrost, Mohseni and Lloyd [1] uses a least square reimplementation of the classic kernelized SVM so as to implicate the efficient quantum matrix inversion of Harrow, Hassidim & Lloyd [10]. The problem to be solved now becomes:

$$F\begin{pmatrix} b \\ \alpha \end{pmatrix} \doteq \begin{pmatrix} 0 & \mathbf{1}^T \\ \mathbf{1} & K+\gamma^{-1}I \end{pmatrix}\begin{pmatrix} b \\ \alpha \end{pmatrix} = \begin{pmatrix} 0 \\ y \end{pmatrix} \quad \mathbf{1}^T \equiv (1,1,1\ldots)^T \tag{1}$$

where K is the kernel matrix (i.e. a permissible generalization of the Gram matrix satisfying Mercer's condition), γ^{-1} is the trade-off parameter between the SVM optimization and accuracy. Training object classifications are denoted by the vector $y \in ([-1, 1]^M)^T$ for the M training objects order-correlated with the kernel matrix K (training object vectors x_k are represented in their own basis). Finally, α and b (the object of the optimization) are respectively the weight and bias offset parameters of the decision hyperplane within the Mercer embedding space induced by the kernel (though note that here the alpha represent distances from the margin).

Consequently, quantum matrix inversion of F solves for the SVM parameters α, b, producing the solution state:

$$|\alpha, \beta\rangle = \frac{1}{b^2 + \sum_{k=1}^{M} \alpha_k^2} \left(b |0\rangle + \sum_{k=1}^{M} \alpha_k |k\rangle \right) \qquad (2)$$

Utilization of these parameters for classification of novel data requires the implementation of a *query oracle* implicating all of the labeled data:

$$|\tilde{u}\rangle = \frac{1}{\left(b^2 + \sum_{k=1}^{M} \alpha_k^2 |x_k|^2 \right)^{\frac{1}{2}}} \left(b |0\rangle |0\rangle + \sum_{k=1}^{M} |x_k| \, \alpha_k \, |k\rangle \, |x_k\rangle \right) \qquad (3)$$

and also the query state:

$$|\tilde{x}\rangle = \frac{1}{M |x|^2 + 1} \left(|0\rangle |0\rangle + \sum_{k=1}^{M} |x_k| \, |k\rangle \, |x_k\rangle \right) \qquad (4)$$

($|k\rangle$ is thus an index state over training vectors)

The classification is then carried out as the inner product of the two states, i.e. by performing a swap test and allocating class labels on the basis of the inner product probability being greater or less than $\frac{1}{2}$ (the swap test is performed via the use of an ancilla to construct the state $\frac{1}{\sqrt{2}}(|0\rangle |\tilde{u}\rangle + |1\rangle |\tilde{x}\rangle)$ which is then measured in the basis $\frac{1}{\sqrt{2}}(|0\rangle - |1\rangle)$).

Bootstrap Aggregation and Attribute Bootstrap Aggregation. Standard bootstrap aggregation is an effective approach for stabilizing unstable classifiers such as decision trees and neural networks [11]. It consists in randomly sampling, with replacement, d groups from the total set of training samples M, training the resulting classifiers and combining the output either via decision fusion (such as majority voting) or averaging in the case of regression-like classifiers. Each set can be expected to have $M(1 - e^{-m/M})$ unique training vectors on average for draw size m.

It may be shown, via bias/variance analysis [12], that bagging can be considered primarily as a method for reducing variance with respect to training-set permutation/sampling. It is therefore be employed predominantly on low-bias classifiers, since classifiers must necessarily trade-off variance against bias in their design (bias is in this sense the expected discrepancy from Bayes optimality).

Bootstrap aggregation is therefore notably less effective for an idealized SVM (or in completely linearly separable problems) owing to the intrinsic variance-resilience implied in the definition of the maximum margin SVM classifier in terms of the support objects -i.e. those objects for which, in which the dual form of SVM optimization problem, the Lagrangian multipliers are non-zero [9]. Typically, these are highly sparse, and therefore training set sub-sample permutation has no effect unless explicitly excluding these objects.

There are, however, techniques for artificially adjusting bias/variance within SVMs. The parameter γ^{-1} above dictates the trade off between data fitting and maximization of the margin. Favoring the former should therefore reduce the bias. An alternative strategy for bias reduction applicable to the quantum SVM applies when considering the polynomial kernel: $K(\boldsymbol{x}_j, \boldsymbol{x}_k) = (\boldsymbol{x}_j \cdot \boldsymbol{x}_k)^D \equiv \phi(\boldsymbol{x}_j) \cdot \phi(\boldsymbol{x}_k)$. Here, D can control bias via the relationship between polynomial degree and functional localization.

The most generally effective strategy for bootstrap aggregation, however, utilizes feature subspaces (referred to as either 'attribute bagging' or the 'random subspace method (RSM)'). Here, it is the selection of the features for classification that constitutes the bootstrap set. Subspace remapping is, however, also a natural quantum operation (implemented by projectors). Thus, if the set of training vectors $\boldsymbol{x}_k$ are represented within an orthonormal Hilbert basis, we are implicitly concerned with the projectors $\{\,|\mathcal{P}_1\rangle\langle\mathcal{P}_1|\,,\,|\mathcal{P}_2\rangle\langle\mathcal{P}_2|\,,\ldots\}$ in carrying out subspace selection within a quantum context, where the $\mathcal{P}_i$ are Hilbert space vectors with spans corresponding to the feature subsets P_i. We will thus utilize this approach in the following to define distinct set of classifiers constituting the ensemble.

Critically, from the point of view of efficiently quantizing attribute bagging, we do not require individual classifier decisions to be identified as such within the final ensemble decision: in effect, the collective classifier acts as a single composite classifier. In quantum terms, this implies that classifiers are able to exist as a superposition without individual measurement prior to the final decision output.

3   Proposed Attribute Bootstrap Aggregation Method

The standard attribute bootstrap aggregation algorithm proceeds as follows: for M training objects with N features, we individually train S classifiers on the respective feature sets $d_s = \{d_s \subset N\,|\ \,|d_s|\ < N\}$, either with or without replacement. To classify test objects, we combine the S classifier outputs by e.g. majority vote or summation over posterior probabilities.

In the following quantum implementation of attribute bootstrap aggregation our objective will thus be to set up a quantum superposition of classifier decision hyperplanes associated with each attribute selection. This will give rise to an ensemble sum over decisions for which it may be demonstrated that a collective measurement is sufficient for ensemble classification (we are thus implicitly opting for the 'summation over posterior probability' form of attribute bootstrap aggregation.)

We initialize our approach by selecting a total of S random selections, p_s, from N features, either with or without replacement, such that $p_s \in \{0,1\}^N$. p_s is hence a characteristic function indexing basis states $|k\rangle$. For each projector indexed by s we can thus train an SVM: $F_s^{-1}\left(\phi(P_s x_j)^T \phi(P_s x_k), y\right)$ where P_s is the projection matrix corresponding to p_s (i.e. P_s is the diagonal matrix having the binary values of p_s on its leading diagonal; $P_s\{i,j\} = 0$ if $i \neq j$, $P_s\{i,i\} = p_s(i) \; \forall i,j \in \{1,2,\ldots,N\}$).

In quantum terms, this means that we can construct a solution state superposition over training vector basis states in order to construct the query oracle (Note that the bootstrap sets occupy the full training vector Hilbert space, irrespective of the differential subspace dimensionalities, so that we are free to form a superposition over projected vectors; thus we do not consider explicit sums over projectors, $\sum_{s=1}^{S} |\mathcal{P}_s\rangle\langle\mathcal{P}_s|$, or density operators, such as would be implicit in a statistical ensemble approach).

Hence, (setting ϕ to the identity for convenience) we can construct the quantum state:

$$|\tilde{u_B}\rangle = \frac{1}{S^{\frac{1}{2}}} \sum_{s=1}^{S} |\alpha_s, \beta_s\rangle \equiv \mathcal{N} \sum_{s=1}^{S} \left(b_s |0\rangle |0\rangle + \sum_{k=1}^{M} |P_s x_k |\alpha_{(k,s)}|k\rangle |\mathcal{P}_s\rangle\langle\mathcal{P}_s| |x_k\rangle \right)$$

$$\text{where} \quad \mathcal{N} = \frac{1}{\left(\sum_{s=1}^{S} b_s^2 + \sum_{k=1}^{M} \alpha_{(k,s)}^2 |P_s x_k|^2\right)^{\frac{1}{2}}}$$

(implicitly obtaining the quantum speed up for each SVM implementation within the superposition).

A key point to note is that the set of $\alpha_{(k,s)}$'s for some arbitrary S acts over all of the M training vectors in order to define the decision hyperplane (in contrast to the Lagrange dual SVM formulation), each defining a distance from the optimal margin. As such, the set $\{\alpha_{(k,s)}\}$ defines a unique subspace of dimensionality $|p_s| - 1$ within the subspace subtended by the $\{P_s x_k\}$ (i.e. the decision hyperplane), where $|p_s|$ here indicates the Hamming weight. However, the *same* $\{\alpha_{(k,s)}\}$ also define a unique subspace of dimensionality $N - 1$ within X, namely the direct product of the decision hyperplane with the null space of P_s. We may therefore, (in constructing the solution state only, and absolutely not the SVM matrix inversion) treat $|\mathcal{P}_s\rangle\langle\mathcal{P}_s| |x_k\rangle$ and $|x_k\rangle$ equivalently with regard to the $\{\alpha_{(k,s)}\}$ (though not the $|x_k|$).

If we thus set $\alpha'_k = \left(\sum_{s=1}^{S} \alpha_{(k,s)}\right)$, $b'_k = \left(\sum_{s=1}^{S} b_s\right)$ and $|x'_k| = |\,|P_s x_k|$, then it may be seen (by moving the summation inside the bracket and gathering terms) that the following equivalences and equalities hold:

$$|\tilde{u_B}\rangle = \frac{1}{S^{\frac{1}{2}}} \sum_{s=1}^{S} |\alpha_s, \beta_s\rangle = \mathcal{N}\left(\sum_{s=1}^{S} b_s |0\rangle |0\rangle + \sum_{k=1}^{M} \sum_{s=1}^{S} |P_s x_k |\alpha_{(k,s)}|k\rangle |\mathcal{P}_s\rangle\langle\mathcal{P}_s| |x_k\rangle \right)$$

$$\equiv \mathcal{N}\left(\sum_{s=1}^{S} b_s |0\rangle |0\rangle + \sum_{k=1}^{M} \sum_{s=1}^{S} |x'_k |\alpha_{(k,s)}|k\rangle |x_k\rangle \right)$$

$$\equiv \text{normalisation const.} \times \left(b' |0\rangle |0\rangle + \sum_{k=1}^{M} |x'_k| \, \alpha'_k |k\rangle |x_k\rangle \right)$$

It may thus be seen that the modified basis is identical to the previous basis, and the ensemble training-data oracle has the same overall form as the original training oracle. Critically, this means that the training oracle is thus represented in the same basis as the query state $\tilde{x}$; i.e. the sum over projectors $|\mathcal{P}_s\rangle\langle\mathcal{P}_s|$ has not altered the representation of the final decision state within the training vector basis, a result that comes about because of the linear separability of training weights in the least squares SVM implementation.

The solution is therefore read off as before (i.e. by using an ancilla to construct the state $\frac{1}{\sqrt{2}}(|0\rangle|\tilde{u_B}\rangle + |1\rangle|\tilde{x}\rangle)$ measured in the basis $\frac{1}{\sqrt{2}}(|0\rangle - |1\rangle)$).

Individual classification decisions are thus no longer resolvable in the swap measurement; only the ensemble decision is measurable. Importantly, no new logic gates or oracle basis is implicated in this construction. Consequently, bootstrap aggregation is "free" within the Rebentrost, Mohseni and Lloyd framework.

4   Conclusion

We have demonstrated that it is possible to implement quantum bootstrap aggregation, specifically quantum attribute bootstrap aggregation, without penalty in quantum machine learning scenarios, using as an exemplar the Rebentrost, Mohseni and Lloyd SVM model. Thus, we can harness the stabilizing characteristics of bagging without requiring either additional logical gates or computation time. To do so, we exploit quantum superposition in such a way as to guarantee that stochastic measurement of the output state will give rise to an aggregate (i.e. ensemble) decision without destroying the superposition over feature subsets induced within the SVM implementation. This is enabled by the linear decomposability of decision boundary parameters within the Kernel-induced Mercer embedding space.

Acknowledgment. The first author would like to acknowledge financial support from the Horizon 2020 European Research project DREAMS4CARS (#731593). The second author is partially supported by EU ICT COST Action IC1405 "Reversible Computation—Extending Horizons of Computing".

References

1. Rebentrost, P., Mohseni, M., Lloyd, S.: Quantum support vector machine for big data classification. Phys. Rev. Lett. **113** (2014). 130501
2. Aïmeur, E., Brassard, G., Gambs, S.: Quantum speed-up for unsupervised learning. Mach. Learn. **90**(2), 261–287 (2013)
3. Altaisky, M., Zolnikova, N., Kaputkina, N., Krylov, V., Lozovik, Y.E., Dattani, N.S.: Towards a feasible implementation of quantum neural networks using quantum dots, arXiv preprint arXiv:1503.05125
4. Lloyd, S., Mohseni, M., Rebentrost, P.: Quantum principal component analysis. Nat. Phys. **10**(9), 631–633 (2014)
5. Barry, J., Barry, D.T., Aaronson, S.: Quantum partially observable markov decision processes. Phys. Rev. A **90**(3), 032311 (2014)

6. Lu, S., Braunstein, S.L.: Quantum decision tree classifier. Quantum Inf. Process. **13**(3), 757–770 (2014)
7. Tucci, R.R.: Quantum circuit for discovering from data the structure of classical bayesian networks, arXiv preprint arXiv:1404.0055
8. Wiebe, N., Kapoor, A., Svore, K.: Quantum algorithms for nearest-neighbor methods for supervised and unsupervised learning, arXiv preprint arXiv:1401.2142
9. Cortes, C., Vapnik, V.: Support-vector networks. Mach. Learn. **20**(3), 273–297 (1995). doi:10.1007/BF00994018
10. Harrow, A.W., Hassidim, A., Lloyd, S.: Quantum algorithm for linear systems of equations. Phys. Rev. Lett. **103**(15), 150502 (2009). arXiv:0811.3171
11. Breiman, L.: Bagging predictors. Mach. Learn. **24**(2), 123–140 (1996)
12. Valentini, G., Dietterich, T.G.: Low bias bagged support vector machines. In: International Conference on Machine Learning, ICML-2003, pp. 752–759. Morgan Kaufmann (2003)

Categorical Compositional Cognition

Yaared Al-Mehairi, Bob Coecke, and Martha Lewis[✉]

Department of Computer Science, University of Oxford, Oxford, UK
yaared.almehairi@gmail.com, {coecke,marlew}@cs.ox.ac.uk

Abstract. We accommodate the Integrated Connectionist/Symbolic Architecture (ICS) of [32] within the categorical compositional semantics (CATCO) of [13], forming a model of categorical compositional cognition (CATCOG). This resolves intrinsic problems with ICS such as the fact that representations inhabit an unbounded space and that sentences with differing tree structures cannot be directly compared. We do so in a way that makes the most of the grammatical structure available, in contrast to strategies like circular convolution. Using the CATCO model also allows us to make use of tools developed for CATCO such as the representation of ambiguity and logical reasoning via density matrices, structural meanings for words such as relative pronouns, and addressing over- and under-extension, all of which are present in cognitive processes. Moreover the CATCOG framework is sufficiently flexible to allow for entirely different representations of meaning, such as conceptual spaces. Interestingly, since the CATCO model was largely inspired by categorical quantum mechanics, so is CATCOG.

1 Introduction

A key question in artificial intelligence and cognition is how symbolic reasoning can be accomplished with distributional representations. [32] present a view of cognition called the *Integrated Connectionist/Symbolic Architecture* (ICS) that incorporates two levels of formal description: "the continuous, numerical lower-level description of the brain", characterized by a connectionist network, and "the discrete, structural higher-level description of the mind", characterized in terms of symbolic rules. ICS is a hybrid approach to the computational modelling of the mind which uses vectors to represent *roles*, from which symbolic structures may be built, and *fillers*, the objects to be manipulated. These roles and fillers are then combined using the tensor product. However, as argued by [7], the tensor product representations used to codify the isomorphism between connectionist and symbolic representations reveal shortcomings. Firstly, the representational space of a concept grows in size as more elements are added to the compound. Secondly, it is unclear how to compare representations that have differing underlying structures. For example, the concepts *joke* and *funny joke*, have structurally different representations, and it is not obvious how one relates

---

B. Coecke and M. Lewis—gratefully acknowledge AFSOR funding on grant 'Algorithmic and Logical Aspects of Composing Meanings'.

J.A. de Barros et al. (Eds.): QI 2016, LNCS 10106, pp. 122–134, 2017.
DOI: 10.1007/978-3-319-52289-0_10

to the other. The third and last problem is to do with particular implementations of ICS. [15,33] use tensor binding representations to model grammar in the following manner: words such as *funny* or *joke* are tagged with their parts of speech. This tagging takes the following form. Each part of speech is assigned a vector, and each word token is assigned a vector. The outer product of the word vector and the part of speech vector is taken, giving a matrix. Circular convolution [26], consisting of taking the sum over diagonals of the matrix, is then used to reduce the matrix back down to a vector. However, this ignores the fact that parts of speech have different roles and structures.

The problem of unifying symbolic and distributional representations has been addressed in the field of computational linguistics. Distributional semantics [30,34] provides vector meanings for words, but has no clear compositional structure. In contrast, compositional approaches such as that of [23] are able to compute the meanings of phrases, but must take the meanings of words as given. The CATCO model of [13] unifies the distributional theory of meaning in terms of vector space models and the compositional theory of grammatical types. It utilises grammar to derive the meaning of a sentence, represented by a vector, from the word vectors that make up the sentence. This model uses composite spaces without increase in size of the resulting meaning space and allows composite concepts to be directly compared with their constituents of the same type, as well as the meaning of sentences of varying length and structure to be compared. Further, this model explicitly recognises the differing structures of parts of speech, and uses these structures to compute the meaning of the sentence. We use the ideas in CATCO to improve the representation of grammar in connectionist frameworks. At the same time, we reformulate the representations in CATCO so that compositionality can be implemented in a more cognitively realistic setting.

We accommodate ICS within CATCO, forming a new model of categorical compositional cognition (CATCOG). The CATCO model was greatly inspired by the categorical semantics for quantum teleportation [6] and nicely matches the template of a quantum-like logic of interaction [8]. Hence, we obtain a model for cognition that draws inspiration from quantum theory.

2   ICS Architecture

In [32], the authors implement symbolic structures within a connectionist architecture. They use vectors and tensor products to represent objects, roles, and structures. Recursive structures such as trees can be represented. The contents of the leaves are encoded in the fillers, and role vectors encode the tree structure. Fillers are bound to roles using the tensor product, and collections of roles and fillers are combined using vector addition.

Recursive Connectionist Realization. Embedding and recursion require the tensor product representation to handle embedded structure, where the filler is itself a complex structure, and not an atomic symbol. The binding $\mathbf{f}/r$ of a filler $\mathbf{f}$ to a role r is realized as a vector $\mathbf{f}/\mathbf{r} = \mathbf{f} \otimes \mathbf{r}$ that is the tensor product of a vector $\mathbf{f}$ realizing $\mathbf{f}$ with a vector $\mathbf{r}$ realizing r. A sentence $\mathbf{s}$ is represented as a sum of filler/role bindings $\sum_i \mathbf{f}_i \otimes \mathbf{r}_i$, and these can be applied recursively. For example, let $\mathbf{s} = \mathtt{[NP\ VP]}$ be a binary tree with left and right subtrees $\mathtt{NP}$ and $\mathtt{VP}$. Let $\mathbf{s}, \mathbf{v}_1, \mathbf{v}_2$ be the vectors realizing $\mathbf{s}, \mathtt{NP}, \mathtt{VP}$. The connectionist realization of $\mathbf{s}$ is:

$$\mathbf{s} = \mathbf{v}_1 \otimes \mathbf{r}_0 + \mathbf{v}_2 \otimes \mathbf{r}_1 \tag{1}$$

If $\mathtt{VP}$ is a tree rather than an atomic symbol, it can be expressed in terms of its left and right subtrees $\mathtt{VP} = \mathtt{[Vt\ NP]}$. If $\mathbf{v}_3, \mathbf{v}_4$ represent the trees $\mathtt{Vt}, \mathtt{NP}$, then the structure $\mathbf{s} = \mathtt{[NP\ [Vt\ NP]]}$ has the following representation:

$$\mathbf{s} = \mathbf{v}_1 \otimes \mathbf{r}_0 + (\mathbf{v}_3 \otimes \mathbf{r}_0 + \mathbf{v}_4 \otimes \mathbf{r}_1) \otimes \mathbf{r}_1 \tag{2}$$
$$= \mathbf{v}_1 \otimes \mathbf{r}_0 + \mathbf{v}_3 \otimes (\mathbf{r}_0 \otimes \mathbf{r}_1) + \mathbf{v}_4 \otimes (\mathbf{r}_1 \otimes \mathbf{r}_1) \tag{3}$$
$$\equiv \mathbf{v}_1 \otimes \mathbf{r}_0 + \mathbf{v}_3 \otimes \mathbf{r}_{01} + \mathbf{v}_4 \otimes \mathbf{r}_{11} \tag{4}$$

The notable feature of this representation is that the vector space in which concepts live must be arbitrarily large, depending on the size of the structure to be represented. Symbols at depth d in a binary tree are realized by $\mathcal{S}_{(d)}$, the FR^d-dimensional vector space formed from vectors of the form $\mathbf{f} \otimes \mathbf{r}_i \otimes \mathbf{r}_j \otimes \cdots \otimes \mathbf{r}_k$ with d role vectors, where F is the dimension of the filler vectors $\mathbf{f}$ and R is the dimension of the individual role vectors $\mathbf{r}_i$. A vector space containing all vectors in $\mathcal{S}_{(d)}$ for all d is:

$$\mathcal{S}^* \equiv \mathcal{S}_{(0)} \oplus \mathcal{S}_{(1)} \oplus \mathcal{S}_{(2)} \oplus \cdots \tag{5}$$

Vectors $\mathbf{s}_{(i)}$ are embedded into this space, meaning that the normal operation of vector addition can be used to combine sentence components.

Symbol Processing. Information is processed in the mind/brain by widely distributed connection patterns (i.e. weight matrices $\mathbb{W}$) that, for central aspects of higher cognition, possess global structure describable through symbolic expressions for recursive functions. [32] show how basic symbol manipulation can be achieved using a distributed system via matrix multiplication. Central aspects of many higher cognitive domains (including language) are realized via recursive processing. Feed-forward networks and recurrent networks provide a mechanism to compute a large class of cognitive functions with recursive structure. In either case, $\mathbb{W}$ is a finite matrix of weights that specifies a particular function (Table 1).

Table 1. Space of descriptions in ICS

Structure	Symbolic	Connectionist
Set	$\mathbf{f}$	$\mathbf{f} \in V_F$
String	$\mathbf{f}_i/r_i$	$\mathbf{f}_i \otimes \mathbf{r}_i$
Tree	$\mathbf{s} = \{\mathbf{f}_i/r_i\}$	$\mathbf{s} = \sum_i \mathbf{f}_i \otimes \mathbf{r}_i \in \mathcal{S}^*$

3   CatCo Semantics

In this section, we summarize the categorical compositional semantics introduced in [13], describing a method for constructing the meanings of sentences from the meanings of words using syntactic structure.

3.1   Pregroup Grammars

Lambek's pregroup grammars [20] are used to describe syntactic structure. This choice of grammar is not essential, and other forms of categorial grammar can be used, as argued in [10]. A pregroup $(P, \leq, \cdot, 1, (-)^l, (-)^r)$ is a partially ordered monoid $(P, \leq, \cdot, 1)$ where each element $p \in P$ has a left adjoint p^l and a right adjoint p^r, such that the following inequalities hold:

$$p^l \cdot p \leq 1 \leq p \cdot p^l \quad \text{and} \quad p \cdot p^r \leq 1 \leq p^r \cdot p \tag{6}$$

The pregroup grammar $\mathsf{Preg}_\mathcal{B}$ over an alphabet $\mathcal{B}$ is freely constructed from the atomic types in $\mathcal{B}$. In what follows, $\mathcal{B} = \{n, s\}$. The type s is used to denote a declarative sentence and n to denote a noun. A transitive verb can then be denoted as $n^r s n^l$. If a string of words and their types reduce to the type s, the sentence is judged grammatical. The sentence *Clowns tell jokes* is typed $n \ (n^r s n^l) \ n$, and can be reduced to s as follows:

$$n \ (n^r s n^l) \ n \leq 1 \cdot s n^l n \leq 1 \cdot s \cdot 1 \leq s \tag{7}$$

This symbolic reduction can also be expressed graphically, as shown in Eq. 8. In this diagrammatic notation, the elimination of types by means of the inequalities $n \cdot n^r \leq 1$ and $n^l \cdot n \leq 1$ is denoted by a 'cup', while the fact that the type s is retained is represented by a straight wire.

3.2   Categorical Compositional Models

The symbolic account and distributional approaches are linked by the fact that they share the common structure of a compact closed category. This compatibility allows the compositional rules of the grammar to be applied in the vector space model, so that sentences may be mapped into one shared meaning space.

A *compact closed category* is a monoidal category in which for each object A there are left and right dual objects A^l and A^r, and corresponding unit and counit morphisms $\epsilon^l : A^l \otimes A \to I$, $\eta^l : I \to A \otimes A^l$, $\epsilon^r : A \otimes A^r \to I$, $\eta^r : I \to A^r \otimes A$ such that the *snake equations* hold. The morphisms of compact closed categories can be expressed in a convenient graphical calculus [19].

The underlying poset of a pregroup can be viewed as a compact closed category with monoidal structure given by the pregroup monoid, and morphisms $\epsilon^l, \eta^l, \epsilon^r, \eta^r$ witnessing the inequalities of (6). Distributional vector space models live in the compact closed category **FHilb** of finite dimensional real

Hilbert spaces and linear maps. Given a fixed basis $\{\mathbf{v}_i\}_i$ of V, ϵ and η are defined by:

$$\epsilon : V \otimes V \to \mathbb{R} :: \sum_{ij} c_{ij}\mathbf{v}_i \otimes \mathbf{v}_j \mapsto \sum_i c_{ii}, \quad \eta : \mathbb{R} \to V \otimes V :: 1 \mapsto \sum_i \mathbf{v}_i \otimes \mathbf{v}_i$$

3.3   Grammatical Reductions in Vector Spaces

Following [27], reductions of the pregroup grammar may be mapped into the category **FHilb** of finite dimensional Hilbert spaces and linear maps using an appropriate strong monoidal functor $Q : \mathbf{Preg} \to \mathbf{FHilb}$. Strong monoidal functors automatically preserve the compact closed structure. For $\mathbf{Preg}_{\{n,s\}}$, we must map noun and sentence types to appropriate finite dimensional vector spaces:

$$Q(n) = N \qquad Q(s) = S$$

Composite types are then constructed functorially using the corresponding structure in **FHilb**. Each morphism α in the pregroup is mapped to a linear map interpreting sentences of that grammatical type. Then, given word vectors $\mathbf{w}_i$ with types p_i, and a type reduction $\alpha : p_1 p_2 ... p_n \to s$, the meaning of the sentence $w_1 w_2 ... w_n$ is generated by:

$$\mathbf{w}_1\mathbf{w}_2...\mathbf{w}_n = Q(\alpha)(\mathbf{w}_1 \otimes \mathbf{w}_2 \otimes \cdots \otimes \mathbf{w}_n)$$

For example, as described in Sect. 3.1, transitive verbs have type $n^r s n^l$, and can therefore represented in **FHilb** as a rank-3 space $N \otimes S \otimes N$. The transitive sentence *Clowns tell jokes* has type $n(n^r s n^l)n$, which reduces to the sentence type s via $\epsilon^r \otimes 1_s \otimes \epsilon^l$. So if we represent **tell** by:

$$\mathbf{tell} = \sum_{ijk} c_{ijk}\mathbf{e}_i \otimes \mathbf{s}_j \otimes \mathbf{e}_k$$

using the definitions of the counits in **FHilb** we then have:

$$\begin{aligned}
\mathbf{Clowns\ tell\ jokes} &= \epsilon_N \otimes 1_S \otimes \epsilon_N(\mathbf{Clowns} \otimes \mathbf{tell} \otimes \mathbf{jokes}) \\
&= \sum_{ijk} c_{ijk}\langle \mathbf{Clowns} \,|\, \mathbf{e}_i \rangle \otimes \mathbf{s}_j \otimes \langle \mathbf{e}_k \,|\, \mathbf{jokes} \rangle \\
&= \sum_j \mathbf{s}_j \sum_{ik} c_{ijk}\langle \mathbf{Clowns} \,|\, \mathbf{e}_i \rangle \langle \mathbf{e}_k \,|\, \mathbf{jokes} \rangle
\end{aligned}$$

This equation has the graphical representation given in 8:

$$\tag{8}$$

Meanings of sentences are compared using the cosine distance between vector representations. Detailed presentations of the ideas in this section are given in [13,27], and an introduction to relevant category theory is provided in [12].

4   Categorical Compositional Cognition

Within both ICS and CATCO, we can view sentence meanings in the following way: the semantics of the individual words of the sentence are given as vectors, and the grammar of the sentence is given as an n-linear map, which is linear in each component. In this section, we map the ICS model to the CATCO model, creating a model for categorical compositional cognition, or CATCOG.

The representation in [32] is of the following form:

$$\sum_i \mathbf{f}_i \otimes \mathbf{r}_i \in \bigoplus_i V \otimes \mathcal{R}_{(i)}$$

The index i here is general, but if we are considering the set of roles to describe a binary tree, then the i corresponds to the depth of the tree.

By using carefully chosen matrices, described in [32], this representation can be written as:

$$\mathbb{W} \cdot \mathbf{f}$$

where here, $\mathbf{f} = \bigoplus \mathbf{f}_i$. This representation allows the sentence to be processed by matrix multiplication, changing order and meaning of words.

In the CATCO model, the representation starts with a tensor product of semantic fillers, represented by triangles in the graphical calculus, and then applies an n-linear map. In order to bring this application in line with the ICS representation, we should represent these fillers as a direct sum. There is a map from a direct sum of vectors to a tensor product of vectors expressed as:

$$\bigoplus_i \mathbf{v}_i \mapsto \bigotimes_i \mathbf{v}_i \tag{9}$$

Given a direct sum of vectors, we firstly convert this to a tensor product of vectors. For example, suppose we have vectors $\mathbf{a} = [a_1, ..., a_n]^\top$ and $\mathbf{b} = [b_1, ..., b_m]^\top$. The direct sum of these is essentially the vector formed by concatenation, $[\mathbf{a}, \mathbf{b}]^\top$. From this, we can map to the tensor product of the two vectors, which in this case can be viewed as the outer product, i.e. the matrix with elements $\{a_i b_j\}_{i=1...n, j=1...m}$. We then apply the n-linear map formed of ϵ, η, 1 that corresponds to the grammatical structure of the sentence. The action of this linear map is the same as tensor contraction, of which matrix-vector multiplication is an instance. This maps the vectors we start out with down to one sentence vector. All such sentence representations inhabit one finite shared meaning space, rather than the unbounded meaning spaces required in [32]. The CATCO model shows how tensor contraction can be used to form sentence meanings in a way that fully utilizes grammatical structure. This comparison is given in diagrammatic form in Fig. 1.

Now that we can see that ICS and CATCO have the same sort of structure, we can cross-fertilize in order to reap the maximum benefit from each representation. The ICS representation has been developed with connectionist implementations in mind, and therefore methods developed in [32], and implementations such as [14–16,33] can be used to develop the CATCO model into a cognitive system rather than the purely linguistic system that it is currently used for.

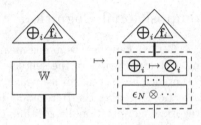

Fig. 1. Comparison of ICS (left) and CATCO (right). In ICS, the string of filler vectors is sent to a linear map which forms a structured tree, represented by thick lines. In CATCO, the string of filler vectors, again represented by a thick line, is first sent to a tensor product of vectors, represented by multiple thin lines. An n-linear map is then applied mapping the string of vectors down to one vector - a single thin line.

ICS is able to characterise a notion of approximate grammatical parsing, called *harmony* that the CATCO model currently lacks. Relationships between the two are explored in [21]. Implementation of the CATCO model within a cognitive framework will also allow for richer representations. Currently, this model is limited to linguistic representations, where meanings of words are derived from text corpora. However, the compositionality that CATCO is able to carry out should transfer very well to meanings derived from other stimuli, such as sound, vision, and so on.

5   Semantic Roles in CatCog

In Fig. 1, we showed how the grammatical structure of a sentence in the CATCO model is viewed as a linear map that corresponds to the matrices used to encode grammatical structure in ICS. However, we may want to enrich the roles from a purely grammatical map to having some semantic content. This would be useful if we wish to utilise the idea of having semantic roles as well as purely formal roles. Semantic roles are discussed in [31,32]. These essentially allow the role vectors to have some semantic content of their own. For example, a proposition 'John gave Mary the book' can be analyzed as having three semantic roles: the giver, the recipient, and the object given. Clearly here, there is more information about the action expressed by the predicate 'give' than is available in purely grammatical roles representing nouns and verbs. This can be implemented within CATCOG by manipulating the diagrams we use. We give here the diagram manipulation and a procedure for bringing semantic content into the role.

$$
\begin{array}{c}
\text{Clowns tell jokes} \\
N \;\; N S N \;\; N
\end{array}
=
\begin{array}{c}
\text{Clowns jokes} \\
N \quad N \\
\text{tell} \\
N \; N \\
S
\end{array}
\equiv
\begin{array}{c}
f \\
N \otimes N \\
W_{\text{tell}} \\
S
\end{array}
\tag{10}
$$

We can also recursively bring more chunks of semantic information into the role vectors if desired. A symbolic structure **s** is represented by a collection of structural roles $\{r_i\}$ represented by $\mathbb{W}_i$ and a base filler $\textbf{f}_1$ represented by a tensor product of atomic fillers $\{\mathbf{a}_j\}$. The realization of **s** is an activation vector $\mathbf{s} = \mathbb{W}_n \cdot \mathbf{f}_n$ that is the recursive matrix-vector multiplication of a matrix $\mathbb{W}_i$ realizing r_i with a vector $\mathbf{f}_i$ realizing a filler/role binding $\textbf{f}_{i-1}/r_{i-1}$, i.e.

$$\mathbb{W}_n \cdot \mathbf{f}_n = \mathbb{W}_n \cdot (\mathbb{W}_{n-1} \cdot \mathbf{f}_{n-1}) \tag{11}$$

$$= \mathbb{W}_n \cdot (\cdots \mathbb{W}_1 \cdot (\mathbf{a}_1 \otimes \cdots \otimes \mathbf{a}_m) \cdots) \tag{12}$$

A simple representation, $\mathbb{W} \cdot \mathbf{f}$, where $\mathbf{f}$ is the tensor product of atomic fillers, for a symbolic structure **s** realized by $\mathbb{W}_n \cdot \mathbf{f}_n$ is as follows:

1. Apply an identity matrix (of the appropriate dimension) to each atomic filler in $\mathbf{f}_n$
2. Pull out the matrix-vector multiplication over tensor products to give $\mathbf{f}_n = \mathbb{W}_{n-1} \cdot \mathbf{f}_{n-1}$
3. Repeat steps 1 and 2 recursively until $\mathbf{f}_i$ is the tensor product of atomic fillers $\mathbb{W} \cdot \mathbf{f} = (\mathbb{W}_n \cdot ... \cdot \mathbb{W}_1) \cdot (\mathbf{a}_1 \otimes \cdots \otimes \mathbf{a}_m)$

This procedure is equivalent to "stretching up" atomic fillers (e.g. nouns in the linguistic case) and "drawing a box" around them to form $\mathbf{f}$ and then "drawing a box" around the rest of the structure to give $\mathbb{W}$, as shown in (10). For example:

$$\textbf{Clowns tell funny jokes} = \mathbb{W}_{\text{tell}} \cdot (\textbf{Clowns} \otimes [\mathbb{W}_{\text{funny}} \cdot \textbf{jokes}]) \tag{13}$$

$$= \mathbb{W}_{\text{tell}} \cdot (\mathbb{I}_{d_N} \otimes \mathbb{W}_{\text{funny}}) \cdot (\textbf{Clowns} \otimes \textbf{jokes}) \tag{14}$$

$$= \mathbb{W}' \cdot (\textbf{Clowns} \otimes \textbf{jokes}) \tag{15}$$

Using this type of representation, we can also represent relative pronouns such as 'which'. The phrase **Clowns who tell jokes** has string diagram

$$\tag{16}$$

To represent this in the ICS format $\mathbb{W} \cdot \mathbf{f}$, we construct matrices implementing the grammatical structure. In CATCO, the grammatical morphisms are $(\mu_N \otimes \iota_S \otimes \epsilon_N)$ which we apply to the vectors $(\textbf{Clowns} \otimes \textbf{tell} \otimes \textbf{jokes})$.

μ can be thought as a multiplication map that pointwise multiplies two vectors together, and ι can be thought of as a deleting map. For a concrete example, suppose $N = \mathbb{R}^2 = S$ and let $\{\mathbf{n}_i\}_i$ and $\{\mathbf{s}_j\}_j$ denote orthonormal bases of N and S respectively. **Clowns, jokes** $\in N$, **tell** $\in N \otimes S \otimes N$ are given in (17). Note that **tell** is a rank-3 tensor with entries $[\textbf{tell}]_{ijk}$. For example, $[\textbf{tell}]_{212} = 9$.

$$\textbf{Clowns}: \begin{bmatrix} 7 \\ 4 \end{bmatrix} \quad \textbf{jokes}: \begin{bmatrix} 5 \\ 1 \end{bmatrix} \quad \textbf{tell}: \begin{bmatrix} 3 & 8 & 4 & 1 \\ 6 & 2 & 9 & 5 \end{bmatrix} \tag{17}$$

From these, matrices are constructed to implement the grammatical structure. $\mathbb{W}_{\mathbf{v}}^{\mu}$ is a matrix that implements the Frobenius multiplication of a vector with $\mathbf{v}$, W_ι is the deleting map, and $\mathbb{W}_{\text{tell}}^{Obj}$ performs application of a verb to an object.

$$\overrightarrow{\textbf{Comedians who tell jokes}} = \mathbb{W}_{\textbf{Comedians}}^{\mu} \cdot (\mathbb{W}_\iota \cdot (\mathbb{W}_{\text{tell}}^{Obj} \cdot (\textbf{jokes}))) \tag{18}$$

$$= \begin{bmatrix} 7 & 0 \\ 0 & 4 \end{bmatrix} \cdot \begin{bmatrix} 1 & 1 & 0 & 0 \\ 0 & 0 & 1 & 1 \end{bmatrix} \cdot \begin{bmatrix} 3 & 8 & 4 & 1 \\ 6 & 2 & 9 & 5 \end{bmatrix}^T \cdot \begin{bmatrix} 5 \\ 1 \end{bmatrix} = \begin{bmatrix} 441 \\ 156 \end{bmatrix} \tag{19}$$

6 Unbinding

The availability of an unbinding mechanism is essential for systematicity in cognitive architectures. This means that given a sentence such as 'Clowns tell jokes', we may access the individual components of the sentence, allowing us to, for example, answer questions about what is going on in the sentence, or allowing us to take the sentence apart and modify it. We propose an approximate unbinding operation which arises naturally from the pulling down of the semantic information into the role information, and hence we use the representation that we introduced in (10).

6.1 Approximate Unbinding

Unbinding is the procedure where we extract a filler from a semantic binding. To achieve this, we require a method to invert $\mathbb{W}_r$, which may not be invertible. We therefore use the Moore-Penrose pseudoinverse for approximate unbinding. For a binding $\mathbb{W}_r \cdot \mathbf{f}$, we approximately unbind $\mathbf{f}$ from $\mathbb{W}_r$ by application of the Moore-Penrose pseudo inverse of $\mathbb{W}_r$: $\mathbb{W}_r^+ \cdot (\mathbb{W}_r \cdot \mathbf{f}) \approx \mathbf{f}$.

Consider $\mathbf{s} = \mathbb{W}_{\text{tell}} \cdot (\textbf{Clowns} \otimes \textbf{jokes})$ where $\textbf{Clowns}, \textbf{jokes} \in N$. We want to insert the adjective *funny*, giving $\mathbf{t}$:

$$\mathbf{t} = \mathbb{W}_{\text{tell}} \cdot (\textbf{Clowns} \otimes [\mathbb{W}_{\text{funny}} \cdot \textbf{jokes}]) \tag{20}$$

This mapping can be done using $\mathbb{W}_{\mathcal{F}} \cdot \mathbf{s}$ where $\mathbb{W}_{\mathcal{F}} = \mathbb{W}_{\text{tell}} \cdot (\mathbb{I}_{d_N} \otimes \mathbb{W}_{\text{funny}}) \cdot \mathbb{W}_{\text{tell}}^+$

$$\mathbb{W}_{\mathcal{F}} \cdot \mathbf{s} = [\mathbb{W}_{\text{tell}} \cdot (\mathbb{I}_{d_N} \otimes \mathbb{W}_{\text{funny}}) \cdot \mathbb{W}_{\text{tell}}^+] \cdot \mathbf{s} \tag{21}$$

$$\approx \mathbb{W}_{\text{tell}} \cdot (\mathbb{I}_{d_N} \otimes \mathbb{W}_{\text{funny}}) \cdot \mathbb{I}_{d_N \cdot d_N} \cdot (\textbf{Clowns} \otimes \textbf{jokes}) \tag{22}$$

$$= \mathbb{W}_{\text{tell}} \cdot (\mathbb{I}_{d_N} \otimes \mathbb{W}_{\text{funny}}) \cdot (\textbf{Clowns} \otimes \textbf{jokes}) \tag{23}$$

$$= \mathbb{W}_{\text{tell}} \cdot (\textbf{Clowns} \otimes [\mathbb{W}_{\text{funny}} \cdot \textbf{jokes}]) = \mathbf{t} \tag{24}$$

7 Consequences of CatCog

The structure of the CatCog model means that all the power of categorical compositional semantics can be leveraged to represent phenomena that are useful in a model of cognitive AI. We give a short description of these structures and how they will be useful.

The representation of ambiguity is important in cognition. How can one representation mean more than one thing, and how does context collapse the ambiguous symbol down to one meaning? CATCO uses quantum theory which has a ready-made structure called a density matrix that can represent ambiguous symbols. These can be used with grammatical composition to model word ambiguity and how the sentence context disambiguates [17,24,25].

Density matrices have also been used to implement logical entailment at the word and the sentence level [1–4]. Results in these papers show how logical entailment between two sentences can be derived as a function of logical entailments between the words in the sentences, within a distributional representation. These results are useful for implementation of logical reasoning, and showing how reasoning at the sentence level will work.

More subtle grammatical structures can be represented such as relative pronouns. Using relative pronouns allows us to form definitional noun phrases such as 'The woman who rules England'. These noun phrases are represented in the same noun space N as their components, and we can therefore compare them directly [18,28,29]. This will be useful in modelling knowledge update.

The CATCO representation has also been used in examining how psychological phenomena such as over- and under-extension of concepts can occur [3,11]. This is a particularly interesting area, since it is not clear that these type of phenomena can be adequately represented using ICS style representations. We give an example to illustrate.

Suppose we take the vectors **pet** and **fish** and suppose we choose role vectors $\mathbf{mod} = [1, 0]^\top$ and $\mathbf{noun} = [0, 1]^\top$. In the ICS representation, we have

$$\mathbf{pet\ fish} = \mathbf{pet} \otimes \mathbf{mod} + \mathbf{fish} \otimes \mathbf{noun}$$

Then, we may wish to compare **goldfish** and **pet fish**. We cannot do this directly without some initial processing. One option might be to form the tensor product **goldfish**⊗**noun**, and use the matrix inner product. However, then, the similarity depends only on the similarity between the noun **goldfish** and the noun **fish**, due to the orthogonality of the role vectors. An objection to this might be that the role vectors do not have to be completely orthogonal, but may be noisy. Then, the similarity is just a noisy similarity to **fish**, and **pet** still plays no real role in the combined meaning.

Another approach would be to use circular convolution [26]. Applying circular convolution to each of **pet**⊗**mod** and **fish**⊗**noun** leaves **pet** as is, but shifts the indices of **fish** by one. These vectors are then summed. If we view the dimensions of the vectors **pet** and **fish** as representing attributes, this gives a notion of interaction between attributes. However, this notion seems ad hoc - why should the indices of the attributes be shifted along by one? In contrast, the CATCO model uses the underlying grammatical structure of the sentence to explain the interactions of attributes [11].

The abstract framework of the categorical compositional scheme is actually broader in scope than natural language applications. It can be applied in other settings in which we wish to compose meanings in a principled manner, guided by structure. Another extension is therefore in using other representational formats such as conceptual spaces [5].

8   Conclusion and Outlook

So what have we achieved with our CATCOG representation in relation to ICS? The benefit of this new recursive representation is that filler/role bindings (i.e. constituents) that make up a symbolic structure **s** are now composed in such a way that all well-formed **s**, with respect to a certain cognitive task, are realized in a *finite shared* meaning space. This allows the comparison of well-formed symbolic structures with different underlying grammatical structures.

This new representation opens up a number of avenues for further work. On the theoretical side, a key line of enquiry will be to push the comparison between ICS and CATCO further. This will allow us to analyse the type of theoretical structure that is used within the $\mathbb{W}$ matrices employed by ICS. In particular, the representations of verbs, adjectives, and other relational words in CATCO inhabit a higher dimensional space than nouns, and therefore it might be thought that there is an unfair comparison between the two models. In fact, it is possible to take a vector representation, and lift it into a higher dimensional space. Investigating how to do this so ICS structure is preserved is future work.

Another current line of research will look at how to properly formalise the notion of knowledge updating. If I tell you that *John runs*, and you previously did not know this, how is your representation of *John* updated? Again, architectures including ICS and [16] will feed into this research.

On the implementation side, future work in this area will be to apply the theory within a model such as Nengo [14] or LISA [16]. These implementations already use tensor product representations, and therefore have the right kind of underlying structure to serve as a good implementation. Extensions of approaches such as [22,31] will also be fruitful.

CATCOG draws inspiration from categorical quantum mechanics, and therefore techniques and structures from quantum theory can be incorporated into the formalism. Further uses concern phases and (strong) complementarity [9].

While our examples are all linguistic, our model accounts for general cognitive tasks that manipulate filler and roles. We therefore leave with a programme for producing compositional structure within distributed representation of cognitive processes.

References

1. Balkır, E.: Using density matrices in a compositional distributional model of meaning. Master's thesis, University of Oxford (2014)
2. Balkır, E., Kartsaklis, D., Sadrzadeh, M.: Sentence entailment in compositional distributional semantics. In: ISAIM 2016 (2015, to appear)
3. Bankova, D.: Comparing meaning in language and cognition. Master's thesis, University of Oxford (2015)

4. Bankova, D., Coecke, B., Lewis, M., Marsden, D.: Graded entailment for compositional distributional semantics (2016). arXiv:1601.04908
5. Bolt, J., Coecke, B., Genovese, F., Lewis, M., Marsden, D., Piedeleu, R.: Interacting conceptual spaces (2016, Submitted)
6. Clark, S., Coecke, B., Grefenstette, E., Pulman, S., Sadrzadeh, M.: A quantum teleportation inspired algorithm produces sentence meaning from word meaning and grammatical structure. Malays. J. Math. Sci. **8**, 15–25 (2014). arXiv:1305.0556
7. Clark, S., Pulman, S.: Combining symbolic and distributional models of meaning. In: Quantum Interaction, pp. 52–55 (2007)
8. Coecke, B.: The logic of quantum mechanics – take II. In: Chubb, J., Eskandarian, A., Harizanov, V. (eds.) Logic and Algebraic Structures in Quantum Computing, pp. 174–198. Cambridge University Press (2016). arXiv:1204.3458
9. Coecke, B., Duncan, R.: Interacting quantum observables: categorical algebra and diagrammatics. New J. Phys. **13**, 043016 (2011). arXiv:quantph/09064725
10. Coecke, B., Grefenstette, E., Sadrzadeh, M.: Lambek vs Lambek: functorial vector space semantics and string diagrams for Lambek calculus. Ann. Pure Appl. Logic **164**, 1079–1100 (2013)
11. Coecke, B., Lewis, M.: A compositional explanation of the 'Pet Fish' phenomenon. In: Atmanspacher, H., Filk, T., Pothos, E. (eds.) QI 2015. LNCS, vol. 9535, pp. 179–192. Springer, Heidelberg (2016). doi:10.1007/978-3-319-28675-4_14
12. Coecke, B., Paquette, E.: Categories for the practising physicist (2009). arXiv:0905.3010
13. Coecke, B., Sadrzadeh, M., Clark, S.: Mathematical foundations for a compositional distributional model of meaning. Linguist. Anal. **36**(1–4), 345–384 (2011)
14. Eliasmith, C.: How to Build a Brain: A Neural Architecture for Biological Cognition. OUP, Oxford (2013)
15. Eliasmith, C., Thagard, P.: Integrating structure and meaning: a distributed model of analogical mapping. Cognit. Sci. **25**(2), 245–286 (2001)
16. Hummel, J.E., Holyoak, K.J.: Distributed representations of structure: a theory of analogical access and mapping. Psychol. Rev. **104**(3), 427 (1997)
17. Kartsaklis, D.: Compositional distributional semantics with compact closed categories and frobenius algebras. Ph.D. thesis, University of Oxford (2015)
18. Kartsaklis, D., Sadrzadeh, M., Pulman, S., Coecke, B.: Reasoning about meaning in natural language with compact closed categories and Frobenius algebras. In: Logic and Algebraic Structures in Quantum Computing, p. 199 (2013)
19. Kelly, M., Laplaza, M.L.: Coherence for compact closed categories. J. Pure Appl. Algebra **19**, 193–213 (1980)
20. Lambek, J.: Type grammar revisited. Log. Asp. Comput. Linguist. **1582**, 1–27 (1999)
21. Lewis, M., Coecke, B.: Harmonic grammar in the disco model of meaning, ADS@IWCS (2015)
22. Milajevs, D., Kartsaklis, D., Sadrzadeh, M., Purver, M.: Evaluating neural word representations in tensor-based compositional settings. EMNLP (2014)
23. Montague, R.: The proper treatment of quantification in ordinary english. In: Hintikka, K.J.J., Moravcsik, J.M.E., Suppes, P. (eds.) Approaches to natural language, pp. 221–242. Springer, Heidelberg (1973)
24. Piedeleu, R.: Ambiguity in categorical models of meaning. Master's thesis, University of Oxford (2014)
25. Piedeleu, R., Kartsaklis, D., Coecke, B., Sadrzadeh, M.: Open system categorical quantum semantics in natural language processing. CALCO (2015)

26. Plate, T.: Holographic reduced representations. Neural Netw. **6**(3), 623–641 (1995)
27. Preller, A., Sadrzadeh, M.: Bell states and negative sentences in the distributed model of meaning. ENTCS **270**(2), 141–153 (2011)
28. Sadrzadeh, M., Clark, S., Coecke, B.: The Frobenius anatomy of word meanings I. J. Logic Comput., ext044 (2013)
29. Sadrzadeh, M., Clark, S., Coecke, B.: The Frobenius anatomy of word meanings II. J. Logic Comput., exu027 (2014)
30. Schütze, H.: Automatic word sense discrimination. Comput. Linguist. **24**(1), 97–123 (1998)
31. Shastri, L., Ajjanagadde, V.: From simple associations to systematic reasoning. Behav. Brain Sci. **16**(03), 417–451 (1993)
32. Smolensky, P., Legendre, G.: The Harmonic Mind. MIT Press, Cambridge (2005)
33. Thagard, P., Stewart, T.C.: The AHA! experience: creativity through emergent binding in neural networks. Cognit. Sci. **35**(1), 1–33 (2011)
34. Turney, P.D., Pantel, P., et al.: From frequency to meaning: vector space models of semantics. J. Artif. Intell. Res. **37**(1), 141–188 (2010)

Graded Vector Representations of Immunoglobulins Produced in Response to West Nile Virus

Trevor Cohen[1]([✉]), Dominic Widdows[2], Jason A. Vander Heiden[3],
Namita T. Gupta[3], and Steven H. Kleinstein[4]

[1] University of Texas School of Biomedical Informatics, Houston, TX, USA
trevor.cohen@uth.tmc.edu
[2] Grab Technologies, Inc., Seattle, WA, USA
[3] Interdepartmental Program in Computational Biology and Bioinformatics,
Yale University, New Haven, CT, USA
[4] Departments of Pathology and Immunobiology, Yale School of Medicine,
New Haven, CT, USA

Abstract. Semantic vector models generate high-dimensional vector representations of words from their occurrence statistics across large corpora of electronic text. In these models, an occurrence of a word or number is treated as a discrete event, including numerical measurements of continuous properties. Furthermore, the sequence in which words occur is often ignored. In earlier work we have developed approaches to address these limitations, using graded *demarcator vectors* to represent measured distances in high-dimensional space. This permits incorporation of continuous properties, such as the position of a character within a term or a year of birth, into semantic vector models. In this paper we extend this work by developing a novel representational approach for protein sequences, in which both the positions and the properties of the amino acid components of protein sequences are represented using graded vectors. Evaluation on a set of around 100,000 immunoglobulin receptor sequences derived from subjects recently infected with West Nile Virus (WNV) suggests that encoding positions and properties using graded vectors increases the similarity between immunoglobulin receptor sequences produced by cells from ancestral lines known to have developed in response to WNV, relative to those from other cell lines.

Keywords: Distributional semantics · Vector Symbolic Architectures · Binary Spatter Code · Quantum Interactions · Computational immunology

1 Introduction

The application of compositional operators to semantic vector representations — vectors that encode the distribution of terms across large text corpora — has been an active area of inquiry for the Quantum Interactions community since

© Springer International Publishing AG 2017
J.A. de Barros et al. (Eds.): QI 2016, LNCS 10106, pp. 135–148, 2017.
DOI: 10.1007/978-3-319-52289-0_11

its inception [1]. In these models, the presence of a term in a particular context is considered as a discrete event - the term is either present or absent, though it may be present more than once. However, as we have argued previously [2], a vector space model providing a holistic account of conceptual representation would also need to represent continuous properties. Consider the phrase "has an average high temperature of 106 °F in July", which refers to the city of Phoenix, Arizona. A semantic vector representation for Phoenix could take into account that the term "106" had been observed, but this would result in a vector representation that is dissimilar to a similarly constructed vector for the city of Las Vegas, which has an average high temperature of 105 °F in the same month. Ideally, these semantic vectors would accommodate continuous values of this sort, resulting in proximal vector representations when similar measurements are encountered.

To this end, in our recent work we have developed an approach to represent both discrete events and continuous measurements with semantic vector models, using a quantization technique similar to that employed to model angular momentum in quantum mechanics [3]. This approach was originally developed to encode orthographic similarity between words, such that words with matching characters in proximal positions will have similar vector representations [4]. Subsequently, these methods were extended to the more general case of encoding continuous properties of tabular data [2]. In this paper, we develop these ideas further by encoding both sequence and continuous properties, to generate vector representations of protein sequences.

The paper proceeds as follows. First we provide some context for the current work, in relation to immunology and prior Quantum Interactions contributions. Then we introduce the mathematical structures to-be-employed, and their application for the purpose of representing protein sequences. We then proceed to the empirical component of this paper, in which we evaluate the extent to which variants of this approach lead to similar vector representations for collections of immunoglobulin (Ig) receptors expressed by B cell clones from the blood of subjects recently infected with West Nile Virus (WNV).

2   Background

The human immune system is a complex learning network of cells and molecules that are responsible for eliminating infections. Despite its inherent complexity, aspects of the immune system are amenable to computational modeling [5]. B cells are members of the adaptive immune system that recognize foreign organisms and molecules (antigens), using a receptor known as the Ig receptor. Once a B cell recognizes an antigen, it undergoes a process of rapid cell division, mutation and selection that leads to generation of cells with receptor variants having increasing affinity for the antigen. B cells that, through mutation, develop receptors with high affinity for an intruding antigen survive and multiply. Those with receptors having low affinity do not. In this way, the immune system adapts to this antigen by customizing the population of B cells to favor those with Ig receptors that recognize it effectively. Through several experimental steps, the DNA sequence of the Ig receptor's antigen binding region can be determined. This DNA sequence can then be translated into the sequence of component amino acids that, in part, encode the binding affinity of the Ig receptor protein.

The technology is available to accomplish such sequencing quickly and inexpensively [6]. These high-throughput sequencing technologies lead to the generation of large numbers of such sequences, which raises the informatics problem of how best to index, retrieve and analyze them. Historically, sequence comparisons have been conducted with algorithms that determine the minimum cost of pairwise alignment, using variants of string edit distance calculated via dynamic programming approaches [7]. A scalable alternative involves utilizing the hamming distance, which calculates the number of amino acids in common at matched positions, without considering approximate relationships in position [8]. These algorithms represent amino acids as discrete symbols, without considering their chemical properties. Alternatively, the average score of amino acid properties in a particular region may be considered [9], or the similarity between vector representations of "bags" of amino acids, discrete properties [10], or shorter subsequences [11] may be estimated. Such metrics discard information concerning position within a sequence. An algorithm for rapid pairwise comparison addressing both variations in local sequence and biochemical properties is a desirable alternative.

3 Mathematical Structures and Methods

3.1 Random Indexing

Random Indexing (RI) is an efficient method of generating semantic vector representations of words [12]. The starting point for RI involves generation of random vectors for the contexts in which terms occur. For example, each document may have a random vector. Random vectors are high-dimensional in nature (d on the order of 1,000 for real vectors), and are generated by assigning a small number (on the order of 10) of the elements of a zero vector to $+1$ or -1 at random. On account of the statistical properties of high-dimensional space, such vectors have a high probability of being mutually close-to-orthogonal. This is reasonably intuitive when considering sparse vectors with a small number of non-zero values. However, it is also the case that randomly-constructed densely populated vectors have a high probability of being far apart in high dimensions [13], including the binary vectors with an equal probability of one or zero in each dimension that provide the fundamental unit of representation for the current experiments [14]. RI utilizes several of the operators used in this research. Firstly, RI involves the generation of mutually close-to-orthogonal random vectors as a fundamental representational unit. In the current paper, and in accordance with our previous work, we will refer to such vectors as *elemental vectors*, and the elemental vector for a term will be denoted $E(\text{term})$. We will use the term "semantic vector" and the denotation $S(\text{term})$ to refer to vectors that are generated through superposition of component vectors, and the symbol $+$ to indicate the superposition operation. For example, RI generates semantic word vectors by superposing (adding) the random vectors representing each of the n contexts a word occurs in, and normalizing the resulting vector.

3.2 Vector Symbolic Architectures

Our approach to encoding sequence and properties draw on a family of representational approaches known as Vector Symbolic Architectures [15] (VSAs). VSAs emerged in response to the critique that connectionist representations, such as neural networks, could not support composition of nested structures thought to underlie reasoning and language, and as such could not provide a comprehensive account of cognition [16]. In connectionist models, the unit of representation is a vector of activation weights. VSAs provide the means to generate compositional structures from such vectors, by providing space-efficient alternatives to Smolensky's initial application of the tensor product for this purpose [17]. These alternatives include circular convolution [18] and element-wise exclusive or (XOR) [19]. In the latter case, the underlying representational unit is a high- (or hyper-) dimensional binary vector, and the VSA is known as the Binary Spatter Code (BSC) [19]. These operators, which are known as *binding* operators, and will be depicted in this paper with the symbol $\otimes$, provide the means for composition. For example, if "temperature" and "106" are represented by vectors, the bound product of these vectors, $\overrightarrow{temperature} \otimes \overrightarrow{106}$, can be used to implement binding of the value "106" to the variable "temperature". A key feature of binding operators is that they are invertible, albeit approximately in some cases. Consequently, we would anticipate if $C = A \otimes B$ then $B \approx C \oslash A$, where $\oslash$ represents the inverse of the binding operator. This mechanism can recover the value bound to a variable, or the variable to which a particular value is bound. VSAs also employ superposition ($+$) as a compositional operator. Of note, for the current research the symbol $+$ here indicates probabilistic superposition of binary vectors rather than the majority rule that is prescribed by the BSC. The number of 1s and 0s in each dimension are tallied across the component vectors, and the superposition is generated probabilistically, such that $P(x = 1)$ in any dimension is equal to $count(x = 1) \div count(x = 1 \cup x = 0)$.

These operators have different functions. Superposition of two vectors produces a vector that is similar to both of its components. Binding produces a vector that is dissimilar from them. In particular, the use of elemental vectors to represent variables entails that values bound to different variables will not be confused with one another: if $E(\text{born}) \approx\perp E(\text{died})$, then $E(\text{born}) \otimes E(1917) \approx\perp E(\text{died}) \otimes E(1917)$. However, relaxing the constraint that these units of representation be mutually close-to-orthogonal provides the means to encode continuous values, such as relative position within a sequence, into semantic vector representations.

3.3 Encoding Sequence

Our approach to encoding sequences was initially developed to encode orthographic representations of words [4]. Consider the word "monk". One way to use

VSAs to generate an orthographic representation of this term would be to treat positions as variables, and characters as values [20], exemplifying an approach that is known as "slot coding" [21]. We can then generate an orthographic vector for "monk" as follows:

$$O(monk) = E(\text{m}) \otimes E(1) + E(\text{o}) \otimes E(2) + E(\text{n}) \otimes E(3) + E(\text{k}) \otimes E(4)$$

However, this approach would result in orthographic vector representations that are similar only for two terms with identical characters in identical positions. This is inconsistent with the flexible nature of human orthographic encoding, which is robust to transposition of characters, amongst other perturbations of sequence. This limitation also applies to VSA-based approaches where a permutation is applied to elemental vectors to encode relative position [22]. A more flexible VSA-based approach involves the generation of bound products representing n-grams, such as the bigram $E(\text{w}) \otimes E(\text{o})$ [20,23]. However, the need to encode multiple n-grams and the encoding of "skip-grams" that permit wildcard characters results in a large number of encoding operations - for example, up to fifteen superpositions and sixteen binding operations to generate a bi- and uni-gram based orthographic representation of a five-letter word [24]. In addition, the resulting representations would only be similar for terms with identical n-grams (or skipgrams). Similarity is a measure of the extent to which discrete symbolic representations of character subsequences match one another exactly.

Our approach to encoding sequence is different, in that character positions are treated continuously. This is accomplished by generating a pair of mutually close-to-orthogonal *demarcator* vectors, and interpolating between them[1]. Consider again the word "monk". Given four character positions, p_1, p_2, p_3 and p_4, and the approximately orthogonal demarcator vectors $D(\alpha)$ and $D(\omega)$, we would construct demarcator vectors for these positions such that $D(p_1) = \frac{4}{5}D(\alpha) + \frac{1}{5}D(\omega)$, $D(p_2) = \frac{3}{5}D(\alpha) + \frac{2}{5}D(\omega)$, $D(p_3) = \frac{2}{5}D(\alpha) + \frac{3}{5}D(\omega)$, and $D(p_4) = \frac{1}{5}D(\alpha) + \frac{4}{5}D(\omega)$[2]. In high dimensions, this results in a set of demarcator vectors in which $sim(D(p_1), D(p_2)) \approx sim(D(p_2), D(p_3)) > sim(D(p_1), D(p_3)) > sim(D(p_1), D(p_4))$ [4]. With these demarcator vectors established an orthographic vector for the word monk, and similarly for any other four-letter word, can be generated as follows:

$$O(monk) = E(\text{m}) \otimes D(\text{p}_1) + E(\text{o}) \otimes D(\text{p}_2) + E(\text{n}) \otimes D(\text{p}_3) + E(\text{k}) \otimes D(\text{p}_4)$$

The resulting representation will be similar to the orthographic vectors for words that have the same characters in similar positions. Better character alignment results in higher similarity. Examples and results are presented in [4], which also discusses the fit between the model and findings from cognitive research on human word recognition.

---

[1] A similar approach, with interpolation between random matrices rather than random vectors, has recently been proposed as a way to represent the positions of pixels within images [25].

[2] With binary vectors, superposition occcurs probabilistically - if $D(\alpha)$ has a 1 as its first element and $D(\omega)$ does not, $D(p_1)$ is generated with a 0.8 probability of a one in this position.

3.4   Encoding Properties with Graded Values

Subsequently, this approach was generalized as a means to encode continuous values. The procedure in this case involves generating $D(\alpha)$ and $D(\omega)$ for each continuous property of a concept to be represented with a semantic vector. For example, the vector for a city may encode its average temperature, population and square mileage. Then, the minimum (v_{min}) and maximum (v_{max}) of each property is calculated. A vector representing any value $v(c)$ of this continuous property is then generated by interpolation:

$$D(vc) = \frac{v_{max} - v(c)}{v_{max} - v_{min}} D(\alpha) + \frac{v(c) - v_{min}}{v_{max} - v_{min}} D(\omega).$$

For a concept with multiple attributes, an elemental vector is generated for each attribute. A semantic vector for this concept can then be generated by binding the elemental vector for each attribute, $E(A_i)$ to the demarcator vector representing this attribute's value $D(V_i)$, and superposing the resulting attribute-value bound product vectors: $S(C) = \sum_{i=1}^{n} E(A_i) \otimes D(V_i)$. Examples and results are presented in [2].

3.5   Quantum Structures

The encoding process utilized for this purpose draws upon a number of mathematical structures that relate to Quantum Theory. The quantization procedure for generating demarcator vectors is similar to that used to model angular momentum in quantum mechanics [3]. The binding operator employed is equivalent to the use of circular convolution in Circular Holographic Reduced Representations, a complex vector based VSA, with phase angles quantized to 0 and π [18]. Circular convolution in turn derives from the tensor product (for a concise account of the relationship between the tensor product and the binding operators of different VSAs, see [26]), used in quantum mechanics to represent composite systems. As has been noted previously, superpositions of role-filler bound products (such as $E(m) \otimes D(p_1)$) constitute entangled states [27]. Finally, the variant of the hamming distance employed to compare sequence vectors to one another is equivalent to the cosine metric, and as such bears correspondence to the use of projection operators to estimate the probability of observations.

4   Protein Sequences and Amino Acid Properties

In this section, we will describe how we combine our approach to encoding sequence with our approach to encoding continuous values, to generate vector representations of protein sequences. In addition, we employ a permutation operator to enable the algorithm to distinguish between regions of interest. The permutation operator is used in the context of VSAs to dissociate vectors from one another [28]. The general idea is that, once permuted, a high-dimensional vector is highly likely to be close-to-orthogonal to all other vectors in the space - including the vector to which the permutation operator was applied. In the context of modeling sequence, permutation has been used to ensure that words in each position of a sliding window are treated differently [22]. Following this approach, we use a permutation operation in which we shift the bits of a binary vector n positions to the right, with a different n for each region of interest. For computational convenience we perform this operation blockwise, shifting 64-bit blocks to the right rather than individual bits. Figure 1 provides an overview of our approach to encoding sequence. The enumerated list below refers back to the numbers in this figure.

1. DNA sequences are segmented into three-character codons, and translated into amino acids in accordance with the genetic code [29] where mapping is possible.
2. Representations of amino acids are composed from demarcator and elemental vectors representing property value pairs, as described in Sect. 3.4. Encoded properties are shown in Table 1. For charge, amino acids without charge are given the value of zero, and other values are converted to charge at pH 7.4 using the Hendersen-Hasselbach equation, such that $charge = (1 + 10^{(7.4-pK[X])})^{-1}$ for $pK[X] \in \{pK[R], pK[H], pK[K]\}$ and $charge = -(1 + 10^{-(7.4-pK[X])})^{-1}$ for $pK[X] \in \{pK[D], pK[E], pK[C], pK[Y]\}$ where $pK[X]$ is the negative log of the acid dissociation constant for the amino acid residue X. Categorical values are encoded as the bound products of elemental vectors representing the categories and values concerned. Unmapped codons are represented by elemental vectors.

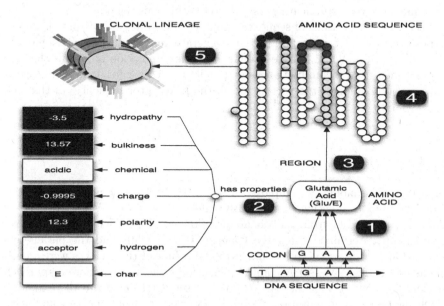

Fig. 1. Overview of encoding processes.

Table 1. Encoded properties for partial list of amino acids (10 of 20).

	Hydropathy	Bulkiness	Chemical	Charge	Polarity	Hydrogen	Char
Ala	1.8	11.5	Aliphatic	0	8.1	None	A
Arg	−4.5	14.28	Basic	0.9999	10.5	Donor	R
Asn	−3.5	12.82	Amide	0	11.6	Donor/acceptor	N
Asp	−3.5	11.68	Acidic	−0.9997	13	Acceptor	D
Cys	2.5	13.46	Sulfur	−0.0736	5.5	None	C
Gln	−3.5	14.45	Amide	0	10.5	Donor/acceptor	Q
Glu	−3.5	13.57	Acidic	−0.9995	12.3	Acceptor	E
Gly	−0.4	3.4	Aliphatic	0	9	None	G
His	−3.2	13.69	Basic	0.1118	10.4	Donor/acceptor	H
Ile	4.5	21.4	Aliphatic	0	5.2	None	I

3. Permutation is applied to differentiate regions of a protein sequence from one another. We applied permutations to distinguish between each of the Complementarity Determining Regions (CDR1-3) and Framework Regions (FWR1-3), as defined by the IMGT numbering scheme [30], when encoding structure. These regions were assigned permutations of 1 through 6 64-bit blocks to the right (P^{+1} to P^{+6}).
4. Graded vectors are employed to encode position within a region. For each encoded region, the vector representation of each amino acid is bound to a demarcator vector indicating its position within this region.
5. Vector representations of sequences, composed from region vectors via superposition, are in turn superposed to generate representations of clonal lineages, where a clonal lineage is defined as the population of B cells that are descended from a common ancestor B cell. The vector for a clonal lineage is the superposition of the vectors for all the Ig receptor sequences of that cell population.

5   Evaluation

To evaluate the model, we employed a set of 98,402 Ig sequences derived from three individuals identified as recently infected with the WNV [31]. These sequences originated from 52,505 unique clonal lineages, with clonal lineage membership determined using the Change-O [32] toolkit and the parameters specified in Tsioris and Gupta et al., 2015 [31]. Three of these clones were identified as producing WNV-specific antibodies using a single-cell nanowell approach to identify WNV-specific B cells [31,33]. We set out to evaluate the extent to which the vector representation of each WNV-specific clonal lineage could serve as a cue to retrieve the remaining two, amongst the 52,504 possibilities (the probability of this occurring by chance is vanishingly small, at $3.8092e^{-5}$).

Table 2. Summary of models across 36 cue-by-target-by-dimensionality combinations. Rgn = region encoded via permutation. Pos = position encoded, either with graded vectors (Gr), or with slot coding (Sl). Prp = Properties encoded. AA = Amino Acid.

Model	Rgn	Pos	Prp	Description
GrSP	✓	Gr	✓	"Graded Structure and Properties": property-based AA vectors bound to graded position vectors, with permuted regions.
GrS	✓	Gr		"Graded Structure": elemental AA vectors bound to graded position vectors, with permuted regions.
BoP			✓	"Bag-of-Properties": sum of property-derived AA vectors.
BoAA				"Bag-of-amino-acids": sum of elemental vectors for AAs.
SloP		Sl	✓	"Slotted Properties": BoP + bind to elemental position vectors.
SloAA		Sl		"Slotted Amino Acids": BoAA + bind to elemental position vectors.

To evaluate the utility of encoding structure and amino acid properties, we tested several configurations of the model, shown in Table 2. These include graded-vector encoding structure and properties in accordance with the entirety of Fig. 1 (GrSP); encoding structure only, without encoding properties (GrS); ignoring structure and treating the protein sequences as "bags" of amino acids (BoAA) or amino acid properties (BoP); and "slot coding" approaches in which vector representations of amino acids (SloAA) or amino acid properties (SloP) are bound to elemental vectors representing their position within the protein sequence, such that the similarity function requires finding an identical (SloAA) or similar (SloP) amino acid in exactly the same position as in a cue sequence. In all cases, 52,205 "clone vectors" were generated, each one representing the repertoire of Ig sequences derived from a single clonal lineage.

For each of the model variants in Table 2, we generated binary vectors at six different dimensionalities between 1024 and 32,768 ($2^{10} - 2^{15}$). For the sake of reproducibility, we generated elemental vectors using a deterministic approach in which the pseudo-random number generator is seeded by applying a hash function to the term-to-be-represented [34]. This preserves the desirable property of near-orthogonality, while ensuring that the influence of random overlap between elemental vectors is consistent across experiments. For each model, and at each dimensionality, we used the vector representations of each of the three WNV-specific clones as cues. Each cue vector was compared against the other 52,504 clone vectors in the space, which were rank ordered with respect to their similarity, with similarity estimated as $1 - \frac{2}{n}$ hamming distance (HD)[3]. Generation and

---

[3] This corresponds to the cosine metric if binary vectors are treated as vectors in $\{1,-1\}$ not $\{1,0\}$. For example, $1 - (2/4) * \text{HD}(1110, 1111) = 0.5$, and $\cos((0.5, 0.5, 0.5, -0.5), (0.5, 0.5, 0.5, 0.5)) = 0.5$ (with 0.5 for normalized vector components after division by $\sqrt{4}$).

comparison of high-dimensional binary vectors, including graded vectors, was conducted using the open source Semantic Vectors package [35]. In each case, the ranks of the vectors for the other two WNV-specific clones were recorded.

6   Results

The results of these experiments are shown in Table 3, which provides the median and minimum rank across the 36 searches (6 dimensionalities × 3 cues × 2 targets), and counts of the number of these examples that fell within the top-ranked results at different thresholds. All of the models evaluated reliably recover WNV-specific clonal lineages within the top 1,000 results (the probability of this occurring at random is around .02). The graded vector based methods (GrSP and GrS) retrieve the most WNV-specific lineages within the top 100 results, and the GrSP method has the lowest median rank of retrieval across all cases.

Table 3. Summary of results across all examples and dimensionalities. Best results in each row are in **bold**. Models incorporating amino acid properties are in grey columns.

	GrSP	GrS	BoP	BoAA	SloP	SloAA
MEDIAN	**877.5**	3857.5	4980	1416	2940.5	6051.5
MIN	5	4	33	98	34	26
<= 10	4	3	0	0	0	0
<= 50	7	6	1	0	2	1
<= 100	**10**	**10**	1	1	4	1
<= 500	12	14	13	**17**	10	5
<= 1000	**18**	15	17	**18**	11	7

Incorporating information about amino acid properties (grey columns) improves the performance of models that incorporate structure (GrSP > GrS and SloP > SloAA), and vice-versa - GrSP and SloP also outperform BoP with respect to proximal (e.g. recall within top 100) and overall (median rank) performance. However, the effect of incorporating property information when structure is ignored (BoP vs. BoAA) is more nuanced, with slightly better recall of higher-ranked results but worse performance overall. These two structure-agnostic models are competitive with respect to their ability to recover WNV-specific lineages in the top 1,000 results, but seldom recover these within the top 100. Of the models that incorporate structure, the graded vector approaches, which accommodate approximate alignment, outperform the tighter constraints of the "slot coding" approaches. SloAA performs worst by most metrics, which is not surprising as it is the model with the tightest constraints, with insistence upon an exact match between both position and specific amino acid. Table 4 summarizes performance for productive cue:target pairs, excluding 125584:68974 which was not retrieved within the top 1000 results in either orientation. This pattern

Table 4. Minimum, median and maximum rank for productive cue:target pairs ($\frac{MIN;MED}{MAX}$). Best MIN in **bold**, best MED <u>underlined</u>, best MAX in *italics* if ≤ 1000. Ranks > 1000 in grey text. Models incorporating properties in grey columns. C/T = $\frac{Cue}{Target}$.

C/T	GrSP	GrS	BoP	BoAA	SloP	SloAA
125584	**26**; <u>54</u>	45; 57.5	116; 267.5	107; 227.5	228; 349.5	1632; 5342.5
314052	*111*	9323	337	306	14489	7292
314052	510; 1000	3584; 7608	324; <u>429</u>	**317**; 472.5	1917; 2296.5	1802; 8434.5
125584	3056	32883	745	*599*	39694	9512
314052	520; 877.5	**96**; <u>560.5</u>	15230; 20214	10711; 14808	1997; 3199	409; 2208
68974	16851	4131	42451	16032	10117	2842
68974	**5**; <u>9</u>	**4**; 12.5	33; 501.5	98; 165	34; 53.5	26; 350.5
314052	*317*	387	8390	418	339	924

suggests one target, 314052, is more readily retrieved than others. One explanation for this might be that more Ig sequences related to this clone appear in the data set ($n = 44$ vs. $n = 5$ and $n = 12$ for 68974 and 125584 respectively). So the clone vector representing it exhibits a broader range of WNV-related characteristics. Superposition of these sequences will emphasize characteristics that are preserved across the ancestral lineage. From a biological perspective, these should be the characteristics that define specificity for WNV.

7   Discussion

In this paper, we develop and evaluate a method through which the position and properties of components of a protein sequence are encoded into high-dimensional vector representations, such that proteins with similar amino acids in similar positions will have similar vectors. These vectors can be compared efficiently using a variant of the hamming distance, and superposed to represent the Ig sequence collection of a clonal lineage. Evaluation reveals encoding amino acid properties improves retrieval of one WNV-binding clonal lineage when another is used as a cue, if sequence and structure are also encoded. Encoding sequence and structure improves retrieval with or without encoding properties, if position is not rigidly encoded. Of note, it is not necessarily the case that clonal lineages ranked higher than the desired targets are *not* WNV-specific. Rather, our approach may have identified other sensitized clones, a possibility that would need to be evaluated empirically. Nonetheless, these results suggest our approach provides scalable solution for approximate matching of protein sequences, a fundamental problem in computational genomics. In future work we will incorporate a broader range of amino acid properties, and conduct evaluation using larger data sets.

8   Conclusion

In this work, we adapt approaches to encoding sequence and continuous values into semantic vector representations to the task of representing protein sequences. Evaluation suggests that encoding amino acid properties is of value for the identification of proteins with similar immunological specificity, if and only if the position of these amino acids is encoded also. However, it is preferable that this encoding be flexible, permitting approximate match in position. Our approach transforms the computationally demanding task of approximate alignment of sequence into the computationally convenient task of measuring the similarity between semantic vector representations. Consequently, it may be applicable to situations requiring rapid evaluation of large numbers of sequences.

Acknowledgments. This research was supported by NIH/BD2K supplement R01LM011563-S1 and NIH/BD2K supplement R01AI104739-S1.

References

1. Clark, S., Pulman, S.: Combining symbolic, distributional models of meaning. In: AAAI Spring Symposium: Quantum Interaction, pp. 52–55 (2007)
2. Widdows, D., Cohen, T.: Graded semantic vectors: an approach to representing graded quantities in generalized quantum models. In: Atmanspacher, H., Filk, T., Pothos, E. (eds.) QI 2015. LNCS, vol. 9535, pp. 231–244. Springer, Heidelberg (2016). doi:10.1007/978-3-319-28675-4_18
3. Bohm, D.: Quantum Theory. Prentice-Hall, New York (1951). Republished by Dover, 1989
4. Cohen, T., Widdows, D., Wahle, M., Schvaneveldt, R.: Orthogonality and orthography: introducing measured distance into semantic space. In: Atmanspacher, H., Haven, E., Kitto, K., Raine, D. (eds.) QI 2013. LNCS, vol. 8369, pp. 34–46. Springer, Heidelberg (2014). doi:10.1007/978-3-642-54943-4_4
5. Kleinstein, S.H.: Getting started in computational immunology. PLoS Comput. Biol. **4**(8), e1000128 (2008)
6. Benichou, J., Ben-Hamo, R., Louzoun, Y., Efroni, S.: Rep-seq: uncovering the immunological repertoire through next-generation sequencing. Immunology **135**(3), 183–191 (2012)
7. Durbin, R., Eddy, S.R., Krogh, A., Mitchison, G.: Biological Sequence Analysis: Probabilistic Models of Proteins and Nucleic Acids. Cambridge University Press, Cambridge (1998)
8. Tsioris, K., Gupta, N.T., Ogunniyi, A.O., Zimnisky, R.M., Qian, F., Yao, Y., Wang, X., Stern, J.N., Chari, R., Briggs, A.W., et al.: Neutralizing antibodies against West Nile virus identified directly from human B cells by single-cell analysis and next generation sequencing. Integrative Biol. **7**(12), 1587–1597 (2015)
9. Wu, Y.-C., Kipling, D., Leong, H.S., Martin, V., Ademokun, A.A., Dunn-Walters, D.K.: High-throughput immunoglobulin repertoire analysis distinguishes between human IgM memory and switched memory B-cell populations. Blood **116**, 1070–1078 (2010)
10. Ganapathiraju, M.K., Klein-Seetharaman, J., Balakrishnan, N., Reddy, R.: Characterization of protein secondary structure. IEEE Signal Process. Mag. **21**(3), 78–87 (2004)

11. Asgari, E., Mofrad, M.R.: Continuous distributed representation of biological sequences for deep proteomics and genomics. PloS One **10**(11), e0141287 (2015)
12. Kanerva, P., Kristofersson, J., Holst, A.: Random indexing of text samples for latent semantic analysis. In: Proceedings of the 22nd Annual Conference of the Cognitive Science Society, vol. 1036 (2000)
13. Widdows, D., Cohen, T.: Reasoning with vectors: a continuous model for fast robust inference. Logic J. IGPL **23**(2), jzu028 (2015)
14. Kanerva, P.: Sparse distributed memory. The MIT Press, Cambridge (1988)
15. Gayler, R.W.: Vector symbolic architectures answer Jackendoff's challenges for cognitive neuroscience. In: Slezak, P. (ed.) ICCS/ASCS International Conference on Cognitive Science, University of New South Wales, Sydney, Australia, pp. 133–138, (2004)
16. Fodor, J.A., Pylyshyn, Z.W.: Connectionism and cognitive architecture: a critical analysis. Cognition **28**(1–2), 3–71 (1988)
17. Smolensky, P.: Tensor product variable binding and the representation of symbolic structures in connectionist systems. Artif. Intell. **46**(1), 159–216 (1990)
18. Plate, T.A.: Holographic Reduced Representations: Distributed Representation for Cognitive Structures. CSLI Publications, Stanford (2003)
19. Kanerva, P.: Binary spatter-coding of ordered k-tuples. In: Artificial Neural Networks–ICANN 1996, pp. 869–873 (1996)
20. Hannagan, T., Dupoux, E., Christophe, A.: Holographic string encoding. Cogn. Sci. **35**(1), 79–118 (2011)
21. Davis, C.J., Bowers, J.S.: Contrasting five different theories of letter position coding: Evidence from orthographic similarity effects. J. Exp. Psychol. Hum. Percept. Perform. **32**(3), 535 (2006)
22. Sahlgren, M., Holst, A., Kanerva, P.: Permutations as a means to encode order in word space. In: Proceedings of the 30th Annual Meeting of the Cognitive Science Society, CogSci 2008, 23–26 July, Washington D.C., USA (2008)
23. Jones, M.N., Kintsch, W., Mewhort, D.J.: High-dimensional semantic space accounts of priming. J. Mem. Lang. **55**(4), 534–552 (2006)
24. Cox, G.E., Kachergis, G., Recchia, G., Jones, M.N.: Toward a scalable holographic word-form representation. Behav. Res. Methods **43**(3), 602–615 (2011)
25. Gallant, S.I., Culliton, P.: Positional binding with distributed representations. In: ICIVC, Portsmouth, UK (2016)
26. Aerts, D., Czachor, M., De Moor, B.: Geometric analogue of holographic reduced representation. J. Math. Psychol. **53**(5), 389–398 (2007)
27. Aerts, D., Czachor, M.: Quantum aspects of semantic analysis and symbolic artificial intelligence. J. Phys. A Math. Gen. **37**, L123–L132 (2004)
28. Kanerva, P.: Hyperdimensional computing: an introduction to computing in distributed representation with high-dimensional random vectors. Cogn. Comput. **1**(2), 139–159 (2009)
29. Crick, F., Barnett, L., Brenner, S., Watts-Tobin, R.J.: General nature of the genetic code for proteins. Nature **192**, 1227–1232 (1961). Macmillan Journals Limited
30. Lefranc, M.-P., Pommié, C., Ruiz, M., Giudicelli, V., Foulquier, E., Truong, L., Thouvenin-Contet, V., Lefranc, G.: IMGT unique numbering for immunoglobulin and T cell receptor variable domains and IG superfamily V-like domains. Dev. Comp. Immunol. **27**(1), 55–77 (2003)

31. Tsioris, K., Gupta, N.T., Ogunniyi, A.O., Zimnisky, R.M., Qian, F., Yao, Y., Wang, X., Stern, J.N.H., Chari, R., Briggs, A.W., Clouser, C.R., Vigneault, F., Church, G.M., Garcia, M.N., Murray, K.O., Montgomery, R.R., Kleinstein, S.H., Love, J.C.: Neutralizing antibodies against West Nile virus identified directly from human B cells by single-cell analysis and next generation sequencing. Integr. Biol. **7**(12), 1587–1597 (2015)
32. Gupta, N.T., Heiden, J.A.V., Uduman, M., Gadala-Maria, D., Yaari, G., Kleinstein, S.H.: Change-O: a toolkit for analyzing large-scale B cell immunoglobulin repertoire sequencing data: table 1. Bioinformatics **31**, 3356–3358 (2015)
33. Ogunniyi, A.O., Thomas, B.A., Politano, T.J., Varadarajan, N., Landais, E., Poignard, P., Walker, B.D., Kwon, D.S., Love, J.C.: Profiling human antibody responses by integrated single-cell analysis. Vaccine **32**, 2866–2873 (2014)
34. Wahle, M., Widdows, D., Herskovic, J.R., Bernstam, E.V., Cohen, T.: Deterministic binary vectors for efficient automated indexing of medline/pubmed abstracts. In: AMIA Annual Symposium Proceedings, American Medical Informatics Association, vol. 2012, p. 940 (2012)
35. Widdows, D., Cohen, T.: The semantic vectors package: new algorithms and public tools for distributional semantics. In: Fourth IEEE International Conference on Semantic Computing (ICSC) (2010)

Contextuality and Foundations of Probability

Testing Contextuality in Cyclic Psychophysical Systems of High Ranks

Ru Zhang[1,2(✉)] and Ehtibar N. Dzhafarov[1]

[1] Purdue University, West Lafayette, USA
[2] Indiana University, Bloomington, USA
{zhang617,ehtibar}@purdue.edu

Abstract. Contextuality-by-Default (CbD) is a mathematical framework for understanding the role of context in systems with deterministic inputs and random outputs. A necessary and sufficient condition for contextuality was derived for cyclic systems with binary outcomes. In quantum physics, the cyclic systems of ranks $n = 5$, 4, and 3 are known as systems of Klyachko-type, EPR-Bell-type, and Leggett-Garg-type, respectively. In earlier publications, we examined data collected in various behavioral and social scenarios, from polls of public opinion to our own experiments with psychophysical matching. No evidence of contextuality was found in these data sets. However, those studies were confined to cyclic systems of lower ranks ($n \leq 4$). In this paper, contextuality of higher ranks ($n = 6, 8$) was tested on our data with psychophysical matching, and again, no contextuality was found. This may indicate that many if not all of the seemingly contextual effects observed in behavioral sciences are merely violations of consistent connectedness (selectiveness of influences).

Keywords: Contextuality · Contextuality-by-default · Cyclic systems · Consistent connectedness · Psychophysical matching

1 Introduction

Consider a system having two external factors (or inputs) α and β, which can be deterministically manipulated, and two random outputs A and B that we interpret as responses to, or measurements of, α and β, respectively. The system can belong to any empirical domain, from quantum physics to behavioral sciences. If manipulating β does not change the marginal distribution of A and manipulating α does not change the marginal distribution of B, we say that the system is consistently connected. Physicists traditionally test contextuality by assuming consistent connectedness (referred to as "no-signaling," "no-disturbance," etc.). However, even in quantum experiments inconsistent connectedness may occur, e.g., because of context-dependent errors in measurements. In behavioral sciences inconsistent connectedness is ubiquitous. The Contextuality-by-Default (CbD) theory allows one to detect and measure contextuality, or to determine that a system is non-contextual, irrespective of whether it is consistently connected [1–8]. In quantum

© Springer International Publishing AG 2017
J.A. de Barros et al. (Eds.): QI 2016, LNCS 10106, pp. 151–162, 2017.
DOI: 10.1007/978-3-319-52289-0_12

physics, many experiments and theoretical considerations demonstrate the existence of contextual systems [9–15], including in cases when consistent connectedness is violated [8]. By contrast, we found no evidence of contextuality in various social and behavioral data sets, from polls of public opinion to visual illusions to conjoint choices to word combinations to psychophysical matching [16,17].

Most of the experimental studies of contextuality, both in quantum physics and in behavioral and social sciences, have been confined to cyclic systems [4,6,8], in which each entity being measured or responded to enters in two contexts and each context contains exactly two entities. In this paper we only deal with cyclic systems of even ranks, those that can be formed using the paradigm with two experimental factors (or inputs) α, β and two outputs in response to the two factors. A cyclic system of an even rank $2n \geq 4$ can be extracted from a design in which α and β vary on n levels each, denoted $\alpha_1, \alpha_2, \ldots, \alpha_n$ and $\beta_1, \beta_2, \ldots, \beta_n$. Out of n^2 possible treatments one extracts $2n$ pairs, we call contexts, whose elements form a cycle, e.g.,

$$
\begin{array}{cccc}
\text{Context 1} & \text{Context 2} & \ldots & \text{Context } (2n-1) & \text{Context } 2n \\
(\alpha_1, \beta_1) & (\beta_1, \alpha_2) & \ldots, & (\alpha_n, \beta_n) & (\beta_n, \alpha_1)
\end{array}
\tag{1}
$$

This is a cyclic system of rank $2n$. The outputs of the system corresponding to these $2n$ contexts are $2n$ pairs of random variables

$$
(A_{11}, B_{11}), (B_{21}, A_{21}), \ldots, (A_{nn}, B_{nn}), (B_{1n}, A_{1n}),
\tag{2}
$$

where A_{ij} is interpreted as a response to (measurement of) α_i in the context (α_i, β_j), and B_{ij} is interpreted as a response to (measurement of) β_j in the same context, where $i, j \in \{1, \ldots, n\}$. It is assumed in addition that each random output is binary, with values denoted $-1, +1$. The random variables A_{ij} and B_{ij} (recorded in the same context) are jointly distributed, so that, e.g., the joint probability of $A_{ij} = 1$ and $B_{ij} = -1$ is well-defined. However, according to CbD, any two random outputs recorded in different contexts, such as A_{ij} and $B_{i'j'}$ or A_{ij} and $A_{i'j'}$, with $(i,j) \neq (i',j')$, are stochastically unrelated, have no joint distribution [3–5,7,8,16].

In CbD, the system just described is considered noncontextual if and only if the $2n$ pairs of random variables in (2) can be coupled (imposed a joint distribution on) so that any two random variables responding to the same factor point in different contexts (i.e., A_{ij} and $A_{ij'}$, or B_{ij} and $B_{i'j}$) are equal to each other with maximal possible probability, given their individual distributions [4,5,7,8,16,17]. A necessary and sufficient condition for noncontextuality of a cyclic system (2) was derived in Refs. [4,6]:

$$
\Delta C = s_1 \left(\langle A_{11} B_{11} \rangle, \langle B_{21} A_{21} \rangle, \ldots, \langle A_{nn} B_{nn} \rangle, \langle B_{1n} A_{1n} \rangle \right)
$$
$$
- \mathsf{ICC} - (2n - 2) \leq 0,
\tag{3}
$$

where $\langle \cdot \rangle$ denotes expected value, $s_1(x_1, \ldots, x_k)$ is the maximum of all linear combinations $\pm x_1 \pm \ldots \pm x_k$ with odd numbers of minuses, and

$$\mathsf{ICC} = |\langle A_{11} \rangle - \langle A_{1n} \rangle| + |\langle B_{11} \rangle - \langle B_{21} \rangle|$$
$$+ \ldots + |\langle A_{n(n-1)} \rangle - \langle A_{nn} \rangle| + |\langle B_{nn} \rangle - \langle B_{1n} \rangle|. \tag{4}$$

If a system is consistently connected, ICC vanishes.

Experimental studies of cyclic systems in quantum physics were confined to ranks 3, 4, and 5 (see Refs. [4,8] for an overview). In behavioral and social experiments and surveys the ranks of the cyclic systems explored were 2, 3, and 4 (see Refs. [16,17] for an overview). In the present study, we analyze cyclic systems of ranks 4, 6, and 8.

2 Experiments

The experimental design and procedure were described in detail in Ref. [17]. Three different psychophysical matching tasks were used (Fig. 1): dot position reproduction task (Experiment 1(a) and 1(b)), concentric circles reproduction task (Experiment 2(a), 2(b) and 2(c)), and floral shape reproduction task (Experiment 3(a) and 3(b)). Each of the seven experiments was conducted on three participants.

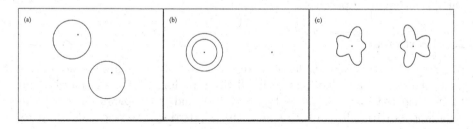

Fig. 1. Stimuli used in the (a) dot position reproduction task, (b) concentric circles reproduction task, and (c) floral shape reproduction task.

In each experimental trial, the participants were shown two stimuli on a computer screen, as shown in Fig. 1. One was a fixed stimulus, the other stimulus was adjustable, by means of rotating a trackball. The participants were required to change this stimulus until it appeared to match the position or shape of the fixed target stimulus. Once a match was achieved, she or he clicked the button on the trackball to terminate the trial. Each stimulus was characterized by two parameters. For the target stimulus these parameters are denoted as α and β, and their values in each trial were generated from a pre-defined set of numbers. The values of the same parameters in the matching stimulus are denoted A

Table 1. External factors (α, β) and random outputs (A, B) for the three types of tasks.

Task	α	β	A	B
Dot position reproduction (rectangular coordinates)	Horizontal coordinate of the target dot	Vertical coordinate of the target dot	Horizontal coordinate of the matching dot	Vertical coordinate of the matching dot
Dot position reproduction (polar coordinates)	Radial coordinate of the target dot	Angular coordinate of the target dot	Radial coordinate of the matching dot	Angular coordinate of the matching dot
Concentric circle reproduction	Radius of the target circle 1	Radius of the target circle 2	Radius of the matching circle 1	Radius of the matching circle 2
Floral shape reproduction, see (5)	Amplitude 1 of the target shape	Amplitude 2 of the target shape	Amplitude 1 of the matching shape	Amplitude 2 of the matching shape

and B (as they randomly vary for given values of α and β). Table 1 shows the parameters used.

The trials were separated by .5 s intervals. Each experiment took several days, each of which consisted of about 200 trials with a break in the middle. Each such session began by a practice series of 10 trials (which were not used for data analysis).

The original data sets for all the experiments are available as Excel files online (http://dx.doi.org/10.7910/DVN/OJZKKP). Each file corresponds to one participant in one experiment.

2.1 Participants

All the participants were students at Purdue University. The first author of this paper, labeled as P3, participated in all the experiments. Participants P1 and P2 participated in Experiments 1(a) and 2(a), and Participants P4 and P5 in Experiments 1(b), 2(b), 2(c), 3(a), and 3(b). All participants were about 25 years old and had normal or corrected to normal vision.

2.2 Stimuli and Procedure

Visual stimuli consisting of curves and dots were presented on a flat-panel monitor. The diameter of the dots and the width of the curves was 5 pixels (px). The stimuli were grayish-white on a comfortably low intensity background. The participants viewed the stimuli in darkness using a chin rest with a forehead support at the distance of 90 cm from the monitor, making 1 screen pixel approximately 62 s arc.

Experiment 1. In Experiment 1(a), each trial began with presenting two circles with a dot in the first quadrant of each circle (as shown in Fig. 1(a)). The dot in the upper left circle was fixed at one of randomly chosen six positions. These six positions contained a 2×2 "rectangular" sub-design: $\{32$ px, 64 px$\} \times \{32$ px, 64 px$\}$ and a 2×2 "polar" sub-design: $\{53.67$ px, 71.55 px$\} \times \{63.43$ deg, 26.57 deg$\}$. The coordinates were recorded using the center of the circle as the origin. The position adjustable dot was in the bottom right circle. The task was to move the bottom right dot by rotating the trackball to a position that matched that of the fixed one. There were 1200 trials overall.

Experiment 1(b) was identical to Experiment 1(a) except the horizontal coordinate and vertical coordinate of the target dot were random integers drawn from the interval [20 px, 80 px). This "rectangular" design also contained a "polar" sub-design [40 px, 90 px) $\times$ [30 deg, 60 deg). The overall number of trials for the "rectangular" design was 1800, for the polar sub-design about 900.

Experiment 2. In each trial of Experiment 2(a), the target stimulus on the left consisted of two concentric circles and a dot in their center. The radii of circle 1 and circle 2 were randomly chosen from the sets $\{16$ px, 56 px, 64 px$\}$ and $\{48$ px, 72 px, 80 px$\}$, respectively. At the beginning of each trial the right stimulus was a dot. The participants had to reproduce the target stimulus by rotating the trackball to "blow up" two circles from that dot one by one. They had the freedom to produce the inner or the outer circle first. Once the first matching circle was produced, the participants clicked a button on the trackball to confirm this circle and then the program enabled them to "blow up" the other circle. After the second circle was created, the trial was terminated by clicking the same button. There were 1800 trials overall.

Experiment 2(b) was identical to Experiment 2(a) except that in each trial the radii of the target circles were randomly chosen from four possibilities $\{12$ px, 24 px$\} \times \{18$ px, 30 px$\}$. There were 1600 trials overall.

Experiment 2(c) was identical to Experiment 2(a) except that in each trial the radii of the target circles were numbers randomly chosen from [18 px, 48 px) $\times$ [56 px, 86 px). There were 1800 trials overall.

Experiment 3. Two floral shapes (Fig. 1(c)) were presented simultaneously in each trial in Experiment 3(a). The target one was on the left. The right one was modifiable. Each floral shape was generated by a function

$$x = \cos(.02\pi\Delta)[70 + \alpha\cos(.06\pi\Delta) + \beta\cos(.1\pi\Delta)], \qquad (5)$$
$$y = \sin(.02\pi\Delta)[70 + \alpha\cos(.06\pi\Delta) + \beta\cos(.1\pi\Delta)],$$

where Δ is polar angle and x and y are the horizontal and vertical coordinates (in pixels). For a matching floral shape, α, β are replaced with A, B, respectively. The amplitudes α, β of the target shape were randomly chosen from the sets $\{-18$ px, 10 px, 14 px$\}$ and $\{-16$ px, -12 px, 20 px$\}$, respectively. The two amplitudes of the right shape were randomly initialized from the interval $[-35$ px, 35 px). The participants were asked to match the left shape by modifying the right shape by rotating the trackball. There were 1800 trials overall.

Experiment 3(b) was identical to Experiment 3(a) except that the two amplitudes of the target shape were randomly chosen numbers from the interval
[−30 px, 30 px).

3   Results

In each experiment the matching points that were too far from the target values
were considered outliers and they were removed from data analysis. The outliers
made less than 1% of all data. Ref. [17] briefly reported how contextuality for
cyclic systems of rank 4 was tested using the data collected from our seven
experiments. In this paper, we present the contextuality test for rank 4 in greater
details, and add the analyses for cyclic systems of ranks 6 and 8, using the same
data.

3.1   Testing Contextuality for Rank 4

A cyclic system of rank 4 can be represented by four contexts

$$\begin{array}{cccc} \text{Context 1} & \text{Context 2} & \text{Context 3} & \text{Context 4} \\ (\alpha_1, \beta_1) & (\beta_1, \alpha_2) & (\alpha_2, \beta_2) & (\beta_2, \alpha_1) \end{array}. \tag{6}$$

To form such a system, we chose $\{\alpha_1, \alpha_2\} \times \{\beta_1, \beta_2\} = \{32\,\text{px}, 64\,\text{px}\} \times \{32\,\text{px}, 64\,\text{px}\}$ for the "rectangular" sub-design of Experiment 1(a). The "polar"
sub-designs of Experiment 1(a) and Experiment 2(b) also have 2×2 struc-
tures, and they were presented as cyclic systems analogously. Experiment 2(a)
and Experiment 3(a) have 3×3 factorial designs. We extracted 9 cyclic systems of rank 4 from each of them by selecting two α's and two β's from the
sets of α and β. The "rectangular" design of Experiment 1(b) and the "polar"
sub-designs of Experiment 1(b), Experiment 2(c), and Experiment 3(b) have
external factors spanning certain intervals. In order to have a cyclic system of
rank 4, each interval was dichotomized into two subintervals. For instance, four
experimental conditions $(\alpha_{i_1}, \beta_{i_2})$, $i_1, i_2 \in \{1, 2\}$, are formed in the "rectangular"
design of Experiment 1(b) if one chooses $\alpha_1 = [20\,\text{px}, 50\,\text{px})$, $\alpha_2 = [50\,\text{px}, 80\,\text{px})$,
$\beta_1 = [20\,\text{px}, 50\,\text{px})$, and $\beta_2 = [50\,\text{px}, 80\,\text{px})$. Of course other cut-off points can
be chosen to dichotomize the intervals. In this paper, we only report the results
from the midpoint-dichotomized data sets.

Irrespective of the experiment, the random outputs $A_{i_1 i_2}, B_{i_1 i_2}$ should each
be dichotomized. The two values for each random variable were defined by choosing a value a_{i_1} and a value b_{i_2} and computing

$$A_{1 i_2}^* = \begin{cases} +1 \text{ if } A_{1 i_2} > a_1 \\ -1 \text{ if } A_{1 i_2} \le a_1 \end{cases}, \quad A_{2 i_2}^* = \begin{cases} +1 \text{ if } A_{2 i_2} > a_2 \\ -1 \text{ if } A_{2 i_2} \le a_2 \end{cases},$$

$$B_{i_1 1}^* = \begin{cases} +1 \text{ if } B_{i_1 1} > b_1 \\ -1 \text{ if } B_{i_1 1} \le b_1 \end{cases}, \quad B_{i_1 2}^* = \begin{cases} +1 \text{ if } B_{i_1 2} > b_2 \\ -1 \text{ if } B_{i_1 2} \le b_2 \end{cases}. \tag{7}$$

We chose a value a_1 as any integer (in pixels) between $\max(\min A_{11}, \min A_{12})$ and $\min(\max A_{11}, \max A_{12})$, b_1 as any integer (in pixels or degrees) between $\max(\min B_{11}, \min B_{21})$ and $\min(\max B_{11}, \max B_{21})$, and analogously for a_2 and b_2. The total number of the rank-4 systems thus formed varied from 3024 to 11,663,568 per experiment per participant. For each choice of the quadruple, we applied the test (3)–(4) to the distributions of the obtained A^* and B^* variables. No positive ΔC was observed, indicating the absence of contextuality in the rank 4 cyclic system for each participant in each experiment.

We present an example to illustrate how the test of (non)contextuality was conducted. For participant P3 in the "polar" sub-design of Experiment 1(a), one choice of the quadruple was $(a_1, a_2, b_1, b_2) = (72 \text{ px}, 67 \text{ px}, 60 \text{ deg}, 23 \text{ deg})$. The distributions of the random outputs for the four contexts indexed as in (6) are presented in Table 2, where the numbers in the grids are joint probabilities and the numbers outside are marginal probabilities.

Table 2. Distributions of the random outputs for the cyclic system of rank 4, P3 in the "polar" sub-design of Experiment 1(a).

Context 1	$B_{11} > b_1$	$B_{11} \leq b_1$	
$A_{11} > a_1$	.0056	0	.0056
$A_{11} \leq a_1$	.3944	.6	.9944
	.4	.6	

Context 2	$B_{21} > b_1$	$B_{21} \leq b_1$	
$A_{21} > a_2$	.6403	.3399	.9802
$A_{21} \leq a_2$	.0099	.0099	.0198
	.6502	.3498	

Context 3	$B_{22} > b_2$	$B_{22} \leq b_2$	
$A_{22} > a_2$	.5789	.4167	.9956
$A_{22} \leq a_2$	.0044	0	.0044
	.5833	.4167	

Context 4	$B_{12} > b_2$	$B_{12} \leq b_2$	
$A_{12} > a_1$	.0273	.0219	.0492
$A_{12} \leq a_1$	.4699	.4809	.9508
	.4972	.5028	

We have, in reference to (3)–(4)

$$s_1 \left(\langle A_{11}^* B_{11}^* \rangle, \langle B_{21}^* A_{21}^* \rangle, \langle A_{22}^* B_{22}^* \rangle, \langle B_{12}^* A_{12}^* \rangle \right) = s_1 \left(.2112, .3004, .1578, .0164 \right) = 0.653,$$

$$\begin{aligned}
\text{ICC} &= |\langle A_{11}^* \rangle - \langle A_{12}^* \rangle| + |\langle B_{11}^* \rangle - \langle B_{21}^* \rangle| + |\langle A_{21}^* \rangle - \langle A_{22}^* \rangle| + |\langle B_{22}^* \rangle - \langle B_{12}^* \rangle| \\
&= |(-.9016) - (-.9888)| + |(-.2) - .3004| + |.9604 - .9912| + |.1666 - (-.0056)| \\
&= .7906.
\end{aligned}$$

With $2n - 2 = 4 - 2 = 2$ we obtain

$$\Delta C = -2.1376 < 0,$$

no evidence of contextuality.

3.2 Testing Contextuality for Rank 6

Both Experiment 2(a) and Experiment 3(a) have 3×3 designs: $\{\alpha_1, \alpha_2, \alpha_3\} \times \{\beta_1, \beta_2, \beta_3\}$. From each of them we extracted one cyclic system of rank 6,

$$\begin{array}{cccccc}
\text{Context 1} & \text{Context 2} & \text{Context 3} & \text{Context 4} & \text{Context 5} & \text{Context 6} \\
(\alpha_1,\beta_1) & (\beta_1,\alpha_2) & (\alpha_2,\beta_2) & (\beta_2,\alpha_3) & (\alpha_3,\beta_3) & (\beta_3,\alpha_1)
\end{array}, \tag{8}$$

and labeled the random outputs A, B accordingly.

The "rectangular" design of Experiment 1(b), the "polar" sub-designs of Experiment 1(b), Experiment 2(c), and Experiment 3(b) are the systems with quasi-continuous factors. These factors were discretized into three levels by using the one-third quantile and the two-third quantile of each interval as cut-off points.

Again, the random outputs should be dichotomized in each experiment. We chose a value a_{i_1} and a value b_{i_2}, $i_1, i_2 \in \{1, 2, 3\}$, and defined

$$A^*_{1i_2} = \begin{cases} +1 \text{ if } A_{1i_2} > a_1 \\ -1 \text{ if } A_{1i_2} \le a_1 \end{cases}, \quad A^*_{2i_2} = \begin{cases} +1 \text{ if } A_{2i_2} > a_2 \\ -1 \text{ if } A_{2i_2} \le a_2 \end{cases},$$

$$A^*_{3i_2} = \begin{cases} +1 \text{ if } A_{3i_2} > a_3 \\ -1 \text{ if } A_{3i_2} \le a_3 \end{cases}, \quad B^*_{i_11} = \begin{cases} +1 \text{ if } B_{i_11} > b_1 \\ -1 \text{ if } B_{i_11} \le b_1 \end{cases}, \tag{9}$$

$$B^*_{i_12} = \begin{cases} +1 \text{ if } B_{i_12} > b_2 \\ -1 \text{ if } B_{i_12} \le b_2 \end{cases}, \quad B^*_{i_13} = \begin{cases} +1 \text{ if } B_{i_13} > b_3 \\ -1 \text{ if } B_{i_13} \le b_3 \end{cases}.$$

We chose a_1 as any integer between $\max(\min A_{11}, \min A_{13})$ and $\min(\max A_{11}, \max A_{13})$, b_1 as any integer between $\max(\min B_{11}, \min B_{21})$ and $\min(\max B_{11}, \max B_{21})$, and analogously for a_2, a_3, b_2, and b_3 for the experiments with discrete factor points Experiment 2(a) and Experiment 3(a). For the experiments with quasi-continuous factors, we chose $a_1, a_2, a_3, b_1, b_2, b_3$ as every third integer within the corresponding range. The total number of the rank-6 systems thus formed varied from 18,000 to 31,905,600 per experiment per participant. For each such choice of the sextuple $(a_1, a_2, a_3, b_1, b_2, b_3)$ we conducted the test (3)–(4). No positive ΔC was observed for the systems of rank 6 we investigated.

We present an example of how the test (3)–(4) was conducted. For participant P1 in Experiment 2(a), in which $\{\alpha_1, \alpha_2, \alpha_3\} \times \{\beta_1, \beta_2, \beta_3\} = \{16 \text{ px}, 56 \text{ px}, 64 \text{ px}\} \times \{48 \text{ px}, 72 \text{ px}, 80 \text{ px}\}$, one choice of the sextuple was $(a_1, a_2, a_3, b_1, b_2, b_3) = (16 \text{ px}, 56 \text{ px}, 64 \text{ px}, 48 \text{ px}, 72 \text{ px}, 80 \text{ px})$. The distributions of the random outputs for the six contexts indexed as in (8) are presented in Table 3.

We have

$$s_1 \left(\langle A^*_{11} B^*_{11} \rangle, \langle B^*_{21} A^*_{21} \rangle, \langle A^*_{22} B^*_{22} \rangle, \langle B^*_{32} A^*_{32} \rangle, \langle A^*_{33} B^*_{33} \rangle, \langle B^*_{13} A^*_{13} \rangle \right)$$
$$= s_1 (.1192, .4843, .5116, .4865, .8246, .2736) = 2.4613,$$

$$\text{ICC} = |\langle A^*_{13} \rangle - \langle A^*_{11} \rangle| + |\langle B^*_{11} \rangle - \langle B^*_{21} \rangle| + |\langle A^*_{22} \rangle - \langle A^*_{21} \rangle| + |\langle B^*_{22} \rangle - \langle B^*_{32} \rangle|$$
$$+ |\langle A^*_{32} \rangle - \langle A^*_{33} \rangle| + |\langle B^*_{33} \rangle - \langle B^*_{13} \rangle|$$
$$= |-.0778 - (-.3396)| + |-.1918 - (-.2218)| + |-.3212 - (-.593)|$$
$$+ |-.4302 - (-.0632)| + |-.3424 - (-.7660)| + |-.7778 - (-.4056)|$$
$$= .2618 + 0.03 + .2718 + .367 + .4236 + .3722 = 1.7264,$$

Table 3. Distributions of the random outputs for the cyclic system of rank 6, P1 in Experiment 2(a).

Context 1	$B_{11} > b_1$	$B_{11} \leq b_1$	
$A_{11} > a_1$	.2124	.2487	.4611
$A_{11} \leq a_1$	.1917	.3472	.5389
	.4041	.5959	

Context 2	$B_{21} > b_1$	$B_{21} \leq b_1$	
$A_{21} > a_2$	.2353	.1041	.3394
$A_{21} \leq a_2$	.1538	.5068	.6606
	.3891	.6109	

Context 3	$B_{22} > b_2$	$B_{22} \leq b_2$	
$A_{22} > a_2$	.1221	.0814	.2035
$A_{22} \leq a_2$	.1628	.6337	.7965
	.2849	.7151	

Context 4	$B_{32} > b_2$	$B_{32} \leq b_2$	
$A_{32} > a_3$	.2703	.0586	.3288
$A_{32} \leq a_3$	.1982	.4730	.6712
	.4685	.5316	

Context 5	$B_{33} > b_3$	$B_{33} \leq b_3$	
$A_{33} > a_3$	.0702	.0468	.1170
$A_{33} \leq a_3$	.0409	.8421	.8830
	.1111	.8889	

Context 6	$B_{13} > b_3$	$B_{13} \leq b_3$	
$A_{13} > a_1$	.1321	.1981	.3302
$A_{13} \leq a_1$	.1651	.5047	.6698
	.2972	.7028	

whence

$$\Delta C = 2.4613 - 1.7264 - (6 - 4) = -3.2651 < 0,$$

no evidence of contextuality.

3.3   Testing Contextuality for Rank 8

The "rectangular" design of Experiment 1(b), the "polar" sub-designs of Experiment 1(b), Experiment 2(c), and Experiment 3(b) have quasi-continuous factors. Each factor in each experiment was discretized into four levels in order to form a rank 8 cyclic system. Three points should be chosen for each factor to make this discretization. We chose the first quartile point, the second quartile (median) point, and the third quartile point of each interval. A cyclic system of rank 8 was extracted from each experiment:

$$\begin{array}{cccccccc} \text{Context 1} & \text{Context 2} & \text{Context 3} & \text{Context 4} & \text{Context 5} & \text{Context 6} & \text{Context 7} & \text{Context 8} \\ (\alpha_1, \beta_1) & (\beta_1, \alpha_2) & (\alpha_2, \beta_2) & (\beta_2, \alpha_3) & (\alpha_3, \beta_3) & (\beta_3, \alpha_4) & (\alpha_4, \beta_4) & (\beta_4, \alpha_1) \end{array},$$
$$(10)$$

with the random outputs labeled accordingly.

To dichotomize the outputs, we chose a value a_{i_1} and a value b_{i_2}, $i_1, i_2 \in \{1, 2, 3, 4\}$ to define

$$A^*_{1i_2} = \begin{cases} +1 \text{ if } A_{1i_2} > a_1 \\ -1 \text{ if } A_{1i_2} \leq a_1 \end{cases}, \quad A^*_{2i_2} = \begin{cases} +1 \text{ if } A_{2i_2} > a_2 \\ -1 \text{ if } A_{2i_2} \leq a_2 \end{cases},$$

$$A^*_{3i_2} = \begin{cases} +1 \text{ if } A_{3i_2} > a_3 \\ -1 \text{ if } A_{3i_2} \leq a_3 \end{cases}, \quad A^*_{4i_2} = \begin{cases} +1 \text{ if } A_{4i_2} > a_4 \\ -1 \text{ if } A_{4i_2} \leq a_4 \end{cases},$$

$$(11)$$

$$B^*_{i_1 1} = \begin{cases} +1 \text{ if } B_{i_1 1} > b_1 \\ -1 \text{ if } B_{i_1 1} \leq b_1 \end{cases}, \quad B^*_{i_1 2} = \begin{cases} +1 \text{ if } B_{i_1 2} > b_2 \\ -1 \text{ if } B_{i_1 2} \leq b_2 \end{cases},$$

$$B^*_{i_1 3} = \begin{cases} +1 \text{ if } B_{i_1 3} > b_3 \\ -1 \text{ if } B_{i_1 3} \leq b_3 \end{cases}, \quad B^*_{i_1 4} = \begin{cases} +1 \text{ if } B_{i_1 4} > b_4 \\ -1 \text{ if } B_{i_1 4} \leq b_4 \end{cases}.$$

For each rank 8 cyclic system, we chose a_1 as every sixth integer between $\max(\min A_{11}, \min A_{14})$ and $\min(\max A_{11}, \max A_{14})$, b_1 as every sixth integer between $\max(\min B_{11}, \min B_{21})$ and $\min(\max B_{11}, \max B_{21})$, and analogously for a_2, a_3, a_4, b_2, b_3, and b_4. The total number of the rank-8 systems thus formed varied from 432 to 6,453,888 per experiment per participant. For each thus obtained octuple we conducted the test (3)–(4). No positive ΔC was observed in all the investigated cyclic systems of rank 8.

To give an example, for participant P4 in Experiment 3(b), one choice of the octuple was $(a_1, a_2, a_3, a_4, b_1, b_2, b_3, b_4) =$ (-21 px, -6 px, 6 px, 21 px, -21 px, -9 px, 9 px, 21 px). The distributions of the random outputs for the eight contexts indexed as in (10) are presented in Table 4.

Table 4. Distributions of the random outputs for the cyclic system of rank 8, P4 in Experiment 3(b).

Context 1	$B_{11} > b_1$	$B_{11} \leq b_1$	
$A_{11} > a_1$	.1532	.2823	.4355
$A_{11} \leq a_1$	.1855	.3790	.5645
	.3387	.6613	

Context 2	$B_{21} > b_1$	$B_{21} \leq b_1$	
$A_{21} > a_2$	.1619	.2667	.4286
$A_{21} \leq a_2$	.1905	.3810	.5715
	.3524	.6477	

Context 3	$B_{22} > b_2$	$B_{22} \leq b_2$	
$A_{22} > a_2$	.2759	.2155	.4914
$A_{22} \leq a_2$	.2586	.2500	.5086
	.5345	.4655	

Context 4	$B_{32} > b_2$	$B_{32} \leq b_2$	
$A_{32} > a_3$	.4130	.1739	.5869
$A_{32} \leq a_3$	.1957	.2174	.4131
	.6087	.3913	

Context 5	$B_{33} > b_3$	$B_{33} \leq b_3$	
$A_{33} > a_3$	.2736	.3208	.5944
$A_{33} \leq a_3$	.1604	.2453	.4057
	.4340	.5661	

Context 6	$B_{43} > b_3$	$B_{43} \leq b_3$	
$A_{43} > a_4$	.2460	.3095	.5555
$A_{43} \leq a_4$	.1667	.2778	.4445
	.4127	.5873	

Context 7	$B_{44} > b_4$	$B_{44} \leq b_4$	
$A_{44} > a_4$	.3209	.3134	.6343
$A_{44} \leq a_4$	.1493	.2164	.3657
	.4702	.5298	

Context 8	$B_{14} > b_4$	$B_{14} \leq b_4$	
$A_{14} > a_1$	.1619	.2571	.4190
$A_{14} \leq a_1$	.2381	.3429	.5810
	.4	.6	

We have then

$$s_1 \left(\langle A_{11}^* B_{11}^* \rangle, \langle B_{21}^* A_{21}^* \rangle, \langle A_{22}^* B_{22}^* \rangle, \langle B_{32}^* A_{32}^* \rangle, \langle A_{33}^* B_{33}^* \rangle, \langle B_{43}^* A_{43}^* \rangle, \langle A_{44}^* B_{44}^* \rangle, \langle B_{14}^* A_{14}^* \rangle \right)$$

$$= s_1 \, (.0644, .0857, .0518, .2608, .0377, .0476, .0746, .0096) = .613,$$

$$\begin{aligned} \mathsf{ICC} &= |\langle A_{11}^* \rangle - \langle A_{14}^* \rangle| + |\langle B_{11}^* \rangle - \langle B_{21}^* \rangle| + |\langle A_{22}^* \rangle - \langle A_{21}^* \rangle| + |\langle B_{22}^* \rangle - \langle B_{32}^* \rangle| \\ &\quad + |\langle A_{33}^* \rangle - \langle A_{32}^* \rangle| + |\langle B_{43}^* \rangle - \langle B_{33}^* \rangle| + |\langle A_{44}^* \rangle - \langle A_{43}^* \rangle| + |\langle B_{14}^* \rangle - \langle B_{44}^* \rangle| \\ &= |-.129 - (-.162)| + |-.3226 - (-.2952)| + |-.0172 - (-.1428)| + |.069 - .2174| \\ &\quad + |.1888 - .1738| + |-.1746 - (-.132)| + |.2686 - (.1110)| + |-.2 - (-.0596)| \\ &= .033 + .0274 + .1256 + .1484 + .015 + .0426 + .1576 + .1404 = .6902, \end{aligned}$$

whence
$$\Delta C = .613 - .6902 - (8 - 2) = -6.0772 < 0,$$
no evidence of contextuality.

4   Conclusions

Contextuality-by-default is a mathematical framework that allows to classify systems as contextual or noncontextual. Experimental data suggest that the noncontextuality boundaries are generally breached in quantum physics [8]. In Refs. [16,17] we reviewed several behavioral and social scenarios to conclude that none of them provided evidence for contextuality. By examining the psychophysical data collected in our laboratory, we found no contextuality for cyclic systems of different ranks, including high ranks (6 and 8) that have never been analyzed before. We suspect that it may be generally true that human and social behaviors are not contextual in the same sense in which quantum systems are.

Acknowledgments. This research has been supported by NSF grant SES-1155956, AFOSR grant FA9550-14-1-0318.

References

1. Dzhafarov, E.N., Kujala, J.V.: A qualified kolmogorovian account of probabilistic contextuality. In: Atmanspacher, H., Haven, E., Kitto, K., Raine, D. (eds.) QI 2013. LNCS, vol. 8369, pp. 201–212. Springer, Heidelberg (2014). doi:10.1007/978-3-642-54943-4_18
2. Dzhafarov, E.N., Kujala, J.V.: Embedding quantum into classical: contextualization vs conditionalization. PLoS One **9**(3), e92818 (2014). doi:10.1371/journal.pone.0092818
3. Dzhafarov, E.N., Kujala, J.V.: Contextuality is about identity of random variables. Physica Scripta T **163**, 014009 (2014)
4. Dzhafarov, E.N., Kujala, J.V., Larsson, J.Å.: Contextuality in three types of quantum-mechanical systems. Found. Phys. **7**, 762–782 (2015)
5. Dzhafarov, E.N., Kujala, J.V., Cervantes, V.H.: Contextuality-by-default: a brief overview of ideas, concepts, and terminology. In: Atmanspacher, H., Filk, T., Pothos, E. (eds.) QI 2015. LNCS, vol. 9535, pp. 12–23. Springer, Heidelberg (2016). doi:10.1007/978-3-319-28675-4_2
6. Kujala, J.V., Dzhafarov, E.N.: Proof of a conjecture on contextuality in cyclic systems with binary variables. Found. Phys. **46**, 282–299 (2015)
7. Kujala, J.V., Dzhafarov, E.N.: Probabilistic Contextuality in EPR/Bohm-type systems with signaling allowed. Contextuality from Quantum Physics to Psychology, pp. 287–308. World Scientific, New Jersey (2015)
8. Kujala, J.V., Dzhafarov, E.N., Larsson, J.Å.: Necessary and sufficient conditions for extended noncontextuality in a broad class of quantum mechanical systems. Phys. Rev. Lett. **115**, 150401 (2015)
9. Bell, J.: On the Einstein-Podolsky-Rosen paradox. Physics **1**, 195–200 (1964)
10. Kochen, S., Specker, E.P.: The problem of hidden variables in quantum mechanics. J. Math. Mech. **17**, 59–87 (1967)

11. Clauser, J.F., Horne, M.A., Shimony, A., Holt, R.A.: Proposed experiment to test local hidden-variable theories. Phys. Rev. Lett. **23**, 880–884 (1969)
12. Fine, A.: Joint distributions, quantum correlations, and commuting observables. J. Math. Phys. **23**, 1306–1310 (1982)
13. Fine, A.: Hidden variables, joint probability, and the Bell inequalities. Phys. Rev. Lett. **48**, 291–295 (1982)
14. Leggett, A.J., Garg, A.: Quantum mechanics versus macroscopic realism: is the flux there when nobody looks? Phys. Rev. Lett. **54**, 857–860 (1985)
15. Klyachko, A.A., Can, M.A., Binicioğlu, S., Shumovsky, A.S.: Simple test for hidden variables in spin-1 systems. Phys. Rev. Lett. **101**(2), 020403 (2008)
16. Dzhafarov, E.N., Kujala, J.V., Cervantes, V.H., Zhang, R., Jones, M.: On contextuality in behavioural data. Philos. Trans. R. Soc. A **374**, 20150234 (2016)
17. Dzhafarov, E.N., Zhang, R., Kujala, J.V.: Is there contextuality in behavioral and social systems? Philos. Trans. R. Soc. A **374**, 20150099 (2015)

Probabilistic Programs: Contextuality and Relational Database Theory

P.D. Bruza[1(✉)] and S. Abramsky[2]

[1] Information Systems School, Queensland University of Technology,
Brisbane, Australia
p.bruza@qut.edu.au
[2] Department of Computer Science, Oxford University, Oxford, UK
samson.abramsky@cs.oxford.ac.uk

Abstract. [6] have introduced a contextual probability theory called Contextuality-by-Default (C-b-D) which is based on three principles. The first of these principles states that each random variable should be automatically labeled by all condition under which it is recorded. The aim of this article is to relate this principle to block structured computer programming languages where variables are declared local to a construct called a "scope". In this way a variable declared in two scopes can be safely overloaded meaning that they can have the same label but preserve two distinct identities without the need for the modeller to label each variable in each condition as advocated by C-b-D. A core issue addressed is how to construct a single probabilistic model from the various interim probability distributions returned by each syntactic scope. For this purpose, a probabilistic variant of the natural join operator of relational algebra is used to "glue" together interim distributions into a single distribution. The semantics of this join operator are related to contextual semantics [1].

1 Introduction

[6] have introduced a contextual probability theory called Contextuality-by-Default (C-b-D) which is based on three principles:

1. (Indexation by conditions): A random variable is identified (indexed, tagged) by all conditions under which its realizations are recorded.
2. (Unrelatedness): Two or more random variables recorded under mutually incompatible conditions are stochastically unrelated, i.e., they possess no joint distribution.
3. (Coupling) A set of pairwise stochastically unrelated random variables can be probabilistically coupled, i.e., imposed a joint distribution on; the choice of a coupling is generally non-unique.

Its curious with respect to the first principle that a similar line of thinking emerged in the field of computer programming languages in the nineteen sixties, particularly with the advent of a radical new language called ALGOL-60. Before ALGOL-60,

© Springer International Publishing AG 2017
J.A. de Barros et al. (Eds.): QI 2016, LNCS 10106, pp. 163–174, 2017.
DOI: 10.1007/978-3-319-52289-0_13

programming languages such as FORTRAN featured variables that are always accessible from any part of the program. These variables were termed "global" variables because of this property. As programming languages evolved, global variables were seen as a cause of errors, because a variable may be inadvertently used for two different functional purposes at different points in the program. In order to help counter such errors so called block structured programming languages were developed.

A block is sometimes referred to as a "lexical scope", which is a syntactically delineated fragment of a program within which program constructs such as variable definitions are defined as being local to the scope. As a consequence, the same variable name can be "overloaded" meaning it can be used in two different scopes but preserve unique "identities", where the identity is defined by its particular functional use in a given scope. This offers advantages to the probabilistic modeller as it maybe natural or convenient for the modeller to overload a variable while developing their model - the question is how to do this safely.

The use of syntactic scopes has two consequences. Firstly, it allows random variables be safely overloaded in a way that accords with the first principle of C-b-D. Secondly, as P-programs may have multiple scopes, each scope returns a probability distribution as an interim result. As it is desirable that a P-program returns a single model, the question arises as how to combine these interim results into a single probability distribution. This question is related to contextuality in the following way. [3] have shown that contextuality can be abstractly formalized by obstructions to the existence of global sections in sheaf theory. The advantage of the sheaf-theoretic approach is that it provides the foundations of a *general* semantics of contextuality. In addition, [1] has discovered that an instance of this general formulation of contextuality is surprisingly present in relational database theory where the problem is to determine whether a universal relation exists for a set of relations such that the component relations can be recovered from the universal relation via projection. This formulation of contextuality is very similar to the problem just posed regarding the composition of interim results. This article will attempt to further develop this connection by investigating how the join operation in relational database theory can be used to provide the semantics of the composition, and how these semantics relate to contextuality.

2   An Example P-program

Figure 1 tries to convey an impression of P-program syntax based on the open source programming language called "Julia" [4]. (This syntax is an operational refinement of the syntax presented in [5])

The using pProgram statement loads a module to interpret P-program syntax and operational semantics into the Julia execution framework. An innovative feature of P-programs syntax is the notion of a context which is intended to correspond to a measurement context related to the phenomenon being modelled. Scopes x1 and x2 define two measurement contexts. Note that the variable T is declared local to both contexts and is thus overloaded. The semantics to be presented below will ensure that this overloading can be safely handled by renaming the variable as necessary in accord with the first principle of C-b-D. Contexts can also access global variables as needed, e.g., variable V is used in both scopes. Global variables reflect the modeller's assumption that their marginal distribution will not vary across measurement contexts.

The P-program statement p = ProbFrame(T,U,V) defines a probability distribution labeled p local to the scope labeled x1. Such a distribution will be referred to as a probabilistic table, or p-table for short, as these are a natural probabilistic extension to the tables defined in relational databases. (Examples of p-tables are given below). The p-table is populated with data using the p = readtable(exp1.csv) statement. In this way, empirically collected data can be incorporated into a P-program for processing.

Finally, each context in a P-program returns an interim probability distribution representing the model of the phenomenon in that measurement context. Special syntax, e.g., pjoin(x1,x2) allows interim distributions from different contexts to be "glued together" to form a single distribution which is returned as the final result of the program. In the semantics to follow, we will investigate standard operations used in database theory to glue p-tables together to form a universal p-table.

3   Joining Distributions

The second last line of the P-program in Fig. 1 is p ~ pjoin(x1,x2). Consider Fig. 2 which depicts two p-tables returned by scopes x1 and x2 of our example P-program. The semantics of pjoin(x1,x2) differ depending on whether the marginal distribution of variable T across the p-tables x1 and x2. This is the only variable shared between the distributions returned by the respective scopes. If the marginal distributions of T differ across the scopes, i.e., $\Psi_{x1}^{\downarrow T} \neq \Psi_{x2}^{\downarrow T}$, then this means that variable T has different identities in each scope. In this case, Cartesian product of two tables can be used resulting in a table where each row in one table is concatenated with each row in the other table and the variable T renamed according to the first principle of C-b-D. (See the left p-table in Fig. 3).

Now consider the second case where the marginal distribution of T *does not* vary across the scopes x1 and x2, i.e., $\Psi_{x1}^{\downarrow T} = \Psi_{x2}^{\downarrow T}$. In this case the variable T is assumed to have single identity across both scopes and this no renaming is needed. In this case a subset of the Cartesian product can be formed where rows are stitched together based on the columns that are common to both tables resulting in p-table with 16 rows. [10] refers to the result as the "product join", denoted $x \times y$, which is depicted as the p-table on the right in Fig. 3. The product join does not deliver a p-table because the probabilities are not normalized. In order to normalize the probabilities, we adopt the same approach as [10] by using inverted p-tables. An inverted p-table is one in which for each row, the probability p is replaced by $1/p$. For instance, the inverted p-table x1 (see Fig. 2), denoted $x1^{-1}$, is a table where the column p now contains the value $1/p_1$ instead of p_1 etc.

[10] shows that in order to normalize the probabilities of the product join depicted on the right of Fig. 3, then this product join must be product joined

```
 1  # load the P-program package
 2        using pProgram
 3  # declare global variable V
 4        global V in {0,1}
 5
 6  # define scope x1 for experiment 1
 7        context x1()
 8  # declare  T,U to be local to scope x1
 9            local T,U in {0,1}
10  # form a distribution using data
11            p = ProbFrame(T,U,V)
12            p = readtable(exp1.csv)
13  # form the marginal distribution p1
14            p1 ˜ p(T,U)
15  # return model for scope x1
16            p1
17        end
18
19  # define scope x2 for experiment 2
20        context x2()
21            local T in {0,1}
22            p = ProbFrame(T,V)
23            p = readtable(exp2.csv)
24  # return result for scope x2
25            p
26        end
27  # Glue models from scopes x1 and x2
28        p = ProbFrame()
29        p ˜ pjoin(x1,x2)
30  # Final model
31        p
```

Fig. 1. Example P-program

	T	U	p		T	V	p
	1	1	p_1		1	1	q_1
x1:	1	0	p_2	x2:	1	0	q_2
	0	1	p_3		0	1	q_3
	0	0	p_4		0	0	q_4

Fig. 2. p-tables corresponding to distributions returned by scope x1 (left) and scope x2 (right)

with the inversion of a marginal distribution defined by the shared variable T, or more formally, $x1 \times x2 \times (\Psi_{x1}^{\downarrow T})^{-1}$. (As we know the marginal probabilities of T are the same across p-tables x1 and x2, this could equivalently be written as $x1 \times x2 \times (\Psi_{x2}^{\downarrow T})^{-1}$). [10] refers to the result as a "generalized join", denoted $x1 \otimes x2$ as it is a probabilistic extension of the natural join found in relational database theory.

p:

T1	T2	U	V	p
1	1	1	1	$p_1 q_1$
1	1	1	0	$p_1 q_2$
1	1	0	1	$p_1 q_3$
1	1	0	0	$p_1 q_4$
1	0	1	1	$p_2 q_1$
1	0	1	0	$p_2 q_2$
1	0	0	1	$p_2 q_3$
1	0	0	0	$p_2 q_4$
0	1	1	1	$p_3 q_1$
0	1	1	0	$p_3 q_2$
0	1	0	1	$p_3 q_3$
0	1	0	0	$p_3 q_4$
0	0	1	1	$p_4 q_1$
0	0	1	0	$p_4 q_2$
0	0	0	1	$p_4 q_3$
0	0	0	0	$p_4 q_4$

p:

T	U	V	p
1	1	1	$p_1 q_1$
1	1	0	$p_1 q_2$
1	0	1	$p_2 q_1$
1	0	0	$p_2 q_2$
0	1	1	$p_3 q_3$
0	1	0	$p_3 q_4$
0	0	1	$p_4 q_3$
0	0	0	$p_4 q_4$

Fig. 3. Joining tables via Cartesian product (left) and product join (right)

The generalized join of our example is therefore defined as follows: $x1 \otimes x2 = x1 \times x2 \times (\Psi_{x1}^{\downarrow T})^{-1}$ (or $x1 \otimes x2 = x1 \times x2 \times (\Psi_{x2}^{\downarrow T})^{-1}$). The resulting p-table is displayed in Table 1. Figure 4 depicts the semantics of `pjoin(x1,x2)` using the database language SQL which provides a more readable semantics than relational algebra. These semantics are dependent on the set of variables common to the distributions represented by the p-tables x1 and x2, in this case {T}. When the marginal distribution of variable T is not the same across scopes x1 and x2, the Cartesian product of p-tables returned by these scopes is employed with the automatic renaming of common variable T (x1.T and x2.T) of both contexts into T1 and T2. In this way the semantics adhere to the first principle of C-b-D *without* the programmer having to explicitly rename the variables.

Table 1. p-table resulting from the generalized join $x1 \otimes x2 = x1 \times x2 \times (\Psi_{x1}^{\downarrow T})^{-1}$

T	U	V	p
1	1	1	$\frac{p_1 q_1}{(p_1+p_2)}$
1	1	0	$\frac{p_1 q_2}{(p_1+p_2)}$
1	0	1	$\frac{p_2 q_1}{(p_1+p_2)}$
1	0	0	$\frac{p_2 q_2}{(p_1+p_2)}$
0	1	1	$\frac{p_3 q_3}{(p_3+p_4)}$
0	1	0	$\frac{p_3 q_4}{(p_3+p_4)}$
0	0	1	$\frac{p_4 q_3}{(p_3+p_4)}$
0	0	0	$\frac{p_4 q_4}{(p_3+p_4)}$

```
1   [[pjoin(x1,x2)]]{T} =
2   IF   ([[x1(T)]] ≁ [[x2(T)]])
3               SELECT x1.T AS T1,x2.T AS T2,x2.U AS U,x1.V AS V,x1.p*x2.p AS p
4               FROM x1,x2;
5   ELSE
6               SELECT x1.T AS T, x2.U AS U,x1.V AS V, x1.p * x2.p * inv.p AS p
7               FROM x1,x2, (SELECT T, 1/p AS p
8                                     FROM x1
9                                     GROUP BY T) AS inv
10              WHERE x1.T = x2.T AND x1.T = inv.T;
```

Fig. 4. Complete SQL semantics of `pjoin(x1,x2)`

If, however, the marginal distributions are the same, then the SQL semantics of the generalized join are employed. Here we can see inversion necessary for normalization as the sub-SELECT in the FROM clause. This results in the table labelled "inv". Other than that, the SELECT statement has the form of the natural join between two tables commonly found in relational databases. These semantics show the structure of the resulting p-table differs from the Cartesian product as there is a single instantiation of the variable T via x1.T as in this case the variable has a single identity across scopes x1 and x2. In order to form the natural join, the condition x1.T = x2.T in the WHERE clause specifies that rows of the respective p-tables x1 and x2 are "stitched together" where the values of T across the rows of the respective component tables are equal. Stitching the rows together in this way delivers the required set of rows to form the basis of the joint distribution across the three columns: x1.T, x2.U,x1.V. Similarly, the condition x1.T = inv.T allows these rows to be stitched together with the rows of the inverted table labelled "inv", which allows normalized probabilities to be computed via "x1.p * x2.p * inv.p" with the resulting column labelled "p" as is required for a p-table.

Generalized `pjoin` Semantics

Consider the two P-programs in Fig. 5. These programs differ only in the local variable declarations in scope P4. The left hand program declares variables A3, B2 in this scope and the right hand one declares variables A2 and B2. In both cases the programs return a single distribution P by joining the distributions $P1,\ldots,P4$ returned by each of the scopes P1 ... P4. Recall that if the distribution (universal p-table) P can be formed such that $P1,\ldots,P4$ are marginal distributions of P, then the phenomenon being modelled by the P-program is not contextual.

Relational database theory tells us that a key consideration in this problem turns out to be whether the database schema comprising constituent relations (p-tables) are cyclic or acyclic. A database schema is deemed "acyclic" iff the hypergraph $H(N,E)$ can be reduced into an empty graph using the Graham procedure [8]. In our case, the nodes N of the hypergraph are the the individual variables in the p-table headers and the edges correspond to the sets of variables in these headers, i.e., there will be one edge corresponding to each

```
 1  # load the P-program package
 2      using pProgram
 3
 4  # define context (a1,b1) for experiment 1
 5      context P1()
 6  # declare  A1,B1
 7          local A1,B1 in {0,1}
 8  # form a distribution using data
 9          p = ProbFrame(A1,B1)
10          p = readtable(exp1.csv)
11  # return model
12          p
13      end
14
15  # define context (a1,b2) for experiment 2
16      context P2()
17  # declare  A1,B2
18          local A1,B2 in {0,1}
19  # form a distribution using data
20          p = ProbFrame(A1,B2)
21          p = readtable(exp2.csv)
22  # return model
23          p
24      end
25
26  # define context (a2,b1) for experiment 3
27      context P3()
28  # declare  A2,B1
29          local A2,B1 in {0,1}
30  # form a distribution using data
31          p = ProbFrame(A2,B1)
32          p = readtable(exp3.csv)
33  # return model
34          p
35      end
36
37  # define context (a3,b2) for experiment 4
38      context P4()
39  # declare  A3,B2
40          local A3,B2 in {0,1}
41  # form a distribution using data
42          p = ProbFrame(A3,B2)
43          p = readtable(exp4.csv)
44  # return model
45          p
46      end
47  # Glue models from scopes
48      p = ProbFrame()
49      p = pjoin(P1,P2,P3,P4)
50  # Final model
51      p
```

(a) P-program 1

```
 1  # load the P-program package
 2      using pProgram
 3
 4  # define context (a1,b1) for experiment 1
 5      context P1()
 6  # declare  A1,B1
 7          local A1,B1 in {0,1}
 8  # form a distribution using data
 9          p = ProbFrame(A1,B1)
10          p = readtable(exp1.csv)
11  # return model
12          p
13      end
14
15  # define context (a1,b2) for experiment 2
16      context P2()
17  # declare  A1,B2
18          local A1,B2 in {0,1}
19  # form a distribution using data
20          p = ProbFrame(A1,B2)
21          p = readtable(exp2.csv)
22  # return model
23          p
24      end
25
26  # define context (a2,b1) for experiment 3
27      context P3()
28  # declare  A2,B1
29          local A2,B1 in {0,1}
30  # form a distribution using data
31          p = ProbFrame(A2,B1)
32          p = readtable(exp3.csv)
33  # return model
34          p
35      end
36
37  # define context (a2,b2) for experiment 4
38      context P4()
39  # declare  A2,B2
40          local A2,B2 in {0,1}
41  # form a distribution using data
42          p = ProbFrame(A2,B2)
43          p = readtable(exp4.csv)
44  # return model
45          p
46      end
47  # Glue models from scopes
48      p = ProbFrame()
49      p = pjoin(P1,P2,P3,P4)
50  # Final model
51      p
```

(b) P-program 2

Fig. 5. Two P-programs

p-table in the pjoin expression, where the edge is the set of variables defining the header of that p-table. For example, the database schema corresponding to P-program 1 in is depicted in Fig. 6. In this case, $N = \{A_1, A_2, A_3, B_1, B_2\}$ and $E = \{\{A_1, B_1\}, \{A_1, B_2\}, \{A_2, B_1\}, \{A_3, B_2\}\}$ The Graham procedure is applied to the hypergraph H until no further action is possible:

– delete every edge that is properly contained in another one
– delete every node that is only contained in one edge

A1	B1	p
1	1	0.5
1	0	0
0	1	0
0	0	0.5

P1:

A1	B2	p
1	1	0.5
1	0	0
0	1	0
0	0	0.5

P2:

A2	B1	p
1	1	0.5
1	0	0
0	1	0
0	0	0.5

P3:

A3	B2	p
1	1	0.5
1	0	0
0	1	0
0	0	0.5

P4:

Fig. 6. Example acyclic database of the four p-tables returned by P-program 1

The following details the steps of the Graham procedure to the example:

1. $\{A_1, B_1\}, \{A_1, B_2\}, \{A_2, B_1\}, \{A_3, B_2\}$
2. $\{A_1, B_1\}, \{A_1, B_2\}, \{A_2, B_1\}, \{B_2\}$
3. $\{A_1, B_1\}, \{A_1, B_2\}, \{A_2, B_1\}$
4. $\{A_1, B_1\}, \{A_1, B_2\}, \{B_1\}$
5. $\{A_1, B_1\}, \{A_1, B_2\}$
6. $\{A_1, B_1\}, \{A_1\}$
7. $\{A_1, B_1\}$
8. $\{A_1\}$
9. $\emptyset$

The Graham procedure results in an empty hypergraph, so the schema is deemed "acyclic". Note, however, that the set of edges corresponding to P-program 2 in Fig. 5 is

$$E = \{\{A_1, B_1\}, \{A_1, B_2\}, \{A_2, B_2\}, \{A_2, B_1\}\}$$

and the hypergraph cannot be reduced to an empty set of edges, so the schema of this P-program is termed "cyclic".

There are a number of theoretical results in relational database theory which make "acyclic" hypergraphs significant to providing the semantics of joining p-tables. [10] detailed the relationship between a Markov network and a relational database model. The key idea behind this connection was the discovery of the equivalence between probabilistic conditional independence and a generalized form of multivalued dependency (GEMVD). Multivalued dependencies are a particular form of mathematical function which are used define constraints on the data stored within the database. This connection allows a Markov distribution to be constructed by joining component distributions together. [10] described this relationship between Markov distributions and relational database theory as "generalized acyclic join dependency" (GAJD) which was formalized in an extended relational database model. GAJDs are in turn related to acyclic hypergraphs. The connection with GAJDs and hypergraphs is the following: A joint distribution factorized on a acyclic hypergraph is equivalent to a GAJD [11].

Consider once again the acyclic schema in Fig. 6. There are four p-tables, $P = \{P_1, P_2, P_3, P_4\}$. As the hypergraph is acyclic, there is a so called join tree construction, denoted $\otimes\{S_1, \ldots, S_n\}$, that satisfies the GAJD. The practical consequence of this is that there is a join expression of the form: $(((S_1 \otimes S_2) \otimes S_3) \otimes S_4)$ where the sequence $S_1, \ldots, S_4$ is a tree construction ordering derived from the acyclic hypergraph and each S_i denotes a unique p-table in the set P. In summary, if the hypergraph constructed from the schema comprising n p-tables $\{P_1, P_2, P_3, \ldots P_n\}$ is acyclic, then a generalized join expression $(\ldots (S_1 \otimes S_2) \otimes S_3) \ldots \otimes S_n)$ exists which joins the p-tables into a single probability distribution P such that each $P_i, 1 \leq i \leq n$ is a marginal distribution of P.

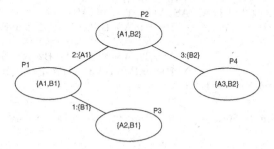

Fig. 7. Join tree of the p-tables P_1, P_2, P_3, P_4 to be joined

In order to gain some intuition about how this plays out in practice, the acyclic database schema depicted in Fig. 6 results in the join tree depicted in Fig. 7. The nodes depict the variables in the respective p-tables, and the edges represent the overlap between the sets of variables in the respective headers. The numbers on the edges denote the ordering used to produce the join expression: $(((P_3 \otimes P_1) \otimes P_2) \otimes P_4)$. Under the assumption that the probability distributions represented in the nodes have identical distributions when marginalized by the variable associated with the edge, we can see how the hypertree produces a Markov network which, in turn, specifies the probabilistic join of the constituent p-tables [9]:

$$P(A_1, A_2, A_3, B_1, B_2) = \frac{P(A_2, B_1)P(A_1, B_1)P(A_1, B_2)P(A_3, B_2)}{P(B_1)P(A_1)P(B_2)} \quad (1)$$

Observe how the structure of equation mirrors the graph in Fig. 7 where the numerator corresponds to the nodes of the join tree and the denominator corresponds to terms which normalize the probabilities. Using the Wong formalism of the previous section, this same distribution is expressed as follows:
$$(((P_3 \otimes P_1) \otimes P_2) \otimes P_4) = (((P_3 \times P_1 \times (\Psi_{P_3}^{\downarrow B_1})^{-1}) \times P_2 \times (\Psi_{P_2}^{\downarrow A_1})^{-1}) \times P_4 \times (\Psi_{P_4}^{\downarrow B_2})^{-1})$$

3.1 pjoin **Semantics of Cyclic Join Dependencies**

The semantics of pjoin(P1,P2,P3,P4) in the previous section relied on the schema of the constituent p-tables to be acyclic. Attention is now turned to the

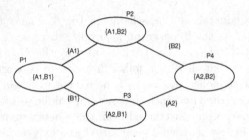

Fig. 8. Cyclic schema of the p-tables P_1, P_2, P_3, P_4

```
1  [pjpoin(P1,P2,P3,P4)] A1,B1,A2,B2 =
2    SELECT P1.A1 AS A11, P2.A1 AS A12,
3                  P1.B1 AS B11, P3.B1 AS B12,
4                  P3.A2 AS A21, P4.A2 AS A22,
5                  P2.B2 AS B21, P4.B2 AS B22,
6                  P1.p*P2.p*P3.p*P4.p AS p
7  FROM P1,P2,P3,P4;
```

Fig. 9. SQL semantics of an example cyclic schema

case when the schema is cyclic. Figure 8 depicts a cyclic schema of four p-tables $P1, P2, P3$ and $P4$ returned by P-program 2 of Fig. 5.

There is a substantial literature in relational database theory surrounding cyclic schemas. For example, [8] states the following: "Cyclicity implies that one or more attributes of the database are 'overloaded' ..... The reason why a database attribute such as PRODUCT might become overloaded is that it has more than one function; it might mean a product that is being supplied and a product being purchased". [8] suggest that a way to deal with cyclicity is to "split the 'overloaded' attributes into two or more new attributes" in order to render the schema acyclic. This is clearly similar to the first principle of C-b-D which would view PRODUCT as one variable in two conditions, hence according to this principle, PRODUCT should not be a single attribute, but two attributes: PRODUCT_SUPPLIED and PRODUCT_PURCHASED, a unique attribute for each condition. [8] show that in some cases a cyclic hypergraph can be decomposed into two hypergraphs; one acyclic and the other cyclic. They prove that the cyclic sub-graph is not further decomposable. Such cyclic graphs are referred to as "supercycles".

The cyclic schema depicted in Fig. 8 is an example a simple supercycle. Here the overloaded variables are denoted on the edges of the graph. In such cases, each overloaded variable should be renamed into two variables. A straightforward semantics forms the Cartesian product of the four p-tables where renaming automatically occurs with respect to the overloaded variables.

By way of illustration, the semantics of the super-cycle depicted in Fig. 8 are expressed in Fig. 9. These semantics define a p-table in which the overloaded variables have been split and renamed. In this example, all the variables happen to be overloaded.

4   Broader Discussion on `pjoin` Semantics and Contextuality

Recall that [1] establishes connections between relational databases and contextuality theory and suggests further connections could be made with probabilistic databases. The present work can be considered as a step in this direction. The p-tables presented in this article are probabilistic variants of tables commonly found in relational databases. The semantics of the `pjoin` are designed to "glue" p-tables together, which is analogous to the glueing of local sections in the sheaf-theoretic definition of contextuality [3]. The question now arises what the `pjoin` semantics say about contextuality.

For a system of p-tables with acyclic schema, there are two cases: (1) When the marginal distributions of the overlapping variables of the p-tables being glued *do not* agree, the semantics deem the phenomenon modelled by the P-program to be contextual. (In this case there will be automatic renaming of variables according to the first principle of C-b-D) (2) When the marginals of the p-tables being glued *do* agree, the `pjoin` semantics yields a joint distribution, which implies that the phenomenon is not contextual. (This case corresponds to the "Vorob'ev condition" [1]). In other words, glueing the component p-tables together into a universal p-table succeeds such that each component table can be recovered by projection For a system of p-tables with cyclic schema, the semantics of the `pjoin` cannot determine whether the system is contextual.

In short, a simple approach using semantics based on the p-table - a simple probabilistic extension of the notion of table in a relational databases together with straightforward adaptions of the Cartesian product and natural join to provide means to glue p-table together is unfortunately not particularly effective in diagnosing contextuality. It is an open question whether more sophisticated methods from relational database theory can be informative with respect to contextuality to the same degree that linear programming methods can [2,7].

References

1. Abramsky, S.: Contextual semantics: from quantum mechanics to logic, databases, constraints, and complexity. Bull. EATCS **2**(113) (2015)
2. Abramsky, S., Barbosa, R., Mansfield, S.: Quantifying contextuality via linear programming. In: Proceedings of the 13th Interational Conference on Quantum Physics and Logic (QPL 2016) (2016)
3. Abramsky, S., Brandenburger, A.: The sheaf-theoretic structure of non-locality and contextuality. New J. Phys. **13**(11), 113036 (2011)
4. Benazson, J., Karpinski, S., Shah, V., Edelman, A.: Julia: a fast dynamic language for technical computing. arXiv:1209.5145 (2012)

5. Bruza, P.D.: Syntax and operational semantics of a probabilistic programming language with scopes. J. Math. Psychol. (2016, in press). doi:10.1016/j.jmp.2016.06.006
6. Dzhafarov, E., Kujala, J.: Probabilistic contextuality in EPR/Bohm-type systems with signaling allowed. In: Dzhafarov, E. (ed.) Contextuality from Quantum Physics to Psychology, chap. 12, pp. 287–308. World Scientific Press, New Jersey (2015)
7. Dzhafarov, R., Kujala, J.: Selectivity in probabilistic causality: where psychology runs into quantum physics. J. Math. Psychol. **56**(1), 54–63 (2012)
8. Gyssens, M., Paredaens, J.: A decomposition methodology for cyclic databases. In: Gallaire, H., Minker, J., Nicolas, J.M. (eds.) Advances in Database Theory, vol. 2, pp. 85–122. Springer, New York (1984)
9. Liu, W., Yue, K., Li, W.: Constructing the Bayesian network structure from dependencies implied in multiple relational schemas. Expert Syst. Appl. **38**, 7123–7134 (2011)
10. Wong, S.: An extended relational model for probabilistic reasoning. J. Intell. Inf. Syst. **9**, 181–202 (1997)
11. Wong, S.: The relational structure of belief networks. J. Intell. Inf. Syst. **16**, 117–148 (2001)

On Peculiar Relations Between Measurement Incompatibility and Contextuality

Dagomir Kaszlikowski[1,2(✉)] and Paweł Kurzyński[1,3]

[1] Centre for Quantum Technologies, National University of Singapore,
3 Science Drive 2, Singapore 117543, Singapore
`phykd@nus.edu.sg`
[2] Department of Physics, National University of Singapore,
2 Science Drive 3, Singapore 117542, Singapore
[3] Faculty of Physics, Adam Mickiewicz University,
Umultowska 85, 61-614 Poznań, Poland
`pawel.kurzynski@amu.edu.pl`

Abstract. We use algorithmic information to define co-measurability of observables and investigate its relation to the phenomenon of quantum contextuality.

Keywords: Contextuality · Quantum correlations · Quantum measurement · Information distance

1 Introduction

Quantum theory (QT) of matter is extremely successful in its explanations of the building blocks of the universe. At the moment there is not even a single experiment that cannot be explained by it and thus there is no need to amend it in any way. However, there has not been any other physical theory as controversial as quantum mechanics. Since the inception of QT in the early 30s, many scientists have been struggling with its philosophical consequences or at least spent a thought or two on the topic. Ironically, Planck and Einstein, two of the prominent founding fathers of the theory, could not accept its consequences as it undermined their preferred views on how the universe should look like.

What is it in QT that makes people uncomfortable? It is difficult to say as opinions vary but all problems seem to originate from an attempt to implant notions of classical physics into QT. One such notion, which we would like to discuss in this article, is an assumption that all observables should be co-measurable with arbitrary precision. This is a basic assumption in classical physics but an anathema in QT where non-commuting observables are non-commeasurable. A classic example is a particle's position and momentum measurement. Perfectly all right to be co-measured in classical physics but forbidden in QT because of the famous relation $\mathbf{XP} - \mathbf{PX} = i\hbar$.

Mathematically, the fact that non-commuting observables cannot be co-measured is a consequence of Gleason theorem [1] that ties this with the Born

© Springer International Publishing AG 2017
J.A. de Barros et al. (Eds.): QI 2016, LNCS 10106, pp. 175–181, 2017.
DOI: 10.1007/978-3-319-52289-0_14

rule as long as the dimension of the quantum system under consideration is 3 or more (and there is little doubt it should be different for a physical system of the dimension 2). If $\mathbf{A}$ and $\mathbf{A}'$ do not commute (we assume here that $\mathbf{A}$ and $\mathbf{A}'$ are nonorthogonal projectors), one cannot find a joint probability distribution $p(\mathbf{A} = a, \mathbf{A}' = a')$ where a, a' are measurement outcomes.

Physical meaning of the above assertion is that it is impossible or at least no one knows how to build a physical apparatus capable of co-measuring $\mathbf{A}$ and $\mathbf{A}'$. You can either measure $\mathbf{A}$ or $\mathbf{A}'$ or you can measure them sequentially but never together.

What if QT is not right about this issue? What if our experiments are crude? After all, not being able to do something does not amount to its impossibility. However outrageous those questions appear they have been asked again and again since the birth of QT. The most famous attempt to disqualify QT was the famous Einstein-Podolsky-Rosen [2] paper that gave birth to works of John Bell [3] and Kochen-Specker [4] and ultimately lead us to a blooming field of quantum information science, and a much better understanding of QT.

In this paper we ask the following question: *Is it possible to define co-measurability of non-compatible observables that is consistent with all experimental data?* We will answer this question and relate it to the phenomenon of quantum contextuality [3,4].

2   Preliminaries

Co-measurability of $\mathbf{A}$ and $\mathbf{A}'$ can be understood as existence of a joint probability distribution for these observables, i.e., $p(\mathbf{A} = a, \mathbf{A}' = a')$. This is the standard and already discussed interpretation [3,11,12]. However, it can also be understood in a more fundamental way without invoking probabilistic interpretation of QT. In fact, every quantum experiment is a series of detection events that can be encoded as 0s and 1s (0 means 'no detection' and 1 means 'detection'). After a series of measurements we obtain some binary strings A and A' that are *primitives* of any experimental test.

Now, we need to define what we mean by co-measurability of $\mathbf{A}$ and $\mathbf{A}'$ given bit strings A and A'. We propose an algorithmic approach: $\mathbf{A}$ and $\mathbf{A}'$ are jointly measurable if the strings A and A' can be jointly generated by a universal deterministic Turing machine (UTM). This is in line with a physical version of the Church-Turing hypothesis: *a universal computing device can simulate every physical process* [6].

The possibility of generating bit string A is described by algorithmic information $K(A)$ [9] that is defined as the length (in bits) of the minimal program on a UTM that outputs the string A. In general, such a program exists but is uncomputable just like the Turing halting problem – the analogon of Goedel's incompleteness theorem. If $K(A)$ is much shorter than the string A it means that this string can be compressed, i.e., it is not random; if $K(A)$ is comparable to the length of A it means that A cannot be compressed and it is random.

Can we have a UTM generating A and A'? If yes, then there must exist algorithmic information $K(A, A')$, i.e., there exists a program generating both strings in one go. Our goal is to find *if and when* this can happen.

2.1 Information Distance

In order to answer our question we need to use tools developed and studied extensively in [7]. We introduce, following [7] the so called *information theoretic metric* that measures similarity between bit strings A and A'

$$d(A, A') = K(A|A') + K(A'|A), \tag{1}$$

where $K(A'|A)$ is a conditional algorithmic information, i.e., the shortest program generating A' from A. Conditional algorithmic information can be also expressed as

$$K(A'|A) = K(A, A') - K(A), \tag{2}$$

therefore

$$d(A, A') = 2K(A, A') - K(A) - K(A'). \tag{3}$$

The above expression is a metric (up to irrelevant logarithmic corrections $\log|A|$), i.e., it is (i) non-negative and equal to zero if and only if $A = A'$, (ii) symmetric when A and A' are swapped and most importantly (iii) it obeys triangle inequality

$$d(A, A') \le d(A, B) + d(B, A') \tag{4}$$

for arbitrary bit strings A, A', B.

Note, that (i) holds because the program generating A twice is practically the same program as the one generating A once, i.e., $K(A, A) = K(A)$. In addition, it is clear that (ii) holds. Finally, note that

$$K(A|B) + K(B|A') \ge K(A|A'). \tag{5}$$

This is because the shortest program generating A from A' cannot be longer than the sum of lengths of shortest programs generating B from A' and A from B. In worst case scenario the shortest program generating A from A' would generate B as an intermediate step and we would have equality. Similarly,

$$K(B|A) + K(A'|B) \ge K(A'|A). \tag{6}$$

By combining (5) and (6) we get (4). Finally, we have

$$\max\{K(A), K(A')\} \le K(A, A') \le K(A) + K(A'), \tag{7}$$

and the distance is bounded

$$|K(A) - K(A')| \le d(A, A') \le K(A) + K(A'). \tag{8}$$

2.2 Contextuality

The triangle inequality is directly related to the phenomenon of contextuality [13–15]. Here we simply define contextuality as a dependence of a measurement of **B** on whether it is co-measured with **A** or with **A'**. In such scenarios one would generate pairs of bit strings $\{A, B_A\}$ and $\{A', B_{A'}\}$. We explicitly denote context dependence of two bit strings B_A and $B_{A'}$ generated in a measurement of **B**. However, as discussed in [14], the algorithmic version of non-contextuality assumption implies that both bit strings have the same algorithmic information $K(B_A) = K(B_{A'}) = K(B)$ because they describe the information content of the same physical process and we assume that this process is context-independent. Thus, we have $K(A, B_A) = K(A, B)$ and $K(A', B_A;) = K(A', B)$.

One can study $d(A, B)$, $d(A', B)$ and $d(A, A')$ and identify contextuality with a violation of any distance property. Here we focus on the triangle inequality. In this case we need to consider a distance $d(A, A')$ for the two observables that constitute two different contexts for the measurement of **B**. It may happen that such a distance is not directly measurable due to incompatibility of the two contexts.

2.3 Bounds on Incompatible Measurements

Although we may be unable to jointly measure two observables and the corresponding distance, we can find an upper bound on it via triangle inequality and an additional measurement B, which is jointly measurable with both observables

$$d(A, A') \leq d(A, B) + d(B, A'). \tag{9}$$

In a similar way we can find a lower bound using a different measurement **B'**

$$d(A, A') \geq d(A, B') - d(B', A'). \tag{10}$$

The reason why we use two different measurements, **B** and **B'**, is that we want to minimise the upper bound and at the same time maximise the lower bound. However it is not guaranteed that both optimisations can be done with the same measurement.

Next, we plug (3) into (9) and (10) and obtain

$$K(A, B') - K(A', B') + K(A') \leq K(A, A') \leq K(A, B) + K(A', B) - K(B). \tag{11}$$

The crucial observation is that $K(A, A')$ exists only if the upper bound is greater or equal to the lower bound. Thus, we arrive at a quadrangle inequality

$$d(A, B) + d(B, A') + d(A', B') - d(B', A) \geq 0. \tag{12}$$

This is an information-theoretic Bell-type inequality. An experimental violation of an equivalent inequality was recently reported in [14], where uncomputable algorithmic information was approximated by realistic compression software.

3   Incompatible Algorithmic Information

For the rest of this paper we assume that incompatible measurements $\mathbf{A}$ and $\mathbf{A}'$ are done on a qubit, however our discussion can be generalised to higher-dimensional systems as well. Therefore, the measurements $\mathbf{B}$ and $\mathbf{B}'$ have to be performed on an ancilliary system.

The problem considered by us differs from the usual Bell scenario in which two parties are given a bipartite system and they try to find optimal measurements to violate a Bell inequality. Here, the state of Alice's system and the two incompatible measurements $\mathbf{A}$ and $\mathbf{A}'$ are fixed. The only optimisation is done over two measurements $\mathbf{B}$ and $\mathbf{B}'$ and over a state of the joint system, which is constrained to reproduce Alice's state when the ancilla is discarded.

Now, we provide two important examples supporting our thesis. We show that in quantum theory two different situations can occur: (i) one can always define algorithmic information for incompatible observables or (ii) one can never define it.

3.1   Pure State

Let us first assume that the state on which the incompatible measurements are performed is pure. In this case the ancilliary system must separate from it and the joint system is in a product state $|\psi\rangle\langle\psi| \otimes \rho_{anc}$. For such cases quantum theory predicts that measurements on both systems are uncorrelated and therefore

$$K(X,Y) = K(X) + K(Y), \tag{13}$$

where X and Y are outcome strings of arbitrary measurements performed on the original system and ancilla, respectively. The bounds on algorithmic information (11) read

$$K(A) \leq K(A, A') \leq K(A) + K(A') + K(B). \tag{14}$$

The lower bound does not depend on any ancilliary measurement, whereas the upper bound is minimised for $K(B) = 0$, which leads to

$$K(A) \leq K(A, A') \leq K(A) + K(A'). \tag{15}$$

We see that for pure states algorithmic information for any pair of incompatible observables can be defined.

3.2   Mixed State

If the incompatible measurements are performed on a mixed state, the ancilliary system can be correlated with it. The state of the joint system can be pure and entangled.

In order to show that algorithmic information for incompatible measurements on an entangled state cannot exist one needs to observe that (12) is violated. This inequality takes the following form

$$K(A, B) + K(B, A') + K(A', B') - K(A') - K(B) \geq K(A, B'). \tag{16}$$

In case of maximally entangled states local measurements produce random strings, therefore $K(A') = K(B) = N$, where N is the number of bits in each string. The violation occurs if there are weak correlations (or no correlations) between **A** and **B'** and strong correlations between the remaining three pairs.

Unfortunately, bipartite entangled states cannot provide us with maximal correlations for all pairs of measurements and we need to consider joint algorithmic information for which

$$\max\{K(X), K(Y)\} < K(X, Y) < K(X) + K(Y). \tag{17}$$

This means that we cannot reduce all joint algorithmic information to algorithmic information of single measurements and in order to detect violations we need to compare their values.

The problem is that algorithmic information is in most cases uncomputable. In order to be able to detect some violation we need to make additional assumptions. Such assumptions allow us to approximate algorithmic information with some other computable functions like realistic compression software [16]. Indeed, using compression algorithms on experimentally generated data it was shown that for a state of two maximally polarisation-entangled photons and two incompatible polarisation measurements **A** and **A'** one can obtain a violation of (12). The polarisation measurements were separated by an angle $\theta \approx 17.2^\circ$. The observed violation (normalised by the length of bit strings) was 0.0494 ± 0.0076 per bit. This indicates that for such scenarios one cannot define algorithmic information for incompatible observables **A** and **A'**.

4   Summary and Discussion

In this work, we approach the problem of co-measurability of incompatible observables in quantum mechanics with the help of algorithmic information. Our starting point is an assumption that it makes sense to talk about co-measurability of observables **A** and **A'** on some state ρ if there exists a program which, when executed on a universal Turing machine, produces two binary strings of outcomes A and A' corresponding to the joint measurements of the given observables. Moreover, the strings A and A' must be compatible with all possible experiments that can be performed on the state ρ.

We show that the requirement of compatibility imposes a lower and upper bound on the joint algorithmic complexity $K(A, A')$ of the computed strings A and A'. These bounds are uniquely tied to the phenomenon of quantum contextuality in the algorithmic sense. It says that computability of the strings A and A' must be independent of the context they are computed with, i.e., in the presence of the measurement of some observable B or some other observabale B'.

We prove that for measurements of any two incompatible observables on a qubit in a pure state it is always possible to find a program on a universal Turing machine that does the job. It is not always true for the qubit in a mixed state. This is because any mixed state can be viewed as a result of entanglement with some other quantum system, which can provide a context for the computation of A and A'. When the state is pure, no entanglement with any other system is possible and no context is provided.

We would like to mention that our approach differs from that presented in [11] where the problem of co-measurability is formulated as a problem of the existence of a joint probability distribution for the observables $\mathbf{A}$ and $\mathbf{A'}$. Assuming a probabilistic structure for bit strings produced in an experiment is unnecessary as we demonstrated here.

Acknowledgements. DK was supported by National Research Foundation & Ministry of Education in Singapore, PK was supported by the National Science Centre in Poland through the NCN Grant No. 2014/14/E/ST2/00585.

References

1. Gleason, A.M.: Measures on the closed subspaces of a Hilbert space. Indiana Univ. Math. J. **6**, 885–893 (1957)
2. Einstein, A., Podolsky, B., Rosen, N.: Can quantum-mechanical description of physical reality be considered complete? Phys. Rev. **47**, 777 (1935)
3. Bell, J.S.: Physics **1**, 195 (1964)
4. Kochen, S., Specker, E.P.: The problem of hidden variables in quantum mechanics. J. Math. Mech. **17**, 59–87 (1967)
5. Wolfram, S.: A New Kind of Science. Wolfram Media Inc., Champaign (2001)
6. Deutsch, D.: Proc. Roy. Soc. A **4**, 0097117 (1985)
7. Li, M., Chen, X., Li, X., Ma, B., Vitanyi, P.M.B.: IEEE Trans. Inf. Theory **50**, 3250 (2004)
8. Cilibrasi, R., Vitanyi, P.M.B.: IEEE Trans. Inf. Theory **51**, 1523 (2005)
9. Li, M., Vitanyi, P.M.B.: An Introduction to Kolmogorov Complexity and Its Applications. Texts in Computer Science. Springer, New York (2009)
10. Cover, T.M., Thomas, J.A.: Elements of Information Theory, 2nd edn. Wiley, New York (2006)
11. Andersson, E., Barnett, S.M., Aspect, A.: Phys. Rev. A **72**, 042104 (2005)
12. Fine, A.: Phys. Rev. Lett. **48**, 291 (1982)
13. Kurzynski, P., Kaszlikowski, D.: Phys. Rev. A **89**, 012103 (2014)
14. Poh, H.S., et al.: New J. Phys. **18**, 035011 (2016)
15. Schumacher, B.W.: Phys. Rev. A **44**, 7047 (1991)
16. Cilibrasi, R., Vitanyi, P.M.B.: IEEE Trans. Inf. Theory **51**, 1523–1545 (2005)

Exploration of Contextuality in a Psychophysical Double-Detection Experiment

Víctor H. Cervantes[(⊠)] and Ehtibar N. Dzhafarov

Purdue University, West Lafayette, USA
{cervantv,ehtibar}@purdue.edu

Abstract. The Contextuality-by-Default (CbD) theory allows one to separate contextuality from context-dependent errors and violations of selective influences (aka "no-signaling" or "no-disturbance" principles). This makes the theory especially applicable to behavioral systems, where violations of selective influences are ubiquitous. For cyclic systems with binary random variables, CbD provides necessary and sufficient conditions for noncontextuality, and these conditions are known to be breached in certain quantum systems. We apply the theory of cyclic systems to a psychophysical double-detection experiment, in which observers were asked to determine presence or absence of a signal property in each of two simultaneously presented stimuli. The results, as in all other behavioral and social systems previously analyzed, indicate lack of contextuality. The role of context in double-detection is confined to lack of selectiveness: the distribution of responses to one of the stimuli is influenced by the state of the other stimulus.

Keywords: Contextuality · Cyclic systems · Inconsistent connectedness · Psychophysics

The Contextuality-by-Default (CbD) theory [9,10] describes systems of measurements with respect to the conditions under which they are recorded and determines the tenability of a non-contextual description of the system. In this paper, we study the double-detection paradigm suggested in Refs. [6,8]. In this paradigm, two stimuli are presented to an observer simultaneously (left-right), each on one of several possible levels. The observer is asked to state (Yes/No), for each of the two observation areas, whether it contains a particular target property (signal). The signal is objectively present in a subset of levels of a stimulus. When such experimental situation includes only two levels for each stimulus (e.g., present/absent), the system of measurements is formally equivalent to that of the Einstein– Podolski– Rosen/Bohm (EPR/B) paradigm (see e.g., Ref. [6]).

1 Contextuality in CbD

We briefly recapitulate the concepts of the CbD, to make this paper self-sufficient. For detailed discussions see Refs. [9,10]; the proofs may be found in Refs. [11,14,15].

© Springer International Publishing AG 2017
J.A. de Barros et al. (Eds.): QI 2016, LNCS 10106, pp. 182–193, 2017.
DOI: 10.1007/978-3-319-52289-0_15

Definition 1 (System of measurements). *A system of measurements is a matrix $\mathfrak{R}_{n \times m}$, in which columns correspond to the properties $\{q_1, \ldots, q_n\}$ and rows to the contexts $\{c_1, \ldots, c_m\}$. A cell (i, j) contains the random variable R_i^j if q_i is measured in context c_j, and the cell is left empty otherwise.*

When adopting the CbD framework, the first goal is to produce a matrix $\mathfrak{R}$ that formally represents the experiment and its results.

Definition 2 (Connections and bunches). *The random variables in any column of a system of measurements form a* connection *for the corresponding property; denote the connection for property q_i by $\mathfrak{R}_i$. Those in any row form a* bunch *representing the corresponding context; denote the bunch for context c_j by R^j.*

Note that elements of a connection are necessarily ("by default") pairwise distinct and pairwise stochastically unrelated, i.e., no R_i^j and R_i^k with $k \neq j$ have a joint distributions. Consequently, the system $\mathfrak{R}$ does not have a joint probability distribution including all of its elements. See Refs. [5, 10].

Definition 3 (Coupling). *Let X_i, with $i \in I$, an index set, be a random variable on a probability space (X_i, Σ_i, P_i). Let $\{Y_i : i \in I\}$ be a collection of jointly distributed random variables (i.e., a random variable in its own right) on a probability space (Y, Ω, p). The random variable $\{Y_i : i \in I\}$ is called a* coupling *of the collection $\{X_i : i \in I\}$ if for all $i \in I$, $Y_i \overset{d}{=} X_i$, where $\overset{d}{=}$ denotes identity in distribution.*

Definition 4 (Maximal coupling). *Let $Y = (Y_i : i \in I)$ be a coupling of a collection $\{X_i : i \in I\}$. And let M be the event where $\{Y_i = Y_j \text{ for all } i, j \in I\}$. If $\Pr(M)$ is the largest possible among all couplings of $\{X_i : i \in I\}$, then Y is a* maximal coupling *of $\{X_i : i \in I\}$.*

Definition 5 (Contextual system). *Let $\mathfrak{R}$ be a system of measurements. Let S be a coupling of $\mathfrak{R}$ such that for each $c_j \in \{c_1, \ldots, c_m\}$, S^j is a coupling of R^j contained in S. The system $\mathfrak{R}$ is said to be* non-contextual *if it has a coupling S such that for all $q_i \in \{q_1, \ldots, q_n\}$, the coupling S_i is a maximal coupling.*

Definition 6 (Cyclic system with binary variables). *Let $\mathfrak{R}$ be a system of measurements such that (a) each context contains two properties; (b) each property is measured in two different contexts; (c) no two contexts share more than one property; and (d) each measurement is a binary random variable, with values ± 1. Then the system $\mathfrak{R}$ is a* cyclic system with binary variables *and in the following will be simply called a* cyclic system.

Remark 1. Note that a cyclic system is composed of the same number n of connections and of bunches, and it contains $2n$ random variables. We shall say that a cyclic system has rank n or is of rank n to explicitly refer to this number.

Definition 7 (Consistent connections). *Let $\mathfrak{R}_i$ be a connection in a system $\mathfrak{R}$. It is said that $\mathfrak{R}_i$ is a consistent connection if for all $c_j, c_k \in \{c_1, \ldots, c_m\}$ such that R_i^j and R_i^k are defined (i.e., both cells (i,j) and (i,k) of $\mathfrak{R}$ are not empty), $R_i^j \overset{d}{=} R_i^k$.*

Definition 8 (Consistently connected system). *A system of measurements $\mathfrak{R}$ is said to be consistently connected if for all $q_i \in \{q_1, \ldots, q_n\}$, the connection $\mathfrak{R}_i$ is a consistent connection. For a cyclic system, define*

$$ICC = \sum_{i=1}^{n} \left| \left\langle R_i^j \right\rangle - \left\langle R_i^k \right\rangle \right|.$$

ICC provides a measure of how inconsistent the connections are in the system.

Definition 9 (Contextuality in cyclic systems). *Let $\mathfrak{R}$ be a cyclic system with n binary variables. Let*

$$s_1(x_1, x_2, \ldots, x_n) = \max \left\{ \sum_{k=1}^{n} a_k x_k : a_k = \pm 1 \ and \ \prod_{k=1}^{n} a_k = -1 \right\}.$$

Let

$$\Lambda C = s_1 \left(\left\{ \left\langle R_i^j R_{i'}^j \right\rangle : q_i, q_{i'} \ measured \ in \ c_j, \ and \ c_j \in \{c_1, \ldots, c_m\} \right\} \right)$$

Let $\Delta C = \Lambda C - ICC - (n-2)$. The quantity ΔC is a measure of contextuality for cyclic systems.

Theorem 1 (Cyclic system contextuality criterion, [14]). *A cyclic system $\mathfrak{R}$ is contextual if and only if $\Delta C > 0$.*

Remark 2. ΔC for a consistently connected cyclic system with $n = 4$ reduces to the Bell/CHSH inequalities [3,10].

2   Contextuality in Behavioral and Social Data

In Ref. [13] many empirical studies of behavioral and social systems were reviewed. Most of those systems come from social data; that is, an observation for each measurement was the result of posing a question to a person, and the set of observations comes from questioning groups of people. For all the studies considered there, the CbD analyses showed that the systems, treated as cyclic systems ranging from rank 2 to 4, were non-contextual. Only one of the studies reviewed in Ref. [13] dealt with responses from a single person to multiple replications of stimuli.

Now, a key modeling problem in cognitive psychology has been determining whether a set of inputs selectively influences a set of response variables (Refs. [4, 16–18]). The formal theory of selective influences has been developed for the case of consistent connectedness, which has been treated as a necessary condition of selective influences; it follows from this formalism that selectiveness of influences in a consistently connected system is negated precisely in the case where it is contextual [6].

However, in most, if not all, behavioral systems, some form of influence upon a given random output is expected from most, if not all, of the system's inputs (Ref. [17]). This means that in the behavioral domain inconsistently connected systems are ubiquitous. While the presence of inconsistent connections rules out the possibility of selective influences, it does not imply that the full behavior of the system is accounted for by the direct action of inputs upon the outputs; an inconsistently connected behavioral system may still be contextual in the sense of CbD.

The double detection paradigm suggested in [6,8] provides a framework where both (in)consistent connectedness and contextuality can be studied in a manner very similar to how they are studied in quantum-mechanical systems (or could be studied, because consistent connectedness in quantum physics is often assumed rather than documented).

3   Method

3.1   Participants

Three volunteers, two females and one male, graduate students at Purdue University, served as participants for the experiment, including the first author of this paper. They were recruited and compensated in accordance to Purdue University's IRB protocol #1202011876, for the research study "Selective Probabilistic Causality As Interdisciplinary Methodology" under which this experiment was conducted. All participants reported normal or corrected to normal vision and were aged around 30. They are identified as $P1 - P3$ in the text and their experience with psychophysical experiments ranged from none to more than three previous participations.

3.2   Apparatus

The experiment was run using a personal computer with an Intel® Core™ processor running Windows XP, a 24-in. monitor with a resolution of 1920×1200 pixels (px), and a standard US 104-key keyboard. A chin-rest with forehead support was used so that the distance between subject and monitor was kept at 90 cm; this made each pixel on the screen to occupy about 62 s arc of the subjects' visual field.

3.3   Stimuli

The stimuli were similar to those from Refs. [1,12]. They consisted of two circles drawn in solid grey (RGB 100, 100, 100) on a black background in a computer

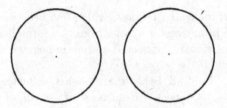

Fig. 1. Stimulus example

screen, with a dot drawn at or near their center. The circles radius was 135 px with their centers 320 px apart; the dots and circumference lines were 4 px wide. The offset of each dot with respect to the center of each circle, when they were not presented at the center, was 4 px. An example of the stimuli (in reversed contrast) is shown in Fig. 1.

3.4 Procedure

Each participant performed nine experimental sessions. At the beginning of each experimental session, the chin-rest and chair heights were adjusted so that the subject could sit and use the keyboard comfortably. The time available for each session was 30 min, during which the participants responded in 560 (non-practice) trials (except for participant $P3$ in the sixth session, who only responded in 557 trials) preceded by up to 30 practice trials. The number of practice trials was set to 30 during the first two sessions and reduced to 15 during subsequent sessions. After each practice trial, the subject received feedback about whether their response for each circle was correct or not. The responses to practice trials were excluded from the analyses. Additionally, depending on their previous experience in psychophysical experiments the participants had up to three training sessions, also excluded from subsequent analyses.

Instructions for the experiment were presented to each participant verbally and written in the screen. In each trial the participant was required to judge for each circle whether the dot presented was displaced from the center or not. The stimuli were displayed until the subject produced their response. The responses were given by pressing and holding together two keys, one for each circle. Then, the dots in each circle were removed and a "Press the space bar to continue" message was flashed on top of the screen. After pressing the space bar, the message was removed and the next stimuli pair were presented after 400 ms. (Reaction times were measured from the onset of stimulus display until a valid response was recorded, but they were not used in the data analysis.)

3.5 Experimental Conditions

In each of two circles the dot presented could be located either at its center, or 4 px above, or else 4 px under the center. These locations produce a total of nine experimental conditions.

Table 1. Probabilities with which a trial was allocated to one of the 9 experimental conditions.

	Center	Up	Down
Center	1/4	1/8	1/8
Up	1/8	1/16	1/16
Down	1/8	1/16	1/16

During each session, excepting the practice trials, the dot was presented at the center in a half of the trials; above the center in a quarter of them; and below the center in the remaining quarter, for each of the circles. Table 1 presents the proportions of allocations of trials to each of the 9 conditions.

For each session, each trial was randomly assigned to one of the conditions in accordance with Table 1. The number of experimental sessions was chosen so that the expected number of (non-practice) trials in the conditions with lowest probabilities was at least 300. This number of observations was chosen based on Ref. [2], whose results show that coverage errors with respect to nominal values are below 1% for almost all confidence intervals for proportions with $n > 300$.

4   Analyses

Based on the experimental design depicted in Table 1, we specify the following properties:

- l_c: a dot is presented in the center of the left circle;
- r_c: a dot is presented in the center of the right circle;
- l_u: a dot is presented above the center of the left circle;
- r_u: a dot is presented above the center of the right circle;
- l_d: a dot is presented below the center of the left circle; and
- r_d: a dot is presented below the center of the right circle.

The 9 experimental conditions (contexts) then are denoted $l_c r_c, l_c r_u$, etc. Thus, the system of measurements depicted by the matrix in Fig. 2 represents the complete 3×3 design given in Table 1.

We approach the exploration of this system through the theory of contextuality for cyclic systems in two ways. Firstly, note that from the system in Fig. 2 we can extract six different cyclic subsystems of rank 6 and nine of rank 4. One of the rank 4 subsystems is presented in the left matrix in Fig. 3. One of the rank 6 subsystems is shown in the right matrix in Fig. 3.

Secondly, in addition to the definition of the quantities as presented above, there are several interesting systems produced by redefining these quantities.[1] From the description of the double-detection paradigm, one can argue, e.g., that

---

[1] There are also several uninteresting ways to construct systems of measurements for the conditions and measurements in this experiment. Examples of how to construct them and why they are not interesting may be found in Ref. [7].

	l_c	r_c	l_u	r_u	l_d	r_d
$l_c r_c$	$R_{l_c}^{l_c r_c}$	$R_{r_c}^{l_c r_c}$	.	.	.	.
$l_u r_c$	.	$R_{r_c}^{l_u r_c}$	$R_{l_u}^{l_u r_c}$	.	.	.
$l_u r_u$	.	.	$R_{l_u}^{l_u r_u}$	$R_{r_u}^{l_u r_u}$	.	.
$l_d r_u$	.	.	.	$R_{r_u}^{l_d r_u}$	$R_{l_d}^{l_d r_u}$	.
$l_d r_d$	.	.	.	.	$R_{l_d}^{l_d r_d}$	$R_{r_d}^{l_d r_d}$
$l_c r_u$	$R_{l_c}^{l_c r_u}$	.	.	$R_{r_u}^{l_c r_u}$	.	.
$l_u r_d$	.	.	$R_{l_u}^{l_u r_d}$	.	.	$R_{r_d}^{l_u r_d}$
$l_d r_c$	.	$R_{r_c}^{l_d r_c}$	.	.	$R_{l_d}^{l_d r_c}$	.
$l_c r_d$	$R_{l_c}^{l_c r_d}$	.	.	.	.	$R_{r_d}^{l_c r_d}$

Fig. 2. System of measurements for double detection experiment.

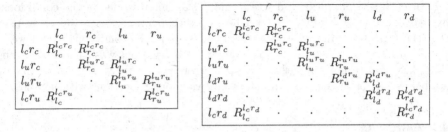

	l_c	r_c	l_u	r_u
$l_c r_c$	$R_{l_c}^{l_c r_c}$	$R_{r_c}^{l_c r_c}$	.	.
$l_u r_c$	.	$R_{r_c}^{l_u r_c}$	$R_{l_u}^{l_u r_c}$	.
$l_u r_u$	.	.	$R_{l_u}^{l_u r_u}$	$R_{r_u}^{l_u r_u}$
$l_c r_u$	$R_{l_c}^{l_c r_u}$	.	.	$R_{r_u}^{l_c r_u}$

	l_c	r_c	l_u	r_u	l_d	r_d
$l_c r_c$	$R_{l_c}^{l_c r_c}$	$R_{r_c}^{l_c r_c}$	.	.	.	.
$l_u r_c$	.	$R_{r_c}^{l_u r_c}$	$R_{l_u}^{l_u r_c}$	.	.	.
$l_u r_u$	.	.	$R_{l_u}^{l_u r_u}$	$R_{r_u}^{l_u r_u}$	.	.
$l_d r_u$	.	.	.	$R_{r_u}^{l_d r_u}$	$R_{l_d}^{l_d r_u}$	.
$l_d r_d$	.	.	.	.	$R_{l_d}^{l_d r_d}$	$R_{r_d}^{l_d r_d}$
$l_c r_d$	$R_{l_c}^{l_c r_d}$	.	.	.	.	$R_{r_d}^{l_c r_d}$

Fig. 3. Examples of cyclic subsystems of rank 4 and 6.

the center location may be viewed as a signal to be detected, with either of the two off-center locations being treated as absence of the signal. This way of looking at the stimuli induces the following definition of the properties to be measured:

– l_c: a dot is presented in the center of the left circle;
– r_c: a dot is presented in the center of the right circle;
– l_{ud}: a dot is presented off-center in the left circle;
– r_{ud}: a dot is presented off-center in the right circle.

Analogously one could also consider $l_{cu}, l_{cd}, r_{cu}, r_{cd}$, as properties to be measured in appropriately chosen contexts.

Another way of dealing with our data is to consider the locations of the dots as properties to be measured (by responses attributing to them to a left or to a right circle). For instance, a pair of properties can be chosen as

– c: a dot is presented in the center of a circle; and
– ud: a dot is presented off the center of a circle.

A systematic application of both of these redefinitions leads to also consider quantities $l_{cu}, l_{cd}, r_{cu}, r_{cd}, u, cd, d$, and cu with the analogous interpretations. In this way, six systems of rank 2 and 27 systems of rank 4 may be constructed. Thus, we shall consider systems with the structures depicted by the matrices in Figs. 4, 5, and 6.

	x	y
$l_x r_y$	$R_x^{l_x r_y}$	$R_y^{l_x r_y}$
$l_y r_x$	$R_x^{l_y r_x}$	$R_y^{l_y r_x}$

Fig. 4. Rank 2 systems structure where (x, y) is any of (c, ud), (cu, d), (cd, u), (c, u), (c, d), (u, d).

	l_x	r_x	l_y	r_y
$l_x r_x$	$R_{l_x}^{l_x r_x}$	$R_{r_x}^{l_x r_x}$	.	.
$l_y r_x$	.	$R_{r_x}^{l_y r_x}$	$R_{l_y}^{l_y r_x}$	.
$l_y r_y$	.	.	$R_{l_y}^{l_y r_y}$	$R_{r_y}^{l_y r_y}$
$l_x r_y$	$R_{l_x}^{l_x r_y}$	.	.	$R_{r_y}^{l_x r_y}$

Fig. 5. Rank 4 systems structure where (l_x, l_y) is any of (l_c, l_{ud}), (l_{cu}, l_d), (l_{cd}, l_u), (l_c, l_u), (l_c, l_d), (l_u, l_d), and (r_x, r_y) is any of $\{(r_c, r_{ud}), (r_{cu}, r_d), (r_{cd}, r_u), (r_c, r_u), (r_c, r_d), (r_u, r_d)\}$.

	l_x	r_x	l_y	r_y	l_z	r_z
$l_x r_x$	$R_{l_x}^{l_x r_x}$	$R_{r_x}^{l_x r_x}$	.	.	.	.
$l_y r_x$	.	$R_{r_x}^{l_y r_x}$	$R_{l_y}^{l_y r_x}$	.	.	.
$l_y r_y$	.	.	$R_{l_y}^{l_y r_y}$	$R_{r_y}^{l_y r_y}$	.	.
$l_z r_y$	.	.	.	$R_{r_y}^{l_z r_y}$	$R_{l_z}^{l_z r_y}$	.
$l_z r_z$	.	.	.	.	$R_{l_z}^{l_z r_z}$	$R_{r_z}^{l_z r_z}$
$l_x r_z$	$R_{l_x}^{l_x r_z}$	.	.	.	.	$R_{r_z}^{l_x r_z}$

Fig. 6. Rank 6 systems structure where (x, y, z) is any of (c, u, d), (c, d, u), (u, c, d), (d, c, u), (u, d, c), (d, u, c).

5   Results

5.1   Results for Cyclic Subsystems

Table 2 presents the individual data for all of the expectations used in the calculations of all subsystems. Note that the statistics associated with the redefined quantities are obtained by an appropriate linear combination of those in Table 2 with weights proportional to the number of trials of the combined conditions.

Table 3 presents the values of ΛC, ICC, and ΔC calculated for each participant and each of the rank 6 cyclic subsystems. Table 4 presents the respective values for each of the rank 4 cyclic subsystems. For all participants, the subsystems are noncontextual.

Table 2. Individual level data

l	r	P1			P2			P3		
		$\langle R_l^{lr} \rangle$	$\langle R_r^{lr} \rangle$	$\langle R_l^{lr} R_r^{lr} \rangle$	$\langle R_l^{lr} \rangle$	$\langle R_r^{lr} \rangle$	$\langle R_l^{lr} R_r^{lr} \rangle$	$\langle R_l^{lr} \rangle$	$\langle R_r^{lr} \rangle$	$\langle R_l^{lr} R_r^{lr} \rangle$
l_c	r_c	0.4349	0.2730	0.4825	0.7317	0.5683	0.3984	0.3582	0.1946	−0.0913
l_c	r_u	0.6190	−0.5397	−0.2095	0.7016	−0.0825	−0.2413	0.6762	−0.8508	−0.6159
l_c	r_d	−0.1873	0.2698	0.4095	0.8857	−0.8635	−0.7937	0.3937	−0.3524	−0.3429
l_u	r_c	−0.5048	0.1175	0.2254	−0.2063	0.5238	−0.5302	−0.7302	0.6603	−0.5683
l_u	r_u	0.0476	−0.0286	0.4794	0.1111	0.1683	0.2190	−0.4904	−0.6624	0.4459
l_u	r_d	−0.8476	−0.0857	0.1619	0.2254	−0.7778	−0.4222	−0.7643	−0.2166	0.0446
l_d	r_c	0.5873	−0.3937	−0.0825	−0.6667	0.7810	−0.5238	−0.4159	0.3429	−0.4762
l_d	r_u	0.5619	−0.9111	−0.5365	−0.7333	0.2635	−0.4286	−0.2508	−0.7079	0.0095
l_d	r_d	0.5111	0.3016	0.4730	−0.5175	−0.5937	0.5810	−0.3079	−0.1746	0.0413

Table 3. Contextuality cyclic subsystems of rank 6

System $(l_x, l_y, l_z), (r_x, r_y, r_z)$	P1			P2			P3		
	ΛC	ICC	ΔC	ΛC	ICC	ΔC	ΛC	ICC	ΔC
$(l_c, l_d, l_u), (r_d, r_u, r_c)$	1.6254	2.4127	−4.7873	2.4571	1.3714	−2.9143	2.0382	1.0779	−3.0397
$(l_d, l_c, l_u), (r_c, r_d, r_u)$	1.7143	2.4889	−4.7746	2.4508	1.4286	−2.9778	2.4078	1.3138	−2.9060
$(l_d, l_u, l_c), (r_c, r_u, r_d)$	1.9873	3.4476	−5.4603	2.3476	0.7286	−2.3810	1.4104	0.8040	−3.3936
$(l_c, l_u, l_d), (r_d, r_c, r_u)$	2.6063	2.2952	−3.6889	2.9508	1.0968	−2.1460	1.4991	1.0213	−3.5222
$(l_u, l_c, l_d), (r_d, r_u, r_c)$	1.7238	2.7206	−4.9968	2.3857	0.9413	−2.5556	1.7151	1.0784	−3.3633
$(l_u, l_d, l_c), (r_c, r_d, r_u)$	1.7651	1.4921	−3.7270	2.1190	1.2524	−3.1333	1.3708	1.0598	−3.6890

Table 4. Contextuality cyclic subsystems of rank 4

System $(l_x, l_y), (r_x, r_y)$	P1			P2			P3		
	ΛC	ICC	ΔC	ΛC	ICC	ΔC	ΛC	ICC	ΔC
$(l_c, l_u), (r_c, r_u)$	1.3968	1.4032	−2.0063	0.9508	0.6429	−1.6921	1.7213	1.2118	−1.4904
$(l_c, l_u), (r_c, r_d)$	0.9556	1.4762	−2.5206	2.1444	0.7159	−0.5714	1.0470	0.6711	−1.6241
$(l_c, l_u), (r_u, r_d)$	1.2603	2.5683	−3.3079	1.6762	0.6349	−0.9587	1.3600	0.8806	−1.5206
$(l_c, l_d), (r_c, r_u)$	1.3111	1.2476	−1.9365	1.5921	0.6556	−1.0635	1.1929	0.7742	−1.5812
$(l_c, l_d), (r_c, r_d)$	1.4476	1.3968	−1.9492	1.5000	0.7857	−1.2857	0.9517	0.4694	−1.5177
$(l_c, l_d), (r_u, r_d)$	1.2095	1.2603	−2.0508	2.0444	1.0159	−0.9714	0.9905	0.6603	−1.6698
$(l_u, l_d), (r_c, r_u)$	1.1587	1.9714	−2.8127	1.7016	0.7365	−1.0349	1.4808	0.7678	−1.2870
$(l_u, l_d), (r_c, r_d)$	0.9429	1.3175	−2.3746	2.0571	1.0222	−0.9651	1.0478	0.5015	−1.4538
$(l_u, l_d), (r_u, r_d)$	1.6508	2.2159	−2.5651	1.2127	0.6095	−1.3968	0.5222	0.4185	−1.8963

5.2   Results for Cyclic Systems with Redefined Quantities

Table 5 presents the values of ΛC, ICC, and ΔC calculated for each participant for each of the rank 2 cyclic systems, and Table 6 shows those for the rank 4 cyclic systems. Note that for participant $P3$, two of the rank 2 systems, those with $(x, y) = (c, d)$ and $(x, y) = (cu, d)$, have a positive ΔC value, which might suggest that these two systems show contextuality. However, their respective

Table 5. Contextuality cyclic systems of rank 2

System (x,y)	P1			P2			P3		
	AC	ICC	ΔC	AC	ICC	ΔC	AC	ICC	ΔC
(c, ud)	0.0286	0.5302	−0.5016	0.0095	0.1778	−0.1683	0.0429	0.0619	−0.0190
(cd, u)	0.5228	0.5947	−0.0720	0.1905	0.2286	−0.0381	0.0430	0.0631	−0.0201
(cu, d)	0.5608	0.5862	−0.0254	0.1778	0.2032	−0.0254	0.1003	0.0695	0.0308
(c, u)	0.4349	0.5365	−0.1016	0.2889	0.3016	−0.0127	0.0476	0.1365	−0.0889
(c, d)	0.4921	0.5238	−0.0317	0.2698	0.3016	−0.0317	0.1333	0.1143	0.0190
(u, d)	0.6984	0.7111	−0.0127	0.0063	0.0825	−0.0762	0.0351	0.0906	−0.0556

Table 6. Contextuality cyclic systems of rank 4

System $(l_x, l_y), (r_x, r_y)$	P1			P2			P3		
	AC	ICC	ΔC	AC	ICC	ΔC	AC	ICC	ΔC
$(l_c, l_{ud}), (r_c, r_{ud})$	0.6556	0.7032	−2.0476	1.4556	0.5921	−1.1365	1.2281	0.7648	−1.5367
$(l_c, l_{ud}), (r_{cd}, r_u)$	0.7926	1.1228	−2.3302	0.6720	0.5238	−1.8519	1.3525	0.9192	−1.5667
$(l_c, l_{ud}), (r_{cu}, r_d)$	0.9407	1.3937	−2.4529	1.2857	0.7460	−1.4603	0.9247	0.5181	−1.5934
$(l_c, l_{ud}), (r_c, r_u)$	0.7349	0.9286	−2.1937	1.2714	0.5381	−1.2667	1.4568	0.9931	−1.5363
$(l_c, l_{ud}), (r_c, r_d)$	1.1381	1.4048	−2.2667	1.6397	0.7063	−1.0667	0.9993	0.5365	−1.5371
$(l_c, l_{ud}), (r_u, r_d)$	0.9079	1.5111	−2.6032	1.2190	0.8254	−1.6063	1.1431	0.7703	−1.6271
$(l_{cd}, l_u), (r_c, r_{ud})$	0.7841	0.4688	−1.6847	1.0423	0.6106	−1.5683	1.3443	0.7911	−1.4469
$(l_{cd}, l_u), (r_{cd}, r_u)$	1.3418	1.6402	−2.2984	1.0681	0.4804	−1.4123	1.4357	0.9428	−1.5070
$(l_{cd}, l_u), (r_{cu}, r_d)$	0.8127	1.6275	−2.8148	0.9975	0.5284	−1.5309	0.7726	0.5453	−1.7727
$(l_{cd}, l_u), (r_c, r_u)$	1.3175	1.3683	−2.0508	0.9619	0.6106	−1.6487	1.6412	1.0639	−1.4227
$(l_{cd}, l_u), (r_c, r_d)$	0.7884	1.2159	−2.4275	1.3788	0.7037	−1.3249	1.0473	0.5867	−1.5394
$(l_{cd}, l_u), (r_u, r_d)$	1.3905	2.4508	−3.0603	1.2804	0.4487	−1.1683	1.0235	0.6986	−1.6751
$(l_{cu}, l_d), (r_c, r_{ud})$	0.6212	0.9725	−2.3513	0.9153	0.6868	−1.7714	0.9903	0.4030	−1.4127
$(l_{cu}, l_d), (r_{cd}, r_u)$	1.0328	1.3848	−2.3520	0.6603	0.6145	−1.9541	0.8142	0.5372	−1.7230
$(l_{cu}, l_d), (r_{cu}, r_d)$	1.3051	1.4399	−2.1347	1.7129	0.8698	−1.1570	0.8240	0.2918	−1.4677
$(l_{cu}, l_d), (r_c, r_u)$	0.9958	1.4889	−2.4931	1.1291	0.6423	−1.5132	0.9988	0.5452	−1.5464
$(l_{cu}, l_d), (r_c, r_d)$	1.2794	1.3704	−2.0910	1.6857	0.8646	−1.1788	0.9818	0.2608	−1.2790
$(l_{cu}, l_d), (r_u, r_d)$	1.3566	1.5788	−2.2222	1.7672	0.8804	−1.1132	0.5084	0.5496	−2.0412
$(l_c, l_u), (r_c, r_{ud})$	0.9286	0.5571	−1.6286	1.5476	0.6492	−1.1016	1.3842	0.9073	−1.5231
$(l_c, l_u), (r_{cd}, r_u)$	1.3513	1.7915	−2.4402	0.9534	0.5069	−1.5534	1.6014	1.1021	−1.5007
$(l_c, l_u), (r_{cu}, r_d)$	0.8095	1.6328	−2.8233	1.6815	0.6296	−0.9481	0.8847	0.6947	−1.8101
$(l_c, l_d), (r_c, r_{ud})$	0.6333	1.1063	−2.4730	1.3635	0.6238	−1.2603	1.0723	0.6218	−1.5495
$(l_c, l_d), (r_{cd}, r_u)$	1.1016	1.1968	−2.0952	0.8265	0.7757	−1.9492	1.1043	0.7363	−1.6320
$(l_c, l_d), (r_u, r_d)$	1.3683	1.3513	−1.9831	1.6815	0.8624	−1.1810	0.9647	0.4479	−1.4833
$(l_u, l_d), (r_c, r_{ud})$	0.5968	0.9143	−2.3175	1.2317	0.8127	−1.5810	1.2643	0.5585	−1.2942
$(l_u, l_d), (r_{cd}, r_u)$	1.3228	1.7608	−2.4381	1.2974	0.6180	−1.3206	1.1044	0.6240	−1.5195
$(l_u, l_d), (r_{cu}, r_d)$	1.1788	1.6169	−2.4381	1.7757	0.8847	−1.1090	0.5485	0.4365	−1.8880

confidence intervals, $\Delta C_{(cu,d)} \in (−0.267, 0.241)$ and $\Delta C_{(c,d)} \in (−0.233, 0.215)$,[2] indicate that the values are consistent with lack of contextuality.

---

[2] 95% confidence intervals corrected by Bonferroni for the number of tests for ΔC values in the experiment. However, it should be noted that even uncorrected intervals covered the value 0.

6   Conclusions

The experiment presented in this paper illustrates the use of the double factorial paradigm in the search of contextuality in behavioral systems, namely in the responses of human observers in a double-detection task. This paradigm provides the closest analogue in psychophysical research to the Alice-Bob EPR/Bohm paradigm.

We have found that for the participants in the study there was no evidence of contextuality in their responses. These results add to the existing evidence that points towards lack of contextuality in psychology (cf. Ref. [13].)

References

1. Allik, J., Toom, M., Rauk, M.: Detection and identification of spatial offset: double-judgment psychophysics revisited. Attention Percept. Psychophysics **76**, 2575–2583 (2014)
2. Cepeda Cuervo, E., Aguilar, W., Cervantes, V.H., Corrales, M., Díaz, I., Rodríguez, D.: Intervalos de confianza e intervalos de credibilidad para una proporción. Revista Colombiana de Estadística **31**, 211–228 (2008)
3. Clauser, J.F., Horne, M.A., Shimony, A., Holt, R.A.: Proposed experiment to test local hidden-variable theories. Phys. Rev. Lett. **23**, 880–884 (1969)
4. Dzhafarov, E.N.: Selective influence through conditional independence. Psychometrika **68**, 7–25 (2003)
5. Dzhafarov, E.N.: Stochastic unrelatedness, couplings, and contextuality. J. Math. Psychol. (in Press)
6. Dzhafarov, E.N., Kujala, J.V.: Quantum entanglement and the issue of selective influences in psychology: an overview. In: Busemeyer, J.R., Dubois, F., Lambert-Mogiliansky, A., Melucci, M. (eds.) Quantum Interaction. LNCS, vol. 7620, pp. 184–195. Springer, Heidelberg (2012)
7. Dzhafarov, E.N., Kujala, J.V.: Context-content systems of random variables: the contextuality-by-default theory. J. Math. Psychol. arXiv preprint arXiv:1511.03516 (in Press)
8. Dzhafarov, E.N., Kujala, J.V.: Probability, random variables, and selectivity. In: Bachtelder, W., Colonius, H., Dzhafarov, E.N., Myung, J.I. (eds.) The New Handbook of Mathematical Psychology. Cambridge University Press (in Press)
9. Dzhafarov, E.N., Kujala, J.V., Cervantes, V.H.: Contextuality-by-default: a brief overview of ideas, concepts, and terminology. In: Atmanspacher, H., Filk, T., Pothos, E. (eds.) Quantum interaction. LNCS, vol. 9535, pp. 12–23. Springer, Heidelberg (2016)
10. Dzhafarov, E.N., Kujala, J.V., Cervantes, V.H., Zhang, R., Jones, M.: On contextuality in behavioral data. Philos. Trans. Roy. Soc. A **374**, 20150234 (2016)
11. Dzhafarov, E.N., Kujala, J.V., Larsson, J.Å.: Contextuality in three types of quantum-mechanical systems. Found. Phys. **45**, 762–782 (2015)
12. Dzhafarov, E.N., Perry, L.: Matching by adjustment: if X matches Y, does Y match X? Front. Psychol. **1**, 24 (2010). doi:10.3389/fpsyg.2010.00024
13. Dzhafarov, E.N., Zhang, R., Kujala, J.V.: Is there contextuality in behavioural and social systems? Philos. Trans. Roy. Soc. A **374**, 20150099 (2015)
14. Kujala, J.V., Dzhafarov, E.N.: Proof of a conjecture on contextuality in cyclic systems with binary variables. Found. Phys. **46**, 282–299 (2015)

15. Kujala, J.V., Dzhafarov, E.N.: Probabilistic contextuality in EPR/Bohm-type systems with signaling allowed. In: Dzhafarov, E.N., Jordan, S., Zhang, R., Cervantes, V.H. (eds.) Contextuality from quantum physics to psychology. Advanced Series on Mathematical Psychology, vol. 6, pp. 287–308. World Scientific, New Jersey (2016)
16. Sternberg, S.: The discovery of processing stages: extensions of Donders method. Acta Psychologica **30**, 276–315 (1969)
17. Townsend, J.T.: Uncovering mental processes with factorial experiments. J. Math. Psychol. **28**, 363–400 (1984)
18. Zhang, R., Dzhafarov, E.N.: Noncontextuality with marginal selectivity in reconstructing mental architectures. Front. Psychol. **6**, 735 (2015). doi:10.3389/fpsyg.2015.00735

On the Interpretation of Probabilities in Generalized Probabilistic Models

Federico Holik[1(✉)], Sebastian Fortin[2], Gustavo Bosyk[1], and Angelo Plastino[1]

[1] National University La Plata and CONICET IFLP-CCT,
C.C. 727, 1900 La Plata, Argentina
holik@fisica.unlp.edu.ar
[2] University of Buenos Aires - CONICET, Buenos Aires, Argentina

Abstract. We discuss generalized probabilistic models for which states not necessarily obey Kolmogorov's axioms of probability. We study the relationship between properties and probabilistic measures in this setting, and explore some possible interpretations of these measures.

Keywords: Quantum probability · Generalized probabilistic models · Interpretations of probability theory

1   Introduction

The debate regarding the interpretation of probability theory remains still open in the literature [3]. And these interpretational problems become particularly important when the probabilities arising in quantum phenomena are considered [37]. The statistical nature of Quantum Theory posed intriguing questions since its beginnings. This was expressed, for example, by R. P. Feynman [51], who stressed the radical changes needed in the methods for computing probabilities:

> I should say, that in spite of the implication of the title of this talk the concept of probability is not altered in quantum mechanics. When I say the probability of a certain outcome of an experiment is p, I mean the conventional thing, that is, if the experiment is repeated many times one expects that the fraction of those which give the outcome in question is roughly p. I will not be at all concerned with analyzing or defining this concept in more detail, for no departure of the concept used in classical statistics is required. What is changed, and changed radically, is the method of calculating probabilities.

The sum rule of probability amplitudes giving rise to interference terms was rapidly recognized as a non-classical feature [5]. Later, it was discovered that this was strongly related to the nonexistence of joint distributions for noncommuting observables. These peculiarities and formal aspects of the probabilities involved in quantum theory have been vastly studied in the literature [6–12].

J.A. de Barros et al. (Eds.): QI 2016, LNCS 10106, pp. 194–205, 2017.
DOI: 10.1007/978-3-319-52289-0_16

One of the most important axiomatizations in probability theory is due to Kolmogorov [13]. In his approach, probabilities are considered as measures defined over a Boolean sigma algebra of a sample space, i.e., as positive maps defined on certain subsets of a given set. Interestingly enough, states of classical statistical theories can be described using Kolmogorov's axioms, because they define measures over the sigma algebra of measurable subsets of phase space. An interesting approach to the statistical character of quantum systems consists in considering quantum states as measures over the non-Boolean structure of projection operators in a Hilbert space [4,5,8]. As is well known, projection operators can be used to describe elementary experiments (the analogue of this notion in the classical setting is represented by subsets of phase space). In this way, a comparison between quantum states and classical probabilistic states can be traced in formal and conceptual grounds. The equivalence between this approach and the usual one, based on the Born's rule [26], is provided by Gleason's theorem [35,36]. This is the reason why quantum states are termed "non-Boolean or non-Kolmogorovian" probability measures [8].

It is important to remark that a generalization of Kolmogorov's axioms can be given in terms of measures over arbitrary orthomodular lattices (instead of Boolean algebras) [6,23,24]. This approach contains quantum and classical statistical models as particular instances [5,8]. Another way to put this in a more general setting, is to consider a set of states of a particular probabilistic model as a convex set [5]. While classical systems can be described as simplexes, nonclassical theories can display a more involved geometrical structure. These models can go far beyond classical and quantum mechanics, and can be used to described different theories (see for example [28,29] and references therein). We will discuss these notions in Sect. 2 of this work.

The fact that states can be considered as measures over different sets of possible experimental results, reveals an essential structural feature of a vast family of physical statistical theories. A statistical model must specify the probabilities of actualization of all possible measurable quantities of the system involved: this is a feature which is common to all models, no matter how different they are. In this paper, we want to study which are the possible ontologies compatible with the general features arising in generalized probabilistic models. The fact that generalized models of physical theories can be characterized using very precise mathematical structures, should allow us to draw conclusions about possible interpretations. A study of the ontological constrains imposed by this general structure was not addressed previously in the literature. As we shall see, the algebraic and geometric features of the event structures defined by these measurable properties imposes severe restrictions on the interpretation of the probabilities defined by generalized states. In Sect. 3 we will show that a novel approach, based on putting constrains on degrees of belief functions defined over arbitrary orthomodular lattices [37,38], is particularly suitable for an extension of the Bayesian interpretation to arbitrary contextual probabilistic models. We will also see that, an ontology based on bundles of *actual* properties poses serious difficulties in most models of interest (specially, in all those which are not classical). An approach based on bundles of *possible* properties is discussed as an alternative [52]. Finally, we draw our conclusions in Sect. 4.

2   Non-Kolmogorovian Probabilistic Models

Suppose that we have a physical system whose states are given by measures which yield definite probabilities for the different outcomes of all possible experiments. From an operational perspective, these probabilities can be understood first in the sense used by Feynman in the quotation of Sect. 1. Then, for an experiment E with discrete outcomes $\{E_i\}_{i=1,..,n}$, a state ν gives us a probability $p(E_i, \nu) := \nu(E_i) \in [0, 1]$ for each possible value of i. The real numbers $p(E_i, \nu)$ must satisfy $\sum_{i=1}^{n} p(E_i, \nu) = 1$; otherwise, the probabilities would not be normalized. In this way, each state ν defines a concrete probability for each possible experiment. A crucial assumption here is that the set of all possible states $\mathcal{C}$ is convex: this assumption allows to form new states by mixing old ones and [29,34]. In formulae, if ν_1 and ν_2 are states in $\mathcal{C}$, then

$$\nu = \alpha\nu_1 + (1 - \alpha)\nu_2 \tag{1}$$

belongs to $\mathcal{C}$ for all $\alpha \in [0, 1]$. We will also assume that it is a compact set. This mixing property can be extended trivially to finite mixtures with more than two elements. Notice that each possible outcome E_i of each possible experiment E, induces a linear functional $E_i(...) : \mathcal{C} \longrightarrow [0, 1]$, with $E_i(\nu) := \nu(E_i)$. Functionals of this form are usually called *effects*. Thus, an experiment will then be a collection of effects (functionals) satisfying $\sum_{i=1}^{n} E_i(\nu) = 1$ for all states $\nu \in \mathcal{C}$. In other words, the functional $\sum_{i=1}^{n} E_i(...)$ equals the identity functional $\mathbf{1}$ (which satisfies $\mathbf{1}(\nu) = 1$ for all $\nu \in \mathcal{C}$). Any compact convex set $\mathcal{C}$ can be canonically embedded as a base for the positive cone $V_+(\mathcal{C})$ of a regularly ordered linear $V(\mathcal{C})$ (see [30,31] for details). This means that for every element z in $V_+(\mathcal{C})$, we can write $z = t\nu$ in a unique way, with $t \geq 0$ and $\nu \in \mathcal{C}$.

In this way, any possible experiment that we can perform on the system, is described as a collection of effects represented mathematically by affine functionals in an affine space $V^*(\mathcal{C})$. A model represented by a convex set $\mathcal{C}$ will be said to be finite dimensional if and only if $V(\mathcal{C})$ is finite dimensional. As in the quantum and classical cases, extreme points of the convex set of states will represent pure states.

It is important to remark the generality of the framework described above: all possible probabilistic models with finite outcomes can be described in such a way. Furthermore, if suitable definitions are made, it is possible to include continuous outcomes in this setting.

A *face* F of a convex set $\mathcal{C}$ is a convex subset of it satisfying that for all μ, if $\mu = \alpha\mu_1 + (1-\alpha)\mu_2$ with $\alpha \in [0, 1]$, then $\mu \in F$ if and only if $\mu_1 \in F$ and $\mu_2 \in F$. Faces can be interpreted geometrically as subsets that are stable under mixing and purification. Faces are very important for our discussion, because it can be proved that the set of all possible faces of any convex set forms a lattice. For very important models this lattice is an orthomodular one, and can be put in connection with the approach described below [1,24]. In particular, the lattice of faces of the convex set of states of a quantum system is isomorphic to the lattice of projection operators in the associated Hilbert space [1,24]. A similar result holds for classical statistical models: the lattice of faces is a Boolean one. This means that, at least for very important models, there exists a strong connection between the geometry of a convex set of states and the propositional algebra associated to the system in question [37,47]. This connection can be exploited in order to draw conclusions about how to interpret the states of the given model.

Birkhoff and von Neumann showed [4] that the empirical propositions associated to a classical system can be naturally organized as a *Boolean algebra* (which is an orthocomplemented distributive lattice [6,16]). While classical observables are defined as functions over phase space and form a commutative algebra, quantum observables are represented by self adjoint operators, which fail to be commutative. Due to this fact, empirical propositions associated to quantum systems are represented by projection operators, which are in one to one correspondence to closed subspaces related to the projective geometry of a Hilbert space [27,32]. Thus, empirical propositions associated to quantum systems form a non-distributive—and thus non-Boolean—lattice.

An important example of a classical probabilistic model is provided by a point particle moving in space time whose states are described by probability functions over $\mathbb{R}^6$. Suppose that A represents an observable quantity (i.e., it is a function defined over the phase space). Then, the proposition "the value of A lies in the interval Δ", defines a *testable* proposition, which we denote by A_Δ. The proposal of [4] is to associate A_Δ to the measurable set $f^{-1}(\Delta)$, which is the set of all states that make the proposition true. If the probabilistic state of the system is given by μ, the corresponding probability of occurrence of f_Δ will be given by $\mu(f^{-1}(\Delta))$. The situation is analogous for more general classical probabilistic systems. There is a strict correspondence between a classical probabilistic state and the axioms of classical probability theory. Indeed, the axioms of Kolmogorov [13] define a probability function as a measure μ on a sigma-algebra Σ such that

$$\mu : \Sigma \to [0,1] \tag{2}$$

which satisfies

$$\mu(\emptyset) = 0 \tag{3}$$

$$\mu(A^c) = 1 - \mu(A), \tag{4}$$

where $(\ldots)^c$ means set-theoretical-complement. For any pairwise disjoint denumerable family $\{A_i\}_{i \in I}$,

$$\mu(\bigcup_{i \in I} A_i) = \sum_i \mu(A_i). \tag{5}$$

A state of a classical probabilistic theory will be defined as a Kolmogorovian measure with $\Sigma = \mathcal{P}(\Gamma)$ (where Γ and $\mathcal{P}(\Gamma)$ denote the phase space of the system and its measurable subsets, respectively). It is straightforward to show that the set of all possible measures of this form is convex.

Quantum models can be described in an analogous way, but using operators acting on Hilbert spaces instead of functions over a phase space. If **A** represents the self adjoint operator associated to an observable of a quantum system, the proposition "the value of **A** lies in the interval Δ" will define a testable experiment represented by the projection operator $\mathbf{P_A}(\Delta) \in \mathcal{P}(\mathcal{H})$, i.e., the projection that the spectral measure of **A** assigns to the Borel set Δ [25]. The probability assigned to the event $\mathbf{P_A}(\Delta)$, given that the system is prepared in the state ρ, is computed using Born's rule [1,26]:

$$p(\mathbf{P_A}(\Delta)) = \mathrm{tr}(\rho \mathbf{P_A}(\Delta)). \tag{6}$$

Born's rule defines a measure on $\mathcal{P}(\mathcal{H})$ with which it is possible to compute all probabilities and mean values for all physical observables of interest [1,26]. It is well known that, due to Gleason's theorem [35,36], a quantum state can be defined by a measure s over the orthomodular lattice[1] of projection operators $\mathcal{P}(\mathcal{H})$ as follows [8,26]:

$$s : \mathcal{P}(\mathcal{H}) \to [0;1] \tag{7}$$

such that:

$$s(\mathbf{0}) = 0 \; (\mathbf{0} \text{ is the null subspace}). \tag{8}$$

$$s(P^{\perp}) = 1 - s(P), \tag{9}$$

and, for a denumerable and pairwise orthogonal family of projections P_j

$$s\left(\sum_j P_j\right) = \sum_j s(P_j). \tag{10}$$

As in the classical case, the set of states defined by the above equations is also convex. Despite their mathematical resemblance, there is a big difference between classical and quantum measures. In the latter case, the Boolean algebra Σ is replaced by $\mathcal{P}(\mathcal{H})$, and the other conditions are the natural generalizations of the classical event structure to the non-Boolean setting. The fact that $\mathcal{P}(\mathcal{H})$ is not Boolean lies behind the peculiarities of probabilities arising in quantum phenomena. In articular, their geometrical features as convex sets are very different; while classical models are simplexes, models arising in quantum systems have a more involved geometry [28]. As an example, the set of probabilistic states of a classical bit (a classical system with only two possible outcomes) forms a line segment, while the set of states of its quantum version, the qubit (a quantum system represented by a two dimensional Hilbert space) has the form of a sphere. As the dimensionality grows, the geometrical features of sets of quantum states becomes more and more involved [1]. The fact that classical states are always

---

[1] An *orthomodular lattice* $\mathcal{L}$, is defined as an orthocomplemented lattice satisfying that, for any a, b and c, if $a \leq c$, then $a \vee (a^{\perp} \wedge c) = c$. In the Hilbert space case, projection operators are in one to one correspondence to closed subspaces. These form an orthomodular lattice with "$\vee$" representing the closure of the sum of two subspaces, "$\wedge$" its intersection, and "$(...)^{\perp}$" representing the orthogonal complement of a given subspace. "$\leq$" means subspace inclusion. See [23] for a detailed exposition.

simplexes, implies that each point has a unique decomposition in terms of pure states; but this property does no longer holds in the quantum case, posing a serious problem for the attempts to give an ignorance interpretation of mixed states.

In a series of papers Murray and von Neumann searched for algebras more general than $\mathcal{B}(\mathcal{H})$ [43–46]. The new algebras are known today as von Neumann algebras, and their elementary components can be classified as Type I, Type II and Type III factors. It can be shown that, the projective elements of a factor form an orthomodular lattice. Classical models can be described as commutative von Neumann algebras. The models of standard quantum mechanics can be described by using Type I factors (Type I_n for finite dimensional Hilbert spaces and Type I_∞ for infinite dimensional models). These are algebras isomorphic to the set of bounded operators of a Hilbert space. Further work revealed that a rigorous approach to the study of quantum systems with infinite degrees of freedom needed the use of Type III factors, as is the case in the axiomatic formulation of relativistic quantum mechanics [8,48,49]. A similar situation holds in algebraic quantum statistical mechanics [8,50]. In these models, states are described as complex functionals satisfying certain normalization conditions, and when restricted to the projective elements of the algebras, obey laws similar to those given by Eq. 7. In other words, they define measures over lattices which are not the same to those of standard quantum mechanics. This opens the door to a meaningful generalization of Kolmogorov's axioms to a wide variety of orthomodular lattices. Thus, a general probabilistic framework can be described by the following equations. Let $\mathcal{L}$ be an orthomodular lattice. Then, define

$$s : \mathcal{L} \rightarrow [0;1],\tag{11}$$

($\mathcal{L}$ standing for the lattice of all events) such that:

$$s(\mathbf{0}) = 0.\tag{12}$$

$$s(E^\perp) = 1 - s(E),\tag{13}$$

and, for a denumerable and pairwise orthogonal family of events E_j

$$s\left(\sum_j E_j\right) = \sum_j s(E_j).\tag{14}$$

where $\mathcal{L}$ is a general orthomodular lattice (with $\mathcal{L} = \Sigma$ and $\mathcal{L} = \mathcal{P}(\mathcal{H})$ for the Kolmogorovian and quantum cases respectively).

Equations 11–14 define what is known as a *non-commutative probability theory* [8]. It is very important to remark that the above measures do not exist for certain orthomodular lattices; for a detailed or a detailed discussion on the conditions under which these measures are meaningful, see [24], Chap. 11. It suffices for us that the most important physical examples fall into this scheme, and this is indeed the case.

3 Different Ontologies

Now a question arises. Can we say something about the nature of probabilities by simply looking at the structural properties of the above described general framework? Is it possible to find a theoretical framework which allows us to give a general interpretation of probabilistic statistical models? The generalized setting is a mathematical framework capable of accommodating models of a very different nature. Given that it contains classical statistical mechanics and quantum mechanics as particular instances, we know that the models involved can be very different. But there are some specific features which allow us to extract some structural conclusions by studying the relationship between the lattice of properties and the geometry of the set of states.

In order to find an answer to the above questions, let us start first by considering an approach based on the restrictions imposed by the algebraic features of the event structure on the probability measures which can be defined in a compatible way. When the property lattice is Boolean, R. T. Cox [14,15] showed that the only measures compatible with the algebraic symmetries of the lattice are those which obey the usual Kolmogorov's axioms. Furthermore, in this approach, Shannon's entropic measure appears as the most natural information measure for these models [20]. Cox approach works as follows. Start with a Boolean algebra $\mathcal{B}$, representing the domain of possible events available to a rational agent (which could be an automata). The algebra is assumed to be distributive, because this fact reflects that the logic used by the agent is classical. The agent has to put a numerical valuation to each possible proposition with a degree of belief function φ. This is done in a conditional way. Thus, for example, the real number $\varphi(a|b)$ represents the degree of belief of the agent that a is true given that b is true. This works as a sort of inference calculus: when we have complete certainty, the agent uses classical logic in order to make deductions; when he has no certainty, he must use a degree of belief function. But it turns out that, if the function φ has to be compatible with the algebraic properties of $\mathcal{B}$, there are not too many options at hand: φ has to satisfy, up to rescaling, a set of laws which are equivalent to those given by Kolmogorov's axioms. This approach has been modified and used to derive Feynman laws of probability in the quantum setting [17–20].

But as we have seen in Sect. 2, if the lattice of properties involved is not Boolean, non-Kolmogorovian measures appear. This is the case for standard non-relativistic quantum mechanics and many other statistical models of interest, such as those provided by algebraic quantum field theory and quantum statistical mechanics. What happens if a rational agent has to define belief functions under the condition that the empirical event structures depart from the Boolean realm of classical physics?

Indeed, if the lattice of properties is represented by the orthomodular lattice of projection operators in a Hilbert space, it is possible to show that the only consistent possibility is given by the Born's rule [37]. Moreover, if the lattices are more general and non-Boolean, it can be shown that the probability measures will not be Kolmogorovian either [37]. In this approach, the Shannon's information measure must be replaced by the von Neumann's entropy in the quantum case and the measurement entropy in the general case [38]. Let us briefly describe how this method works in the general case. One first starts by identifying the algebraic structure of the event structure of a given theory T. In many cases of interest, this will be specified as a particular orthomodular lattice $\mathcal{L}$. Notice that, in principle, this could be considered as empirical information available to the agent. Once the algebraic properties of the event structure are determined, a variant of Cox method can be applied by studying the constrains imposed on the degree of belief functions. The crucial point here is that event structures are not always organized as Boolean lattices. Thus, in order to determine the general properties of the probabilities of a given theory, Cox's method has to be applied to lattices more general than Boolean ones.

The existence of this approach opens an interesting perspective for the Bayesian interpretation of probabilities. The interpretation would be as follows. There is an empirical scenario in which a rational agent[2] (which could be an automata) must take a decision, and with that aim, he must define a degree of belief function. Different possible experiments and results are available and they are organized in an event structure, assumed to be an orthomodular lattice. If the lattice of events that he is facing is Boolean (as in Cox's approach), then the measures of degree of belief of the rational agent will obey laws equivalent to those of Kolmogorov. On the contrary, if the state of affairs that the agent must face presents contextuality (as in standard quantum mechanics), the measures involved must be non-Kolmogorovian. The natural information measures will be Shannon's or more general ones, according to the algebraic structure of the context involved [38]. This kind of approach would allow for a natural justification for the peculiarities of probabilities arising in quantum phenomena from the standpoint of the Bayesian approach.

But one of the problems of the Bayesian interpretation of probabilities is that it says nothing about ontology in a deliberate way. What can we do if we want to go beyond the subjective approach and say something about the nature of the models involved? As we have seen, a generalized probabilistic model establishes a relationship between the state of the system and the results of possible experiments to be performed on the system. Is it possible to assign concrete properties of the system to these experiments? In the Kolmogorovian setting, it is possible to find global valuations of the Boolean lattice to the set $\{0, 1\}$. In other words, for each possible property, we can consistently affirm that the system either possesses that property or does not possess it. Thus, at least in principle, we can consider classical models as objects with definite properties. The probabilities would simply reflect our subjective ignorance about this objective situation.

The situation changes radically in the quantum case. The Kochen-Specker (KS) theorem poses a serious threat for the interpretation of a quantum system as

---

[2] It is important to notice here that different notions of "rational agent" could be used. In particular, it would be interesting to study the possibility of using *Dutch Book Arguments* in the generalized setting.

an object with definite properties: it is not possible to establish a global Boolean valuation to the elements of the lattice of projection operators. Of course, this problem can be solved if hidden variables are assumed, as in the Bohmian formulation of quantum theory (where the interpretation displays highly non-local features). But one thing we know for sure: we cannot interpret the elements of the event structure as representing definite properties of the system. The trick of considering the state of the system as the quantum logical conjunction of all actual properties (i.e., those properties for which the probability of occurrence is equal to one in a given state), becomes untenable when entangled states and improper mixtures are considered [53].

What about an interpretation in terms of bundles of properties for quantum systems? One may think that the problem of the interpretation of quantum systems is related to the assumption of an ontology of substances and properties, being the system a sort of 'carrier' of its actual properties. In order to avoid this, one may try to think quantum systems not as individual objects, but as *bundles of properties*. According to this interpretation, properties have an ontological priority, and there is no individual substratum acting as a carrier. In other words, an object is no longer considered as an individual substratum possessing properties, but simply a convergent bundle of properties without any substratum. But again, the KS theorem threatens the interpretation of a quantum system as a bundle of *actual* properties. For this reason, some authors have attempted an interpretation of standard quantum mechanics based on bundles of *possible* properties (see for example, [52] and references therein). The fact that possible properties do not pertain to the realm of actuality, would avoid the problems imposed by the KS theorem.

But the above considerations with regard to the impossibility of considering the elements of the event structure as a set of definite (or actual) properties, imposes a severe restriction on the interpretation of probabilities arising in quantum phenomena: an ignorance interpretation will be problematic, due to the fact that, in these interpretations, there will always exist sets of properties for which definite values cannot be consistently assigned previously to the measurement process. For these reasons, it seems natural to take quantum probabilities as ontological (provided that we want to avoid hidden variable models).

One of the key features that allows for the existence of the KS theorem is the fact that the orthomodular lattice of projections is not Boolean. Indeed, in [40], a detailed study of the orthomodular structures underlying the Kochen-Speker construction is presented. As we have seen, the event structures associated to more generalized probabilistic models can be non-Boolean in the general case. This means that, for a vast family of non-Kolmogorovian models, we will not be able to think about the elements of the event structure as representing actual properties of an individual system. And with regard to the algebraic formulation of physical probabilistic theories, a generalized version of the KS theorem exists for von Neumann algebras [41] (see also [42]). Due to the existence of these results, an interpretation based on bundles of actual properties for generalized probabilistic models seems to be problematic. As in the quantum case, the approach based on bundles of *possible* properties could be used instead [52].

But again, as in the standard quantum mechanics example, the probabilities involved will no longer admit an ignorance interpretation for generalized probabilistic models showing contextuality.

4 Conclusions

In this work we have discussed the connection between the event structures associated to general non-Kolmogorovian models and measures representing states. We reviewed an approach in which states are regarded as functions measuring the degree of belief of a rational agent, and find that a Bayesian interpretation seems to be suitable for the most important probabilistic models, provided that contextual phenomena is accepted as a starting point. Of course, this program should be worked out with more detail, specially with regard to the study of conditional probabilities and the Bayes' rule in the generalized setting.

In order to go beyond the subjective interpretation, we also discussed the conditions under which the event structures can be related to properties of a system, and inquired on the ontological aspects of such an association. Due to the existence of generalized versions of the KS theorem, we find that for the majority of models the description of systems as bundles of actual properties will be problematic. This opens the door to a generalization of previous approaches in which bundles of possible properties are the elementary bricks out of which reality is constructed. But in all these interpretations, an ignorance interpretation of probabilities will no longer be possible.

Acknowledgments. The Authors acknowledge CONICET and UNLP (Argentina). We are grateful to the anonymous reviewers, whose comments have helped to improve the manuscript. This publication was also made possible through the support of grant 57919 from the John Templeton Foundation. The opinions expressed in this publication are those of the authors and do not necessarily reflect the views of the John Templeton Foundation. FH also is grateful to the participants of the Conference "Quantum interactions - 2016" (San Franciso, July 2016), for the stimulating and lively discussions that have enriched this work.

References

1. Bengtsson, I., Zyczkowski, K.: Geometry of Quantum States: An Introduction to Quantum Entanglement. Cambridge University Press, Cambridge (2006)
2. Holik, F., Plastino, A., Saenz, M.: Natural information measures in Cox' approach for contextual probabilistic theories. Quantum Inf. Comput. **16**(1 & 2), 0115–0133 (2016)
3. Rocchi, P.: Janus-faced Probability. Springer, Cham (2014)
4. Birkhoff, G., von Neumann, J.: The logic of quantum mechanics. Ann. Math. **37**, 823–843 (1936)
5. Gudder, S.P.: Stochastic Methods in Quantum Mechanics, North Holland, New York (1979)
6. Dalla Chiara, M.L., Giuntini, R., Greechie, R.: Reasoning in Quantum Theory. Kluwer Academic Pubulisher, Dordrecht (2004)

7. Rédei, M.: Quantum Logic in Algebraic Approach. Kluwer Academic Publishers, Dordrecht (1998)
8. Rédei, M., Summers, S.: Studies in history and philosophy of science part B: studies in history and philosophy of modern physics. Probab. Quantum Mech. **38**(2), 390–417 (2007)
9. Davies, E., Lewis, J.: An operational approach to quantum probability. Commun. Math. Phys. **17**, 239–260 (1970)
10. Srinivas, M.: Foundations of a quantum probability theory. J. Math. Phys. **16**(8), 1672–1685 (1975)
11. Anastopoulos, C.: Annals Of Physics **313**, 368–382 (2004)
12. Rau, J.: On the relation between quantum mechanical probabilities and event frequencies. Ann. Phys. **324**, 2622–2637 (2009)
13. Kolmogorov, A.N.: Foundations of Probability Theory. Springer, Berlin (1933)
14. Cox, R.T.: Probability, frequency, and reasonable expectation. Am. J. Phys. **14**, 1–13 (1946)
15. Cox, R.T.: The Algebra of Probable Inference. The Johns Hopkins Press, Baltimore (1961)
16. Boole, G.: An Investigation of the Laws of Thought. Macmillan, London (1854)
17. Knuth, K.H.: Deriving laws from ordering relations. In: Erickson, G.J., Zhai, Y. (eds.) Proceedings of 23rd International Workshop on Bayesian Inference and Maximum Entropy Methods in Science and Engineering, American Institute of Physics, New York, NY, USA, pp. 204-235 (2004)
18. Knuth, K.H. Measuring on lattices. In: Goggans, P., Chan, C.Y. (eds.) Proceedings of 23rd International Workshop on Bayesian Inference and Maximum Entropy Methods in Science and Engineering, American Institute of Physics, New York, NY, USA, Volume 707, pp. 132-144 (2004)
19. Knuth, K.H.: Valuations on lattices and their application to information theory. In: Proceedings of the 2006 IEEE World Congress on Computational Intelligence, Vancouver, Canada, July 2006
20. Knuth, K.H.: Lattice duality: the origin of probability and entropy. Neurocomputing **67C**, 245–274 (2005)
21. Goyal, P., Knuth, K.: Quantum theory and probability theory: their relationship and origin in symmetry. Symmetry **3**, 171–206 (2011). doi:10.3390/sym3020171
22. Goyal, P., Knuth, K.H., Skilling, J.: Origin of complex quantum amplitudes and Feynman's rules. Phys. Rev. A **81**, 022109 (2010)
23. Kalmbach, G.: Orthomodular Lattices. Academic Press, San Diego (1983)
24. Beltrametti, E.G., Cassinelli, G.: The Logic of Quantum Mechanics. Addison-Wesley, Reading (1981)
25. Reed, M., Simon, B.: Methods of modern mathematical physics I: functional analysis. Academic Press, New York (1972)
26. Holik, F., Massri, C., Plastino, A., Zuberman, L.: On the lattice structure of probability spaces in quantum mechanics. Int. J. Theor. Phys. **52**(6), 1836–1876 (2013)
27. Bub, J.: Quantum computation from a quantum logical perspective. Quant. Inf. Process. **7**, 281–296 (2007)
28. Holik, F., Bosyk, G.M., Bellomo, G.: Quantum information as a non-kolmogorovian generalization of Shannon's theory. Entropy **17**, 7349–7373 (2015). doi:10.3390/e17117349
29. Holik, F., Plastino, A., Mechanics, Q.: A new turn in probability theory. In: Zoheir, E. (ed.) Contemporary Research in Quantum Systems. Nova Publishers, New York (2014)

30. Alfsen, E.M.: Compact Convex Sets and Boundary Integrals. Springer, Heidelberg (1971)
31. Barnum, H., Duncan, R., Wilce, A.: Symmetry, compact closure and dagger compactness for categories of convex operational models. J. Philos. Logic **42**, 501–523 (2013)
32. Stubbe, I., Steirteghem, B.V.: Propositional systems, Hilbert lattices and generalized Hilbert spaces. In: Engesser, K., Gabbay, D.M., Lehmann, D. (eds.) Handbook Of Quantum Logic and Quantum Structures: Quantum Structures (2007)
33. Barnum, H., Barret, J., Leifer, M., Wilce, A.: Generalized no-broadcasting theorem. Phys. Rev. Lett. **99**, 240501 (2007)
34. Barnum, H., Wilce, A.: Information processing in convex operational theories. Electron. Not. Theor. Comput. Sci. **270**(1), 3–15 (2011)
35. Gleason, A.: Measures on the closed subspaces of a Hilbert space. J. Math. Mech. **6**, 885–893 (1957)
36. Buhagiar, D., Chetcuti, E., Dvurečenskij, A.: On Gleason's theorem without Gleason. Found. Phys. **39**, 550–558 (2009)
37. Holik, F., Saenz, M., Plastino, A.: A discussion on the origin of quantum probabilities. Ann. Phys. **340**(1), 293–310 (2014)
38. Holik, F., Plastino, A., Saenz, M.: Natural information measures for contextual probabilistic models. Quantum Inf. Comput. **16**(1 & 2), 0115–0133 (2016)
39. Svozil, K.: Quantum Logic. Springer, Verlag (1998)
40. Svozil, K., Tkadlec, J.: Greechie diagrams, nonexistence of measures in quantum logics, and Kochen–Specker-type constructions. J. Math. Phys. **37**, 5380–5401 (1996)
41. Doring, A.: Kochen-Specker theorem for von neumann algebras. Int. J. Theor. Phys. **44**(2) (2005)
42. Smith, D.: Orthomodular Bell-Kochen-Specker theorem. Int. J. Theor. Phys. **43**(10) (2004)
43. Murray, F.J., von Neumann, J.: On rings of operators. Ann. Math. **37**, 116–229 (1936)
44. Murray, F.J., von Neumann, J.: On rings of operators II. Trans. Am. Math. Soc. **41**, 208–248 (1937)
45. von Neumann, J.: On rings of operators III. Ann. Math. **41**, 94–161 (1940)
46. Murray, F.J., von Neumann, J.: On rings of operators IV. Ann. Math. **44**, 716–808 (1943)
47. Holik, F.: Logic, geometry and probability theory. SOP Trans. Thoer. Phys. **1**, 128–137 (2014)
48. Halvorson, H., Müger, M.: Algebraic Quantum Field Theory. In: Butterfield, J.B., Earman, J.E. (eds.) Philosophy of Physics, Elsevier, Amsterdam, The Netherlands, pp. 731–922 (2006)
49. Yngvason, J.: The role of type III factors in quantum field theory. Rep. Math. Phys. **55**, 135–147 (2005)
50. Bratteli, O., Robinson, D.W.: Operator Algebras and Quantum Statistical Mechanics: Volumes 1 and 2. Springer, Heidelberg (2012)
51. Feynman, R.P.: The concept of probability in quantum mechanics. In: Proceedings of Second Berkeley Symposium on Mathethical Statistical and Probability, University of California Press, pp. 533–541 (1951)
52. da Costa, N., Lombardi, O., Lastir, M.: A modal ontology of properties for quantum mechanics. Synthese **190**(17), 3671–3693 (2013)
53. Domenech, G., Holik, F., Massri, C.: A quantum logical and geometrical approach to the study of improper mixtures. J. Math. Phyys. **51**(5), 052108 (2010)

An Introduction to Symmetric Inflated Probabilities

Mark Burgin[(✉)]

University of California, 520 Portola Plaza, Los Angeles, CA 90095, USA
mburgin@math.ucla.edu

Abstract. Traditionally, probability is treated as a function that takes values in the interval [0, 1]. All conventional interpretations of probability support this assumption, while all popular formal descriptions, e.g., axioms for probability, such as Kolmogorov's axioms, canonize this premise. However, researchers found that negative, as well as larger than 1 probabilities could be a useful tool in physics. Some even assert that probabilities that can be negative, larger than 1 or less than −1 are necessary for physics. Here we develop an axiomatic system for such probabilities, which are called symmetric inflated probabilities and reflect interaction of particles and antiparticles, and study their properties.

Keywords: Negative probability · Antiparticle · Annihilation · Symmetry · Axiom · Additivity · Frequency · Inflation

1 Introduction

Traditionally, probability is regarded as a function that takes values in the interval [0, 1]. However, researchers found that probabilities values of which did not belong to this interval could be useful in various situations. For instance, negative probabilities have been applied to a number of theoretical and practical problems.

Historically, Hermann Weyl was the first researcher to unconsciously encounter negative probability in (Weyl 1927). Explicitly, negative probabilities emerged in physics in works of Dirac (1930a) and Heisenberg (1931) within the context of quantum theory. However, both physicists missed its significance and possibility to take negative values, using this distribution as an approximation to the full quantum description of a system such as the atom. In contrast to this, Wigner (1932) came to the conclusion that quantum corrections often lead to negative probabilities, or as some prefer to say *quasi-probabilities*.

The importance of Wigner's construction for foundational problems was not recognized until much later when Wigner quasi-probability distribution little by little has become very popular in physics finding application to many different physical problems, including quantum optics, statistical mechanics, hydrodynamics, nuclear theory and quantum field theory (Hillery, et al. 1984).

Later Dirac (1942) in his work on the quantization of electromagnetic field did not only support Wigner's approach but also introduced the physical concept of negative energy strongly connected to negative probabilities. It was discovered that physical theories operating in a Hilbert space with indefinite metric entail negative probabilities

© Springer International Publishing AG 2017
J.A. de Barros et al. (Eds.): QI 2016, LNCS 10106, pp. 206–223, 2017.
DOI: 10.1007/978-3-319-52289-0_17

(Dirac 1942; Pauli 1943; Le Couteur 1949; Gupta 1957; Howard et al. 1961; Sudarshan 1961).

Dirac (1974) and Feynman (1987) described various useful physical interpretations of negative probabilities to demonstrate importance of negative probabilities in physics.

A little by little, negative probabilities were becoming more and more popular in physics (cf., for example, (Dirac 1943; Bartlett 1945; Feynman 1950; 1987; Baker 1958; Mückenheim 1986; 1988; Sokolovski and Connor 1991; Scully et al. 1994; Belinskii 1994; Han et al. 1996)). Now negative probabilities is a commonplace tool for many physicists (cf., for example, (Youssef 2001; Curtright and Zachos 2001; Galvao 2005; Sokolovski 2007; Bednorz and Belzig 2009; Hofmann 2009; Kronz 2009; Gell-Mann and Hartle 2011; Abramsky and Brandenburger 2014; de Barros and Oas 2015)).

Negative probabilities also came to economics and finance (Duffie and Singleton 1999; Forsyth et al. 2001; Haug 2004; Székely 2005; Kronz 2009; Burgin and Meissner 2010). Besides, according to (Ferrie and Emerson 2008), several finite dimensional quasi-probability representations of quantum states have been proposed to study various problems in quantum information theory.

In addition, negative probabilities were used in social and behavioral sciences (cf., for example, (de Barros 2014; de Barros and oas 2014)).

At the same time, larger than 1 probabilities, also called above unity probabilities or bigger than one probabilities, i.e., probabilities values of which can be larger than 1, have received less attention. One of the few to address them was Nobel Prize laureate Paul Dirac who wrote (1943):

"The various parts of the wave function which referred to the existence of positive and negative-energy photons in the old interpretation now refer to the emissions and absorptions of photons. The probabilities, equal to 2 and −2, are not physically understandable, but one can use them mathematically in accordance with the rules for working with a Gibbs ensemble."

However, even before Dirac used and contemplated larger than 1 probabilities, they were intrinsically brought into play by other physicists. In his fundamental review on extended probabilities, Mückenheim (1986) explains how such probabilities emerge by extending the quantum theoretical description of radiation given by Weisskopf and Wigner (1930). They calculated the natural linewidth of radioactive decay of an excited atom in which the normalized decay probability density $\rho(E, t)$ can take on negative values, as well as values exceeding unity. As a result, the corresponding normalized probability, which is an observable quantity, may violate both the lower and the upper limit in Kolmogorov's axioms (Mückenheim 1986). It is important that these results were verified by experiments, demonstrating that utilization of larger than 1 probabilities well reflected physical reality (Holland et al. 1960; Lynch et al. 1960; Wu et al. 1960).

One more Nobel Prize laureate Richard Feynman (1987) also argued that larger than 1 probabilities could be useful for probability calculations in different problems of quantum physics.

Later larger than 1 probabilities have been considered in physics, biology and finance in the works of Mack (2002), Sjöstrand (2006), Venter (2007), and Nyambuya (2011). Some of the researchers did not want to accept meaningfulness of larger than 1 probabilities and tried to eliminate them by some artificial transformations. For instance,

Mack (2002) tries to get rid of larger than 1 probabilities by reducing the probability mass at zero. Other researchers recognized as an inherent property of the studied phenomena. For instance, Haug (2004) argued that negative, as well as larger than 1 probabilities could be a useful tool in enhancing financial modeling. Even more, Kronz (2009) explains necessity of greater than one probabilities demonstrating that one can account for constructive quantum interference, if probability values greater than one are allowed.

Gell-Mann and Hartle (2011) extended probability ensemble interpretation by including real numbers that may be negative or greater than 1 as the probability values and providing an unconventional interpretation of such probabilities. According to them, such extended probabilities obey the usual rules of probability theory except that they can be negative or greater than one for an alternative for which it cannot be determined whether it occurs or not (as on the alternative histories in the two-slit experiment).

In addition, larger than 1 (inflated) probabilities are specifically useful in finance as they, for example, were successfully applied to solving problems in financial modeling (Burgin and Meissner 2012a).

Looking into the history of mathematics and physics, we see that the evolution of negative, as well as larger than 1 probabilities is similar to many new concepts in mathematics, which were initially met with skepticism. When negative numbers came from India and China to Europe, critics dismissed their sensibility. Some of the European mathematicians, such as d'Alembert or Frend, rejected the sensibility of negative numbers until the 18th century and referred to them as 'absurd' or 'meaningless' (Kline 1980; Mattessich 1998). Even in the 19th century, it was a common practice to ignore any negative results derived from equations, on the assumption that they were meaningless (Martinez 2006). For instance, Lazare Carnot (1753–1823) affirmed that the idea of something being less than nothing is absurd (Mattessich 1998). Such outstanding mathematicians as William Hamilton (1805–1865) and August De Morgan (1806–1871) had similar opinions. Likewise, irrational numbers and later imaginary numbers were firstly rejected.

It is interesting that analogous situations happen even now. For instance, Blass and Gurevich (2015) declared that "negative probabilities were obviously inconsistent with the frequentist interpretation" 5 years after a frequentist interpretation had been published in (Burgin 2010). Other researchers also emphasized that interpreting negative probabilities is a difficult problem (Halliwell and Yearsley 2013; Oas et al. 2014).

Today irrational, negative and imaginary numbers are accepted and applied in numerous scientific and practical fields, such as physics, chemistry, biology and finance.

In a similar way, negative, as well as larger than 1 probabilities are finding more and more practical applications. There were axiomatic mathematical theories of negative probabilities and of inflated (larger than 1) probabilities: partial axiomatization was given in (Allen 1976); axiomatization for p-adic negative probabilities was given in (Khrennikov 2009); axiomatization for regular negative probabilities used in physics and finance was given in (Burgin 2009; 2013; Burgin and Meissner 2010; 2012), while axiomatization for inflated (larger than 1) probabilities was given in (Burgin and Meissner 2012a). The goal of this paper to elaborate an axiomatic mathematical theory that includes both negative probabilities and of inflated (larger than 1) probabilities. This theory describes symmetric inflated probabilities.

2 Mathematical Foundations of Symmetric Inflated Probability

Let us consider a set Ω, which consists of two irreducible disjoint parts (subsets) Ω^+ and Ω^-, i.e., neither of these parts is equal to its proper subset. Elements from the set Ω^+ are called *elementary positive events*, while elements from the set Ω^- are called *elementary negative events* or *antievents*. Subsets of the set Ω^+ are called *positive events*, while subsets of the set Ω^- are called *negative events* or *antievents*. All other subsets of the set Ω are *mixed events*.

The following axiom defines a correspondence between positive and negative events.

Axiom SIP1 (*Order structure*). There is a graded with respect to Ω^+ and Ω^- involution α: $\Omega \to \Omega$, i.e., α is a mapping with the following properties: α^2 is an identity mapping on Ω, $\alpha(w) = -w$ for any element w from Ω, $\alpha(\Omega^+) \supseteq \Omega^-$, and if $w \in \Omega^+$, then $\alpha(w) \notin \Omega^+$.

If $w \in \Omega^+$, then $-w$ is called the *antievent* of w. We assume that $-(-w) = w$.

There are different examples of negative events (antievents). They are usually connected to negative objects. For instance, encountering a negative object is a negative event.

An example of negative objects is given by antiparticles, which form an antimatter counterpart of quantum particles. For instance, the antiparticle of the electron e^- is called the positron and denoted by e^+. The discovery of the positron has an interesting history. When Paul Dirac extended quantum mechanics to include special relativity, he derived a formula known as the Dirac equation. This equation had two solutions. One of them described the electron, while the other one predicted that an electron should have a positively charged counterpart (Dirac 1930b). However, other physicists did not accept this conclusion and even mocked at Dirac for his innovation. In spite of this negative attitude, this particle, the positron, was soon discovered in the cosmic radiation by Carl Anderson in 1932. It was not easy to find positrons because the positrons produced in natural radioactive decay quickly annihilate themselves with electrons, producing pairs of gamma rays.

Another example of negative objects is given by antipatterns, which are negative design patterns in the software industry field (Koenig, 1995; Laplante and Neill 2005). A software design pattern is an *antipattern* if it is a repeated pattern of action, process or structure that initially appears to be beneficial, but ultimately produces more bad consequences than beneficial results, and for which an alternative solution exists that is clearly documented, proven in actual practice and repeatable.

Observations of subatomic particles have persuasively demonstrated that when a particle meets its antiparticle, they annihilate each other and disappear, their combined rest energies becoming available to appear in other forms (Feynman 1987a). These processes are described by creation and annihilation operators.

Note that annihilation occurs not only in physics where particles and antiparticles annihilate one another, but also in ordinary life of people. For instance, Alice has stocks of two companies. If in 2009, the first set of stocks gave profit $1,000, while the second set of stocks dropped by $1,000, then the combined income was $0. The loss annihilated the profit.

Here is even a simpler example. Bill finds $20 and loses $10. As the result, the amount of this person's money has increased by $10. The loss annihilated a part of the gain.

Thus, it is natural to assume that if an event contains an elementary event w and its antievent $-w$, then w and $-w$ annihilate one another. To formalize this situation, we introduce additional equality relation determined by the following formula

$$\{v_i, w, - w; \ v_i, \ w \in \Omega \ \& \ i \ \in \ I\} \equiv \{v_i; \ v_i \in \ \Omega \ \& \ i \in I\}$$

This allows us to define the union with annihilation of two subsets X and Y of Ω by the following formula:

$$X \oplus Y = (X \cup Y) \setminus [(X \cap - Y) \cup (-X \cap Y)]$$

Here $-X = \{-w; w \in X\}$ and the set-theoretical operation \ represents annihilation, while sets $X \cap -Y$ and $X \cap -Y$ are formed from annihilating entities.

Some properties of the new set operation $\oplus$ are the same as properties of the union $\cup$.

Lemma 2.1

(a) $X \oplus X \equiv X$ for any subset X of Ω.
(b) $X \oplus Y \equiv X \cup Y$ for any subsets X and Y of Ω.
(c) $X \oplus \emptyset = X$ for any subset X of Ω.
(d) $X \oplus (Y \oplus Z) \equiv (X \oplus Y) \oplus Z$ for any subsets X, Y and Z of Ω.
(e) $X \oplus Y = Y \oplus X$ for any subsets X and Y of Ω.

At the same time, other properties of operations $\oplus$ and $\cup$ are different. For instance, operations $\cap$ and $\cup$ are not distributive with respect to the operation $\oplus$.

Lemma 2.2

(a) It is possible that $Z \cup (X \oplus Y) \neq (Z \cup X) \oplus (Z \cup Y)$ for some subsets X, Y and Z of Ω.
(b) It is possible that $X \oplus (Y \cap Z) \neq (X \oplus Y) \cap (X \oplus Z)$ for some subsets X, Y and Z of Ω.
(c) It is possible that $X \oplus (Y \cup Z) \neq (X \oplus Y) \cup (X \oplus Z)$ for some subsets X, Y and Z of Ω.
(d) It is possible that $Z \cap (X \oplus Y) \neq (Z \cap X) \oplus (Z \cap Y)$ for some subsets X, Y and Z of Ω.

Proof

(a) Let us take $\Omega = \{w_1, w_2, w_3, -w_1, -w_2, -w_3\}$, $Z = \{w_1, w_2, -w_1, -w_2\}$, $X = \{w_1, w_2\}$ and $Y = \{-w_1, -w_2\}$. Then $X \oplus Y = \emptyset$, $Z \cup X = Z$, $Z \cup Y = Z$, $Z \cup (X \oplus Y) = Z$, and $(Z \cup X) \oplus (Z \cup Y) = Z \oplus Z = \emptyset$. Thus, $Z \cup (X \oplus Y) \neq (Z \cup X) \oplus (Z \cup Y)$.

(b) Let us take $\Omega = \{w_1, w_2, w_3, -w_1, -w_2, -w_3\}$, $X = \{w_1, w_2, -w_1, -w_2\}$, $Z = \{w_1\}$ and $Y = \{-w_2\}$. Then $Y \cap Z = \emptyset$, $X \cap Z = Z = \{w_1\}$, $X \cap Y = Y = \{-w_2\}$, $X \oplus (Y \cap Z) = X = \{w_1, w_2, -w_1, -w_2\}$, while $(X \oplus Y) \cap (X \oplus Z) = \emptyset$. Thus, $X \oplus (Y \cap Z) \neq (X \oplus Y) \cap (X \oplus Z)$.

(c) Let us take $\Omega = \{w_1, w_2, w_3, -w_1, -w_2, -w_3\}$, $X = \{w_1, w_2, -w_1, -w_2\}$, $Z = \{w_1\}$ and $Y = \{-w_2\}$. Then $Y \cup Z = \{w_1, -w_2\}$, $X \oplus Z = \{w_1, w_2, -w_2\}$, $X \oplus Y = \{w_1, -w_1, -w_2\}$, $X \oplus (Y \cup Z) = \{w_1, -w_2\}$, while $(X \oplus Y) \cup (X \oplus Z) = \{w_1, w_2, -w_1, -w_2\}$. Thus, $X \oplus (Y \cup Z) \neq (X \oplus Y) \cup (X \oplus Z)$.

(d) Let us take $\Omega = \{w_1, w_2, w_3, -w_1, -w_2, -w_3\}$, $Z = \{w_1, w_2, -w_1\}$, $X = \{w_1, w_2\}$ and $Y = \{-w_1, -w_2\}$. Then $X \oplus Y = \emptyset$, $Z \cap X = X = \{w_1, w_2\}$, $Z \cap Y = \{-w_1\}$, $Z \cap (X \oplus Y) = \emptyset$, and $(Z \cap X) \oplus (Z \cap Y) = \{w_2\}$. Thus, $Z \cap (X \oplus Y) \neq (Z \cap X) \oplus (Z \cap Y)$.

Lemma is proved.

Lemma 2.3. $Z \cap (X \oplus Y) \subseteq (Z \cap X) \oplus (Z \cap Y)$ for all subsets X, Y and Z of Ω.

Proof. If $w \in Z \cap (X \oplus Y)$, then $w \in Z$ and $w \in X \oplus Y$. The second membership means that either ($w \in X$ and $-w \notin Y$) or ($w \in Y$ and $-w \notin X$). In the first case, $w \in Z \cap X$ and $-w \notin Z \cap Y$. In the second case, $w \in Z \cap Y$ and $-w \notin Z \cap X$. So, in both cases, $w \in (Z \cap X) \oplus (Z \cap Y)$. Thus, $Z \cap (X \oplus Y) \subseteq (Z \cap X) \oplus (Z \cap Y)$.

Lemma is proved.

As α is an involution of the whole space, we have the following result.

Lemma 2.4. α is a one-to-one mapping and $|\Omega^+| = |\Omega^-|$.

Corollary 2.1 (*Domain symmetry*). $w \in \Omega^+$ if and only if $-w \in \Omega^-$.

Corollary 2.2 (*Element symmetry*). $-(-w) = w$ for any element w from Ω.

Corollary 2.3 (*Event symmetry*). $-(-X) \equiv X$ for any event X from Ω.

Lemma 2.5. $\alpha(w) \neq w$ for any element w from Ω.

Proof. For any $w \in \Omega^+$ this is true by Axiom SIP1. If for some $w \in \Omega^-$, we have $\alpha(w) = w$, then $\alpha(v) = w$ for some element v from Ω^+ because by Axiom SIP1, α is a projection of Ω^+ onto Ω^-. Consequently, we have

$$\alpha(\alpha(v)) = \alpha(w) = w$$

However, α is an involution, and we have $\alpha(\alpha(v)) = v$. This results in the equality

$$v = w.$$

Consequently, we have $\alpha(v) = v$. This contradicts Axiom SIP1 because $v \in \Omega^+$. Lemma is proved.

Lemma 2.6

$$\Omega^+ \cap \Omega^- \equiv \emptyset.$$

Proof. Let $w \in \Omega^+ \cap \Omega^-$. Then by Axiom EP1, $-w \in \Omega \setminus \Omega^+ = \Omega^- \setminus \Omega^+$ as $\Omega = \Omega^- \cup \Omega^+$. Thus, we can define $\Omega_0^- = \Omega^- \setminus \{w\}$ and take $\Omega = \Omega_0^- \cup \Omega^+$. However, this contradicts irreducibility of Ω^-.

Proposition is proved by contradiction.

Corollary 2.4. For any element w from Ω, $w \in \Omega^+$ if and only if $-w \in \Omega^-$.

For any set $X \subseteq \Omega$, we define:

$$X^+ = X \cap \Omega^+$$

$$X^- = X \cap \Omega^-$$

$$-X = \{-w, w \in X\}$$

An important property of the basic set-theoretical operations is that it is possible to perform operations separately on positive and negative components of sets and then to combine these results.

Lemma 2.7. $A \cup B = (A^+ \cup B^+) \cup (A^- \cup B^-)$ for any subsets A and B of Ω.

Indeed, as $A \equiv A^+ \cup A^-$ and $B \equiv B^+ \cup B^-$, we have

$$A \cup B = (A^+ \cup A^-) \cup (B^+ \cup B^-) = (A^+ \cup B^+) \cup (A^- \cup B^-)$$

Lemma 2.8. $A \cap B \equiv (A^+ \cap B^+) \oplus (A^- \cap B^-)$ for any subsets A and B of Ω.

Indeed, as $A \equiv A^+ \cup A^-$ and $B \equiv B^+ \cup B^-$, we have

$$A \cap B = (A^+ \cup A^-) \cap (B^+ \cap B^-) \equiv$$
$$(A^+ \cap B^+) \cup (A^+ \cap B^-) \cup (A^- \cap B^+) \cup (A^- \cap B^-) \equiv (A^+ \cap B^+) \oplus (A^- \cap B^-)$$

because $(A^+ \cap B^-) \equiv \emptyset$ and $(A^- \cap B^+) \equiv \emptyset$.

In a similar way, we prove the following result.

Lemma 2.9. $A \setminus B \equiv (A^+ \setminus B^+) \oplus (A^- \setminus B^-)$ for any subsets A and B of Ω.

Lemma 2.10. $X \equiv X^+ \oplus X^- = X^+ \cup X^-$ for any set X from **F**.

Indeed, as $X \subseteq \Omega$, $X^+ = X \cap \Omega^+$, $X^- = X \cap \Omega^-$, and $\Omega = \Omega^+ \cup \Omega^-$, we have $X = X^+ \cup X^-$. In addition, $X^+ \oplus X^- = X^+ \cup X^-$ because by Lemma 2.6, we have $X^+ \cap X^- = \emptyset$.

Lemma 2.11. $A \oplus B \equiv (A^+ \oplus B^+) \oplus (A^- \oplus B^-)$ for any sets X and Y from **F**.

Indeed, as by Lemma 2.10, $A \equiv A^+ \oplus A^-$ and $B \equiv B^+ \oplus B^-$, we have

$$A \oplus B \equiv (A^+ \oplus A^-) \oplus (B^+ \oplus B^-) \equiv (A^+ \oplus B^+) \oplus (A^- \oplus B^-)$$

because by Lemma 2.1, operation $\oplus$ is commutative and associative.

The main idea behind probability is that probability is defined only for random events. Although the concept of randomness has different interpretations and formalizations, here we follow the classical approach developed by Kolmogorov, in which the set **F** of random events consists of subsets of Ω and is simply defined by its formal properties. This approach allows treating different types of random events. Even more, it makes possible inclusion of all events considered in the theory of hyperprobability into the general schema (Burgin and Krinik 2009).

Axiom SIP2 (*Algebraic structure*). $\mathbf{F}^+ = \{X \in \mathbf{F}; X \subseteq \Omega^+\}$ is a set algebra that has Ω^+ as its element.

We remind that a collection of sets **A** is a *set algebra* if it is closed with respect to union, intersection and difference of sets, while a set algebra **B** closed with respect to complements of its elements is called a *set field* (Kolmogorov and Fomin 1999). For any set algebra **A**, the empty set $\emptyset$ belongs to **A** and for any set field **B** in Ω, the set Ω belongs to **B**.

Axiom SIP3 (*Operational structure*). **F** is closed with respect to annihilation, i.e., if $X \equiv Y$ and $X \in \mathbf{F}$, then $Y \in \mathbf{F}$.

Elements from **F**, i.e., subsets of Ω that belong to **F**, are called *random events*.
Elements from $\mathbf{F}^+ = \{X \in \mathbf{F}; X \subseteq \Omega^+\}$ are called *positive random events*.
Elements from $\mathbf{F}^- = \{-A; A \in \mathbf{F}^+\}$ are called *negative random events* or *random antievents*.
Elements from Ω^+ that belong to $\mathbf{F}^+$ are called *elementary positive random events* or *elementary random events*.
Elements from Ω^- that belong to $\mathbf{F}^-$ are called *elementary negative random events* or *elementary random antievents*.
Note that the model is symmetric because positive events are, in this sense, antievents of the corresponding negative events, e.g., E is the antivent of $-E$.
If $A \in \mathbf{F}^+$, then $-A$ is called the *antievent* of A.

Axiom SIP4 (*Composition*). $\mathbf{F} \equiv \{X; X^+ \subseteq \mathbf{F}^+ \,\& \, X^- \subseteq \mathbf{F}^- \,\& \, X^+ \cap -X^- \equiv \emptyset \,\& \, X^- \cap -X^+ \equiv \emptyset\}$

This axiom means that in a general case, each element from **F** consists of two parts – one from $\mathbf{F}^+$ and another from $\mathbf{F}^-$ although one of these parts may be empty.

We remind that a set algebra is called a set field if it has the largest element and is closed with respect to complement (Kolmogorov and Fomin 1999).

Properties of the structure $\mathbf{F}^+$ are inherited by the structure $\mathbf{F}^-$.

Theorem 2.1 (*Algebra symmetry*). If $\mathbf{F}^+$ is a set algebra (set field), then $\mathbf{F}^-$ is a set algebra (set field).

Proof. Let us assume that $\mathbf{F}^{+}$ is a set algebra and take two negative random events H and K from $\mathbf{F}^{-}$. By the definition of $\mathbf{F}^{-}$, $H = -A$ and $K = -B$ for some positive random events A and B from $\mathbf{F}^{+}$. Then we have

$$H \cap K = (-A) \cap (-B) = -(A \cap B)$$

As $\mathbf{F}^{+}$ is a set algebra, $A \cap B \in \mathbf{F}^{+}$. Thus, $H \cap K \in \mathbf{F}^{-}$.

In a similar way, we have

$$H \cup K = (-A) \cup (-B) = -(A \cup B)$$

As $\mathbf{F}^{+}$ is a set algebra, $A \cup B \in \mathbf{F}^{+}$. Thus, $H \cup K \in \mathbf{F}^{-}$. By the same token, we have $H \setminus K \in \mathbf{F}^{-}$.

Besides, if $\mathbf{F}^{+}$ has a unit element E, then $-E$ is a unit element in $\mathbf{F}^{-}$.

Thus, $\mathbf{F}^{-}$ is a set algebra.

Now let us assume that $\mathbf{F}^{+}$ is a set field and $H \in \mathbf{F}^{-}$. Then by the definition of $\mathbf{F}^{-}$, $H = -A$ for a positive random event A from $\mathbf{F}^{+}$. It means that $C_{\Omega+}A = \Omega^{+} \setminus A \in \mathbf{F}^{+}$. At the same time,

$$C_{\Omega^-} H = \Omega^{-} \setminus H = (-\Omega^{+}) \setminus (-A) = -(\Omega^{+} \setminus A) = -C_{\Omega^+}A$$

As $C_{\Omega+} A$ belongs to $\mathbf{F}^{+}$, the complement $C_{\Omega-} H$ of H belongs to $\mathbf{F}^{-}$. Consequently, $\mathbf{F}^{-}$ is a set field.

Theorem is proved.

Properties of the structure $\mathbf{F}^{+}$ are inherited by the structure $\mathbf{F}$.

Theorem 2.2 (*Algebraic completeness*). If $\mathbf{F}^{+}$ is a set field (set algebra), then $\mathbf{F}$ is a set field (set algebra) with respect to operations $\cup$ and $\cap$.

Proof. Let us assume that $\mathbf{F}^{+}$ is a set algebra and take two random events A and B from $\mathbf{F}$. Then by Theorem 2.1, $\mathbf{F}^{-}$ is a set algebra. By Lemma 2.10, $A = A^{+} \cup A^{-}$ and $B = B^{+} \cup B^{-}$. By Axiom SIP4, $A^{+}, B^{+} \in \mathbf{F}^{+}, A^{-}, B^{-} \in \mathbf{F}^{-}$, while by Lemma 2.6, $A^{+} \cap A^{-} = \emptyset, B^{+} \cap B^{-} \equiv \emptyset, A \equiv A^{+} \cup A^{-}$, and $B \equiv B^{+} \cup B^{-}$.

By Lemma 2.8, we have $A \cap B \equiv (A^{+} \cap B^{+}) \cup (A^{-} \cap B^{-})$. Thus, $(A \cap B)^{+} \equiv A^{+} \cap B^{+}$ and $(A \cap B)^{-} \equiv A^{-} \cap B^{-}$. As $\mathbf{F}^{+}$ is a set algebra, $(A \cap B)^{+} \equiv A^{+} \cap B^{+} \in \mathbf{F}^{+}$. As by Theorem 2.1, $\mathbf{F}^{-}$ is a set algebra, $(A \cap B)^{-} \equiv A^{-} \cap B^{-} \in \mathbf{F}^{-}$. Consequently, $A \cap B \in \mathbf{F}$.

By Lemma 2.9, $A \setminus B \equiv (A^{+} \setminus B^{+}) \cup (A^{-} \setminus B^{-})$. Thus, $(A \setminus B)^{+} \equiv A^{+} \setminus B^{+}$ and $(A \setminus B)^{-} \equiv A^{-} \setminus B^{-}$. As $\mathbf{F}^{+}$ is a set algebra, $(A \setminus B)^{+} \equiv A^{+} \setminus B^{+} \in \mathbf{F}^{+}$. As by Theorem 2.1, $\mathbf{F}^{-}$ is a set algebra, $(A \setminus B)^{-} \equiv A^{-} \setminus B^{-} \in \mathbf{F}^{-}$. Consequently, $A \setminus B \in \mathbf{F}$.

By Lemma 2.11, $A \cup B \equiv (A^{+} \cup B^{+}) \cup (A^{-} \cup B^{-})$. Thus, $(A \cup B)^{+} \equiv A^{+} \cup B^{+}$ and $(A \cup B)^{-} \equiv A^{-} \cup B^{-}$. As $\mathbf{F}^{+}$ is a set algebra, $(A \cup B)^{+} \equiv A^{+} + B^{+} \equiv A^{+} \cup B^{+} \in \mathbf{F}^{+}$. As by Theorem 2.1, $\mathbf{F}^{-}$ is a set algebra, $(A \cup B)^{-} \equiv A^{-} \cup B^{-} \in \mathbf{F}^{-}$. Consequently, $A \cup B \in \mathbf{F}$.

Besides, if $\mathbf{F}^+$ has a unit element E, then $-E$ is a unit element in $\mathbf{F}^-$ and $E \cup -E$ is a unit element in $\mathbf{F}$.

Thus, $\mathbf{F}$ is a set algebra.

Now let us assume that $\mathbf{F}^+$ is a set field and $A \in \mathbf{F}$. Then by Theorem 2.1, $\mathbf{F}^-$ is a set field. By Lemma 2.10, $A \equiv A^+ + A^-$. As by Lemma 2.6, $\Omega^+ \cap \Omega^- = \emptyset$, we have

$$C_\Omega A = C_{\Omega_+} A^+ + C_{\Omega_-} A^-$$

Then $C_{\Omega_+} A^+$ belongs to $\mathbf{F}^+$ as $\mathbf{F}^+$ is a set field, while as it is proved in Theorem 2.1, $C_{\Omega_-} A^-$ belongs to $\mathbf{F}^-$. Consequently, $C_\Omega A$ belongs to $\mathbf{F}$ and $\mathbf{F}$ is a set field.

Theorem is proved.

Now it is possible to give an axiomatic definition of a probability function for symmetric inflated probability. Here we treat only the finite case when $\Omega = \{w_1, w_2, w_3, \ldots, w_n, -w_1, -w_2, -w_3, \ldots, -w_n\}$, $\Omega^+ = \{w_1, w_2, w_3, \ldots, w_n\}$ and $\Omega^- = \{-w_1, -w_2, -w_3, \ldots, -w_n\}$.

Definition 2.1. A function P from $\mathbf{F}$ to the set R of real numbers is called a *symmetric inflated probability function*, if $\mathbf{F}$ satisfies axioms SIP1 – SIP4 and P satisfies the following axioms:

Axiom SIP5 (*Upper normalization*). $0 \le P(\Omega^+) \le m$ for some natural number m.

Axiom SIP6 (*Lower normalization*). $0 \le P(A)$ for all $A \in \mathbf{F}^+$.

Axiom SIP7 (*Finite additivity*)

$$P(A \cup B) = P(A) + P(B)$$

for all sets $A, B \in \mathbf{F}$ such that

$$A \cap B \equiv \emptyset$$

Axiom SIP8 (*Adequacy*). If $A \equiv B$ and $A \in \mathbf{F}$, then $P(A) = P(B)$.

For instance, $P(\{w, -w\}) = P(\emptyset) = 0$.

We can see that Axioms SIP1–SIP8 establish a connection between symmetric inflated probabilities and signed measures in the same way as Kolmogorov axioms determine a connection between conventional probabilities and measures (Billingsley 1995).

Theorem 2.3. The system of Axioms SIP1–SIP8 is consistent.

Indeed, we can take $\Omega = \{w, -w\}$, $\Omega^+ = \{w\}$, $\Omega^- = \{-w\}$, $\mathbf{F} = \{\emptyset, \{w, -w\}, \{w\}, \{-w\}\}$ and assign $P(\emptyset) = 0$, $P(\{w, -w\}) = 0$, $P(\{w\}) = 1$, and $P(\{-w\}) = -1$. Then it is easy to check that P satisfies all Axioms SIP1–SIP7.

Definition 2.2

(a) The triad $(\Omega, \mathbf{F}, P)$ is called a *symmetric inflated probability space*.

(b) If $A \in \mathbf{F}$, then the number $P(A)$ is called the *symmetric inflated probability* or simply *siprobability* of the event A.

Let us obtain some properties of symmetric inflated probability.

Proposition 2.1. $0 \leq P(A) \leq P(\Omega^+)$ for all $A \in \mathbf{F}^+$.

Proof. $\Omega^+ = A \cup B$ for the event $B = \Omega^+ \setminus A$. As $A \in \mathbf{F}^+$ and $\mathbf{F}^+$ is a set algebra, we have $B \in \mathbf{F}^+$. Thus, the probability $P(B)$ is defined and by Axioms SIP7, $P(\Omega^+) = P(A) + P(B)$. Consequently, $P(A) = P(\Omega^+) - P(B)$. As by Axioms SIP6, $P(B) \geq 0$, we have $P(A) \leq P(\Omega^+)$ and by Axioms SIP6, $P(A) \geq 0$.
Proposition is proved.

Corollary 2.5. $0 \leq P(A) \leq m$ for some natural number m and all $A \in \mathbf{F}^+$.

Lemma 2.12. $P(\emptyset) = 0$.
Indeed, by Axiom SIP7, we have $P(A \cup \emptyset) = P(A) + P(\emptyset)$. Thus, $P(\emptyset) = P(A \cup \emptyset) - P(A) = P(A) - P(A) = 0$.
Lemma 2.12 has the following interpretation. In each trial (experiment), something happens. Therefore, the extended probability that nothing happens is equal to zero.
Lemma 2.1 and Axioms SIP4 and SIP8 imply the following result.

Proposition 2.2. $P(X \oplus Y) = P(X \cup Y)$ for any two random events X and Y from $\mathbf{F}$.
Axioms imply symmetry of the probability P.

Proposition 2.3 (Symmetry). $P(-A) = -P(A)$ for any random event A from $\mathbf{F}$.

Proof. By Lemma 2.6, $A \cup -A = \emptyset$. By Axiom SIP8, $P(A \cup -A) = P(\emptyset)$. By Axiom SIP7, $P(A \cup -A) = P(A) + P(-A)$ as $A \cap -A = \emptyset$. By Lemma 2.12, $P(\emptyset) = 0$. Thus, $P(A) + P(-A) = 0$ and $P(-A) = -P(A)$ for any random event A from $\mathbf{F}$.
Proposition is proved.

Note that this mathematical result supports and is supported by intuition of physicists with respect to negative probability. For instance, Dirac (1942) compared negative probability to (the probability of) a negative sum of money, i.e., to a debt. Indeed, debts annihilate (to some extent) those amounts of money that people have. In a similar way, Belinskii (1994) writes, "a negative probability *reduces* the probability for events corresponding to it and *increases* the probability for opposite events."

Corollary 3.5 (*Non-positivity*). $P(A) \leq 0$, for all $A \in \mathbf{F}^-$.

Proposition 2.4. $0 \geq P(C) \geq P(\Omega^-)$ for all $C \in \mathbf{F}^-$.

Proof. By Proposition 2.3, $P(C) = -P(A)$ for some random event $A \in \mathbf{F}^+$ and $P(\Omega^-) = -P(\Omega^+)$. By Proposition 2.1, $0 \leq P(A) \leq P(\Omega^+)$. Thus, $0 \geq P(C) \geq P(\Omega^-)$.

Proposition is proved.
The extended probability of a random event is composed from two components as the following theorem shows.

Proposition 2.5. $P(A) = P(A^+) - P(-A^-) = P(A^+) + P(A^-)$ for any random event $A \in \mathbf{F}$.

Proof. As $A = A^+ \cup A^-$, by Axiom SIP7, $P(A) = P(A^+) + P(-A^-)$ because by Lemma 2.6, $A^+ \cap A^- = \emptyset$ for any subset A of Ω. By Proposition 2.3, $P(A^-) = -P(-A^-)$. Consequently, $P(A) = P(A^+) - P(-A^-)$.

Propositions 2.1, 2.4 and 2.5 imply the following result.

Theorem 2.4. $P(\Omega^-) \le P(A) \le P(\Omega^+)$ for all $A \in \mathbf{F}$.

Indeed, by Propositions 2.5, $P(A) = P(A^+) - P(-A^-)$ and $P(-A^-) \ge 0$. Thus, $P(A) \le P(A^+) \le P(\Omega^+)$.

At the same time, $P(\Omega^-) \le P(A^-) \le P(A)$.

Proposition 2.6. $P(\Omega) = 0$.

Indeed, $P(\Omega) = P(\Omega^-) + P(\Omega^+)$ and $P(\Omega^-) = -P(\Omega^+)$.

Proposition 2.6 has the following interpretation. The set Ω cannot exist (be stable) due to annihilation. So, its extended probability, or more adequately, the extended probability of its existence, is equal to zero.

Proposition 2.7. If $A = \{w_1, w_2, w_3, \ldots, w_k\}$ belongs to $\mathbf{F}$ and all $w_1, w_2, w_3, \ldots, w_k$ belongs to $\mathbf{F}$, then $P(A) = P(w_1) + P(w_2) + P(w_3) + \cdots + P(w_k)$.

Proposition 2.7 directly follows from Axiom SIP7 because A is a set of elementary random events.

Proposition 2.8. Any probability function P is monotone on $\mathbf{F}^+$, i.e., if $A \subseteq B$ and $A, B \in \mathbf{F}^+$, then $P(A) \le P(B)$, and is antimonotone on $\mathbf{F}^-$, i.e., if $H \subseteq K$ and $H, K \in \mathbf{F}^-$, then $P(H) \ge P(K)$.

Proof. Let us consider two random events A and B from $\mathbf{F}^+$, such that $A \subseteq B$. In this case, $B = A \cup C$ for some random event C from $\mathbf{F}^+$ where $A \cap C = \emptyset$. By Axiom SIP7, $P(B) = P(A) + P(C)$ and by Proposition 2.1, both $P(A)$ and $P(C)$ are non-negative numbers. Thus, $P(A) \le P(B)$.

Let us consider two random events H and K from $\mathbf{F}^-$, such that $H \subseteq K$. In this case, $K = H \cup G$ for some random event G from $\mathbf{F}^-$ where $H \cap G = \emptyset$. By Axiom SIP7, $P(K) = P(H) + P(G)$ and by Proposition 2.4, both $P(H)$ and $P(G)$ are not positive numbers. Thus, $P(K) \le P(H)$.

Proposition is proved.

3 Frequency Interpretation of Symmetric Inflated Probability

We have constructed an axiomatic system for a function called symmetric inflated probability. Some properties of this function are the same as properties of the conventional probability, for example, additivity. However, there are important properties of symmetric inflated probability that are essentially different from properties of the conventional probability. For instance, symmetric inflated probability can take negative values and the probability of the maximal event represented by the space Ω is equal to zero. The frequency interpretation for a probability function with these properties is given in (Burgin 2010). This interpretation provides real-life semantics for the axiomatic system constructed in this paper. One more interpretation of probability taking both positive and negative values is considered in (Abramsky and Brandenburger 2014).

However, not all unusual properties of symmetric inflated probability were represented by those interpretations. For instance, it was not explained how probability can be larger than 1 or how it is possible that the probability of the maximal positive event represented by the space Ω^+ can be less than 1. Therefore, here we give explanation of these properties using the most popular in physics frequency interpretation. Note that probabilities of positive events encompass the conventional probability.

To understand probability larger than 1, we have to assume that in contrast to the conventional schema of probability described, for example, in (Kolmogorov 1933), outcomes of experiments are not necessary events and one outcome is exactly one event from the set 2^Ω, but an outcome is a multiset (Knuth 1997) of events in a general case. It means, for example, that one outcome can contain two different events and three events identical to the first of those two events. Thus, the totality of events in this outcome is equal to four. To understand how it can be in real life, let us consider the following examples.

Example 3.1. In a trial, three coins are tossed. The conventional question is: What is the probability of getting, at least, one head in one toss? To calculate this probability, we assume that all coins are without defects and all tosses are fair and independent. Thus, the probability of having the head on one tossed coin is $p_1(h) = 0.5$. The same is true for tails. Consequently, the probability of having no heads or what is the same, three tails in one toss is $p(3t) = 0.5 \times 0.5 \times 0.5 = 0.125$.

At the same time, we may ask the question: What is the probability of getting heads in one toss? To answer this question, let us suppose that probability reflects not only the limit average number of getting heads but also the limit average number of obtained heads in one toss. In this case, the probability of having heads in tossing three coins is $p_3(h) = 0.5 + 0.5 + 0.5 = 1.5$.

Note that with the growth of the number of the tossed coins, the probability of having heads also grows being larger than 1 when there are more than two coins.

Example 3.2. In an experiment, 10 dice are rolled. Let us ask the question: What is the probability of showing three spots in one experiment? To calculate this probability, we assume that all dice are without defects and all trials are fair and independent. In this case, the probability of having three spots in one rolling is $p_1 = 1/6$ for one die and $p_{10} = 10/6$ for ten dice.

Now let us describe the formal definition of the frequency interpretation.

Taking a event $A = \{w_{i1}, w_{i2}, w_{i3}, \ldots, w_{ir}\}$ and a sequence of N trials, each of which gives some outcome, we denote by n the sum of multiplicities of positive events from A that occur during this sequence of trials and by m the sum of multiplicities of negative events from A that occur during this sequence of trials.

Then we have the frequency

$$r_N(A) = n/N - m/N$$

In contrast to the conventional approach, it is possible that $r_N(A) > 1$ or $r_N(A) < -1$.

Let us consider the set $\mathbf{P}_A$ of all events A such that limits $\lim_{N \to \infty} n/N$ and $\lim_{N \to \infty} m/N$ exist. We call these events *quasi-random*. Random events satisfy additional conditions considered by different authors. Then we define the *symmetric inflated frequency probability* of the event A equal to

$$p(A) = \lim_{N \to \infty} r_N(A)$$

In other words, when the number N of trials goes to infinity ($N \to \infty$) the number $r_N(A)$ approaches the symmetric inflated frequency probability of the event A. The regularity of $r_N(A)$ converging to a number characterizes the meaning of the probability of the event A.

Now let us treat the situations when the probability of the maximal positive event represented by the space Ω^+ is less than 1.

In the classical probability theory, it is assumed that the space Ω of elementary events provides a representation of all possible outcomes of the considered system of trials (Kolmogorov 1933). As a result, the event represented by Ω always happens in each trial. In contrast to this, there are many situations when the set of all possible outcomes is unknown. For instance, a biologist goes to jungles. Is it possible to know in advance what species she will find in the jungles? One more example is the situation when somebody uses the Internet. Is it possible to know in advance what viruses she will encounter there?

This example shows that there are situations when the outcome of a trial does not always consist of elementary events from Ω. In such a situation, taking the frequency m/n where m is the number of trials when the event (represented by) Ω happened in n trials, we see that it is possible that $m/n < 1$ and the sequence of these frequencies m/n will converge to a number p less than 1 when m tends to infinity. In the frequency interpretation, p is the probability of the event represented by Ω and it is less than 1.

4 Conclusion

The developed theory of symmetric inflated probabilities shows that in the context of quantum interaction, negative probabilities reflect existence of antiparticles, as well as the possibility to encounter antiparticles in experiments represent interaction of particles and antiparticles when an antiparticle annihilates interacting with a corresponding particle. This approach allows consistent frequency interpretation of negative and inflated, that is, larger than 1, probabilities.

In addition, the developed theory employs the principle of symmetry, which is basic in physics in general and in quantum physics, in particular.

This shows that symmetric inflated probability essentially employs ideas and structures from theoretical physics in general and in quantum physics, in particular.

It is also possible to suggest open problems for further research.

In (Burgin 2010), the frequency interpretation, which is the most important and popular in physics, is developed for symmetric probabilities in general and negative probabilities, in particular.

Problem 1. Build other types of interpretations, e.g., the propensity interpretation for symmetric probabilities and negative probabilities.

In this paper, the frequency interpretation, which is the most important and popular in physics, is developed for symmetric inflated probabilities in general and probabilities larger than 1, in particular.

Problem 2. Build other types of interpretations, e.g., the propensity interpretation for symmetric probabilities and probabilities larger than 1.

There are two basic types of axiomatics for probabilities – quantitative and qualitative. In this paper, a quantitative axiomatics is developed for symmetric inflated probabilities in general and negative probabilities, in particular.

Problem 3. Construct qualitative axiomatics for symmetric probabilities and negative probabilities.

To conclude, it is necessary to remark that negative probabilities, introduced in quantum physics, have become useful tools in social and behavioral sciences, machine learning, quantum computation, psychology, economics and finance, in particular, the mathematical theory of symmetric inflated probabilities presented in this paper also has other interpretations, which allow their applications to problems in economics and finance (Burgin and Meissner 2012; 2012a).

References

Abramsky, S., Brandenburger, A.: An operational interpretation of negative probabilities and no-signalling models. In: Breugel, F., Kashefi, E., Palamidessi, C., Rutten, J. (eds.) Horizons of the Mind. A Tribute to Prakash Panangaden. LNCS, vol. 8464, pp. 59–75. Springer, Heidelberg (2014). doi:10.1007/978-3-319-06880-0_3

Allen, E.H.: Negative probabilities and the uses of signed probability theory. Philos. Sci. **43**(1), 53–70 (1976)

Baker, G.A.: Formulation of quantum mechanics based on the quasi-probability distribution induced on phase space. Phys. Rev. **109**, 2198 (1958)

de Barros, J.A.: Decision making for inconsistent expert judgments using negative probabilities. In: Atmanspacher, H., Haven, E., Kitto, K., Raine, D. (eds.) QI 2013. LNCS, vol. 8369, pp. 257–269. Springer, Heidelberg (2014). doi:10.1007/978-3-642-54943-4_23

de Barros, J.A., Oas, G.: Negative probabilities and counter-factual reasoning in quantum cognition. Phys. Scr. **T163**, 014008 (2014)

de Barros, J.A., Oas, G.: Quantum cognition, neural oscillators, and negative probabilities. In: Haven, E., Khrennikov, A. (eds.) The Palgrave Handbook of Quantum Models in Social Science: Applications and Grand Challenges. Palgrave MacMillan, Basingstoke (2015)

Bartlett, M.S.: Negative Probability. Math. Proc. Camb. Philos. Soc. **41**, 71–73 (1945)

Bednorz, A., Belzig, W.: On the problem of negative probabilities in time-resolved full counting statistics, 25th international conference on low temperature physics (LT25). J. Phys. Conf. Ser. **150**, 022005 (2009)

Belinskii, A.V.: How could you measure a negative probability? JETP Lett. **59**, 301–311 (1994)

Billingsley, P.: Probability and Measure. Wiley-Interscience, Hoboken (1995)

Blass, A., Gurevich, Y.: Negative probability. Preprint in Physics, quant-ph/1502.00666 (2009). http://arXiv.org

Burgin, M.: Extended probabilities: mathematical foundations. Preprint in Physics, math-ph/0912.4767 (2009). http://arXiv.org

Burgin, M.: Interpretations of negative probabilities. Preprint in Quantum Physics, quant-ph/1008.1287, 17 p. (2010). http://arXiv.org

Burgin, M.: Negative probability in the framework of combined probability. Preprint in Probability (math.PR), 1306.1166 (2013). http://arXiv.org

Burgin, M., Krinik, A.C.: Probabilities and hyperprobabilities. In: 8th Annual International Conference on Statistics, Mathematics and Related Fields, Conference Proceedings, Honolulu, Hawaii, pp. 351–367 (2009)

Burgin, M., Meissner, G.: Negative probabilities in modeling random financial processes. Integr. Math. Theor. Appl. **2**(3), 305–322 (2010)

Burgin, M., Meissner, G.: Negative probabilities in financial modeling. Wilmott Magazine, pp. 60–65 (2012)

Burgin, M., Meissner, G.: Larger than one probabilities in mathematical and practical finance. Rev. Econ. Financ. **2**(4), 1–13 (2012)

Curtright, T., Zachos, C.: Negative probability and uncertainty relations. Mod. Phys. Lett. **A16**, 2381–2385 (2001)

Dirac, P.A.M.: Note on exchange phenomena in the Thomas atom. Proc. Camb. Philos. Soc. **26**, 376–395 (1930a)

Dirac, P.A.M.: A theory of electrons and protons. Proc. R. Soc. Lond. Ser. A **126**, 360–365 (1930b)

Dirac, P.A.M.: The physical interpretation of quantum mechanics. Proc. R. Soc. Lond. Ser. A **180**, 1–39 (1942)

Dirac, P.A.M.: Quantum electrodynamics. Commun. Dublin Inst. Adv. Stud. **1**, 1 (1943)

Dirac, P.A.M.: Spinors in Hilbert Space. Plenum, New York (1974)

Duffie, D., Singleton, K.: Modeling term structures of defaultable bonds. Rev. Financ. Stud. **12**, 687–720 (1999)

Ferrie, C., Emerson, J.: Frame representations of quantum mechanics and the necessity of negativity in quasi-probability representations. J. Phys. A: Math. Theor. **41**, 352001 (2008)

Feynman, R.P.: The concept of probability theory in quantum mechanics. In: The Second Berkeley Symposium on Mathematical Statistics and Probability Theory. University of California Press, Berkeley, California (1950)

Feynman, R.P.: Negative probability. In: Quantum Implications: Essays in Honour of David Bohm, pp. 235–248. Routledge & Kegan Paul Ltd., London & New York (1987)

Feynman, R.P.: The reason for antiparticles. In: Elementary Particles and the Laws of Physics, The 1986 Dirac memorial lectures, pp. 56–59. Cambridge University Press, Cambridge (1987a)

Forsyth, P.A., Vetzal, K.R. Zvan, R.: Negative Coefficients in Two Factor Option Pricing Models. Working Paper (2001). http://citeseer.ist.psu.edu/435337.html

Galvao, E.F.: Discrete Wigner functions and quantum computational speedup. Phys. Rev. A **71**, 04230 (2005)

Gell-Mann, M., Hartle, J.B.: Decoherent Histories Quantum Mechanics with One 'Real' Fine-Grained History. Preprint in Quantum Physics, quant-ph/1106.0767 (2011). http://arXiv.org

Gupta, S.N.: Quantum mechanics with an indefinite metric. Can. J. Phys. **35**, 961–968 (1957)

Halliwell, J., Yearsley, J.: Negative probabilities, Fine's theorem, and linear positivity. Phys. Rev. A **87**(2), 022114 (2013)

Han, Y.D., Hwang, W.Y., Koh, I.G.: Explicit solutions for negative-probability measures for all entangled states. Phys. Lett. A **221**(5), 283–286 (1996)

Haug, E.G.: Why so negative to negative probabilities. Wilmott Magazine, pp 34–38 (2004)

Heisenberg, W.: Über die inkohärente Streuung von Röntgenstrahlen. Physik. Zeitschr. **32**, 737–740 (1931)

Hillery, M., O'Connell, R.F., Scully, M.O., Wigner, E.P.: Distribution functions in physics: fundamentals. Phys. Rep. **106**(3), 121–167 (1984)

Hofmann, H.F.: How to simulate a universal quantum computer using negative probabilities. J. Phys. A Math. Theor. **42**, 275304 (2009). (9 pp)

Holland, R.E., Lynch, F.J., Perlow, G.J., Hanna, S.S.: Time spectra of filtered resonance radiation of Fe. Phys. Rev. Lett. **4**, 181–182 (1960)

Howard, J., Schnitzer, J., Sudarshan, E.C.: Quantum mechanical systems with indefinite metric II. Phys. Rev. **123**, 2193–2201 (1961)

Khrennikov, A.: Interpretations of Probability. Walter de Gruyter, Berlin/New York (2009)

Kline, M.: Mathematics: The Loss of Certainty. Oxford University Press, New York (1980)

Knuth, D.: The Art of Computer Programming. Seminumerical Algorithms, vol. 2. Addison-Wesley, Reading, Mass, Boston (1997)

Kolmogorov, A.N.: Grundbegriffe der Wahrscheinlichkeitrechnung. Ergebnisse Der Mathematik (English translation: Foundations of the Theory of Probability, Chelsea P.C. 1950) (1933)

Kolmogorov, A.N., Fomin, S.V.: Elements of the Theory of Functions and Functional Analysis. Dover Publications, New York (1999)

Koenig, A.: Patterns and antipatterns. J. Object Oriented Program. **8**(1), 46–48 (1995)

Kronz, F.: Actual and virtual events in the quantum domain. Ontol. Stud. **9**, 209–220 (2009)

Laplante, P. A., Neill, C. J.: Antipatterns: Identification, Refactoring and Management. Auerbach Publications, Boca Raton, FL (2005)

Le Couteur, K.J.: The indefinite metric in relativistic quantum mechanics. Proc. R. Soc. Lond. Ser. A Math. Phys. Sci. **196**(1045), 251–272 (1949)

Lynch, F.J., Holland, R.E., Hamermesh, M.: Time dependence of resonantly filtered gamma rays from Fe57. Phys. Rev. **120**, 513–520 (1960)

Mack, T.: Schadenversicherungsmathematik, 2nd edn. Verlag Versicherungswirtschaft (2002)

Martinez, A.A.: Negative Math: How Mathematical Rules Can Be Positively Bent. Princeton University Press, New Jersey (2006)

Mattessich, R.: From accounting to negative numbers: a signal contribution of medieval India to mathematics. Acc. Historians J. **25**(2), 129–145 (1998)

Mückenheim, W.: A review of extended probabilities. Phys. Rep. **133**(6), 337–401 (1986)

Mückenheim, W.: An extended-probability response to the Einstein-Podolsky-Rosen argument. Quantum Mechanics versus Local Realism: The Einstein-Podolsky-Rosen Paradox, pp. 345–364. Plenum Press, New York (1988)

Nyambuya, G.: Deciphering and Fathoming Negative Probabilities in Quantum Mechanics (2011). (viXra.org > Quantum Physics > viXra:1102.0031)

Oas, G., de Barros, J.A., Carvalhaes, C.: Exploring non-signalling polytopes with negative probability. Phys. Scr. **T163**, 014034 (2014)

Pauli, W.: On Dirac's new method of field quantization. Rev. Mod. Phys. **15**(3), 175–207 (1943)

Scully, M.O., Walther, H., Schleich, W.: Feynman's approach to negative probability in quantum mechanics. Phys. Rev. A **49**, 1562 (1994)

Sjöstrand, T.: Monte Carlo generators. In: Fleischer, R (ed.) 2006 European School of High-Energy Physics, CERN-2007-005, pp. 51–73 (2007)

Sokolovski, D.: Weak values, "negative probability", and the uncertainty principle. Phys. Rev. A **76**, 042125 (2007)

Sokolovski, D., Connor, J.N.L.: Negative probability and the distributions of dwell, transmission, and reflection times for quantum tunneling. Phys. Rev. A **44**, 1500–1504 (1991)

Sudarshan, E.C.G.: Quantum mechanical systems with indefinite metric I. Phys. Rev. **123**(6), 2183–2193 (1961)

Székely, G.J.: Half of a coin: negative probabilities. Wilmott Magazine, 66–68, July 2005

Venter, G.: Generalized linear models beyond the exponential family with loss reserve applications. Astin Bull. **37**(2), 345–364 (2007)

Weisskopf, V., Wigner, E.: Berechnung der nat urlichen Linienbreite auf Grund der Diracschen Lichttheorie. Z. Phys. **63**, 54–73 (1930)

Weyl, H.: Quantenmechanik und Gruppentheorie. Z. Phys. **46**, 1–46 (1927)

Wigner, E.P.: On the quantum correction for thermodynamic equilibrium. Phys. Rev. **40**, 749–759 (1932)

Wu, C.S., Lee, Y.K., Benczer-Koller, N., Simms, P.: Frequency distribution of resonance line versus delay time. Phys. Rev. Lett. **5**(9), 432–435 (1960)

Youssef, S.: Physics with exotic probability theory, Preprint hep-th/0110253 (2001). http://arXiv.org

Quantum-Like Measurements

A First Attempt at Ordinal Projective Measurement

Jacob Denolf[(✉)]

Department of Data Analysis, Ghent University,
H. Dunantlaan 1, 9000 Ghent, Belgium
`jacob.denolf@ugent.be`

Abstract. To our knowledge, all applications of the quantum framework in social sciences are used to model measurements done on a discrete nominal scale. However, especially in cognition, experiments often produce data on an ordinal scale, which implies some internal structure between the possible outcomes. Since there are no ordinal scales in physics, orthodox projection-valued measurement (PVM) lacks the tools and methods to deal with these ordinal scales. Here, we sketch out an attempt to incorporate the ordinal structure of outcomes into the subspaces representing these outcomes. This will also allow us to reduce the dimensionality of the resulting Hilbert spaces, as these often become too high in more complex quantum-like models. To do so, we loosen restrictions placed upon the PVM (and even POVM) framework. We discuss the two major consequences of this generalization: scaling and the loss of repeatability. We also present two applications of this approach, one in game theory and one concerning Likert scales.

Keywords: Quantum-like measurement · Ordinal scales · Likert scales

1 Introduction

With the emerging success of applying the quantum probabilistic toolbox in social sciences, there is also an increasing focus on its limitations. In physics, the construction of the needed model is relatively straightforward. However, in quantum cognition, the quite rigid recipe sometimes shows its limits both mathematically and interpretationally [9]. So, it shouldn't come as a surprise that more recent work tries to expand the reach of these tools by looking at possibilities beyond the standard projective measurement (PVM) principles. The best known generalization beyond PVM is the use of Positive Operator Valued Measurement (POVMs) [2], but alternative, sometimes even more general, approaches also arise (e.g. [1,11]). These ventures are mostly theoretical in nature, with applications

The author would like to thank Kirsty Kitto, James Yearsley, Ariane Lambert-Mogiliansky and especially Ismael Martínez-Martínez for the engaging discussions and comments.

© Springer International Publishing AG 2017
J.A. de Barros et al. (Eds.): QI 2016, LNCS 10106, pp. 227–238, 2017.
DOI: 10.1007/978-3-319-52289-0_18

using experimental data being rather sparse. None of these approaches, however, deals with the problem of representing outcomes with an internal structure.

In this paper we present an idea which also goes beyond orthodox quantum-like techniques. This new technique was originally formulated for a specific setting in [10] and further developed and tested in [7]. In these two papers, a model is constructed which deals with the relationship of a participant's beliefs and preferences in a game theoretic setting, taken from [3]. During this process, problems concerning a too high dimension of a Hilbert space arose, which where solved by drawing inspiration from a rotational solution presented in [15] and (ab)using the ordered structure of the possible outcomes. To do so, we opted to loosen certain restrictions which lead to alternative types of projectors. While the solution to these problems served an ad hoc purpose, the question whether this new technique could be applied in different settings presented itself.

Here we argue that this generalization of P(O)VM can be used to model any situation where different outcomes of a measurement have an internal ordinal structure. After defining this generalization, we discuss two consequences of using this new structure and present two possible applications of this approach: the game theoretic one mentioned before and Likert scales in general.

2   Revisiting the Clinton/Gore Example

We take a new look at the quantum-like model concerning public opinion on Bill Clinton and Al Gore. This is one of the go-to introductory examples in quantum cognition, see for example [4]. In a Gallup poll, conducted September 6-7, 1997, participants were asked 2 separate questions: if they think Clinton is trustworthy and if they think Gore is trustworthy. When the Clinton question is posed first, 53% of the participants consider him to be trustworthy and 73% consider Gore to be trustworthy. However, when the question order is reversed, 67% think Gore is trustworthy and 59% think Clinton is trustworthy. This change in attitude indicates an order effect, which suggests a quantum-like approach by considering the Clinton and Gore questions to be incompatible. In the resulting quantum-like model each question is represented by an orthogonal 2 dimensional basis, with each vector representing the relevant 'yes' or 'no' answer and by defining a 2-dimensional Hilbert space containing both bases. The resulting model has a good statistical fit, with only two parameters (one coordinate of the state vector, as the second coordinate is fixed due to the normalization restriction, and one angle between the two bases) to be estimated.

We now identify two properties of this experimental paradigm, which become problematic when we leave this relative simple example for more complex ones. First, the number of possible outcomes is low. Both questions only allow 2 possible replies, while trustworthiness of presidential candidates could be considered far more complex. This gives the resulting Hilbert space a manageable two dimensions. Note that as all measurements are considered incompatible, no tensoring is required, which would increase dimensionality exponentially. Second, there is no structure in the outcomes. The yes and no outcomes are on a discrete nominal scale, with no implicit relationship between them.

Let's make the situation a bit more complex. First, suppose we want to add some more nuance to the questions and allow for more replies: very trustworthy/quite trustworthy/somewhat trustworthy/neutral/somewhat untrustworthy/quite untrustworthy/very untrustworthy. These outcomes clearly have an internal structure, as they are ordered. This extension makes the resulting Hilbert space 7-dimensional. Second, suppose that, for whatever research reasons, a third similar measurement is performed, which also allows for a similar set of 7 outcomes, that does not produce order effects. Even though the situation is not extreme from an experimental point of view, the Hilbert space needed to model this situation would be 49-dimensional. This would increase the amount of parameters needed to fit the state vectors and subspaces dramatically, resulting in an inoperable model. Next to this unwieldy dimensionality, this approach lacks the tools to incorporate the ordinal structure of the outcomes. Since, to our knowledge, no ordinal scales[1] are present in quantum mechanics, where would these tools come from? However, in contrast, ordinal scales are widespread in psychology, with their own distinct theory, framework and statistics.

In what follows, we propose a first attempt at modeling ordinal outcomes, within the quantum-like approach. This attempt also reduces the problematic dimensionality that arises when measurements with more than two outcomes are performed and tensoring is needed, when constructing the relevant bases.

3 Defining the New Ordinal Projectors

Paraphrasing Kirsty Kitto in her QI15 talk, see [2], a quantum(-like) measurement M, with its set of possible outcomes $\{M_i\}$, is represented by a set of subspaces $\{\mathcal{M}_i\}$, where $\mathcal{M}_i$ represents outcome M_i. These subspaces $\mathcal{M}_i$ each define a projector P_i, which projects any vector $|S\rangle$ on the relevant subspace $\mathcal{M}_i$. The state of a system (e.g. a participant in a psychological experiment) is represented by a normalized state vector $|\psi\rangle$. Now, the mathematical rules are quite straightforward:

(i) The probability of obtaining outcome M_i is $\langle\psi|P_i|\psi\rangle$ or, intuitively, the closer the state vector is to the relevant subspace, the higher the probability of obtaining that outcome.

(ii) After obtaining outcome M_i, the state after measurement becomes $\frac{P_i|\psi\rangle}{\sqrt{\langle\psi|P_i|\psi\rangle}}$ or, intuitively, when obtaining an outcome, the state vector becomes a normalized vector in the relevant subspace.

PVM Structure. As is widely known, the orthodox quantum measurement paradigm (Projection-valued measurement or PVM) demands that all subspaces associated with one measurement are orthogonal and, perhaps trivially, that these subspaces span the entire Hilbert space. This ensures that probabilities sum to one and that when a measurement is performed twice, without any

---

[1] Ordinal scales are discrete scales with a well defined order on the outcomes.

manipulation in between both measurements, the same outcome is obtained twice. We call this last property *repeatability*.

POVM Structure. Perhaps less widely known, when we weaken the demand that all subspaces associated with one measurement are orthogonal but still ensure that all probabilities sum to one by demanding that all relevant projector matrices sum to the identity matrix:

$$\sum_i P_i = I, \tag{1}$$

we obtain a more general class of measurements which we call Positive Operator-Valued Measurement (POVMs). Note that POVMs do not adhere to repeatability. This first generalization gives us freedom to incorporate structure in the outcomes, while reducing the dimensionality. However, this solution is still more restrictive then one might think at first, as restriction 1 is still quite strong. More concrete, when a set of outcome vectors is defined, typically an extra outcome vector has to be introduced to ensure all projectors sum to the identity matrix. Take, as an example, a simple two dimensional case. When two non-orthogonal vectors $|M_1\rangle = (1, 0)$ and $|M_2\rangle = (\cos \theta, \sin \theta)$, with projectors

$$P_1 = \begin{pmatrix} 1 & 0 \\ 0 & 0 \end{pmatrix} \text{ and } P_2 = \begin{pmatrix} \cos^2 \theta & \cos \theta \sin \theta \\ \cos \theta \sin \theta & \sin^2 \theta \end{pmatrix}, \tag{2}$$

are needed to model an experimental situation, their projectors sum to:

$$P_1 + P_2 = \begin{pmatrix} 1 + \cos^2 \theta & \cos \theta \sin \theta \\ \cos \theta \sin \theta & \sin^2 \theta \end{pmatrix}. \tag{3}$$

Having the diagonal elements equal to one can easily be achieved by appropriate scaling. However, to have the off-diagonal elements equal to zero, a third outcome vector $|M_3\rangle = (\pm \cos \theta, \mp \sin \theta)$ or $|M_3\rangle = (\pm \sin \theta, \mp \cos \theta)$ must be introduced, even when there is no third possible experimental outcome!

Ordinal Scales. To solve this, we propose to omit the demand that all projectors sum to the identity matrix, effectively losing almost all structure, but use this freedom to add new structure which reflects our ordinal scale, while still adhering to our basic quantum-like rules (i) and (ii). The necessity of generalizing measurement beyond POVMs is not a new idea, as remarked in [9] and discussed in Chap. 8 of [14].

As we only have two mathematical entities at hand (a state vector $|\psi\rangle$ and a set of subspaces $\{\mathcal{M}_i\}$ representing outcomes), this structure has to be incorporated in these two. On the one hand, as the state vector is supposed to represent the particular state of the system, the type of scale of the measurement should not impact this state vector. On the other hand, as the set of subspaces is representing the outcomes, any structure between these outcomes, should be reflected in a structure between the subspaces. This is why we allow subspaces associated with outcomes of the same measurement to be non-orthogonal to each other. Now we can define the notion of a subspace $\mathcal{M}_i$ being *closer* to a subspace $\mathcal{M}_j$ then to a subspace $\mathcal{M}_k$, when $\widehat{\mathcal{M}_i\mathcal{M}_j}$, the angle[2] between $\mathcal{M}_i$ and $\mathcal{M}_j$, is smaller then $\widehat{\mathcal{M}_i\mathcal{M}_k}$ the angle between $\mathcal{M}_i$ and $\mathcal{M}_k$. This gives us a natural way of representing an ordinal scale with outcomes $\boldsymbol{M}_i$ (admitting to a well defined order $\prec$) by demanding that:

Definition 1. *if* $\boldsymbol{M}_i \prec \boldsymbol{M}_j \prec \boldsymbol{M}_k$, *then* $\widehat{\mathcal{M}_i\mathcal{M}_j} \leq \widehat{\mathcal{M}_i\mathcal{M}_k}$ *&* $\widehat{\mathcal{M}_j\mathcal{M}_k} \leq \widehat{\mathcal{M}_i\mathcal{M}_k}$.

Note that the maximum angle between two subspaces is $\pi/2$, so orthogonal subspaces are considered to be the farthest away possible from each other.

The exact value of these angles is an empirical question, which we discuss later. When all relevant subspaces are orthogonal, each subspace adds its own dimension to the total dimension of the encompassing Hilbert space, which is the reason of the exploding dimensionality in the introductory example. As the need for orthogonality is now omitted, the resulting dimensionality can be greatly reduced as compared to the traditional PVM approach. This makes the dimension of the final Hilbert space also an empirical question and/or a deliberate choice, taking into account, e.g., the number of data points or certain demands for elegance or simplicity of the resulting model. The concepts for calculating probabilities (i) and post-measurements states (ii) remain identical to the ones used with PVMs and POVMs. Note that as all considered P_i are projectors, they are still Hermitian positive semi-definite, so $\langle\psi|P_i|\psi\rangle$ is positive and real. Because the state vector still gets projected on the subspace representing the obtained outcome, this approach keeps the quantum-like nature. As a result, all concepts (order effects, contextuality, entanglement...) used in quantum cognition are still a part of this approach because the regular PVM structure is now a specific case of our more general framework.

4   Consequences

Our loosening of restrictions used when defining P(O)VMs has significant consequences. Here, we discuss the major two.

4.1   Sum of Probabilities

As we do not require restriction (1) to hold, it is possible that the sum of the possibilities across all possible outcomes exceeds 1. While this seems problematic at first, two solutions naturally present themselves. First, a scaling factor can be

---

[2] The angle $\widehat{\mathcal{M}_i\mathcal{M}_j}$ between two subspaces $\mathcal{M}_i$ and $\mathcal{M}_j$ is classically defined as $\min(\widehat{V_iV_j})$, with $V_i \in \mathcal{M}_i$ and $V_j \in \mathcal{M}_j$.

introduced. This is the solution used in [7]. Keeping the notations defined as in the previous section, for all $|\psi\rangle$ define C_M as:

$$C_M = \sum_j \langle\psi|P_j|\psi\rangle. \tag{4}$$

This allows us to scale appropriately. Now, we redefine the probability of obtaining outcome M_i as

$$P'(M_i) = \frac{P(M_i)}{C_M} \tag{5}$$

$$= \frac{\langle\psi|P_i|\psi\rangle}{\sum_j \langle\psi|P_j|\psi\rangle}. \tag{6}$$

This gives us

$$\sum_i P'(M_i) = \frac{\sum_i \langle\psi|P_i|\psi\rangle}{\sum_j \langle\psi|P_j|\psi\rangle} \tag{7}$$

$$= 1. \tag{8}$$

While this approach lacks mathematical elegance, it effectively makes the probabilities sum to one.

A second, more elegant, solution is inspired by classical logistic regression. In logistic regression, a function $f(x_1 \ldots x_n)$ is derived, where, given a number of predictors $x_1 \ldots x_n$, the outcome of a binary variable (A or $\neg A$) is estimated. The natural way of predicting a binary outcome would be to estimate the probability of obtaining A. However, as there is no way to ensure that the image of the derived function $f(x_1 \ldots x_n)$ is a subset of $[0, 1]$ (the same problem as with our non-orthogonal subspaces) the odds $\frac{P(A)}{P(\neg A)}$ are modeled, instead of the probability $P(A)$. Since odds only have the restriction that they are positive, this approach can also be successfully introduced here:

$$\text{ODDS}(M_i) = \frac{P(M_i)}{P(\neg M_i)} \tag{9}$$

$$= \frac{\langle\psi|P_i|\psi\rangle}{\langle\psi|I - P_i|\psi\rangle}. \tag{10}$$

Using odds does not introduce any new factors, making it more elegant mathematically. One can easily calculate standard probabilities from these odds since the scaling factor needed beforehand would disappear throughout the calculations. However, odds might be more difficult to interpret. To our knowledge, there are no quantum-like models where these odds are used. It can be easily shown by calculating the odds with the newly defined $P'(M_i)$ that both solutions are identical from a modeling point of view.

4.2   Loss of Repeatability

As a consequence of allowing non-orthogonal subspaces to represent outcomes of the same measurement, we lose repeatability: when a measurement is performed twice, without any manipulation between both measurements, two different outcomes can be obtained. While repeatability seems a necessity at first, multiple instances where it is not required (or is even considered too strict) can be found in, among other fields, cognition. The best known approach lacking repeatability is the use of POVMs, which we defined in Sect. 3. For an in-depth discussion of the use of POVMs in cognition and the relationship to repeatability, we refer to [2,9]. More on the application of POVMs in physics can be found in [13]. Summarizing, models not adhering to repeatability are not only feasible, but also sometimes required within quantum cognition.

What could this loss of repeatability mean within our Clinton/Gore example and ordinal scales in general? When we go back to our 7 outcome ordinal scale 'very trustworthy/quite trustworthy/somewhat trustworthy/neutral/somewhat untrustworthy/quite untrustworthy/very untrustworthy', we claim that some of these outcomes should not exclude each other. To justify this, we introduce the notion of *unsharp measurement*. This idea is already successfully implemented in [7]. We claim that when participants are forced to pick one of these outcomes, their reply does not mean a complete dismissal of another option as these opinions are not completely distinguishable (see also the discussion of 'distinguishing quantum states in 2.2.4 of [14]). When, e.g., a participant replies that he thinks Gore is somewhat trustworthy, the participant does not necessarily disagree with the notion that Gore is quite trustworthy. The more probable it is that two options do not preclude each other, the closer their respective vector spaces should be. While the example might be too simple and underestimating the cognitive abilities of the participants, there is always a tipping point where outcomes do become psychologically indistinguishable. To construct an extreme example, suppose that the trustworthiness question allows for an ordinal scale ranging from 1 (untrustworthy) to 1000 (trustworthy). There is no participant that could successfully fathom the difference between, e.g., replying 503 and replying 504. The internal structure we incorporated, ensures that if repeatability is violated in such cases, the possible outcomes of the repeated questions are neatly scattered around the original answer, as the closer two subspaces are, the more likely it is that the outcomes they represent are obtained after each other. The upper limit case of this is the original outcome, which has the highest probability of being obtained again. The lower limit case of this are outcome vectors orthogonal to the vector representing the original outcome. They can not be obtained in the repeated measurement. As such, the class of measurements where repeatability does occur, is a subclass of the one we propose, by having all relevant outcome vectors orthogonal.

Note that this idea of unsharp measurement can be empirically tested. To do so, simply confront the participant with a different option than the given reply and ask if the participant could agree with it. These ideas allow the model to be constructed in an empirical way: test or argue which outcomes are mutually exclusive and represent these by orthogonal subspaces (this also determines the dimension of the resulting Hilbert space). Observe which outcomes are not excluded and define their subspaces accordingly. We illustrate this type of reasoning in the second example of the next section. Moreover, this approach allows for statistical testing of certain cognitive hypotheses concerning cognitive abilities and/or ordinal scaling by checking if allowing these 'close' subspaces results in (more) satisfying statistical fits of experimental data.

5   Applications

5.1   QP and B Model

A first example where these new types of projectors on non-orthogonal subspaces have already been constructed and successfully applied was presented in [10] and later expanded upon in [7] (including a successful statistical test against experimental data). The incentive of constructing them in this paradigm, lay in the emergence of a problematic dimensionality when following the traditional quantum-like course. A thorough overview of the game theoretic experiment and the resulting model falls outside the scope of this paper. The relevant part in this discussion concerns the part of the experiment where participants are asked to estimate how much of their 9 possible opponents in a game choose to cooperate (as opposed to defect) in a certain step of the experiment. As this measurement allows 10 different outcomes (0 ... 9 opponents believed to be cooperating), it naturally leads to a 10 dimensional Hilbert space. Due to the relationship between other measurements performed in this experiment, two of these Hilbert spaces need to be tensored, resulting in a (problematic) 100-dimensional Hilbert space. Internal structure is clearly present in the replies, as, e.g., replying '6' is closer to replying '7' then it is to replying '8'. Combined with an argument that the '0' and '9' replies should exclude each other, which forces the subspaces representing '0' and '9' to be orthogonal, the resulting subspaces are defined in a 2-dimensional Hilbert space, with reply 'i' being represented by vector $|B_i\rangle$, as can be seen in Fig. 1. Defining the participant's beliefs as projections of the state vector in the same plane doesn't differ much from rotating the state vector by using a Hamiltonian, as is done in a similar prisoner dilemma setting in [5]. However, we opted to still derive probabilities from our projectors, as opposed to just using the rotation for representing a time evolution, as in [5]. This approach reduced the problematic dimensionality, with the final dimension equal to 4, while still retaining the advantages quantum-like models provide (such as modeling order effects) and yielded a very good statistical fit.

It is worth mentioning briefly that the above situation can also be modeled using a POVM structure, with an extra outcome, as mentioned when discussing POVMs in Sect. 3. This approach is taken from [17], where it is described in detail. To do so we keep the definition of the 10 outcome vectors $|B_i\rangle$ as beforehand and define an ad hoc new outcome vector $|B_f\rangle$, representing that 'the measurement has failed', similar to the vector $|M_3\rangle$ in Sect. 3. This $|B_f\rangle$ ensures that all projector matrices sum to the identity matrix. The probabilities in this case

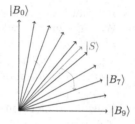

Fig. 1. The outcome 'i' is represented by $|B_i\rangle$. The participant is represented by state vector $|S\rangle$. Here, the participant replies that he thinks 7 opponents have cooperated, projecting/rotating the state vector onto $|B_7\rangle$.

are redefined as the probabilities of obtaining a certain outcome *on the condition that the measurement didn't fail.* When 'the measurement failed' outcome would be (theoretically) obtained, the measurement is supposed to redone immediately. The resulting probabilities are identical to the probabilities obtained by using our new non-POVM ordinal structure. Note that in this experimental setting the measurement never fails, therefor the POVM structure does not represent the experiment in a clean way. This poses a question to the modeler: to stay within the bounds of POVM structures, at the cost of not naturally representing the experiment or to stray beyond POVM structure, but achieving a straightforward representation of the experiment.

5.2   Likert Scales

A second natural candidate for this treatment is the modeling of Likert scales (for an overview on Likert scales, see [16]). Likert scales are used in polling of opinions and consist of multiple Likert items. A Likert item consists of a statement, which the participant evaluates on a given scale. This scale should be *symmetric* (a neutral option and equal number of positive and negative options) and *balanced* (the perceived distance between following options is equal). The format of a typical five level Likert item looks like

strongly disagree (1) - disagree (2) - neutral (3) - agree (4) - strongly agree (5),

which is clearly on an ordinal scale. These Likert scales are widely used in Psychology in general and in opinion polling surveys in particular. The use of quantum-like techniques when dealing with these kind of surveys is already established, as, e.g., they are prone to order effects [12]. Some work has already been done to use quantum-like techniques when dealing with Likert scales [6]. However, this approach suffers from the two problems flagged before. First, the dimension of the used Hilbert spaces gets high very quickly and second, the implicit ordinal structure of the outcomes is represented in the state vector, which should only represent the participant, and not in the outcome vectors. Our view opens up new possibilities to tackle these Likert scales. We construct one as an example, but keep in mind that this particular form has not been tested against any experimental data. We only wish to take some first steps to showcase the flexibility of our approach. When looking at the (1)–(5) scale presented above, we argue that 'strongly disagree (1)', 'neutral (3)' and 'strongly agree (5)' should exclude each other, as we consider them in our example as non-nuanced, very clear opinions. As such, they are represented by orthogonal vectors, called $|1\rangle, |3\rangle$ and $|5\rangle$ respectively, giving us a 3-dimensional Hilbert space $\mathcal{H}$. We also argue that picking options (2) or (4), represented by the vectors $|2\rangle$ and $|4\rangle$, does not necessarily means that the participant disagrees with (1) and (3) or (3) and (5) respectively. Keeping in mind the *balanced* property of Likert scales, places $|2\rangle$ symmetrically between $|1\rangle$ and $|3\rangle$ and $|4\rangle$ symmetrically between $|3\rangle$ and $|5\rangle$. Note that we can easily incorporate assumptions (e.g. *balanced*) from Likert scale theory into our model. This naturally leads to the structure depicted in Fig. 2.

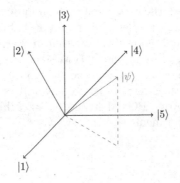

Fig. 2. The outcome '(i)' is represented by $|i\rangle$. The participant is represented by state vector $|\psi\rangle$.

Our implied structure in the outcomes does not impose restrictions on the agents. We can still model a person who doubts between (1) and (5) but not (3), by having a state vector equal to, for example, $|\psi\rangle = (1/\sqrt{2}, 0, 1/\sqrt{2})$.

Our arguments about the (non)-excluding outcomes and resulting dimensions here are very superficial. One could, e.g., argue that option (3) should be symmetrical between (1) and (5), leading to a 2-dimensional Hilbert space. A meticulous investigation of Likert scales in this paradigm falls outside the scope of this paper. We only wish to show that it is possible to represent inherent ordinal structure in the outcomes, possibly combined with other theoretical assumptions or restrictions.

6   Concluding Remarks

In this paper we propose some tentative first steps towards modeling ordinal scales using quantum-like techniques. After losing some of the restrictions used in the construction of projective measurements (and even lose restrictions placed upon POVMs), we use this lack of structure to impose new structure, now originating from the internal structure that ordinal outcomes exhibit. These techniques also allow for a reduction of the resulting dimensionality, as this can become problematic quickly in slightly more complex situations than the common examples seen in quantum cognition. We discuss the two biggest consequences of this approach, the first one being the total sum across all probabilities exceeding one and the second one being the loss of repeatability of outcomes. Exceeding one when adding the probabilities makes scaling necessary or requires the modeling of odds of outcomes instead of probabilities. We argue that the loss of repeatability is not as problematic as it seems at first and provide a possible interpretation of this phenomenon. Finally, we mention two possible applications. First, we give a short overview of an implementation already done in a game theoretic setting. Second, we propose the idea of applying our quantum-like ordinal system to model Likert scales.

This contribution is only a first step into modeling ordinal scales in a quantum-like way. The theoretical side of this story needs to be deepened, with a more thorough discussion of the concepts sketched out in Sect. 3, next to investigating structures similar in role to Naimark's Theorem for POVMs [8]. Also, more data-driven applications than the one presented here need to be formulated and statistically tested to investigate the true merit of this new approach.

References

1. Aerts, D., de Bianchi, M.S.: Beyond-quantum modeling of question order effects and response replicability in psychological measurements. CoRR abs/1508.03686 (2015). http://arxiv.org/abs/1508.03686
2. Aliakbarzadeh, M., Kitto, K.: Applying POVM to model non-orthogonality in quantum cognition. In: Atmanspacher, H., Filk, T., Pothos, E. (eds.) Quantum Interaction. LNCS, vol. 9535, pp. 284–293. Springer, Cham (2016)
3. Blanco, M., Engelmann, D., Koch, A., Normann, H.T.: Preferences and beliefs in a sequential social dilemma. Games Econ. Behav. **87**, 122–135 (2014)
4. Busemeyer, J., Bruza, P.: Quantum Models of Cognition and Decision. Cambridge University Press, Cambridge (2012)
5. Busemeyer, J., Pothos, E., Franco, R., Trueblood, J.: A quantum theoretical explanation for probability judgment errors. Physchol. Rev. **118**(2), 193–218 (2011)
6. Camparo, J.: A geometrical approach to the ordinal data of likert scaling and attitude measurements: the density matrix in psychology. J. Math. Psychol. **57**(1), 29–42 (2013)
7. Denolf, J., Martínez-Martínez, I., Josephy, H., Barque-Duran, A.: A quantum-like model for complementarity of preferences and beliefs in dilemma games. (submitted)
8. Gelfand, I., Neumark, M.: On the imbedding of normed rings into the ring of operators in hilbert space. Mat. Sbornik **54**, 197–217 (1943)
9. Khrennikov, A., Basieva, I., Dzhafarov, E.N., Busemeyer, J.R.: Quantum models for psychological measurements: an unsolved problem. PloS one **9**(10), e110909 (2014)

10. Martínez-Martínez, I., Denolf, J., Barque-Duran, A.: Do preferences and beliefs in dilemma games exhibit complementarity? In: Atmanspacher, H., Filk, T., Pothos, E. (eds.) Quantum Interaction. LNCS, vol. 9535, pp. 142–153. Springer, Cham (2015)

11. Matvejchuk, M., Widdows, D.: Real-orthogonal projections as quantum pseudo-logic. In: Atmanspacher, H., Filk, T., Pothos, E. (eds.) Quantum Interaction. LNCS, vol. 9535, pp. 275–283. Springer, Cham (2015)

12. Moore, D.W.: Measuring new types of question-order effects: additive and subtractive. Pub. Opin. Q. **66**(1), 80–91 (2002)

13. de Muynck, W.: POVMs: a small but important step beyond standard quantum mechanics. In: Nieuwenhuizen, T., Mehmani, B., Špicka, B., Aghdami, M., Khrennikov, A. (eds.)Beyond the Quantum, pp. 69–79 (2007)

14. Nielsen, M.A., Chuang, I.L.: Quantum Computation and Quantum Information. Cambridge University Press, Cambridge (2010)

15. Pothos, E., Busemeyer, J.: A quantum probability explanation for violations of 'rational' decision theory. In: Proceedings of the Royal Society of London B: Biological Sciences, RSPB-2009 (2009)

16. Spector, P.E.: Summated rating scale construction: An introduction. No. 82, Sage (1992)

17. Yearsley, J.M.: Advanced tools and concepts for quantum cognition: a tutorial. J. Math. Psychol. Special Issue on Quantum Probability (in press) (2016)

Eigenlogic: A Quantum View
for Multiple-Valued and Fuzzy Systems

François Dubois[1,2] and Zeno Toffano[3,4(✉)]

[1] LMSSC, Conservatoire National des Arts Et Métiers, Paris, France
francois.dubois@cnam.fr
[2] Department of Mathematics, University Paris-Sud, Orsay, France
[3] Telecom Department, CentraleSuplec, Gif-sur-yvette, France
zeno.toffano@centralesupelec.fr
[4] Laboratoire des Signaux et Systèmes - L2S (UMR8506) - CNRS,
Université Paris-Saclay, Paris, France

Abstract. We propose a matrix model for two- and many-valued logic using families of observables in Hilbert space, the eigenvalues give the truth values of logical propositions where the atomic input proposition cases are represented by the respective eigenvectors. For binary logic using the truth values $\{0, 1\}$ logical observables are pairwise commuting projectors. For the truth values $\{+1, -1\}$ the operator system is formally equivalent to that of a composite spin $1/2$ system, the logical observables being isometries belonging to the Pauli group. Also in this approach fuzzy logic arises naturally when considering non-eigenvectors. The fuzzy membership function is obtained by the quantum mean value of the logical projector observable and turns out to be a probability measure in agreement with recent quantum cognition models. The analogy of many-valued logic with quantum angular momentum is then established. Logical observables for three-value logic are formulated as functions of the L_z observable of the orbital angular momentum $\ell = 1$. The representative 3-valued 2-argument logical observables for the Min and Max connectives are explicitly obtained.

Keywords: Finite elements · Quantum gates · Boolean functions

AMS classification: 03B52 · 81Q99 · 94-04

1 Introduction

Quantum logic developed by Birkhoff and von Neumann in their seminal article in 1936 [1] considers logical propositions as subspaces of a quantum state Hilbert space. As will be shown hereafter and also underlined in [2], these subspaces can be viewed as eigenspaces of projectors, the projectors corresponding to logical propositions. A true proposition is then associated to the eigenvalue $+1$. The representation of logical propositions in a vector space could be of interest in

J.A. de Barros et al. (Eds.): QI 2016, LNCS 10106, pp. 239–251, 2017.
DOI: 10.1007/978-3-319-52289-0_19

modern semantic theories such as distributional semantics, for example using the "Hyperspace Analogue to Language" algorithm as was done in [3], or in connectionist models of cognition [4].

In this work we show that a proposition in a logical system can be represented by an observable in Hilbert space. When interpreted in the context of quantum mechanics this model uses finite dimensional projectors and angular momentum observables. Conversely, a quantum system when considered in its eigenspace is formally equivalent to a logical propositional system. The view here, which comes under the name of "Eigenlogic" (for the original motivation and more detailed discussion see [5]), considers that the eigenvalues of the logical observables are the truth values of a proposition and the associated eigenvectors correspond to the different input atomic propositional cases. When considering vectors outside of the eigensystem this view leads to a "fuzzy" measure of the degree of truth of a logical proposition.

In our model for binary valued logic, using numbers $\{0, 1\}$, the logical observables are pairwise commuting projectors. The model is extended to the other binary system using numbers $\{+1, -1\}$, differences reside in the symmetry of the corresponding logical observables. In the latter case the observables are equivalent to quantum spin $1/2$ observables, no more idempotent projectors but isometric self-inverse reflection observables squaring to 1. These are equivalent to the recently proposed "quantum Boolean functions" [6] developed in the context of the research topic "Fourier analysis of Boolean functions" having many applications in theoretical computer science, information theory and also in social decision and voting theory. We then propose an algebraic generalization, based on the finite-elements method, that can be applied to whatever m-value n-argument logical system.

The paper is organized as follows: we start with Boolean two-valued $\{0, 1\}$ logic and we demonstrate important expressions for the projector observables in the 2-argument case indicating also the general method for n-arguments. The case for binary values $\{+1, -1\}$ is then presented. Then we consider the case for fuzzy logical propositions and give the method for calculating fuzzy membership functions by using the Born rule and show that these functions can be identified with probabilities. The last section is devoted to the many-valued systems ($m > 2$) the case of 3-valued 2-argument logic is discussed with some examples of applications.

2   Two-Valued Eigenlogic

2.1   Projector Two-Valued Logic

We will consider a two-dimensional rank-1 projector $\boldsymbol{\Pi}$ acting on a single set. What are the expected outcomes when applying this projector? If, for example, vector $|a>$ corresponds to an element of the set, the following matrix equation will be verified: $\boldsymbol{\Pi} \cdot |a> = 1 \cdot |a>$. The value 1 being the eigenvalue of the projector associated with the eigenvector $|a>$. Interpretable results [5] considered in a two-value $\{0, 1\}$ logical system will correspond to the possible eigenvalues

0 and 1, where 0 is the result for elements not belonging to the set. So in this way a question concerning the proposition of belonging or not to a particular set, will have as an answer one of the two eigenvalues. The "true" value 1 will correspond to the eigenvector $|a>$, now named $|1>$, and the "false" value 0 will correspond to the complementary eigenvector $|\bar{a}>$, named $|0>$. When these properties are expressed in matrix form: vectors $|1>$ and $|0>$ become 2 dimensional orthonormal column vectors and the projection operators 2×2 square matrices. This gives:

$$|1> = \begin{pmatrix} 0 \\ 1 \end{pmatrix}, \qquad |0> = \begin{pmatrix} 1 \\ 0 \end{pmatrix}.$$

The choice of the position of the value 1 in the column vectors is arbitrary, here it follows the quantum information convention for a "qubit-1" [7]. As usual in Quantum Mechanics we can find the set of projectors that completely represent the quantum system, in particular by lifting the eventual degeneracy of the eigenvalues. Here eigenvalues are always equal to 0 or 1 and the question about the multiplicity of eigenvalues is natural. In this contribution we focus on different projective structures that completely define the logical system. In the very simple case where 0 and 1 are both not degenerate eigenvalues, the projectors relative to the eigenvector basis take the form:

$$\boldsymbol{\Pi}_1 = \boldsymbol{\Pi} = \begin{pmatrix} 0 & 0 \\ 0 & 1 \end{pmatrix}, \qquad \boldsymbol{\Pi}_0 = \boldsymbol{I} - \boldsymbol{\Pi} = \begin{pmatrix} 1 & 0 \\ 0 & 0 \end{pmatrix}. \qquad (1)$$

We systematically consider all the possible structures of such projectors. When representing logic with n atomic propositions using projectors various possibilities are intrinsically present in a unique structure with 2^{2^n} different projectors. Once the eigenbasis is chosen the remaining structure is intrinsic.

For example the two projectors shown in Eq. (1) are complementary and idempotent. One can give a general expression of a one-argument "logical observable" as an expansion over the commuting projectors $\boldsymbol{\Pi}_0$ and $\boldsymbol{\Pi}_1$ spanning the vector space:

$$\boldsymbol{F} = f(0)\,\boldsymbol{\Pi}_0 + f(1)\,\boldsymbol{\Pi}_1 = \begin{pmatrix} f(0) & 0 \\ 0 & f(1) \end{pmatrix} \qquad (2)$$

the coefficients $f(0)$ and $f(1)$ in the expansion are the truth values of the corresponding $\{0, 1\}$ Boolean logical connective. Eq. (2) represents the spectral decomposition of the operator and because the eigenvalues are real the logical operator is Hermitian and can thus be considered as a quantum observable. In this way, in Eigenlogic, the truth values of the logical proposition are the eigenvalues of the logical observable. One can then construct the 4 logical observables corresponding to the 4 one-argument Boolean connectives: $\boldsymbol{A} = \boldsymbol{\Pi}_1$ is the "logical projector" and $\overline{\boldsymbol{A}} = \boldsymbol{I} - \boldsymbol{\Pi}_1 = \boldsymbol{\Pi}_0$ its complement. The "True" operator corresponds here to the identity operator $\boldsymbol{I}$. The "False" observable corresponds to the null operator. These four observables form a complete family of commuting projectors. The extension to more arguments is obtained by using the

Kronecker product $\otimes$ in the same way as for the composition of quantum systems (for technical details on this operation see for example [7]).

In the case of $n = 2$ arguments we will have an expansion over 4 commuting orthogonal rank-1 projectors. Some properties of the Kronecker product on projectors have to be specified: (i) The Kronecker product of two projectors is also a projector; (ii) If projectors are rank-1 projectors (a single eigenvalue is equal to 1, all the others are 0) then their Kronecker product is also a rank-1 projector. Using these properties, the 4 commuting orthogonal rank -1 projectors $\boldsymbol{\Pi}_{00}$, $\boldsymbol{\Pi}_{01}$, $\boldsymbol{\Pi}_{10}$, and $\boldsymbol{\Pi}_{11}$, spanning the 4 dimensional vector space are calculated in a straightforward way:

$$\begin{cases} \boldsymbol{\Pi}_{00} = (\boldsymbol{I} - \boldsymbol{\Pi}) \otimes (\boldsymbol{I} - \boldsymbol{\Pi}), & \boldsymbol{\Pi}_{01} = (\boldsymbol{I} - \boldsymbol{\Pi}) \otimes \boldsymbol{\Pi}, \\ \boldsymbol{\Pi}_{10} = \boldsymbol{\Pi} \otimes (\boldsymbol{I} - \boldsymbol{\Pi}), & \boldsymbol{\Pi}_{11} = \boldsymbol{\Pi} \otimes \boldsymbol{\Pi}. \end{cases}$$

So one can write the logical observable for $n = 2$ arguments:

$$\boldsymbol{F} = f(0,0)\, \boldsymbol{\Pi}_{00} + f(0,1)\, \boldsymbol{\Pi}_{01} + f(1,0)\, \boldsymbol{\Pi}_{10} + f(1,1)\, \boldsymbol{\Pi}_{11}. \tag{3}$$

In an explicit way:

$$\boldsymbol{F} = \begin{pmatrix} f(0,0) & 0 & 0 & 0 \\ 0 & f(0,1) & 0 & 0 \\ 0 & 0 & f(1,0) & 0 \\ 0 & 0 & 0 & f(1,1) \end{pmatrix}.$$

Equation (3) represents a spectral decomposition with the eigenvalues being the truth values, in this case we will have a family of 16 possible different observables. All these observables are pairwise commuting projectors and in general their product (matrix product) is not equal to zero. This last point is essential in the model, because not only mutually exclusive projectors are representative for a logical system, the complete family of projectors must be used. For example the observables for conjunction, AND, and disjunction, OR, which have in common the truth value, $(1, 1)$, for the input combination (True $\equiv$ 1, True $\equiv$ 1), have their matrix product different from zero.

This method can be extended to whatever number of arguments n using the "seed" projector $\boldsymbol{\Pi}$, its complement $(\boldsymbol{I} - \boldsymbol{\Pi})$ and by applying the Kronecker product. So given the number of input arguments n and knowing the truth table of the logical connective one directly obtains the corresponding binary Eigenlogic observable.

Now let's develop the case for $n = 2$ arguments: one can express the connectives corresponding to a "logical projector" according to the composition rule, thus obtaining two commuting projector observables:

$$\boldsymbol{A} = \boldsymbol{\Pi} \otimes \boldsymbol{I}, \quad \boldsymbol{B} = \boldsymbol{I} \otimes \boldsymbol{\Pi}, \quad \boldsymbol{A} \cdot \boldsymbol{B} = \boldsymbol{\Pi} \otimes \boldsymbol{\Pi} \tag{4}$$

the conjunction, AND, observable becomes simply the product of these two logical projectors $\boldsymbol{A} \cdot \boldsymbol{B}$. The disjunction, OR, and exclusive disjunction, XOR, observables are shown on Table 1, where the algebraic expansions for Boolean

Table 1. The sixteen two-argument two-valued logical connectives and the respective Eigenlogic observables for eigenvalues $\{0,1\}$ and $\{+1,-1\}$.

Connective for Boolean A, B	Truth table $\{F, T\}$: $\{0,1\}$; $\{+1,-1\}$	$\{0,1\}$ projective logical observable	$\{+1,-1\}$ isometric logical observable
False F	F F F F	0	$+I$
NOR ; $\overline{A \vee B}$	F F F T	$I - A - B + A \cdot B$	$\frac{1}{2}(+I - U - V - U \cdot V)$
$A \not\Leftarrow B$	F F T F	$B - A \cdot B$	$\frac{1}{2}(+I - U + V + U \cdot V)$
$\overline{A}$	F F T T	$I - A$	$-U$
$A \not\Rightarrow B$	F T F F	$A - A \cdot B$	$\frac{1}{2}(+I + U - V + U \cdot V)$
$\overline{B}$	F T F T	$I - B$	$-V$
XOR; $A \oplus B$	F T T F	$A + B - 2A \cdot B$	$U \cdot V = Z \otimes Z$
NAND; $\overline{A \wedge B}$	F T T T	$I - A \cdot B$	$\frac{1}{2}(-I - U - V + U \cdot V)$
AND; $A \wedge B$	T F F F	$A \cdot B = \Pi \otimes \Pi$	$\frac{1}{2}(+I + U + V - U \cdot V)$
$A \equiv B$	T F F T	$I - A - B + 2A \cdot B$	$-U \cdot V$
B	T F T F	$B = I \otimes \Pi$	$V = I \otimes Z$
$A \Rightarrow B$	T F T T	$I - A + A \cdot B$	$\frac{1}{2}(-I - U + V - U \cdot V)$
A	T T F F	$A = \Pi \otimes I$	$U = Z \otimes I$
$A \Leftarrow B$	T T F T	$I - B + A \cdot B$	$\frac{1}{2}(-I + U - V - U \cdot V)$
OR; $A \vee B$	T T T F	$A + B - A \cdot B$	$\frac{1}{2}(-I + U + V + U \cdot V)$
True T	T T T T	I	$-I$

connectives explicitly derived in [5] are used. Negation (complementation) is obtained by subtracting from the identity operator for projective logical observables and by multiplying by -1 for isometric logical observables (see hereafter). Useful transformations are obtained by De Morgan's theorem (for general theorems in logic see for example Knuth [8]), for the negative conjunction, NAND one has the identity $\overline{A \wedge B} = \overline{A} \vee \overline{B}$ in the same way one can obtain NOR with the identity $\overline{A \vee B} = \overline{A} \wedge \overline{B}$. Implication observables are also shown on Table 1.

2.2   Isometric Reversible Two-Valued Logical Observables

There is a linear bijection (isomorphism) from the projector logical observables F towards reversible observables G:

$$G = I - 2F.$$

The two families of observables commute and have the same system of eigenvectors. Practically to obtain G from F one just has to substitute the eigenvalue 0 with $+1$ and 1 with -1. The observables G are "isometries": unitary reflection operators. From projector Π in Eq. (4) one obtains the observable Z:

$$Z = I - 2\Pi = \begin{pmatrix} +1 & 0 \\ 0 & -1 \end{pmatrix} = \sigma_z$$

which is actually one of the Pauli matrices σ_z and corresponds in quantum mechanics, to the z component of a spin $1/2$ observable $\mathbf{S}_z = (\hbar/2)\,\sigma_z$ where $\hbar$ is the reduced Planck's constant. In the field of quantum information this operator is also named the "Pauli-Z" gate or "phase-π" gate [7]. Here, $U = Z$ designates the "logical projector" connective and $\overline{U} = -Z$ its complement (negation), *nota bene* in this case the connective "logical projector" is not a projection operator, in order to avoid ambiguity it is often named [6] "dictator".

For $n = 2$ arguments one can then write directly the expression for a logical isometric observable by using its spectral decomposition. The logical "dictators" U and V become:

$$U \,=\, Z \otimes I, \qquad V \,=\, I \otimes Z, \qquad U \cdot V \,=\, Z \otimes Z.$$

The exclusive disjunction XOR observable is here simply given by the product of the dictators: $U \cdot V$. Negation is obtained by multiplying by the number -1. From Table 1 one sees that there are more complicated relations, for example the conjunction, AND, observable is:

$$\frac{1}{2}(I + U + V - U \cdot V) = \begin{pmatrix} +1 & 0 & 0 & 0 \\ 0 & +1 & 0 & 0 \\ 0 & 0 & +1 & 0 \\ 0 & 0 & 0 & -1 \end{pmatrix} = C^Z.$$

Those familiar with the domain of quantum information can easily recognize the reversible logical gate "control-Z" or simply named C^Z [7].

3 From Deterministic Logic to Fuzzy Logic

Fuzzy logic deals with truth values that may be any number between 0 and 1, here the truth of a proposition may range between completely true and completely false. It is generally considered that probability theory and fuzzy logic are related to different forms of uncertainty, the first is concerned with how probable it is that a variable belongs to a given set and the second one uses the concept of fuzzy set membership, intended as the degree of membership. This was the first motivation of fuzzy logic [9]. But this distinction when considering the quantum probabilistic Born rule is not so strict from a formal point of view. We will start the discussion by giving the interpretation of a vector state in Eigenlogic.

In the preceding sections we considered operations on the eigenspace of a logical observable family. For example for $n = 2$ arguments a complete family of 16 commuting logical observables represents all possible logical connectives and becomes "interpretable" [5] when applied to one of the four possible canonical eigenvectors of the family. These vectors, corresponding to all the possible atomic input propositional cases, are represented by the vectors $|00>$, $|01>$, $|10>$ and $|11>$ forming a complete orthonormal basis. When applying a logical observable on one of these vectors the resulting eigenvalue will correspond to the truth value for the considered input.

Now what happens when the state-vector is not one of the eigenvectors of the logical system? In quantum mechanics, where vectors operate in Hilbert space, one can always express a state-vector as a decomposition on a complete orthonormal basis. In particular we can express it over the canonical eigenbasis of the logical observable family. For two-arguments this vector can be written as:

$$|\Psi> = C_{00}|00> + C_{01}|01> + C_{10}|10> + C_{11}|11> .$$

We can interpret this in the following way: when only one of the coefficients is non-zero (in this case its absolute value must take the value 1) then we are back in the preceding situation of a determinate input atomic propositional case. But when more than one coefficient is non-zero we are in a "mixed" or "fuzzy" propositional case. Such a state could also possibly be interpreted as a quantum superposition of atomic propositional cases.

We can then calculate the "mean value" of a logical observable. In particular the logical projector observables F will give a "fuzzy measure" of the logical proposition in the form of the "fuzzy membership function" μ. Let's show this on some examples: in the case of one argument one can express an arbitrary 2-dimensional quantum state as: $|\varphi> = \sin\alpha|0> + e^{i\beta}\cos\alpha|1>$ where the "angles" α and β are real numbers. The quantum mean value of the "logical projector" observable $A = \Pi$ can then be calculated using the Born rule:

$$\mu(a) = <\varphi|\Pi|\varphi> = \cos\alpha\,e^{-i\beta}<1|1><1|\cos\alpha e^{i\beta}|1> = \cos^2\alpha;$$

in the same way one can calculate the complement

$$\mu(\bar{a}) = <\varphi|I - \Pi|\varphi> = \sin^2\alpha = 1 - \mu(a).$$

This verifies one of the requirements of fuzzy logic for the complement (negation) of a fuzzy set.

According to standard notations for spin $1/2$ quantum states, or qubits, on the Bloch sphere [7] we use the transformation $\alpha = (\pi-\theta)/2$ and $\beta = \varphi$. A quantum compound state can be built by taking the tensor product of two elementary states: $|\psi> = |\varphi_p> \otimes |\varphi_q>$, where $|\varphi_p> = \cos\frac{\theta_p}{2}|0> + e^{i\varphi_p}\sin\frac{\theta_p}{2}|1>$ (for $|\varphi_q>$ we have a similar expression). Now $\sin^2\frac{\theta_p}{2} = p$ and $\sin^2\frac{\theta_q}{2} = q$ represent the probabilities of being in the "True" state $|1>$ for spins $1/2$ oriented along two different axes θ_p and θ_q.

One can calculate the fuzzy membership function of the corresponding "logical projector" for the two-argument case using Eq. (4).

$$\mu(a) = <\psi|\Pi \otimes I|\psi> = p(1-q) + p\cdot q = p, \quad \mu(b) = <\psi|I \otimes \Pi|\psi> = q.$$

This shows that the mean values correspond to the respective probabilities. Now let's "measure" for example the conjunction and the disjunction, using the observables in Table 1, this gives:

$$\begin{cases} \mu(a \wedge b) = <\psi|\Pi \otimes \Pi|\psi> = p\cdot q = \mu(a)\cdot\mu(b), \\ \mu(a \vee b) = p + q - p\cdot q = \mu(a) + \mu(b) - \mu(a)\cdot\mu(b). \end{cases}$$

Similar results for conjunction and disjunction have been outlined recently, also using projector operators, when considering concept combinations [10] for quantum-like experiments in the domain of quantum cognition.

What happens when the state-vector cannot be put in the form of a tensor product, that is when it corresponds to an entangled state? The problem is outside the scope of this paper but an interesting result can be shown: the mean value of whatever logical observable of the type F on an arbitrary quantum state $|\Psi>$ will always verify the inequality:

$$< \Psi|F|\Psi > = \mathrm{Tr}\left(\rho_\Psi \cdot F\right) \leq 1, \qquad \text{with} \quad \rho_\Psi \equiv |\Psi><\Psi|,$$

and can thus be interpreted as a probability measure.

4 From Two-Valued to Multi-Valued Logic

Multi-valued logic requires a different algebraic structure than an ordinary binary-valued one. Many properties of binary logic do not support set of values that do not have cardinality 2^n. Multi-valued logic is often used for the development of logical systems that are more expressive than Boolean systems for reasoning [11]. Particularly three and four valued systems, have been of interest with applications to digital circuits and computer science.

The total number of possible logical connectives for an m-valued n-argument system is the combinatorial number m^{m^n}, so in particular for a binary 2-valued 2-argument system, as shown above, the number of connectives will be $2^{2^2} = 16$, the complete list indicated on Table 1. For a binary three-argument system, the number increases to $2^{2^3} = 256$. For a 3-valued 1-argument system the number of connectives will be $3^{3^1} = 27$ and for a 3-valued 2-argument system: $3^{3^2} = 19683$. So it is clear that by increasing the values from two to three the possibilities of new connectives becomes intractable for a complete description of a logical system, but some special connectives play important roles and will be illustrated hereafter. We will proceed by showing the general algebraic method.

4.1 Interpolation with Finite Elements

The finite element method (see for example [12]) allows one to interpolate a function, *id est* to make explicit the values $f(x)$ from the given values of specific numbers, the (so-called) degrees of freedom.

Let's consider the following simple example: given the values $f(+1)$, $f(0)$ and $f(-1)$ of a function f at the particular points $x = +1, 0, -1$, and using the appropriate Dirac linear forms, we can write: $< \delta_{+1}, f >= f(+1)$, $< \delta_0, f >= f(0)$ and $< \delta_{-1}, f >= f(-1)$, where $\Sigma \equiv \{\delta_{+1}, \delta_0, \delta_{-1}\}$ is called the set of degrees of freedom. This linear structure shows that it is natural to consider a three-dimensional space. The "basis function" φ_i associated to the set of degrees of freedom Σ and to the polynomial space solves this problem. The three basis functions using degrees of freedom and second-degree polynomials are:

$$\varphi_{+1}(x) = \frac{1}{2}\,x\,(x+1), \quad \varphi_0(x) = 1 - x^2, \quad \varphi_{-1}(x) = \frac{1}{2}\,x\,(x-1). \qquad (5)$$

So in general, an arbitrary function f can be written:

$$f(x) = \sum_{i=+1,0,-1} f(i)\,\varphi_i(x), \qquad \sum_{i=+1,0,-1} \varphi_i(x) \equiv 1 \qquad (6)$$

where the completeness of the basis functions is verified by their sum being 1.

4.2   Formalization of Three-Valued Eigenlogic

We use an operator system which is equivalent to the one of orbital angular momentum $\ell = 1$. In general angular momentum is characterized by two quantum numbers: j the angular momentum number and m_j the magnetic momentum number. Both these numbers must be integer or half integer. The rules are: $j \geq 0$, and attached to this value we have the condition: $-j \leq m_j \leq j$. The value $j = 0$ is possible and gives a single value $m_j = 0$ the next is $j = s = 1/2$ giving two values $m_s = \pm 1/2$ corresponding to the two-valued spin system. The value $j = 1$ gives three possible values $m_j = \{+1, 0, -1\}$ and so on. We consider for $j = \ell = 1$ the z-component orbital angular momentum observable [13]

$$L_z = \hbar\Lambda = \hbar \begin{pmatrix} +1 & 0 & 0 \\ 0 & 0 & 0 \\ 0 & 0 & -1 \end{pmatrix}. \qquad (7)$$

In the above matrix the three eigenvalues $\{+1, 0, -1\}$ will be considered as the logical values. A convention for these values, extending binary logic, is the following: False : $F \equiv +1$, Neutral : $N \equiv 0$, True : $T \equiv -1$.
We can now express the three-value logical observables as spectral decompositions over the rank-1 projectors spanning the vector space: Π_{+1}, Π_0 and Π_{-1}. These operators correspond to the pure state density matrices of the three eigenstates $|+1>$, $|0>$ and $|-1>$ of L_z. The three projectors can be expressed as a function of the dimensionless observable Λ, using directly the expressions given above in (5) where the basis functions φ_i become the projectors and the symbol x the observable Λ given in (7):

$$\Pi_{+1} = \frac{1}{2}\Lambda(\Lambda + I) \qquad \Pi_0 = I - \Lambda^2 \qquad \Pi_{-1} = \frac{1}{2}\Lambda(\Lambda - I) \qquad (8)$$

Then every one-argument "local projector" $F(\Lambda)$ can be obtained using the relation (6).

4.3   Three-Valued, Two-Argument Examples: Min, Max

When considering a 2-argument 3-valued system we find the expansion by using the Kronecker product in the same way as for the binary system in Eq. (3):

$$F = \sum_{i,j=+1,0,-1} f_{ij}\,\Pi_i \otimes \Pi_j, \qquad f_{ij} \in \{+1, 0, -1\}. \qquad (9)$$

these observables are now 9×9 matrices. We can define the two argument "dictators", U and V, simply by the rule of composition, this leads to:

$$U = \Lambda \otimes I \qquad V = I \otimes \Lambda \qquad U \cdot V = \Lambda \otimes \Lambda. \qquad (10)$$

In trivalent logic (see *e.g.* [11]) popular connectives are Min and Max, defined in the maps on Table 2.

Table 2. The Min and Max maps for a three-valued two-argument logic.

Min $U \backslash\!\backslash V$	F	N	T
F $\equiv +1$	+1	+1	+1
N $\equiv 0$	+1	0	0
T $\equiv -1$	+1	0	−1

Max $U \backslash\!\backslash V$	F	N	T
F $\equiv +1$	+1	0	−1
N $\equiv 0$	0	0	−1
T $\equiv -1$	− 1	−1	−1

Here the connectives Min and Max are symmetric, they are equivalent for a complete inversion of signs on inputs and outputs. Using the relations (8), (9) and (10) in conjunction with reduction rules we obtain the following observables:

$$\begin{cases} \text{Min}(U, V) = \dfrac{1}{2} \left(U + V + U^2 + V^2 - U \cdot V - U^2 \cdot V^2\right) \\ \text{Max}(U, V) = \dfrac{1}{2} \left(U + V - U^2 - V^2 + U \cdot V + U^2 \cdot V^2\right) \end{cases} \qquad (11)$$

The proof of the relations (11) is a direct consequence of relations (5) and (9). We have on one hand:

$$\begin{aligned} \text{Min}\,(U, V) &= \varphi_1(U) \otimes \varphi_1(V) + \varphi_1(U) \otimes \varphi_0(V) + \varphi_1(U) \otimes \varphi_{-1}(V) \\ &\quad + \varphi_0(U) \otimes \varphi_1(V) + \varphi_{-1}(U) \otimes \varphi_1(V) - \varphi_{-1}(U) \otimes \varphi_{-1}(V) \\ &= \varphi_1(U) + \varphi_1(V) - \varphi_1(U) \otimes \varphi_1(V) - \varphi_{-1}(U) \otimes \varphi_{-1}(V) \qquad \text{due to (6)} \\ &= \tfrac{1}{2} U\,(U + I) + \tfrac{1}{2} V\,(V + I) - \tfrac{1}{4} U\,(U + I) V\,(V + I) - \tfrac{1}{4} U\,(U - I) V\,(V - I) \\ &= \tfrac{1}{2} \left(U^2 + U + V^2 + V - U^2 V^2 - UV\right) \end{aligned}$$

and the first relation of (11) is proven. On the other hand, we have

$$\begin{aligned} \text{Max}\,(U, V) &= \varphi_1(U) \otimes \varphi_1(V) - \varphi_1(U) \otimes \varphi_{-1}(V) - \varphi_0(U) \otimes \varphi_{-1}(V) \\ &\quad - \varphi_{-1}(U) \otimes \varphi_{-1}(V) - \varphi_{-1}(U) \otimes \varphi_1(V) - \varphi_{-1}(U) \otimes \varphi_0(V) \\ &= \varphi_1(U) \otimes \varphi_1(V) - \varphi_{-1}(U) - \varphi_{-1}(V) + \varphi_{-1}(U) \otimes \varphi_{-1}(V) \qquad \text{due to (6)} \\ &= \tfrac{1}{4} U\,(U + I) V\,(V + I) - \tfrac{1}{2} U\,(U - I) - \tfrac{1}{2} V\,(V - I) + \tfrac{1}{4} U\,(U - I) V\,(V - I) \\ &= \tfrac{1}{2} \left(U^2 V^2 + UV - U^2 - V^2 + U + V\right) \end{aligned}$$

and the second relation of (11) is proven. $\qquad\qquad\qquad\square$

The proof presented above exploits the properties of the Kronecker product and reduction rules due to the completeness of the finite projection space. Reduction of logical expressions is an important topic in logic. In binary logic it is formalized by using Karnaugh maps which represent canonical SOP (Sum Of Products) disjunctive normal forms [8].

Binary logic is "included" in ternary logic, we want to verify this by eliminating the "neutral" state, $N \equiv 0$, and considering only the two logical values $\{+1, -1\}$. In this case we have: $U^2 = V^2 = I$ and so (11) reduces to:

$$\begin{cases} \mathrm{Min}\,(U, V) = \frac{1}{2}\left(I + U + V - U \cdot V\right), \\ \mathrm{Max}\,(U, V) = \frac{1}{2}\left(-I + U + V + U \cdot V\right) \end{cases}$$

considering that for binary logic the Min connective becomes the conjunction, AND, and the Max connective the disjunction, OR, we find the previous results given on Table 1 for binary $\{+1, -1\}$ observables.

5   Discussion and Conclusion

We have presented an operational formalism named "Eigenlogic" using observables in Hilbert space. The original feature being that the eigenvalues of a logical observable represent the truth values of the corresponding logical connective, the associated eigenvectors corresponding to one of the fixed combination of the inputs (atomic propositions). This approach differs from other geometric formalizations of logic (for references and discussion see [5]). Here the outcome of a "measurement" or "observation" on a logical observable will give the truth value of the associated logical proposition, and becomes "interpretable" when applied to the eigenspace leading to a natural analogy with the measurement postulate in quantum mechanics. One of the referees proposed the following diagram to summarize the point of view presented in this contribution:

$$\begin{aligned} \text{eigenvectors in Hilbert space} &\longrightarrow \text{atomic propositional cases} \\ \text{projectors} &\longrightarrow \text{logical connectives} \\ \text{eigenvalues} &\longrightarrow \text{truth values.} \end{aligned}$$

At first sight this method could be viewed as "classical" because exactly the same results are obtained in Eigenlogic as in ordinary propositional logic. This is in itself an important result demonstrating a new method in logic based on linear algebra, the method being also developed in multivalued logic. But when considering vector states, *id est* input propositions, that are not eigenvectors, the measurement outcomes are governed by the quantum Born rule, and interpretable results are then given by the mean values. This fact led us to apply the method to Fuzzy logic.

Another important point is the general algebraic method, based on classical interpolation framework suggested by the finite-element method. Our method can be employed for whatever m-valued n-argument logical system and in each case the corresponding logical observables can be defined. Some observables can be formally compared with angular momentum observables in quantum mechanics. Because of the exponential increase of complexity, an analytical formulation is only tractable for a low number of logical values and arguments. We treated the two-argument binary case completely and the three-valued case using the logical observables Min and Max. An algorithmic approach for logical connectives with a large number of arguments could be interesting to develop using Eigenlogic observables in high-dimensional vector spaces. But because the space grows in dimension very quickly, it may not be particularly useful for practical implementation without logical reduction. It would be interesting to develop specific algebraic reduction methods for logical observables inspired from actual research in the field. For a good synthesis of the state of the art, see *e.g.* [14].

Eigenlogic could create a new perspective in the field of quantum computation because several of the observables turn out to be well-known quantum gates. Here we represent them as diagonal matrices, *id est* in their eigenbasis, other "normal" forms being easily recovered by unitary transformations. It would be interesting to operate quantum gates in our framework. Many-valued logic is being investigated in quantum computation for example with ternary-logic quantum gates using "qutrits". Our formulation of multivalued logical observables could be used for the design of new quantum gates.

Dynamical evolution of the logical system could be included in the model by identifying the appropriate Hamiltonian operators. Standard procedures for expressing interaction Hamiltonians as a function of angular momentum observables could be used [13].

More generally we think that this view of logic could add some insight on more fundamental issues. Boolean functions are nowadays considered as a "toolbox" for resolving many problems in theoretical computer science, information theory and even fundamental mathematics. In the same way Eigenlogic can be considered as a new "toolbox" and could be of interest for the "Quantum Interaction" community where quantum-like approaches in human and social sciences need to be founded on a logical basis.

Acknowledgments. The authors thank both referees for their precise and constructive remarks and suggestions. Some of them have been included in the present version of this contribution.

References

1. Birkhoff, G., von Neumann, J.: The logic of quantum mechanics. Ann. Math. 2nd Ser. **37**(4), 823–843 (1936)
2. Ying, M.S.: Foundations of Quantum Programming. Morgan Kaufmann, Massachusetts (2016)
3. Barros, J., Toffano, Z., Meguebli, Y., Doan, B.-L.: Contextual query using bell tests. In: Atmanspacher, H., Haven, E., Kitto, K., Raine, D. (eds.) QI 2013. LNCS, vol. 8369, pp. 110–121. Springer, Heidelberg (2014). doi:10.1007/978-3-642-54943-4_10
4. Busemeyer, J.R., Bruza, P.D.: Quantum Models of Cognition and Decision. Cambridge University Press, Cambridge (2012)
5. Toffano, Z.: Eigenlogic in the spirit of George Boole. arXiv:1512.06632 (2015)
6. Montanaro, A., Osborne, T.J.: Quantum Boolean functions. arXiv:0810.2435 (2008)

7. Nielsen, M.A., Chuang, I.L.: Quantum Computation and Quantum Information. Cambridge University Press, Cambridge (2000)
8. Knuth, D.E.: The Art of Computer Programming, Volume 4, Fascicle 0: Introduction to Combinatorial Algorithms and Boolean Functions. Addison-Wesley, Reading (2009)
9. Zadeh, L.A.: Fuzzy sets. Inf. Control **8**(3), 338–353 (1965)
10. Aerts, D., Sozzo, S., Veloz, T.: Quantum structure of negation and conjunction in human thought. Front Psychol. **6**, 1447 (2015)
11. Miller, D.M., Thornton, M.A.: Multiple Valued Logic: Concepts and Representations. Morgan & Claypool Publishers, San Rafael (2008)
12. Zienkiewicz, O.Z.: The Finite Element Method in Engineering Science. McGraw-Hill, New York (1971)
13. Schiff, L.I.: Quantum Mechanics. McGraw-Hill, New York (1949)
14. Yanushkevich, S.N., Shmerko, V.P.: Introduction to Logic Design. CRC Press, Boca Raton (2008)

A New Perspective on Observables in the Category of Relations: A Spectral Presheaf for Relations

Kevin Dunne[(⊠)]

University of Strathclyde, Glasgow, Scotland
kevin.dunne@strath.ac.uk

Abstract. We take a first step towards establishing a link between the topos approach to quantum theory and the monoidal approach to quantum theory. The topos approach to quantum theory makes extensive use of categories of commutative C^*-algebras and their corresponding Gelfand spectrum. We generalise these categories of C^*-algebras and generalise the notion of Gelfand spectrum via defining the abstract spectral presheaf. We then characterise this spectral presheaf for the category of sets and relations, and examine how this relates to the notion of observable in this category as studied in the monoidal approach to quantum theory.

1 Introduction

The monoidal category approach to quantum theory [1], and the topos approach to quantum theory [2,3] are two projects which seek to reformulate parts of quantum theory in the language of category theory.

The monoidal approach uses the language of †-symmetric monoidal categories to present a general mathematical framework in which a variety of quantum and quantum-like theories can be studied and compared. In doing so, the monoidal approach abstracts away from the language of Hilbert space or C^*-algebras, to much more general mathematical structures. Monoidal categories admit graphical languages, and hence this general framework presents an intuitive and practical formalism for reasoning about physical theories.

The topos approach to quantum theory addresses unresolved foundational issues of quantum theory, using modern mathematics to attack the old problems of physics and metaphysics.

These approaches use very different kinds of mathematics, and address different questions. This work can be seen as a first step towards establishing a relationship between these two distinct approaches to quantum theory. In particular we use the notion *observable* in each approach as a point of contact.

We first look at this connection for a standard model of quantum theory, the category of finite dimensional Hilbert spaces. We then describe the same relationship for the category of sets and relations. In the topos approach Hilbert spaces, C^*-algebras, and von Neumann algebras remain fundamental concepts,

© Springer International Publishing AG 2017
J.A. de Barros et al. (Eds.): QI 2016, LNCS 10106, pp. 252–264, 2017.
DOI: 10.1007/978-3-319-52289-0_20

and hence we must first generalise aspects of the topos approach before special-
ising to the category of sets and relations.

Definition 1. *A †-category consists of a category $\mathcal{A}$ equipped with a functor
$\dagger : \mathcal{A}^{\mathrm{op}} \to \mathcal{A}$ which is the identity on objects and satisfies $\dagger \circ \dagger = \mathrm{id}_{\mathcal{A}}$.*

*A †-symmetric monoidal category consists of a symmetric monoidal category
$(\mathcal{A}, \otimes, I)$ with a dagger, such that $\dagger$ is a symmetric monoidal functor, and where
all of the natural isomorphisms forming the symmetric monoidal structure are
unitary, i.e. $\alpha^{-1} = \alpha^{\dagger}$.*

Example 1. The archetypal example of a †-symmetric monoidal category is the
category of finite dimensional complex Hilbert spaces, with linear maps, and
usual tensor product $(\mathbf{fdHilb}, \otimes, \mathbb{C})$.

Example 2. The category of sets and relations with monoidal product the cartesian product $(\mathbf{Rel}, \times, \{*\})$ is a †-symmetric monoidal category. The dagger is
given by simply reversing relations in the obvious way.

The category of relations is a simple but non-trivial †-symmetric monoidal
category and hence provides a useful non-standard model of quantum theory.
As such, there is an extensive literature on this category from the perspective of
quantum theory, for example, providing a categorical model for Spekkens Toy
Theory [4,5].

Definition 2. *A unital algebra in a symmetric monoidal category $(\mathcal{A}, \otimes, I)$ consists of an object $C \in \mathcal{A}$ together with morphisms $\mu : C \otimes C \to C$ and $\eta : I \to C$
such that the following diagrams commute*

$$
\begin{array}{ccc}
C \otimes C \otimes C & \xrightarrow{\mathrm{id} \otimes \mu} & C \otimes C \\
\downarrow{\scriptstyle \mu \otimes \mathrm{id}} & & \downarrow{\scriptstyle \mu} \\
C \otimes C & \xrightarrow{\mu} & C
\end{array}
$$

$$
\begin{array}{ccccc}
 & & C \otimes I & \xrightarrow{\mathrm{id} \otimes \eta} & C \otimes C \\
 & {\scriptstyle \rho_C} \nearrow & & & \searrow{\scriptstyle \mu} \\
C & & \xrightarrow{\quad\mathrm{id}\quad} & & C \\
 & {\scriptstyle \lambda_C} \searrow & & & \nearrow{\scriptstyle \mu} \\
 & & I \otimes C & \xrightarrow{\eta \otimes \mathrm{id}} & C \otimes C
\end{array}
$$

Such an algebra is commutative if the following diagram commutes

$$
\begin{array}{ccc}
C \otimes C & \xrightarrow{\mu} & \\
\downarrow{\scriptstyle \sigma_{C,C}} & \searrow & C \\
C \otimes C & \xrightarrow{\mu} &
\end{array}
$$

where σ is the monoidal braiding of $\mathcal{A}$.

A cocommutative counital coalgebra *is a commutative unital algebra in $\mathcal{A}^{\mathrm{op}}$,
i.e. consists of morphisms $\delta : C \to C \otimes C$ and $\varepsilon : C \to I$, such that the reversal
of the above diagrams commute.*

Definition 3. *A special commutative Frobenius algebra in $(\mathcal{A}, \otimes, I)$ consists of a commutative algebra $\eta : I \to C$, $\mu : C \otimes C \to C$ and a cocommutative coalgebra $\varepsilon : C \to I$, $\delta : C \to C \otimes C$ such that the following commute*

$$
\begin{array}{ccc}
C \otimes C & \xrightarrow{\ \mu\ } & C \\
{\scriptstyle \text{id} \otimes \delta} \downarrow & & \downarrow {\scriptstyle \delta} \\
C \otimes C \otimes C & \xrightarrow{\ \mu \otimes \text{id}\ } & C \otimes C
\end{array}
\qquad\qquad
\begin{array}{ccc}
C & \xrightarrow{\ \delta\ } & C \otimes C \\
 & {\scriptstyle \text{id}} \searrow & \downarrow {\scriptstyle \mu} \\
 & & C
\end{array}
$$

If $(\mathcal{A}, \otimes, I)$ is †-symmetric, $(C, \mu, \eta, \delta, \varepsilon)$ is called a †-special commutative Frobenius algebra if $\mu^\dagger = \delta$ and $\eta^\dagger = \varepsilon$.

Let H be a finite dimensional Hilbert space, and let $\{ |e_i\rangle \}_{i \in I}$ be an orthonormal basis. With this data we define the algebra (H, μ, η) as follows

$$
\begin{array}{ccc}
H \otimes H & \xrightarrow{\ \mu\ } & H \\
|e_i\rangle \otimes |e_j\rangle & \longmapsto & \begin{cases} |e_i\rangle & \text{if } i = j \\ 0 & \text{otherwise} \end{cases}
\end{array}
\qquad
\begin{array}{ccc}
\mathbb{C} & \xrightarrow{\ \eta\ } & H \\
1 & \longmapsto & \sum_{i \in I} \frac{1}{|I|} |e_i\rangle
\end{array}
\qquad (1)
$$

It is straightforward to check that this algebra, together with its adjoint maps satisfy the equations of a †-special commutative Frobenius algebra. The following theorem [6, Theorem 5.1] states that these are all of the †-special commutative Frobenius algebras in **fdHilb**.

Theorem 1. *Every †-special commutative Frobenius algebra (H, μ, η) in **fdHilb** is of the form (1) for some orthonormal basis $\{ |e_i\rangle \}_{i \in I}$.*

Hence there is a 1-1 correspondence between orthonormal bases of a finite dimensional Hilbert space H and the †-special commutative Frobenius algebra structures with which H can be endowed. This provides the justification that †-special commutative Frobenius algebras provide an axiomatisation of observables.

For a †-special commutative Frobenius algebra (H, μ, η) in **fdHilb** corresponding with the orthonormal basis $\{ |e_i\rangle \}_{i \in I}$, it is exactly these basis elements which are copied by the comultiplication map, i.e. satisfy $\mu^\dagger(|e_i\rangle) = |e_i\rangle \otimes |e_i\rangle$. These are called the *set-like elements* of the Frobenius algebra and can be defined for Frobenius algebras in an arbitrary category.

Definition 4. *The set-like elements of a †-special commutative Frobenius algebra (X, μ, η) are the points $x : I \to X$ satisfying*

$$
\begin{array}{ccc}
I & \xrightarrow{\ \sim\ } & I \otimes I \\
{\scriptstyle x} \downarrow & & \downarrow {\scriptstyle x \otimes x} \\
X & \xrightarrow{\ \mu^\dagger\ } & X \otimes X
\end{array}
$$

Within the monoidal approach to quantum theory set-like elements can be seen as a generalisation of eigenstates of a non-degenerate self-adjoint operator.

We now discuss the topos approach to quantum theory. Consider the category **Hilb** of Hilbert spaces and bounded linear maps. For each Hilbert space H the set $\mathrm{Hom}(H, H)$ carries the structure of a C^*-algebra. In the topos approach to quantum theory one considers, for a fixed Hilbert space H, the category **Hilb-Alg**(H), whose objects are commutative C^*-subalgebras of $\mathrm{Hom}(H, H)$, and whose morphisms are inclusions of subalgebras, i.e. **Hilb-Alg**(H) is the poset of commutative subalgebras of $\mathrm{Hom}(H, H)$ viewed as a category.

In [3] the full subcategory **Hilb-Alg**$_{\mathrm{vN}}(H) \hookrightarrow$ **Hilb-Alg**(H) of commutative von Neumann subalgebras is considered. Here we focus on the case where H is finite dimensional for which these categories coincide.

Commutative C^*-subalgebras of this kind can be thought of as a "classical snapshots" of a quantum system represented by H; they encode what can be observed of that system.

The topos considered is the category of presheaves $F :$ **Hilb-Alg**$(H)^{\mathrm{op}} \to$ **Set**. One presheaf of particular interest is the spectral presheaf [3], which classifies the Gelfand spectrum of a commutative C^*-algebra.

Definition 5. *The* spectral presheaf $\mathrm{Spec} :$ **Hilb-Alg**$(H)^{\mathrm{op}} \to$ **Set**, *is defined*

$$\mathrm{Spec}(\mathbf{C}) = \{\, \gamma : \mathbf{C} \to \mathbb{C} \mid \gamma \, a \, unital \, C^* - algebra \, homomorphism \,\}$$

while for $i : \mathbf{C}_2 \hookrightarrow \mathbf{C}_1$ *the action on morphisms is given by precomposition*

$$\mathrm{Spec}(\mathbf{C}_1) \xrightarrow{\;\mathrm{Spec}(i)\;} \mathrm{Spec}(\mathbf{C}_2)$$
$$\gamma \longmapsto \gamma \circ i$$

Remark 1. One important feature of the spectral presheaf in topos quantum theory is that the Kochen-Specker theorem, which asserts the contextual nature of quantum theory, is equivalent to the statement that this presheaf has no global sections [3].

We now discuss the passage from an observable in the monoidal approach, to an observable in the topos approach.

For a finite dimensional Hilbert space H, it follows from the Artin Wedderburn Theorem that every commutative C^*-subalgebra of $\mathrm{Hom}(H, H)$ can be decomposed as follows

$$\mathbf{C} \cong p_1 \mathbf{C} \oplus p_2 \mathbf{C} \oplus \ldots \oplus p_n \mathbf{C}$$

where p_i are self-adjoint primitive idempotents, that is, projectors onto orthogonal subspaces of H. The set $\mathrm{Spec}(\mathbf{C})$ is canonically isomorphic to the set of projectors $\{p_i\}_{i \in I}$. In particular, for each $\gamma : \mathbf{C} \to \mathbb{C}$, there is exactly one p_i such that the kernel of γ is the annihilator of the subalgebra $p_i \mathbf{C} \subset \mathbf{C}$.

It is easy to see how a †-special commutative Frobenius algebra (H, μ, η) for finite dimensional H determines an algebra $\mathbf{C}_\mu \in$ **Hilb-Alg**(H). Let $\{|e_i\rangle\}_{i \in I}$ be the set of set-like elements of the Frobenius algebra, and let $\mathbf{C}_\mu$ be the algebra generated by the self-adjoint projectors $p_i = |e_i\rangle \langle e_i|$. Note the canonical correspondence between elements of $\mathrm{Spec}(\mathbf{C}_\mu)$ and the set-like elements of (H, μ, η).

In the sequel we develop the same story as above but having replaced the category of finite dimensional Hilbert spaces with **Rel**. In order to do this we need an appropriate generalisation of the category **Hilb-Alg**(H), abstracting away from Hilbert spaces and C^*-algebras. This is done in Sect. 3 by defining the category $\mathcal{A}$-**Alg**(X) for an arbitrary locally small †-symmetric monoidal category with †-biproducts $\mathcal{A}$. We do this by observing that the sets $\mathrm{Hom}(X, X)$ in such categories carry a rich algebraic structure. We then generalise the Gelfand spectrum of a C^*-algebra by defining an analogous spectral presheaf for these general categories $\mathrm{Spec} : \mathcal{A}$-**Alg**$(X)^{\mathrm{op}} \to$ **Set**. In particular we will give a classification of this spectrum for the case where $\mathcal{A} = $ **Rel**.

This is done using the language of semirings, semimodules, and semialgebras which we review in Sect. 2.

In Sect. 4 we look at how to construct an object of the category **Rel-Alg**(A) from a †-special commutative Frobenius algebra (A, μ, η) in **Rel**. We discuss the advantages of considering the category **Rel-Alg**(A) as opposed to just the †-special commutative Frobenius algebra structures with which A can be endowed.

2   Semirings, Semimodules and Semialgebras

Here we recall some definitions and fix some terminology. The reader familiar with the passage from a commutative ring R, to R-modules, and to R-algebras, will see the exact parallel in developing semirings, semimodules, and semialgebras.

Definition 6. *A semiring consists of a set S equipped with a commutative monoid structure* $+ : S \times S \to S$ *with unit $0 \in S$, and a monoid structure* $\cdot : S \times S \to S$, *with unit $1 \in S$, such that for all $r, s, t \in S$*

1. $t \cdot (r + s) = t \cdot r + t \cdot s$;
2. $(r + s) \cdot t = r \cdot t + s \cdot t$;
3. $0 \cdot s = s \cdot 0 = 0$.

A semiring is called commutative *if $\cdot$ is commutative.*

   A $*$-semiring, *or involutive semiring is one equipped with an operation $*$ such that for all $s, t \in S$*

4. $(s^*)^* = s$;   7. $1^* = 1$;
5. $(st)^* = t^* s^*$;   8. $(s + t)^* = s^* + t^*$.
6. $0^* = 0$;

As the notation suggests we will refer to the monoid operations of a semiring as *addition* and *multiplication* respectively. We will simplify multiplicative notation $s \cdot t = st$, when the intended meaning is clear.

Note that we are assuming all semirings to be unital, i.e. that they have a multiplicative unit 1. A *subsemiring* of S is a subset containing 0 which is closed under addition and multiplication, and contains a multiplicative unit.

Definition 7. *Let S be a commutative semiring. A subset $I \subset S$ is called an ideal if it contains 0, is closed under addition, and such that for all $s \in S$ and $a \in I$, $as \in I$.*

An ideal is called prime *if $st \in I$ implies $s \in I$ or $t \in I$.*

A semiring is called *idempotent* if $s + s = s$ for all $s \in S$.

Lemma 1. *Let S be an idempotent semiring, S comes equipped with a canonical partial order defined $a < b$ iff $a + b = b$.*

Definition 8. *Let S be an idempotent semiring and I an ideal. The* downward closure *of I is defined $\downarrow I = \{ p \in S \mid$ there exists $x \in I$ such that $p < x \}$.*

It is easy to check that $\downarrow I$ is also an ideal. An ideal I is said to be *downward closed* if $I = \downarrow I$.

Definition 9. *Let $(S, \cdot, 1, +, 0)$ be a commutative semiring, an S-semimodule (or a semimodule with scalars S, or simply a semimodule) consists of a commutative monoid $+_M : M \times M \to M$, with unit 0_M, together with a scalar action or* scalar multiplication $\bullet : S \times M \to M$ *such that for all $r, s \in S$ and $m, n \in M$:*

1. $s \bullet (m +_M n) = s \bullet m +_M s \bullet n$;
2. $(r \cdot s) \bullet m = r \bullet (s \bullet m)$;
3. $(r + s) \bullet m = (r \bullet m) +_M (s \bullet m)$;
4. $0 \bullet m = s \bullet 0_M = 0_M$;
5. $1 \bullet m = m$.

A *subsemimodule* of $(M, +_M, 0_M)$ consists of a submonoid which is also a semimodule under the same action of S.

The *annihilator* of an S-semimodule M is the set of elements of $s \in S$ such that $s \bullet m = 0_M$ for all $m \in M$. It is easy to verify annihilators are ideals.

Definition 10. *An S-semialgebra $(M, \cdot_M, 1_M, +_M, 0_M)$ consists of an S-semimodule $(M, +_M, 0_M)$ equipped with a monoid structure $\cdot_M : M \times M \to M$, with unit 1_M, such that $(M, \cdot_M, 1_M, +_M, 0_M)$ forms a semiring, and where the scalar action obeys $s \bullet (m \cdot_M n) = (s \bullet m) \cdot_M n = m \cdot_M (s \bullet n)$.*

An S-semialgebra is called commutative *if $\cdot_M$ is commutative.*

When we talk about the ideals of a semialgebra M we mean the ideals of M as a semiring. Similarly, we call a semialgebra *idempotent* if it is idempotent as a semiring.

Notice that every semiring S is an S-semialgebra, where the action of S is taken to be the usual multiplication in S.

Definition 11. *Let S be a $*$-semiring. A $*$-semialgebra with scalars S consists of an S-semiring $(M, \cdot_M, 1_M, +_M, 0_M)$, with an involution such that the involutions of S and M are compatible, i.e. $(s \bullet m)^* = s^* \bullet m^*$.*

A *subsemialgebra* of M is a subset which is both a subsemiring and a subsemimodule. A $*$-*subsemialgebra* of a $*$-semialgebra is a subsemialgebra closed under taking involutions.

Homomorphisms and kernels of homomorphisms for all of these structures are defined in the obvious ways, preserving the relevant algebraic structure.

3   The Abstract Spectral Presheaf

In this section we show that for a locally small †-symmetric monoidal category with †-biproducts $\mathcal{A}$, each set $\mathrm{Hom}(X, X)$ is naturally equipped with the structure of a $*$-semialgebra. We show that by a direct generalisation of Definition 5 the Gelfand Spectrum of a C^*-algebra can be generalised to these $*$-semialgebras through defining a spectral presheaf for arbitrary $\mathcal{A}$.

Recall a *zero object* in a category is an object, typically denoted 0, which is both initial and terminal. Given a zero object, for any objects X and Y there is a *zero morphism* denoted $0_{XY} : X \to Y$, given by the unique factorisation through the zero object

$$X \xrightarrow{\ !\ } 0 \xrightarrow{\ !\ } Y$$

Definition 12. *Let $\mathcal{A}$ be a †-category. A monoidal product is a* biproduct *if it is both a product and a coproduct.*

A †-biproduct *is a biproduct such that canonical projections π and coprojections κ are related by $\pi^\dagger = \kappa$.*

The following is a well known result in categorical algebra going back at least as far as [7].

Lemma 2. *Locally small categories with biproducts $\oplus$ and a zero object are enriched in the category of commutative monoids, i.e. each hom-set $\mathrm{Hom}(X, Y)$ is a monoid. For morphisms $f, g : X \to Y$, define $f + g : X \to Y$ by*

$$X \xrightarrow{\ \Delta\ } X \oplus X \xrightarrow{\ f \oplus g\ } Y \oplus Y \xrightarrow{\ \nabla\ } Y$$

and where the additive unit is given by the unique zero map $0 : X \to Y$

The categories **fdHilb** and **Rel** have †-biproducts. Biproducts in **fdHilb** are given by the direct sum of the underlying vector spaces. The resulting additive structure on linear maps $f, g : H \to K$ is the pointwise sum.

In **Rel** disjoint union is a biproduct. The resulting additive structure on relations $r, s : A \to B$ is the union of relations.

Definition 13. *In a locally small symmetric monoidal category* $(\mathcal{A}, \otimes, I)$ *we call the set* $\mathrm{Hom}(I, I)$ *the abstract scalars.*

As the name suggests, the abstract scalars come equipped with algebraic structure [8], in particular they form a commutative monoid, with product given by composition, and unit element given by the identity morphism on I. For the categories we are interested in the scalars will have even more structure.

Lemma 3. *For* $(\mathcal{A}, \otimes, I)$ *a locally small* †*-symmetric monoidal category with* †*-biproducts, the set* $\mathrm{Hom}(I, I)$ *is a commutative* *-semiring.*

Proof. Biproducts give the scalars the structure of a semiring. This is folklore, but a proof can be found in [9].

The claim is that the dagger gives us the required involution. To see this we need to verify the remaining equations of Definition 6. Equations 5 and 7 follow from functoriality. Equation 8 follows from addition being defined by a †-biproduct. Equation 4 follows from the equation $† \circ † = Id_{\mathcal{A}}$. *Since the functor* † *is identity on objects, it preserves the zero object and hence preserves zero-morphisms, and hence Eq. 6 holds, as required.* □

Example 3. In **Hilb** the scalars are the set of linear maps $\mathrm{Hom}(\mathbb{C}, \mathbb{C})$, which is canonically isomorphic to the field $\mathbb{C}$. Involution is given by complex conjugation.

The following is shown in [9].

Lemma 4. *Let* $(\mathcal{A}, \otimes, I)$ *be a locally small symmetric monoidal category with biproducts. Each* $\mathrm{Hom}(X, Y)$ *carries the structure of an* S-*semimodule, with scalars* $S = \mathrm{Hom}(I, I)$. *Addition of morphisms is as defined in Lemma 2, and scalar action* $s \bullet f$ *given by*

$$X \xrightarrow{\sim} X \otimes I \xrightarrow{f \otimes s} Y \otimes I \xrightarrow{\sim} Y$$

Lemma 5. *Let* $(\mathcal{A}, \otimes, I)$ *be a locally small* †*-symmetric monoidal category with* †*-biproducts and zero object. For each object* X, $\mathrm{Hom}(X, X)$ *carries the structure of a* *-semialgebra with scalars* $S = \mathrm{Hom}(I, I)$.

Proof. By Lemma 4 $\mathrm{Hom}(X, X)$ *is a semimodule. We define the multiplication to be morphism composition. This distributes over addition by the properties of biproducts [7]. The scalar action being compatible with multiplication follows from the coherence conditions of symmetric monoidal categories.*

The dagger provides the necessary involution by the same argument in the proof of Lemma 3. □

We now have everything we need to give the necessary generalisation of the topos approach to quantum theory, and define the abstract spectral presheaf.

Definition 14. *Let* $(\mathcal{A}, \otimes, I)$ *be a locally small* †-*symmetric monoidal category with* †-*biproducts and zero object. For each object* $X \in \mathcal{A}$ *define the category*

$$\mathcal{A}\text{-}\mathbf{Alg}(X)$$

with objects commutative ∗-*subsemialgebras of* $\mathrm{Hom}(X,X)$, *and morphisms inclusions of* ∗-*subsemialgebras.*

Remark 2. Since there exists a purely algebraic characterisation of the von Neumann algebras in **Hilb-Alg**(H), we can similarly define the subcategory $\mathcal{A}\text{-}\mathbf{Alg}_{\mathrm{vN}}(X) \hookrightarrow \mathcal{A}\text{-}\mathbf{Alg}(X)$ of semialgebras which satisfying the double commutant identity. This will not be discussed further in this work.

Definition 15. *Let* $(\mathcal{A}, \otimes, I)$ *be a locally small* †-*symmetric monoidal category with* †-*biproducts and scalars* $S = \mathrm{Hom}(I, I)$. *The spectral presheaf for* $\mathcal{A}$

$$\mathcal{A}\text{-}\mathbf{Alg}(X)^{\mathrm{op}} \xrightarrow{\text{Spec}} \mathbf{Set}$$

is defined on objects

$$\mathrm{Spec}(\mathbf{A}) = \{\ \rho : \mathbf{A} \to S \mid \rho \, a \, \dagger\text{-}semialgebra \, homomorphism\ \}$$

and on morphisms by precomposition.

By Example 3 we see that this spectral presheaf coincides with Definition 5 when $\mathcal{A} = \mathbf{Hilb}$.

We end this section by considering the case where $(\mathcal{A}, \otimes, I) = (\mathbf{Rel}, \times, \{*\})$, and give a complete characterisation of the spectrum for **Rel**. In **Rel** there are two elements of $\mathrm{Hom}(\{*\}, \{*\})$: the identity and the zero relation. Under the operations defined this gives the Boolean semiring **2** with trivial involution. Since addition in a semialgebra $\mathbf{A} \in \mathbf{Rel}\text{-}\mathbf{Alg}(A)$ is given by union of relations these semialgebras are idempotent, and hence by Lemma 1 are equipped with a partial order.

Theorem 2. *Let* $\mathbf{A} \in \mathbf{Rel}\text{-}\mathbf{Alg}(A)$. *The spectrum* $\mathrm{Spec}(\mathbf{A})$ *is isomorphic to the set of proper downward closed prime ideals of* $\mathbf{A}$.

Proof. It is straightforward to show that an ideal of an arbitrary idempotent semiring $\mathbf{A}$ is prime and downward closed iff it is the kernel of a homomorphism $\rho : \mathbf{A} \to \mathbf{2}$.

It remains to show that for $\mathbf{A} \in \mathbf{Rel}\text{-}\mathbf{Alg}(A)$ the semialgebra homomorphisms into **2** are ∗-semialgebra homomorphisms.

It is enough to show that downwards closed ideals are closed under involutions. Let $p \in I$ be the top element of the ideal I, defined to be the sum of all elements in I. It is easy to see that p is idempotent, and moreover $x \in I$ iff $x < p$. It is easy to verify that $x < y$ implies $x^* < y^*$, hence it is enough to show that p is self-adjoint, i.e. $p = p^\dagger$.

By assumption of commutativity we have $pp^\dagger = p^\dagger p$, and hence $pp^\dagger$ is self-adjoint.

Next we prove $p < pp^\dagger$ directly, using properties of relations. Suppose $a \sim_p b$, then we need to show $a \sim_{pp^\dagger} b$. Note that if $a \sim_p b$ then $b \sim_{pp^\dagger} b$, and hence we have $a \sim_p b \sim_{pp^\dagger} b$. Since $pp^\dagger = ppp^\dagger$ we have $a \sim_{pp^\dagger} b$, and thus $p < pp^\dagger$.

Since $pp^\dagger \in I$, we have $pp^\dagger < p$ and hence $p = pp^\dagger$. Therefore p is self-adjoint, as required.   □

4   Semialgebras of Relations from Frobenius Algebras

Here we give some results which parallel those discussed in Sect. 1. In particular looked at the passage from a †-special commutative Frobenius algebra (H, μ, η) to an object in the category **Hilb-Alg**(H). In the category of sets and relations, given a †-special commutative Frobenius algebra (A, μ, η) we can also construct a semialgebra in **Rel-Alg**(A), however it is slightly more subtle.

A complete classification of †-special commutative Frobenius algebras in **Rel** is given in [10, Theorem 4.4].

Theorem 3. *A †-special commutative Frobenius algebra (A, μ, η) in* **Rel** *is an abelian groupoid, i.e. A is a disjoint union of abelian groups $A = \bigsqcup_{i \in I} G_i$ where the multiplication relation $\mu : A \times A \to A$ is defined by the individual group multiplication maps. The unit of the groupoid is the set of unit elements $e_i \in G_i$ from each group. Comultiplication $\mu^\dagger(g)$ for each $g \in A$ is given by*

$$\mu^\dagger(g) = \{ (h, h') \mid \mu(h, h') = g \}$$

From this it is easy to see that each connected component of the groupoid corresponds with a set-like element.

Definition 16. *Two †-special commutative Frobenius algebras in $\mathcal{A}$ are observationally equivalent if they are isomorphic and have the same set-like elements.*

Remark 3. Observationally equivalent †-special commutative Frobenius algebras in **fdHilb** are necessarily equal, as these Frobenius algebras are completely determined by their set-like elements.

This is not the case in **Rel**. For example, consider the set $A = \{a, b\}$. There are two ways to endow A with the group structure $\mathbb{Z}_2$, by picking either a or b to be the unit element. In either case there is a single set-like element consisting of the whole set A. Hence there are two observationally equivalent †-special commutative Frobenius algebras on A.

Theorem 4. *A †-special commutative Frobenius algebra (A, μ, η) in* **Rel** *determines a ∗-semialgebra denoted $\mathbf{A}_\mu \in$ **Rel-Alg**(A) such that the set $\mathrm{Spec}(\mathbf{A}_\mu)$ is canonically isomorphic to the set of set-like elements of (A, μ, η).*

Moreover, for observationally equivalent †-special commutative Frobenius algebras (A, μ, η) and (A, ν, θ) we have $\mathbf{A}_\mu = \mathbf{A}_\nu$.

Proof. Let (A, μ, η) be a †-*special commutative Frobenius algebra, i.e. a disjoint union of groups* $\bigsqcup_{i \in I} G_i$. *Then there is a family of maps* $\mu_g : A \to A$ *for each* $g \in A$, *with* $\mu_g^\dagger = \mu_{g^{-1}}$. *Take* $\mathbf{A}_\mu$ *to be the closure of this family under the given binary operations.*

Under the construction of $\mathbf{A}_\mu$ *each* G_i *determines an ideal of* $\mathbf{A}_\mu$, *which is also a subsemialgebra, by taking the closure of the family* μ_g *for* $g \in G_i$. *Every prime ideal of* $\mathbf{A}_\mu$ *is of the form* $\mathbf{R}_i = \bigsqcup_{j \neq i} G_j$ *for some* $i \in I$. *This ideal is the annihilator of the subsemiring determined by* G_i. *Hence there is a natural 1-1 correspondence between prime ideals and connected components of the groupoid, i.e. the set-like elements.* □

Example 4. Consider the set $A = \{a, b, c, d\}$ and †-special commutative Frobenius algebra with multiplication $\mu : A \times A \to A$ defined

$$
\begin{aligned}
(a, a) &\longmapsto a & (c, c) &\longmapsto c \\
(a, b) &\longmapsto b & (c, d) &\longmapsto d \\
(b, b) &\longmapsto a & (d, d) &\longmapsto c
\end{aligned}
$$

This is a Frobenius algebra isomorphic to the groupoid $\mathbb{Z}_2 \sqcup \mathbb{Z}_2$. For this Frobenius algebra we have specified the elements a and c to be the identity elements of each respective copy of $\mathbb{Z}_2$. The two set-like elements of this Frobenius algebra are the subsets $\{a, b\}$ and $\{c, d\}$.

The semialgebra $\mathbf{A}_\mu$ determined by this †-special commutative Frobenius algebra is generated by the relation which permutes a and b, acting as the zero map on c and d, and the corresponding relation which permutes c and d acting as the zero map on a and b.

Notice that any whatever choice we make endowing the structure of $\mathbb{Z}_2$ on the subsets $\{a, b\}$ and $\{c, d\}$ yields the same semialgebra $\mathbf{A}_\mu \in \mathbf{Rel\text{-}Alg}(A)$.

Remark 4. A *torsor*, or *principle homogeneous space* consists of a set X upon which a group G acts freely and transitively. One can think of X as the group G having "forgotten" what the identity element is.

It is already known that this precise group structure is not necessary when considering Frobenius algebras as observables in **Rel** [11].

The passage of a †-special commutative Frobenius algebra (A, μ, η) to the †-semialgebra $\mathbf{A}_\mu$ can be seen as going from a disjoint union of abelian groups to a disjoint union of torsors; we retain the essential groupoid structure which we need to reason about important monoidal category quantum–theoretic structures, e.g. *phase groups* [12], but forget the arbitrary choice of identity element.

Considering the $*$-semialgebra $\mathbf{A}_\mu$, rather than (A, μ, η) makes precise the notion that the exact group structure of the Frobenius algebra does not matter.

5   Conclusion and Further Work

This work can be seen as a first step in establishing a connection between the monoidal category and topos theoretic approaches to quantum theory, by providing a necessary abstraction of the topos approach in the form of the categories $\mathcal{A}$-**Alg**(X) and associated spectral presheaves.

Having a firm grasp on concrete cases, e.g. $\mathcal{A} = $ **fdHilb** and $\mathcal{A} = $ **Rel** will be key in understanding the more general connection for arbitrary $\mathcal{A}$. In light of Theorem 4 we pursue a general connection between the †-special commutative Frobenius algebras in $\mathcal{A}$, and the categories $\mathcal{A}$-**Alg**(X), and in particular between the set-like elements of the former and the spectrum of the latter.

We have given only the most preliminary account of the categories **Rel-Alg**(A) and their relation to the †-special commutative Frobenius algebras in **Rel**. Future work will give a comprehensive account of the categories **Rel-Alg**(A), and their relationship to the †-special commutative Frobenius algebras (A, μ, η).

Much more can be said connecting the category **Rel-Alg**(A) with the established concepts in the monoidal category approach to quantum theory, for example phase groups, complementarity [13] and abstract notions of non-locality [14]. Given Remark 4 this seems particularly worthwhile and will be explored further.

There are multiple approaches to contextuality using the language of sheaves for example [15,16]. One can now apply this machinery to the abstract spectral presheaf we have defined. In particular, in light of Remark 1, a version of the Kochen-Specker theorem can now be stated for arbitrary $\mathcal{A}$; we can ask if the abstract spectral presheaf for this category has global sections. This allows us to talk about contextuality in these categories in a way which was previously not possible.

References

1. Abramsky, S., Coecke, B.: A categorical semantics of quantum protocols. In: Symposium on Logic in Computer Science, pp. 415–425 (2004)
2. Isham, C., Butterfield, J.: A topos perspective on the Kochen-Specker theorem: I. quantum states as generalised valuations
3. Doering, A., Isham, C.: What is a thing? In: Coecke, B. (ed.) New Structures in Physics, vol. 813, pp. 753–940. Springer, Heidelberg (2011)
4. Spekkens, R.W.: Evidence for the epistemic view of quantum states: a toy theory. Phys. Rev. A. **75** (2007)
5. Coecke, B., Edwards, B.: Toy quantum categories (extended abstract). Electr. Notes Theor. Comput. Sci. **270**, 29–40 (2011)
6. Coecke, B., Pavlovic, D., Vicary, J.: A new description of orthogonal bases. Math. Struct. Comput. Sci. **23**, 555–567 (2013)
7. Mitchell, B.: Theory of Categories. Academic Press, New York (1965)
8. Kelly, G.M., Laplaza, M.L.: Coherence for compact closed categories. J. Pure Appl. Algebra **19**, 193–213 (1980)
9. Heunen, C.: Semimodule enrichment. Electr. Notes Theor. Comput. Sci. **218**, 193–208 (2008)
10. Pavlovic, D.: Quantum and classical structures in nondeterminstic computation. In: Bruza, P., Sofge, D., Lawless, W., Rijsbergen, K., Klusch, M. (eds.) QI 2009. LNCS (LNAI), vol. 5494, pp. 143–157. Springer, Heidelberg (2009). doi:10.1007/978-3-642-00834-4_13

11. Evans, J., Duncan, R., Lang, A., Panangaden, P.: Classifying all mutually unbiased bases in Rel (2009)
12. Coecke, B., Edwards, B., Spekkens, R.W.: Phase groups and the origin of non-locality for qubits. Electr. Notes Theor. Comput. Sci. **270**, 15–36 (2011)
13. Coecke, B., Duncan, R., Kissinger, A., Wang, Q.: Strong complementarity and non-locality in categorical quantum mechanics. In: Logic in Computer Science, pp. 245–254 (2012)
14. Gogioso, S., Zeng, W.: Mermin non-locality in abstract process theories. In: EPTCS, vol. 195, 228–246 (2015)
15. Abramsky, S., Barbosa, R.S., Kishida, K., Lal, R., Mansfield, S.: Contextuality, cohomology and paradox. In: Logic in Computer Science, pp. 211–228 (2015)
16. Staton, S., Uijlen, S.: Effect algebras, presheaves, non-locality and contextuality. In: Automata, Languages, and Programming, pp. 401–413 (2015)

Language Geometry Using Random Indexing

Aditya Joshi[1]([✉]), Johan T. Halseth[2], and Pentti Kanerva[3]

[1] Department of Mathematics, University of California–Berkeley, Berkeley, USA
adityajoshi@berkeley.edu
[2] Department of Computer Science, University of California–Berkeley, Berkeley, USA
[3] Redwood Center for Theoretical Neuroscience, Berkeley, USA

Abstract. Random Indexing is a simple implementation of Random Projections with a wide range of applications. It can solve a variety of problems with good accuracy without introducing much complexity. Here we demonstrate its use for identifying the language of text samples, based on a novel method of encoding letter N-grams into high-dimensional Language Vectors. Further, we show that the method is easily implemented and requires little computational power and space. As proof of the method's statistical validity, we show its success in a language-recognition task. On a difficult data set of 21,000 short sentences from 21 different languages, we achieve 97.4% accuracy, comparable to state-of-the-art methods.

Keywords: N-gram vector · Language profile · Vector symbolic architecture · Multiply–Add–Permute Algebra

1 Introduction

As humans who communicate through language, we have the fascinating ability to recognize unknown languages in spoken or written form, using simple cues to distinguish one language from another. Some unfamiliar languages, of course, might sound very similar, especially if they come from the same language family, but we are often able to identify the language in question with very high accuracy. This is because embedded within each language are certain features that clearly distinguish one from another, whether it be accent, rhythm, or pitch patterns. The same can be said for written languages, as they all have features that are distinctive. Recognizing the language of a given text is the first step in all sorts of language processing, such as text analysis, categorization, translation and much more.

As popularized by Shannon [1], most language models use distributional statistics to explain structural similarities in various specified languages. The traditional method of identifying languages in the absence of dictionaries consists of counting individual letters, letter bigrams, trigrams, tetragrams, etc., and comparing the frequency profiles of different text samples. As a general principle, the more accurate you want your detection method to be, the more data you have to store about the various languages. For example, Google's recently open-sourced program called Chromium Compact Language Detector uses large

© Springer International Publishing AG 2017
J.A. de Barros et al. (Eds.): QI 2016, LNCS 10106, pp. 265–274, 2017.
DOI: 10.1007/978-3-319-52289-0_21

language profiles built from enormous corpora of data. As a result, the accuracy of their detection, as seen through large-scale testing and in practice, is near perfect [2].

High-dimensional vector models are popular in natural-language processing and are used to capture word meaning from word-use statistics. The vectors are called *semantic vectors* or *context vectors*. Ideally, words with a similar meaning are represented by semantic vectors that are close to each other in the vector space, while dissimilar meanings are represented by semantic vectors far from each other. Latent Semantic Analysis is a well-known model that is explained in detail in [3]. It produces 300-dimensional (more or less) semantic vectors from a singular value decomposition (SVD) of a matrix of word frequencies in a large collection of documents.

An alternative to SVD, based on Random Projections, was proposed by Papadimitriou [4] and Kaski [5]. Random Indexing [6,7] is a simple and effective implementation of the idea. It has been used in ways similar to Mikolov et al.'s Continuous Bag-of-Words Model (KBOW; [8]) and has features similar to Locality-Sensitive Hashing (LSH) but differs from them in its use of high dimensionality and randomness. With the dimensionality in the thousands (e.g., $D = 10{,}000$)—referred to as "hyperdimensional"—it is possible to calculate useful representations in a single pass over the dataset with very little computing.

In this paper, we will present a way of doing language detection using Random Indexing, which is fast, highly scalable, and space efficient. We will also present some results regarding the accuracy of the method, even though this will not be the main goal of this paper and should be investigated further.

2   Random Indexing

Random Indexing represents information by projecting data onto vectors in a high-dimensional space. There exist a huge number of different, nearly orthogonal vectors in such a space [9, p. 19]. This lets us combine two such vectors into a new vector using well-defined vector-space operations, while keeping the information of the two with high probability. In our implementation of Random Indexing, we use a variant of the MAP (Multiply, Add, Permute) coding described in [10] to define the vector space. Vectors are initially taken from a D-dimensional space (with $D = 10{,}000$) and have an equal number of randomly placed 1 s and -1 s. Such vectors are used to represent the basic elements of the system, which in our case are the 26 letters of the Latin alphabet and the (ASCII) Space. These vectors for letters are sometimes referred to as their *Random Labels*.

The binary operations on such vectors are defined as follows. Elementwise *addition* of two vectors A and B, is denoted by $A + B$. Similar, elementwise *multiplication* is denoted by $A * B$. A vector A will be its own multiplicative inverse, $A * A = \mathbf{1}$, where $\mathbf{1}$ is the D-dimensional identity vector consisting of only 1s. The cosine is used to measure the similarity of two vectors. It is defined as $\cos(A, B) = |A' * B'|$, where A' and B' are the normalized vectors of A and B, respectively, and $|C|$ denotes the sum of the elements in C.

Information from a pair of vectors A and B is stored and utilized in a single vector by exploiting the summation operation. That is, the sum of two separate vectors naturally preserves unique information from each vector because of the mathematical properties of the space. To see this, note that $\cos(A, A) = 1$, while for all $B \neq A$, $\cos(A, B) < 1$. The cosine of two random, unrelated vectors tends to be close to 0. Because of this, the vector B can easily be found in the vector $A + B$: $\cos(B, A + B)$ differs significantly from 0.

For encoding a sequence of vectors, we use a random (but fixed throughout all our computations) *permutation* operation ρ of the vector coordinates. Hence, the sequence A-B-C is encoded as the D-dimensional vector ABC by permuting the first vector twice, permuting the second vector once, taking the third vector as is, and by multiplying the tree: $ABC = \rho(\rho(A)) * \rho(B) * C = \rho\rho A * \rho B * C = \rho^2 A * \rho B * C$. This efficiently distinguishes the sequence A-B-C from, say, A-C-B. This can be seen from looking at their cosine (here c is the normalization factor):

$$V_1 = \rho\rho A * \rho B * C$$
$$V_2 = \rho\rho A * \rho C * B$$
$$\implies \cos(V_1, V_2) = c \cdot |(\rho\rho A * \rho B * C) * (\rho\rho A * \rho C * B)|$$
$$= c \cdot |\rho\rho A * \rho\rho A * \rho B * \rho C * C * B)|$$
$$= c \cdot |\rho\rho(A * A) * \rho(B * C) * (B * C))|$$
$$= c \cdot |\mathbf{1} * \rho(B * C) * (B * C))|$$
$$\approx c \cdot 0$$

since a random permutation ρV of a random vector V is uncorrelated to V.

2.1   Making and Comparing of Text Vectors

We use the properties of high-dimensional vectors to extract certain properties of text into a single vector. [11] shows how Random Indexing can be used for representing the contexts in which a word appears in a text, into that word's context vector. We show here how to use a similar strategy for recognizing a text's language by creating and comparing *Text Vectors*: the Text Vector of an unknown text sample is compared for similarity to precomputed Text Vectors of known language samples—the latter are referred to as *Language Vectors*.

Simple language recognition can be done by comparing letter frequencies of a given text to known letter frequencies of languages. Given enough text, a text's letter distribution will approach the letter distribution of the language in which the text was written. The phenomenon is called an "ergodic" process in [1], as borrowed from similar ideas in physics and thermodynamics. This can be generalized to using *letter blocks* of different sizes. By a block of size N, we mean N consecutive letters in the text so that a text of length M would have $M - N + 3$ blocks. When the letters are taken in the order in which they appear in the text, they are referred to as a sequences (of length N) or as N-grams.

As an example, the text "a book" gives rise to the trigrams "a_b", "_bo", "boo", and "ook" (here "_" stands for Space). The frequencies of such letter blocks can be found for a text and compared to known frequencies for different languages. For texts in languages using the Latin alphabet of 26 letters (plus Space), like English, this would lead to keeping track of $27^3 = 19,683$ different trigram frequencies. For arbitrary alphabets of L letters, there would be $(L+1)^N$ N-grams to keep track of. These numbers grow quickly as the block size N increases, yet Random Indexing encodes all N-gram frequencies into a single 10,000-dimensional Text Vector.

The Random Indexing approach for doing language recognition is similar. A text's Text Vector is first calculated by running over all the blocks of size N within the text and creating an N-gram Vector for each. An N-gram Vector is created for the sequence of letters as described earlier. As an example, if we encounter the block "rab", its trigram vector is calculated by performing $\rho\rho R * \rho A * B$, where R, A and B are the Random Labels for r, a, and b—they are random D-dimensional vector with half 1s and half -1s, and the same ones are used with all languages and text samples.

A text's Text Vector is now obtained from summing the N-gram Vectors for all the blocks in the text. This is still an D-dimensional vector and can be stored efficiently. Language Vectors are made in exactly the same way, by making Text Vectors from samples of a known language and adding them into a single vector. Determining the language of an unknown text is done by comparing its Text Vector to all the Language Vectors. More precisely, the cosine measure $d_{\cos}$ between a language vector X and an unknown text vector V is defined as follows:

$$d_{\cos}(X, V) = \frac{X \cdot V}{|X||V|} = \frac{\sum_{i=1}^{D} x_i v_i}{\sqrt{\sum_{j=1}^{D} x_j^2 \sum_{k=1}^{D} v_k^2}}$$

If the cosine is high (close to 1), the trigram frequencies of the text are similar to the trigram frequencies of that language and thus, the text is likely to be written in the same language. Hence, the language that yields the highest cosine is chosen as the system's prediction/guess.

2.2 Complexity

The outlined algorithm for Text Vector generation can be implemented efficiently. For generating a vector for an N-gram, $N - 1$ vector permutations and multiplications are performed. This takes time $O(N \cdot D)$. Looping over a text of M letters, $O(M)$ N-gram Vectors must be created and added together. This clearly implies an $O(N \cdot D \cdot M)$ implementation. This can be improved to $O(D \cdot M)$ by noting that most of the information needed for creating the N-gram Vector for the next block is already contained in the previous N-gram Vector, and can be retrieved by removing the contribution from the letter that is now no longer in the block.

Say we have the N-gram Vector $A = \rho^{N-1} V_1 * \rho^{N-2} V_2 * \ldots * \rho V_{N-1} * V_N$ for block number i, and now want to find the N-gram Vector B for block $i + 1$. We remove from A the vector $\rho^{N-1} V_1$ by multiplying with its inverse (which is the vector itself), which we can do in $O(D)$ time since ρ^{N-1} is just another (pre-calculated) permutation. Then we permute the result once using ρ and multiply that with the Letter Vector V_{N+1} for the new letter in the block. This gives us the new N-gram Vector

$$B = \rho(\rho^{N-1}V_1 * A) * V_{N+1}$$
$$= \rho(\rho^{N-2}V_2 * \ldots * \rho V_{N-1} * V_N) * V_{N+1}$$
$$= \rho^{N-1}V_2 * \ldots * \rho^2 V_{N-1} * \rho V_N * V_{N+1}$$

and so we can create N-gram Vectors for arbitrary size blocks without adding complexity.

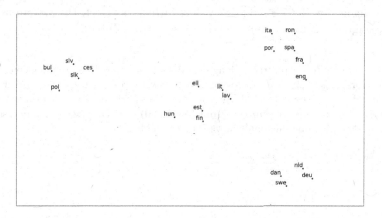

Fig. 1. 10,000-dimensional Language Vectors for 21 languages roughly cluster based on the known relations between the languages. The Language Vectors were based on letter trigrams and were projected onto a plane using t-SNE [12].

3   Experimental Results

The algorithm outlined above was used to create Language Vectors for 21 languages. Texts for the Language Vectors were taken from the Wortschatz Corpora [13] where large numbers of sentences in selected languages can be easily downloaded. Each Language Vector was based on about a million bytes of text. Computing of the Language Vectors corresponds to training the system.

Intuitively, Language Vectors within a language family should be closer to each other than vectors for unrelated languages. Indeed, the hyperdimensional Language Vectors roughly cluster in this manner, as seen in Fig. 1.

To get an idea of how well the actual detection algorithm works, we tested the Language Vectors' ability to identify text samples from the Europarl Parallel Corpus, described in [14]. This corpus includes 21 languages with 1,000 samples of each, and each sample is a single sentence.

Table 1. Percentage of sentences correctly identified as a function of N-gram size.

N	Detection success
1	74.9
2	94,0
3	97.3
4	97.8
5	97.3

Table 1 shows the result for N-gram sizes from 1 to 5 ($N = 1$ is the equivalent of comparing letter histograms). With tetragrams we were able to guess the correct language with 97.8% accuracy. Even when incorrect, the system usually chose a language from the same family, as seen from Table 2.

Table 2. The confusion matrix of language detection using 10,000-dimensional Language Vectors based on letter trigrams. Each row corresponds to the correct label and each column is the predicted label for the Europarl corpus detection test. The entry (i, j) is the number of sentences (out of a 1,000) that language j was guessed for language i. A high value diagonal shows the very high accuracy.

	ell	eng	ita	ces	est	spa	nld	por	lav	lit	ron	pol	fra	bul	deu	dan	fin	hun	swe	slk	slv
ell	987	1	.	.	.	.	3	3	.	.	.	1	.	4	.	.	1	.	.	.	.
eng	2	982	.	4	.	.	1	.	2	.	.	.	6	.	.	1	.	2	.	.	.
ita	.	.	992	.	1	2	.	.	.	.	2	3	.	.	.	.	.	.	.	.	.
ces	1	1	.	940	1	.	.	.	1	1	1	1	.	5	1	.	.	.	.	35	12
est	1	.	.	1	983	.	.	.	3	.	.	.	3	.	1	1	5	1	1	.	.
spa	.	.	6	.	.	946	2	30	8	1	2	.	5	.	.	.	.	.	.	.	.
nld	.	1	.	.	.	.	980	1	.	.	2	1	.	.	5	9	.	.	1	.	.
por	.	1	2	.	.	1	1	991	.	.	.	.	3	1	.	.	.	.	.	.	.
lav	2	.	.	1	.	.	.	2	963	26	.	2	.	2	.	1	.	.	.	1	.
lit	2	.	1	2	1	1	.	2	18	969	.	.	1	.	.	.	.	.	.	1	2
ron	.	.	1	.	.	1	.	2	.	1	987	2	4	2	.	.	.	.	.	.	.
pol	2	1	.	3	1	.	.	.	.	.	.	984	.	4	.	.	.	.	.	4	1
fra	3	.	2	.	.	4	2	1	1	2	1	.	982	.	.	1	.	.	.	1	.
bul	1	.	.	7	.	.	4	.	.	.	.	.	.	984	.	.	.	.	.	3	1
deu	.	2	1	1	.	.	3	.	.	.	.	.	3	.	985	4	.	.	1	.	.
dan	.	2	.	.	.	.	9	.	.	.	.	.	2	.	.	974	.	.	13	.	.
fin	.	.	.	4	.	2	.	1	.	.	.	.	.	.	.	.	993	.	.	.	.
hun	.	.	.	.	.	.	6	1	1	1	.	.	.	.	.	2	.	989	.	.	.
swe	.	1	.	.	.	1	5	.	.	.	4	.	1	.	4	10	.	.	974	.	.
slk	2	.	.	72	.	.	1	.	2	1	4	18	.	6	1	.	.	.	.	881	12
slv	1	.	.	5	2	.	.	1	.	.	1	.	.	6	1	1	.	.	.	.	982

LEGEND: bul = Bulgarian, ces = Czech, dan = Danish, deu = German, ell = Greek, eng = English, est = Estonian, fin = Finnish, fra = French, hun = Hungarian, ita = Italian, lav = Latvian, lit = Lithuanian, nld = Dutch, pol = Polish, por = Portuguese, ron = Romanian, slk = Slovak, slv = Slovene, spa = Spanish, swe = Swedish

It is worth noting that 10,000 small integers keep track of 14,348,907 possible pentagrams just as easily as 19,683 trigrams. The method should be explored further, as explained in the Future Work section.

The arithmetic (algebra) of the operations with which Text Vectors are made—i.e., permutation, multiplication, and addition, and how they work together—make it possible to analyze the Language Vectors and find out, for example, what letters are most likely to follow "th". In English it would be "e", but what is the next most likely? In Table 3, we answer this question using a learnt Language Vector for English.

Table 3. Using the vector operations of multiplication and inverse permutations, and noting that the multiplicative inverse of a random vector with only 1 s and −1s is itself, we find the most likely letter to follow the bigram "th", knowing the answer is encoded in an English Vector. As expected intuitively, the result shows that "e" is the most likely letter. Additionally, we have easily accessible information about the second most likely and so on. We show the top 6. (Note that _ is (ASCII) space.)

Letter	Distance
e	0.31
_	0.063
a	0.049
i	0.024
r	0.024
o	0.018

4   Details of Implementation

The 21 Language Vectors were "trained" with text from the Leipzig Corpora Collection (website http://corpora.uni-leipzig.de/download.html). The file for each language is about a million bytes and contains 10,000 sentences of news material. Letters outside the 26 in the Latin alphabet were replaced by their Latin equivalents by hand-coding and using the Unidecode 0.04.17 package (https://pypi.python.org/pypi/Unidecode), and sequences of nonletters were treated as a single space. The 21,000 test sentences (1,000 per language) came from the European Parliament Proceedings Parallel Corpus 1996–2011 (http://www.statmt.org/europarl/) and were preprocessed the same way as the training corpus.

The "random," fixed permutation ρ was implemented as a rotate by one coordinate position. This is safe because the vectors themselves are random, only one permutation is needed, and the permutation is iterated a few times at most (much fewer than 10,000).

The experiment was programmed in Python and run on a laptop computer. The following run-time statistics are from a 64-bit, 2.70 GHz (100 MHz clock)

Intel processor, 4 cores and 32 GB of 1600 MHz memory (total). Computing a 10,000-dimensional Language Vector from a million bytes of text takes 14.5 s. Computing the 10,000-dimensional Text Vectors for the 21,000 test sentences and comparing them to the 21 Language Vectors, to make the confusion matrix, takes 2 min. The run time for a round of experiments to make Table starting with a random seed is just over 7 min.

5   Discussion

Computing with high-dimensional random vectors is the larger issue addressed by this paper: what are the operations on the vectors, what is their algebra, and what kinds of algorithms the algebra favors? Language identification provides us with an easily understood example of the concepts involved.

The addition and multiplication operations on the vectors form an algebraic structure that approximates a field, which is further complemented by a permutation operation that distributes over both addition and multiplication. These operations constitute a kind of Multiply–Add–Permute (MAP) algebra [15] that seems particularly suited for modeling human cognition and language.

This style of computing goes back to Hinton's Reduced Representation which emphasizes the need to represent sets and their elements with vectors of equal width [16], and to Smolensky's Tensor Product Variable Binding which allows a set of variable–value pairs to be encoded and superposed in a higher-order tensor from which the individual constituents can be extracted [17]. These two ideas are brought together in Plate's Holographic Reduced Representation (HRR; [18,19]), of which the present system is a special case. The idea is to work in a *closed* system—namely, that the outputs of addition, multiplication and permutation have the same dimensionality (and statistical distribution) as the inputs. The term Vector Symbolic Architecture (VSA; [20]) refers to systems of this kind.

VSA systems use either multiplication or permutation for variable binding because they are invertible and they distributes over addition. Here we have encoded N-grams using both. First the letters are bound to their positions within an N-gram with permutations and then the position-encoded letters are "bound" to each other with multiplication—this latter "binding" is a more general mapping because it is not between variables and their values. When the N-gram Vectors for a given text are superposed with vector addition, we get an N-grams profile that can be compared to profiles of other text samples (see Fig. 1 and Table 2).

The example of Table 3 is more subtle, where we query a Language Vector for the letter that appeared most often after "th". The solution can be understood in terms of the vector algebra that makes use of both the inverse permutation and the inverse multiplication. This kind of representation vaguely resembles quantum superposition that allows all the superposed vectors to be operated on in parallel and the results to be extracted with appropriate inverse operations. The simplicity of the algorithm is worth pointing out.

6   Future Work

Many adjustments can be made to improve the efficacy of Random Indexing on language detection. The results of this paper are based mainly on letter trigrams. However, it is a simple matter to add into the Text Vectors single-letter frequencies and bigrams, for example. Also, the vector dimensionality can be reduced to several thousands without markedly affecting the results. Early experiments suggest that this method works well with encoding language information in multilingual texts, which is often much more difficult to do.

Because of the generality of Random Indexing on texts, any time series with a well-defined "alphabet" can be encoded using this scheme. In this way, we propose that our method can be used to do language detection in speech data, addressing our original problem.

7   Conclusion

We have described the use of Random Indexing to language identification. Random Indexing has been used in the study of semantic vectors since 2000 [6,7], and for encoding problems in graph theory [10], but only now for identifying source materials. It is based on simple operations on high-dimensional random vectors: on Random Labels with 0-mean components that allow weak signals to rise above noise as the data accumulate. The algorithm works in a single pass, in linear time, with limited memory, and thus is inherently scalable, and it produces vectors that are amenable to further analysis. The experiments reported in this paper were an easy task for a laptop computer.

Acknowledgments. We thank Professor Bruno Olshausen for providing the setting for this work in his class on Neural Computation, and two anonymous reviewers for their comments that helped us improve the paper. Pentti Kanerva's work was supported by Systems On Nanoscale Information fabriCs (SONIC), one of the six SRC STARnet Centers, sponsored by MARCO and DARPA.

References

1. Shannon, C.E.: A mathematical theory of communication. Bell Syst. Techn. J. **27**(4), 623–656 (1948)
2. McCandless, M.: Accuracy, performance of Google's Compact Language Detector (2011). http://blog.mikemccandless.com/2011/10/accuracy-and-performance-of-googles.html
3. Landauer, T., Dumais, S.: A solution to Plato's problem: the latent semantic analysis theory of acquisition, induction and representation of knowledge. Psychol. Rev. **104**(2), 211–240 (1997)
4. Papadimitriou, C.H., et al.: Latent semantic indexing: a probabilistic analysis. In: Proceedings of 17th ACM Symposium on the Principles of Database Systems, pp. 159–168 (1998)

5. Kaski, S.: Dimensionality reduction by random mapping: fast similarity computation for clustering. In: Proceedings of International Joint Conference on Neural Networks, vol. 1, pp. 413–418 (1998)
6. Kanerva, P., Kristoferson, J., Holst, A.: Random indexing of text samples for latent semantic analysis. In: Gleitman, L.R., Josh, A.K. (eds.) Proceedings of 22nd Annual Conference of the Cognitive Science Society, p. 1036 (2000)
7. Sahlgren, M.: An introduction to random indexing. In: Methods and Applications of Semantic Indexing Workshop at the 7th International Conference on Terminology and Knowledge Engineering (2005)
8. Mikolov, T., et al.: Efficient estimation of word representations in vector space, p. 12, 7 September 2013. arXiv:1301.3781v3 [cs.CL]
9. Kanerva, P.: Sparse Distributed Memory. MIT Press, Cambridge (1988)
10. Levy, S.D., Gayler, R.W.: Lateral inhibition in a fully distributed connectionist architecture. In: Proceedings of the Ninth International Conference on Cognitive Modeling (2009)
11. Kanerva, P.: Computing with 10,000-bit words. In: Proceedings of 52nd Annual Allerton Conference on Communication, Control, and Computing (2014)
12. van der Maaten, L.: Visualizing high-dimensional data using t-SNE. J. Mach. Learn. Res. **9**, 2579–2605 (2008)
13. Quasto, U., Richter, M., Biemann, C.: Corpus portal for search in monolingual corpora. In: Proceedings of the Fifth International Conference on Language Resources and Evaluation, LREC, pp. 1799–1802 (2006)
14. Nakatani, S.: Langdetect is updated (added profiles of Estonian/ Lithuanian/Latvian/Slovene, and so on. http://shuyo.wordpress.com/2011/ 09/29/langdetect-is-updatedadded-profiles-of-estonian-lithuanian-latvian-slovene-and-so-on/. Accessed 16 Dec 2014
15. Gayler, R.W.: Multiplicative binding, representation operators, analogy. In: Kokinov, B., Holyoak, K., Sofia, G.D. (eds.) Advances in Analogy Research, p. 405. New Bulgarian University (1998)
16. Hinton, G.E.: Mapping part-whole hierarchies into connectionist networks. Artif. Intell. **46**(1–2), 47–75 (1990)
17. Smolensky, P.: Tensor product variable binding, the representation of symbolic structures in connectionist networks. Artif. Intell. **46**(1–2), 159–216 (1990)
18. Plate, T.A.: Holographic reduced representations: convolution algebra for compositional distributed representations. In: Mylopoulos, R.R., Mateo, J.S. (eds.) Proceedings of 12th International Joint Conference on Articial Intelligence (IJCAI), pp. 30–35. Kaufmann, CA (1991)
19. Plate, T.A.: Holographic Reduced Representation: Distributed Representation of Cognitive Structure. CSLI, Stanford (2003)
20. Gayler, R.W.: Vector symbolic architectures are a viable alternative for Jackendo's challenges. Behav. Brain Sci. **29**, 78–79 (2006)

Author Index

Abramsky, S.   163
Aerts, Diederik   81
Al-Mehairi, Yaared   122

Basieva, Irina   49
beim Graben, Peter   99
Beltran, Lyneth   81
Blutner, Reinhard   99
Bob, Petr   71
Bosyk, Gustavo   194
Bruza, P.D.   163
Burgin, Mark   206

Cervantes, Víctor H.   182
Coecke, Bob   122
Cohen, Trevor   135

De Assis, Leonardo Guimarães   71
De Assis, Leonardo P.G.   57
de Barros, J. Acacio   57, 71
de Bianchi, Massimiliano Sassoli   81
Denolf, Jacob   227
Dubois, François   239
Dunne, Kevin   252
Dzhafarov, Ehtibar N.   16, 151, 182

Fortin, Sebastian   194

Gupta, Namita T.   135

Halseth, Johan T.   265
Heiden, Jason A. Vander   135
Holik, Federico   194

Joshi, Aditya   265

Kanerva, Pentti   265
Kaszlikowski, Dagomir   175
Khrennikov, Andrei   49
Kleinstein, Steven H.   135
Kujala, Janne V.   16
Kurzyński, Paweł   175

Lewis, Martha   122

Montemayor, Carlos   57

Nagarajan, Rajagopal   115

Plastino, Angelo   194

Sozzo, Sandro   81

Toffano, Zeno   239

van Fraassen, Bas C.   3
Veloz, Tomas   81

Widdows, Dominic   135
Windridge, David   115

Yau, Hou Y.   33

Zhang, Ru   151

Printed in the United States
By Bookmasters